Manifest Destinies

Manifest Destinies

AMERICA'S WESTWARD EXPANSION AND
THE ROAD TO THE CIVIL WAR

Steven E. Woodworth

Alfred A. Knopf · New York · 2010

THIS IS A BORZOI BOOK
PUBLISHED BY ALFRED A. KNOPF

Copyright © 2010 by Steven Woodworth
All rights reserved.
Published in the United States by Alfred A. Knopf,
a division of Random House, Inc., New York, and
in Canada by Random House of Canada Limited, Toronto.

Knopf, Borzoi Books, and the colophon are
registered trademarks of Random House, Inc.

The photograph of Independence Rock appears courtesy of the Library of Congress.
All other images except that of Richard Mentor Johnson and the William S. Jewett
portrait of John C. Frémont appear courtesy of Wikimedia Commons.

Library of Congress Cataloging-in-Publication Data
Woodworth, Steven E.
Manifest destinies : America's westward expansion and the road
to the Civil War / by Steven E. Woodworth.—1st ed.
p.   cm.
ISBN 978-0-307-26524-1
1. United States—Territorial expansion.   2. Manifest Destiny.
3. Mexican War, 1846–1848.   4. United States—History—1815–1861.
5. United States—History—Civil War, 1861–1865—Causes.   I. Title.
E179.5.W65 2010
970.04—dc22   2010016843

Manufactured in the United States of America
First Edition

To seven excellent scholars and colleagues—

Brian Melton, Charles Grear, Jason Frawley,

John Lundberg, David Slay, Paul Schmelzer,

and Leah Tarwater.

To God alone be the glory.

CONTENTS

MAPS

PREFACE

Abraham Lincoln famously referred to the United States, founded "four score and seven years" before the time of his speaking, as a nation "conceived in liberty, and dedicated to the proposition that all men are created equal." On the November day in 1863 when Lincoln spoke those words, he and his audience were painfully aware of the fatal flaw in the Republic the founders had established, the contradiction personified in the life of the very man who had penned the statement to which Lincoln was alluding. Thomas Jefferson, chief author of the Declaration of Independence, with its claim that "all men are created equal," was a slaveholder.

Slavery was the negation of American ideals of liberty, and the founding generation was almost as painfully aware of the fact as was Lincoln's own. That first generation of United States citizens remained blissfully ignorant of the price that inconsistency would ultimately exact on their country, and they could believe, with no more wishful thinking than comes naturally to humans, that the institution of slavery would die a natural death in America within another generation or two. Through the interaction of the cotton gin, the steam loom, the rich expanse of available farmland in the Deep South states, and the worldwide demand for cotton textiles, slavery did not die in America but rather grew. What John C. Calhoun called the South's "peculiar institution" became more than ever the basis of southern wealth, and white southerners, whether slaveholders or not, came to regard it as indispensable not only to their region's economy but also to their social fabric, which was based on the unquestioned supremacy of the white race.

The flaw thus remained in the edifice of American liberty, but for many years the country was able to ignore the issue of slavery and function as though it did not exist. A couple of constitutional provisions and a federal law or two protected the rights claimed by slaveholders, but otherwise the federal government took almost no cognizance of slavery during the nation's first thirty years. During those decades the United States grew in size and strength and in the freedom that it recognized for all its citizens—but not for the slaves. And during those years the American people remained, with few exceptions, oblivious to their nation's chief moral problem and went about their own business, caring for their families, enjoying freedom, and seeking economic success, in many cases by moving west.

Americans had been a westering people since the first hardy pioneers had planted their homesteads just beyond the sight and smell of salt water in the colonies of the early seventeenth century. Freedom, opportunity, and a fresh start all beckoned Americans to the edge of settlement, a line that crept steadily west through colonial times and then, without pause, after independence. When in the middle of the 1840s a New York newspaperman wrote that it was America's "manifest destiny to overspread the continent," he was merely putting into words what the great mass of his countrymen had felt for more than two centuries—that the extension of what Americans liked to call "the Empire of Liberty" to encompass the whole length and breadth of North America was a blessing and an example to all mankind. What was special when John L. O'Sullivan coined that phrase was that his generation of Americans seemed to be rushing toward the culmination of this goal with a speed their forefathers had never imagined. It appeared that the nation could fulfill its great territorial ambition without dealing with the moral problem that contradicted the ideas of liberty on which it prided itself.

The problem of slavery sometimes reared its head to disturb the peace and happiness of the young Republic. Most notably this occurred in 1819 and 1820 after the new state of Missouri petitioned Congress for admission to the Union as a slave state. A slave state that far north, and where no slavery had existed prior to U.S. acquisition, was a disturbing development to northerners who saw in it the proof that slavery was not, in fact, going to wither away, but was instead becoming the normal arrangement of economy and society in the United States. When these northerners objected to Missouri's admission without a provision that its slaves eventually be freed, white southern leaders reacted fiercely, and a crisis developed that the aged Jefferson described as being "like a fire bell in the night [that] awakened and filled me with terror." With difficulty, the politicians of that era worked out a compromise, allowing slavery in some territories and not in others, that once again suppressed the issue of slavery and banished it from the national political arena.

In the two decades after the 1820 Missouri Compromise, Americans reacted to Jefferson's nocturnal fire bell in different ways. White southerners became more committed than ever to slavery, and some of them began to think that the Missouri Compromise had been a bad bargain, that their leaders should never have conceded that Congress or any power had the right to prohibit slavery in any territory of the United States. Northerners were of different minds on the subject. Some accepted slavery as the natural order of things and wanted no one to interfere with it. A small but growing minority took an opposite view, seeing slavery as the moral wrong it was and believing that the country must face that issue squarely and make the right choice by abolishing the "peculiar institution." Still others recognized slavery as a moral wrong but believed that it could be solved better later, or at least that it could not be solved at present. They saw no reason to tear down the American "Temple of Liberty" (another favorite expression in that era) in the vain quest for moral perfection.

The divisions between these various groups would shape the political battles of a generation—but not of that generation, the generation of those whose active adult lives were lived between about 1820 and 1845, with the exception of a few whose long careers spanned several eras. The abolitionists were too few in those days. The combination of southerners who defended slavery, northerners who defended slavery, and northerners who wanted to postpone the question was more than strong enough to drown out the voices of the handful of principled opponents of slavery—fanatics, their contemporaries called them—whose only consolation in the midst of their political futility was the comfort of a clear conscience.

One northerner who believed the question of slavery should be postponed because it was simply too dangerous to handle at present was the New York politician Martin Van Buren, who would serve as president from 1837 to 1841. Van Buren did as much as any other political leader to put together a two-party system that would force political disagreements into safe channels and thus prevent the political cataclysm that a clash on the subject of slavery could bring. Topics that could be safely debated would be represented by one of the two parties, thus giving voters a means of expressing their preferences and participating in the national political debate, but the structure of the party system was such that neither major party could afford to take a strong stand either for or against slavery—especially against. With the deadly issue of slavery thus safely excluded from national debate, the country would be free to pursue its continued growth in freedom, wealth, power, and territory.

As the political battles of the early 1840s were to demonstrate, the two-party system was robust enough to handle almost any political dispute, even issues that moved their advocates to intense feelings. Political leaders of opposing factions might become bitter enough toward each other to resort to personal violence, but the system continued to function. The government and the country held together, and the issue of slavery remained marginalized. As the developments of the late 1840s were to prove, the only thing that could reintroduce the question of slavery to the national political arena, and thus prepare the field for a cataclysmic clash on that subject, was the very culmination of the territorial expansion that Americans had cherished and hoped that they could accomplish while ignoring the fate of the nation's two and a half million slaves. Thus America's manifest destiny to overspread the continent became its manifest destiny finally to face the issue of slavery.

PART ONE

The Two-Party System

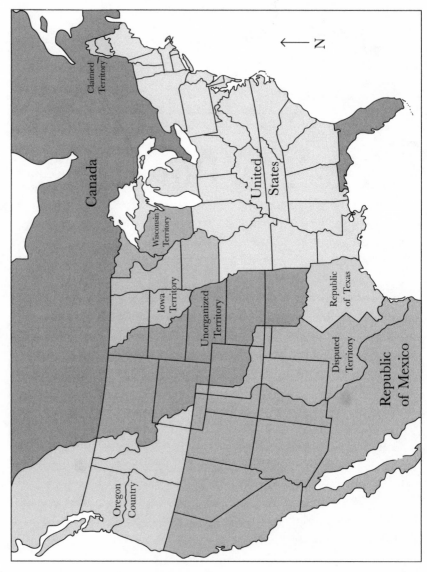

North America in 1840

CHAPTER ONE

The Log Cabin and Hard Cider Campaign

AMERICANS IN 1840 felt confident that their country was on the verge of greatness. The young Republic might be only three score and four years old, but it was already the world's biggest and oldest land governed of, by, and for the people, a self-conscious beacon of freedom to the rest of the world. And the future seemed to stand open to the United States, just like the rest of the North American continent, beckoning bold Americans to stride forward and take possession and thus increase the power and expand the extent of what they liked to call the Empire of Liberty.

America was growing. The census the government would conduct that year would reveal that the Republic's population, centered hypothetically on a point 260 miles west of Washington, D.C., numbered just over seventeen million, an increase of 32.7 percent in the past ten years. New states were joining the Union. Two had joined in the past decade (Arkansas in 1836 and Michigan a few months later in 1837), and more were all but certain to follow in the one now dawning. The Iowa and Wisconsin territories would likely be ready for admission inside the next ten years, and interesting prospects lay farther west, even beyond the broad expanse of the Louisiana Purchase lands that the explorer Meriwether Lewis had described as "the fairest portion of the globe." In 1836 the Christian missionaries Marcus and Narcissa Whitman and Henry and Eliza Spalding had traveled all the way across the Rocky Mountains. Fellow missionary Jason Lee had pushed farther west, to the green and fertile Willamette Valley. Their letters home had brought some of the first reports of that inviting country, and other of their countrymen were already beginning to contemplate migrating.

Even more exciting had been the news in recent years from the Southwest, where Americans had settled the largely empty Mexican province of Tejas at Mexico's invitation. When that country had tried to subject the colonists to despotic government, they had risen up and in 1836 overthrown Mexican rule of the province, claiming it and a vast region beyond the provincial boundary as the new Republic of Texas. There had been talk of Texas joining the United States, and by all accounts its citizens were eager.

The fast-growing adolescent United States was not without problems. Twenty years before, in 1820, intense political strife had arisen from the very issue of expansion itself, specifically the application of the Missouri Territory to enter the Union as a slave state. Some northern congressmen had objected, and the result had been a prolonged political conflict of alarming proportions. The point of strife was a fundamental contradiction in the nation's character. Founded on the self-evident truth that all men are created equal and endowed by their Creator with the rights to life, liberty, and that pursuit of happiness that private property ownership made possible, the "land of the free" counted some two and a half million slaves among its seventeen million inhabitants. The slaves were property, their owners maintained, and therefore had no right to liberty. That this was a gross contradiction of the nation's ideals was once realized even in the South. Now such admissions were out of fashion below the Mason-Dixon Line, and white southerners were asserting with increasing volume that slavery was a positive good for both blacks and whites. Time would tell whether this fundamental flaw would produce serious consequences for the growing nation.

Few in 1840 understood the potential dangers more clearly than the occupant of the White House. Martin Van Buren had recognized, perhaps sooner than anyone else in American national politics, that political conflict was unavoidable and that political parties, far from being the pernicious factions of which James Madison and the other founders had warned, could in fact serve as channels to direct that conflict into safe areas of debate and away from slavery, the one topic that had the potential to destroy the entire system and possibly divide the country. At the time of the Missouri crisis, back in 1820, the country had not possessed a two-party system. All politicians had been at least nominally members of the Republican Party, and this absence of the strife of "factions" had so pleased that generation of Americans that they had referred to the decade after the War of 1812 as the Era of Good Feelings. But feelings had not been at all good when the Missouri issue exploded on the national scene midway through the era. Without the restraints of established political parties, the strife in Congress escalated quickly to a level that former president Thomas Jefferson likened to "a fire bell in the night [that] awakened and filled me with terror." Congress had with difficulty reached a compromise in its dispute, and a much younger Martin Van Buren had taken a lesson from the incident.[1]

Van Buren was born in Kinderhook, New York, in 1782, the son of a tavern keeper of Netherlands descent, and the future president's first language was Dutch. He had received little formal education but had been determined to succeed, studying for six years under a Kinderhook lawyer before being admitted to the bar in 1803. A successful law practice led to an equally successful career in state politics. Van Buren won the nicknames Wizard of the Albany Regency, for his leadership of the state's most powerful political faction, and Red Fox of Kinderhook, for his considerable political skills. He became a U.S. senator from New York in 1821 and then in 1828, in quick succession, governor of New York and secretary of state under the newly elected president, Andrew Jackson. In Jackson's second term Van Buren was vice president, and when Old Hickory followed Washington's example in declining to seek a third term in office, Van Buren was his natural successor. He had won the election of 1836 handily. The eighth president of the United States was very much a self-made man.[2]

Van Buren's ideal of a political party was one that would be national in scope, based on an alliance of North and South. By building a party that drew its strength from every section of the country, Van Buren could force the opposing party to do the same—if it wanted to have any hope of competing successfully for control of Congress and the presidency. Each party would seek to maintain its appeal throughout the nation, and as this pertained to the South, that meant each party would do its best to suppress all criticism of slavery. Once established, the system created a political dynamic that made slavery persistently invisible on the national political stage. Van Buren had done as much as anyone to construct the party system by building the Democratic Party, first as a staunch supporter and trusted advisor of party founder Andrew Jackson and later as the party's victorious standard-bearer. As president he was now the active leader of the more coherent and powerful of the nation's two political parties.[3]

And he had a serious problem. Within weeks of his taking office, the bottom had fallen out of the American economy. In April 1837 some 250 businesses had failed in New York City alone, and by mid-May every bank in the city had suspended payments of gold and silver. By the end of that month total losses from business failures in New York had reached $100 million. Over the months that followed, 40 percent of the nation's banks folded, and many of the others were crippled and on the brink of

collapse. An epidemic of bankruptcies swept the country. Unemploy-
ment was rampant and economic suffering intense as the United States
plunged into a depression that dwarfed any other in the national experience prior to the Great Depression of the 1930s.[4]

Why had all this happened? As usual with economics, the root causes
are hard to untangle, but it seems that British investors had been bullish
on America during the early 1830s, investing so lavishly that the inflow of
their gold effectively doubled the U.S. money supply. At the same time,
U.S. bankers had recklessly expanded credit, with banknotes in circulation jumping from $95 million to $140 million during the middle years of
the decade. With the easy credit provided by scores of eager investors, a
number of state governments foolishly borrowed dizzying sums to
finance lavish programs of transportation improvements—railroads,
canals, and the like. Midway through the decade, the Bank of England
became alarmed at the ongoing export of capital and changed its policies
so as to make investing in Britain more attractive. The resulting diversion
in the flow of British investment capital might at first seem an insignifi-
cant cause for the massive financial crash America suffered in 1837, but
credit bubbles, such as the one that had formed in the United States during the first half of the 1830s, are notoriously skittish. Like a slight vibra-
tion on a snow-covered mountainside, even a small tremor in the money
supply can trigger an avalanche that carries away everything in its path.
So it was with the U.S. economy of the 1830s, as the withdrawal of
British investments triggered an inexorable credit contraction that historians would come to call the Panic of 1837.[5]

Van Buren handled the situation about as well as any president could
have. He resisted the temptation to get the government entangled in the
economy—and thus compound the nation's troubles and prolong the
depression. He worked hard to establish an independent subtreasury system that would keep government funds from distorting the banking and
credit markets, and he did his best to secure the federal government's
financial situation so that it at least would not drag the economy down
further. That was more than could be said of a number of the state governments, several of which defaulted on payments after their mid-decade
binges of unrestrained borrowing for infrastructure spending.

Public opinion, however, was not necessarily going to be shaped by a
calm assessment of Van Buren's performance. As Theodore Roosevelt
would observe more than half a century later, "When the average man
loses his money he is simply like a wounded snake and strikes right and
left at anything, innocent or the reverse, that presents itself as conspicu-

ous in his mind."[6] The president was conspicuous. Unlike Congress, he was a recognizable individual. Thus, if a scapegoat was needed, the public would look first to the White House. The Whigs gleefully did their best to encourage that reaction, with Whig newspaper editors referring to the president as "Van Ruin" and blaming the nation's economic woes squarely on the president's economic policies, such as his opposition to the Bank of the United States and his support for sound money.

Exuberant at their prospects for finally winning a presidential election, the Whigs held their first nominating convention in Harrisburg, Pennsylvania, in December 1839. The Democrats had been holding such conventions for years, but the Whigs had previously nominated their candidates by means of the Whig congressional caucus. Now, eager to copy their opponents' successful tactic, the party embraced the convention system with its (at least theoretically) more democratic mode of choosing a presidential candidate. The Whigs were determined to present their party as more democratic than the Democrats, even if they had to adopt all of the Democratic Party's methods that they had, until recently, been loudly denouncing as demagoguery far below their dignity.[7]

Henry Clay had high hopes that he would be the convention's choice, and a plurality of the delegates agreed with him. If the Whig Party had a father, he was Clay. As the party had coalesced during the 1830s out of every faction and splinter group that opposed Andrew Jackson for any reason whatsoever, Clay had been the most vocal and consistent foe of Old Hickory. To the extent that the party had any coherent program, it was Clay's so-called American System. This consisted of support for a central bank to create inflation, with its illusion of prosperity; high tariffs to protect domestic producers at the expense of foreign trade; and federal taxpayer funding for each locality's pet infrastructure project. It had the makings of a dandy system for buying votes. Clay had been the presidential nominee of the Whigs' predecessor party, the National Republicans, in the election of 1832. He had stood aside in 1836, and now, with Whig chances looking better than ever before, it was his turn again. If ever a party had an obvious choice, Clay was the man for the Whigs in the 1840 race.[8]

Several of the party's major power brokers were of a different mind. They cared much more about a Whig victory than they did about which Whig won that victory. They had no intention of squandering the opportunity afforded their party by the country's gratifyingly miserable current economic condition. Determined to take every possible step to maximize the party's chance of success at the polls, they came to the conclusion that some other candidate might be, in the parlance of the time, more "available," by which they meant more electable. Clay was well known, but so were his positions. He and his American System had come before the voters twice before, in the presidential elections of 1824 and 1832, and lost both times. Furthermore, the party's anti-Masonic bloc, a holdover from a popular movement of the previous decade, opposed Clay, and that bloc still swayed an important number of votes in New York and Pennsylvania. Abolitionists and other opponents of slavery, many of them evangelical Christians, were far from enthusiastic about the slaveholding—and reputedly loose living—Henry Clay. This was all the more true after he made in February 1839 a widely reported Senate speech denouncing abolitionists. And though Clay had as much personal charm as any politician in American history, in twenty-eight years on the national political scene he could hardly have avoided making a number of enemies.[9]

Thus, when the delegates gathered in Harrisburg, certain astute political managers, like New York's jovial Thurlow Weed and his henchman, the newspaper editor Horace Greeley, as well as the humorless Pennsylvanian Thaddeus Stevens, were ready to work such magic as they could in favor of a more available candidate. When Stevens learned that the Virginia delegation was contemplating support for its favorite son, Winfield Scott, the politically ambitious commanding general of the United States Army, he contrived to saunter over to that delegation's part of the hall and drop, quite casually and apparently accidentally, a letter he had somehow obtained, written by Scott to a New York politician aiming to conciliate the abolitionist vote in that state. It did not conciliate Scott's fellow Virginians, who promptly, as Stevens had calculated, dropped Scott from consideration. Having persuaded the convention to adopt the unit rule, mandating a one-state, one-vote nomination, Weed and Stevens then skillfully maneuvered one delegation after another toward their chosen candidate, if not as a first-ballot choice, then as a second. When the wheeling and dealing was finished and the smoke-filled rooms had cleared, the Whigs had passed over Henry Clay and chosen instead the soldier and politician William Henry Harrison of Ohio.[10]

Born at Berkeley Plantation in 1773, Harrison was the youngest son of a wealthy and prominent family of the Virginia Tidewater gentry. His father was a member of the Continental Congress, signed the Declaration of Independence, and subsequently served as governor of Virginia. After his father's death in 1791, young Harrison joined the army, receiving a commission as ensign in the First U.S. Infantry Regiment. Posted to Cincinnati, Harrison became part of General "Mad Anthony" Wayne's army and helped defeat a confederation of Indians at the 1794 Battle of Fallen Timbers. The following year, Harrison was one of the signers of the Treaty of Greenville, by which the Indians ceded much of Ohio for white settlement. In 1797 he resigned from the army to become secretary of the Northwest Territory, and two years later, at the age of twenty-six, he was elected the territory's first delegate to Congress.[11]

In 1800 Congress created the Indiana Territory, separating it from Ohio, which was by then on the fast track to statehood, and President John Adams appointed Harrison its first governor. In 1810 the Shawnee brothers Tecumseh and Tenskwatawa formed a coalition of tribes with the goal of driving the whites out of the lands the Indians had previously occupied north of the Ohio River. The following year, the secretary of war authorized Harrison to raise an army and visit the brothers' village in a show of force that it was hoped would lead to negotiations. On November 6, 1811, his army arrived and encamped near the village, which was located at the confluence of the Tippecanoe and Wabash rivers. Tenskwatawa, in the absence of his brother, requested a truce and a parley to be held the next day. Harrison agreed, but before dawn the next morning the Indians launched a surprise attack on the army encampment. After several hours of fighting, Harrison's troops drove off the attackers, who then abandoned their village in retreat.[12]

The nation hailed Harrison as the victor of what came to be called the Battle of Tippecanoe, and in later years his nickname would be Old Tippecanoe. Despite the fame of the 1811 fight with Tenskwatawa in what would become northwestern Indiana, Harrison's greatest victory came two years later, during the War of 1812, when an army under his command defeated the British at the Battle of the Thames. In that battle, Tecumseh himself, who was fighting for the British, was killed. After the war, Harrison became active in politics. He served as a U.S. commissioner in negotiating two Indian treaties and was elected to a term in the U.S. House of Representatives, another in the Ohio legislature, and one in the U.S. Senate, with an unsuccessful race for governor along the way. He left the Senate in 1828 to accept an appointment as U.S. minister to Colombia, but he held that post for less than three months, leaving office the following March on the inauguration of the new president, Andrew Jackson. Thereafter, Harrison retired to the large farm he had received from his father-in-law. His acres were located near the village of North

Bend, Ohio, on the Ohio River near Cincinnati. He came out of retirement in 1836 for an unsuccessful run for the presidency. Now the Whigs had decided to run him again, under much more favorable auspices.[13]

The convention's choice of Harrison was a bitter pill for the supporters of Henry Clay, who were numerous among the delegates, especially among those from southern states. Some wept openly when Harrison won the nomination. Others were simply furious. To placate them and also to balance the ticket, the convention looked for a southerner and at least a nominal Clay supporter for the vice-presidential nomination. The immediate problem, as it turned out, was in getting such a man to accept the spot. So great was the disgust of the Clay supporters toward the convention's nomination for the top of the ticket that the first four men to whom the vice-presidential nomination was offered turned it down. The man the convention settled on was John Tyler, a stiff, dignified Virginia aristocrat. Tyler was a delegate at the convention and, at least in theory, a supporter of Henry Clay, and he was said to have been among those reduced to tears when the convention's vote for Harrison was announced.[14]

In later months, the question of just how the convention's choice happened to fall on Tyler became one of unusual interest—as well it might, considering that Tyler's political views were the reverse of Clay's on almost every issue. In some ways Tyler could be thought of as a doctrinaire follower of John C. Calhoun of South Carolina, the strident spokesman for the rights of slaveholders and of the South as a special section of the country, but Tyler identified himself with a coterie of Virginia politicians who were hard-core purists for old-style Jeffersonian Republicanism in its most distilled form. In their eyes, Andrew Jackson's sin had lain in his using the powers of the presidency too forcefully. The irony of this, in view of the fact that Jefferson had been a forceful president and that Jackson had been acting forcefully in defense of the very constitutional principles that the hard-core Republicans professed to hold even more stringently than he did, seemed to be lost on Tyler and his band of Virginia true believers. Like Calhoun, Tyler and the Old Republicans maintained a death grip on precise constitutional scruples at least in part because they saw those scruples as the best defense of slavery.[15]

Tyler disagreed with Calhoun on some nuances of the alleged rights of nullification and secession, as well as on such matters as Van Buren's independent treasury and subtreasury program, but in most other respects Tyler would have found himself in agreement with the fiery

South Carolinian. Like Calhoun, Tyler despised all tariffs and the idea of a national bank. The only reason he was in the Whig Party was that he had broken with Jackson over Jackson's determination to enforce the existing tariff in the face of South Carolina's attempt at nullification seven years before. Although Clay and Tyler were said to be personal friends, Tyler had little in common with the Kentuckian politically besides his residence south of the Mason-Dixon Line and his ownership of slaves, but those were definitely factors of importance and apparently enough to secure Tyler's support for Clay among the several potential Whig candidates for 1840.[16]

Tyler's perceived affinity for Clay—and his perceived attractiveness to southern voters—helped win him the nomination, despite his open and avowed opposition to Clay's American System. Whig delegates may also have reasoned that Tyler's presence on the ticket would help hold the allegiance of the Nullifiers and their various southern sympathizers, many of whom, following old Calhoun himself, were already starting to drift back to the Democratic Party. Besides, after several prominent backers of Clay indignantly rejected overtures for the vice presidency, Tyler was at least available. What did his political opinions matter? Vice presidents had always been irrelevant once in office. The Whigs had a ticket: "Tippecanoe and Tyler too." As one Clay supporter noted, "There was rhyme, but no reason in it."[17]

As the convention was winding up, a young delegate ventured to point out that they had not yet adopted a platform. Ought they? The opinion of his colleagues was emphatic that they ought not. In fact, Whig leaders had for some time been discussing the policy of adopting a platform, and they were decidedly against it. Nicholas Biddle, the director of the Second Bank of the United States, who, with Henry Clay, had waged the so-called Bank War against Andrew Jackson, wrote that if the Whigs were to nominate Harrison, "it will be on account of the past, not the future." In that case, Harrison should "rely entirely on the past. Let him say not one single word," Biddle continued, "about his principles, or his creed—let him say nothing—promise nothing." No questioners, the bank director warned, should ever be able to "extract from him a single word, about what he thinks now, or what he will do hereafter."[18]

This policy of blatantly offering the voters a pig in a poke had much to recommend it in a political party composed of various factions that disagreed with one another on many issues of policy. Almost the only matters on which all Whigs were of one mind were that they hated Andrew Jackson and all his adherents and that they wanted very badly to get into office. Northeastern Whigs longed for high tariffs that would shift more of the nation's wealth into the pockets of northeastern business-men. Western Whigs sought federally financed internal improvements that would enhance their region's economic infrastructure at the expense of taxpayers in other regions. Both hoped for the easy credit and per-ceived economic boom times they dreamed would be produced by a powerful central bank. Southern Whigs might or might not favor those programs, but they were eager to vote against the party of Andrew Jack-son, who had made South Carolina back down in the nullification crisis of the early 1830s. Already Whigs in the South were presenting them-selves to voters as the most reliable defenders of slavery, while Whigs in the North billed themselves before the electorate as the only party on which a sensible abolitionist should bestow his vote. For a polyglot party of this sort, discussion of the issues was fraught with danger. Far better, if it could be done, to say nothing at all about the issues and attract votes solely with slogans and hoopla. After making various plans for the cam-paign now beginning, the convention adjourned.[19]

Prior to the convention Henry Clay had written a magnanimous letter all about how he would be happy to let the convention choose whomever it might see as the best candidate and pledging to give his cor-dial support to whomever that should be. Of course, he assumed that it would be himself, despite some forebodings about other candidates and hints party leaders had tried to give him about the inexpediency of his own nomination. Uneasy about the outcome but still not believing the Whigs would dare to pass him over, Clay remained in Washington await-ing news of the convention. On the final day he beguiled the time in the dining room of Brown's Hotel, where he poured one drink after another at a bar that was described as "well-loaded." Clay was too by then, and he launched into a long, loud, and profane rant against his political oppo-nents, much to the astonishment of the others in the dining room. After Clay had staggered off to his boardinghouse, one shocked witness turned to another and said, "That man can never be my political idol again."[20]

Clay was back at the boardinghouse by the time the delegation from the convention in Harrisburg arrived to break the bad news to him. He was sitting down when they told him, but on hearing the news he jumped up and began pacing, stamping his feet, waving his fists in the air, and shouting an almost unbroken stream of curses. "Such an exhibition we never witnessed before," recorded one of those present, "and we pray never again to witness such an ebullition of passion, such a storm of des-peration and curses." "My friends are not worth the powder and shot it would take to kill them!" Clay snarled between imprecations. "If there were two Henry Clays, one of them would make the other President of the United States!" Gradually his rage subsided into a state of lugubrious self-pity. "It is a diabolical intrigue, I now know, which has betrayed me," he moaned. "I am the most unfortunate man in the history of parties; always run by my friends when sure to be defeated, and now betrayed for a nomination when I, or any one, would be sure of an election."[21]

Given time, Clay recovered—and sobered up. Within a week he delivered a speech to a Whig gathering in Washington, proclaiming that it did not matter that the party had passed over him, since the Whig Party had never been about individuals anyway. "No!" Clay intoned. "We have been contending for principles. Not men, but principles, are our rules of action." It was an impressive display of party unity, but it pointedly ignored the fact that the convention had just nominated a man and refused to make any statement whatsoever concerning principles.[22]

Democrats were not slow in reacting to the man—and the lack of principles—put forth by the Whig convention, denouncing Harrison's obvious avoidance of any reference to the issues and styling him "General Mum." They also pointed to his age. At sixty-seven he was the oldest man yet to seek the presidency. Hearing that a disgruntled Clay supporter had complained that they should have left the old general to enjoy his log cabin and his hard cider in peace, a Baltimore Democratic newspaper editor pounced on the remark. "Give him a barrel of hard cider, and settle a pension of two thousand a year on him," he wrote, "and my word for it, he will sit the remainder of his days in his log cabin."[23]

For the astute Whig managers, this was a gift. They were soon trumpeting Harrison as "the people's candidate," "the Log-Cabin Candidate." The *New-York Daily Whig*, not usually considered the voice of the rugged frontiersman, inveighed against the "pampered office-holders" who would "sneer at the idea of making a poor man President of the United States." The Whigs soon had developed a story line much to their liking. Harrison was a simple farmer who lived in a log cabin and drank hard cider, the simple beverage of the common man. Van Buren, on the other hand, was an effete epicure who lived in wanton luxury at public expense, wore silk shirts with ruffles, and drank champagne from fancy glasses. Harrison was a man of the people; Van Buren an aristocrat, disdainful of ordinary mortals. It was utter moonshine, but it became the theme of the campaign. The Whig press took it up virtually in unison.[24]

That William Henry Harrison became the "log cabin candidate" was all the more remarkable in view of the fact that he did not live in a log cabin but in a commodious mansion on his spreading acres at North Bend. He had not been born in a log cabin but in an opulent plantation house. In fact, if he had lived in a log cabin at any period of his life, it had been only when he could not avoid it, and such periods had been few and brief. While serving as governor of the Indiana Territory and holding frequent negotiations with the occasionally hostile tribes, Harrison had commissioned the building of a two-story plantation-style brick mansion named Grouseland in the rough-hewn territorial capital of Vincennes. By birth, background, upbringing, and taste, Harrison was far more the aristocrat than was Van Buren. Nevertheless, the Whigs set out to sell the American people just the opposite story. They had a small log cabin constructed near Harrison's North Bend mansion so that the candidate could at least honestly say that he currently lived in such a structure, and log cabins, in various degrees of miniaturization, appeared at rallies and parades across the country as the leading symbol of Harrison's candidacy.

The Whigs first launched their political campaign in the very halls of Congress itself, and the nation's business had to take a backseat to the party's business. The Twenty-sixth Congress had convened for its first session two days before the Whig convention in Harrisburg. With the campaign now formally under way, congressional Whigs took the floor to denounce the Van Buren administration's conduct of the Second Seminole War, a low-grade conflict that had been simmering for a number of years in the Florida swamps, with the army trying with little success to move the Seminoles from Florida to a projected new home in the Indian Territory (now Oklahoma). Catching the elusive Indians in the trackless swamps had proven well-nigh impossible, and the failure now became grist for the Whigs' campaign mill. They flayed the Van Buren administration mercilessly for allowing the army to use allegedly inhumane methods (bloodhounds to track the Seminoles), but then turned right around and complained that Van Buren had not taken steps strong enough to conclude the war successfully. When the administration requested a reorganization of the militia system, Whig members practically fell over themselves in their haste to raise the hue and cry about this new evidence of Van Buren's plan to create a standing army and have himself crowned "Martin the First, King of North America."[25]

Next the congressional Whigs fastened their outrage on an appropriation bill for $3,665 for the upkeep of the White House. Although the amount was very small for such a large building and the frugal Van Buren would approve only the most necessary repairs and renovations, the Whigs denounced the expenditure as further evidence of Van Buren's royal pretensions. On three successive days in mid-April, Pennsylvania Whig congressman Charles Ogle made an extended speech called "The Regal Splendor of the Presidential Palace." The White House, Ogle maintained, was a "palace as splendid as that of the Caesars, and as richly adorned as the proudest Asiatic mansion." The president, to whom Ogle applied the Whigs' favorite derisive nickname, Sweet Sandy Whiskers, had, Ogle asserted, spent $20,000 on furniture and on having the White House grounds landscaped in obscene representations. Worse, the luxury items with which Van Buren had allegedly stocked the White House were foreign-made. The president might at least have had the decency to buy American. But no, Ogle continued, this "democratic peacock" dressed in foreign finery preened himself in front of oversized gold-framed mirrors, and ate off gold and silver tableware. The congressman concluded by announcing that he was going to vote against the current appropriation because Van Buren might just as well use it to install a throne and buy himself a crown.[26]

This would have been a merited indictment of the president if any part of it had been true. None of it was, and Ogle knew it. He had fabricated the entire story out of whole cloth. An Englishman who visited the White House during Van Buren's residence there told quite a different story. After attending a March 1838 open house, James Silk Buckingham, member of Parliament, wrote that the White House was much more modestly furnished and decorated than a typical English country gentleman's residence. It was "unostentatious . . . without parade or displays . . . well adapted to the simplicity and economy . . . of the republican institutions of the country."[27]

Even some of Ogle's fellow Whigs could not stomach the blatant barrage of lies he had launched in his speech. The very next day Massachusetts Whig representative Levi Lincoln rose in the House to protest Ogle's "unwarranted and undignified attack" on the president, pointing out that Van Buren had spent less money on the White House than any preceding president and "invariably expressed reluctance to have anything expended for that object." Whig newspaper editors, however, seized on the issue with delight, not only reporting it as truth but adding their own embellishments. One editor reported that the speech had so angered Van Buren that he had burst his corset. Another falsehood, but a lie would serve as well as the truth for getting the Whig candidate elected—better, in this case, since suitable truth did not exist. Horace Greeley even pretended to believe that published reports of Levi Lincoln's speech were in fact a Democratic hoax. Ogle, meanwhile, had his speech printed and sent to thousands around the country. Numerous Whig newspapers also helped disseminate their own copies.[28]

Before adjourning their national nominating convention in Harrisburg, the Whig delegates had made plans for conventions—party rallies, in effect—to be held in every state of the Union. The most ambitious of these would be a nationwide Whig Convention of Young Men, to open in Baltimore on the first Monday in May, simultaneously with the Democrats' national nominating convention in that city. The agenda for each of these Whig rallies was flamboyant showmanship and as much noise as possible, as the party continued to drown out its policy differences—both with the American people and within its own ranks—in a cacophony of raucous campaigning.[29]

The Baltimore event was a smashing success. Delegations were on hand from twenty-one of the twenty-six states, for a total crowd variously estimated at from eight thousand to more than three times that number. A grand parade through the streets of the city formed a procession three miles long that took an hour and fifteen minutes to pass any given point, with several marching bands, hundreds of banners, Whig dignitaries in elegant barouches, and no fewer than eight log cabin floats, some of which had come all the way from Pennsylvania. One such mobile log cabin featured smoke emerging from its chimney and, standing in front of its door, a barrel of hard cider, from which the cheerful float riders refreshed themselves more or less continuously. Leading the parade, the Baltimore delegation carried a large white banner with a picture of an eagle and another of a barrel of cider and a twelve-line poem about how the people were rising up to make Harrison president, concluding:

> *Speeds on in his glory Old Tippecanoe*
> *The iron arm'd soldier, the true hearted soldier*
> *The gallant old soldier of Tippecanoe!*[30]

The most celebrated item in the parade, however, was a parade ball, a stuffed leather sphere, eight or nine feet in diameter, decorated with campaign slogans and transfixed horizontally by a long pole along which half a dozen men could stand on each side of the leather globe and "roll the ball," as the saying went, for Old Tippecanoe. In fact, Harrison supporters had rolled this particular ball all the way from Allegany County in western Maryland. Now as eager volunteers rolled the ball along the parade route, marchers and spectators chanted the doggerel inscribed on it:

> *Farewell, dear Van*
> *You're not our man;*
> *To guide the ship*
> *We'll try Old Tip.*[31]

Once the procession reached the spacious grounds of the Canton Race Track, it was the orators' turn, and all the big guns of Whig rhetoric were on hand. "The time for discussion is passed," intoned Henry Clay. "We are all Whigs. We are all Harrison men. We are united. We must triumph." Then Daniel Webster, the foremost orator of the era, took his turn at the podium. "The time has come when the cry is change. Every breeze says change," declaimed Webster, proving that in politics, at least, some things never change. Webster did not specify what sort of change he wanted—as if only one sort of change was possible—but he did not neglect to touch on the campaign's main theme: "We have fallen, gentlemen, upon hard times," he announced, "and the remedy seems to be hard cider." Other speakers followed, but their eloquence was lost on much of the crowd, since a very stiff wind blew throughout the festivities and kept most in attendance from hearing any of the oratory. Nevertheless, the crowd was enthusiastic, with much cheering and singing and drinking of hard cider. It was by all accounts a memorable event.[32]

Meeting simultaneously in Baltimore, within earshot of the raucous parade as it passed through town, was the much smaller and quieter national Democratic nominating convention. The ongoing economic depression gripping the nation would have been enough to cast a pall over an incumbent party's electoral efforts, but the Democrats in 1840 had other problems, of which the noisy Whiggish multitudes in the streets were only a part. The convention duly renominated Van Buren for the top spot on the ticket, but the vice-presidential nomination presented a far thornier question.

A veteran of the War of 1812, Vice President Richard Mentor Johnson had commanded the Kentucky Mounted Rifles and led them in the fierce charge that had not only decided Harrison's victory at the Battle of the Thames but had also killed Tecumseh. Indeed, Johnson himself was reputed to have fired the shot that felled the renowned Shawnee warrior. No one could question the scars of five wounds Johnson had suffered in the desperate fight. His heroism at the Thames, and his killing of Tecumseh, brought him tremendous fame and popularity, especially in the West. In that sense, the Democrats could scarcely have hoped for a better candidate to run as part of their ticket against Old Tippecanoe.[33]

Yet Johnson was not in every way the perfect candidate, even for the vice presidency. At sixty, he was definitely not the dashing fellow who had charmed voters and led men in battle a generation before. Portly and unkempt, he cut an unimpressive figure. He kept a tavern at White Sulphur Spring, Kentucky, when not occupied by his duties as vice president of the United States, and he seemed to enjoy the business of tavern keeping, conversing convivially with his guests. As an added complication, he openly cohabited with one of his slaves.

That last point was by far the most notorious. Johnson had never legally married, but he had lived for years with an octoroon slave of his named Julia Chinn. Despite her pale complexion, Julia's African descent made it illegal for Johnson to marry her. But he had acknowledged her as his common-law wife and had claimed her two daughters as his own, paying for their education and giving them large tracts of land when they married. After Julia died of cholera in 1833, Johnson had started a relationship with another of his female slaves. She ran away but was caught, so Johnson sold her and took up with her sister, also one of his slaves. To say these activities constituted a severe political liability is putting it far too mildly. The South and much of the North as well had no tolerance for interracial unions. No part of the country had much tolerance for cohabitation outside of marriage. Thus Johnson's strong claims to popularity were at least counterbalanced by a personal life that was scandalous by any standard and doubly scandalous in the South. The Whigs, eagerly playing the race card, had made all they could of the matter. "He is married to, or has been in connection with a jet-black, thick-lipped, odoriferous negro wench, by whom he has reared a family of children whom he has endeavoured to force upon society as . . . equals," raged a southern Whig newspaper.[34]

Former president Andrew Jackson was determined that Johnson had to go, as were many other Democrats, particularly in the South. Despite a number of forceful letters from Jackson, however, Van Buren declined to take action to ensure that Johnson would not be on the ticket for his second term. Many northern Democrats still admired Johnson, and Van Buren was unwilling to offend them. Instead, he left the choice of a vice-presidential candidate to the uninfluenced decision of the convention.

The delegates were no more eager to go on record about Johnson than was Van Buren, and their solution was to punt the matter to the states. The Democratic Party in each state was to adopt whomever it might fancy for its vice-presidential candidate. It was, all things considered, about as bad a decision as could readily be conceived and seemed to set the stage for a bizarre situation in which the vice president would be a Whig even if Van Buren won another term in the White House. As it turned out, and somewhat to the Democrats' relief, no other Democratic contenders for the vice presidency put themselves forward. Johnson therefore remained, by default, the party's nationwide vice-presidential candidate.[35]

Before closing their convention, the Democrats adopted a platform that expressed strong opposition to Clay's American System, the presumptive real policy position of the Whigs. The Democratic platform also opposed the idea of any congressional action on the subject of slavery. Complete noninterference was the party's policy toward what Calhoun called the South's "peculiar institution," as it was toward many other aspects of social and economic relations.[36]

And so the campaign continued through the spring and summer and into the fall. Whig rallies took place across the country, as loud and boisterous as the extravaganza in Baltimore and sometimes perhaps even bigger. More than thirty thousand were claimed, albeit by an enthusiastic Whig source, to have attended a May 29 rally at the Tippecanoe battleground in Indiana, featuring numerous bands as well as floats that included a four-ton wheeled replica of a fully rigged sailing ship, drawn by six horses and bearing various banners praising Harrison and denouncing Van Buren. There was a sixty-foot canoe on wheels, pulled by a fine team of horses, and of course the obligatory log cabin "adorned with coon skins, gourds, and a variety of log cabin furniture, and pulled along the parade route by six more stout horses."[37]

A similar rally at Fort Meigs in Ohio, scene of one of Harrison's battles during the War of 1812, featured a stationary log cabin seventy-five feet long as well as the by now customary parade with bands and a giant canoe float. After the parade there were plenty of Whig orators on hand to make speeches denouncing Van Buren, and then, amid the great excitement of his supporters, Harrison himself arrived to help celebrate his past victory and, in a definite breach of etiquette for presidential candidates in those days, stump for his next victory. He wore a broad-brimmed hat in place of his usual high silk hat, since the latter might have looked like the kind of aristocratic paraphernalia that only the likes of Van Buren was supposed to use. Whigs claimed thirty-five thousand in attendance.[38]

At this and other Whig rallies reasonably close to Harrison's home in southwestern Ohio, Old Tippecanoe appeared in person and made a speech. That was a stark departure from the standards of political propriety then prevailing. In imitation of George Washington, a presidential candidate was to remain quietly at home, demurely taking no interest in the political campaign until and unless, with the election finally over, he received formal notification that his fellow citizens had chosen him to assume the presidency. A candidate who appeared at his own rallies and made speeches on his own behalf risked appearing immodest, conceited, and dangerously ambitious. Somehow in the midst of all the mind-numbing hoopla, Harrison got away with what no candidate had previously attempted. It was a not-inconsiderable part of the Whigs' accomplishment that year that their wild electioneering practices seemed to make voters forget all previous standards of electoral propriety. In boldly going where no presidential candidate had gone before, Harrison did not immediately change the customs of American elections. Twenty years later Stephen Douglas would campaign for himself, and another thirty-six years after that, in 1896, William Jennings Bryan would do the same. By the mid-twentieth century, however, such tactics had become accepted, and "front porch campaigns" were quaint memories.[39]

Some estimates put the crowd at a September Whig rally in Dayton, Ohio, at more than one hundred thousand. There marchers chanted:

> *Old Tip he wears a homespun coat;*
> *He has no ruffled shirt-wirt-wirt.*
> *But Mat he has the golden plate,*
> *And he's a little squirt-wirt-wirt.*

Whig rhymesters churned out campaign songs in surprising numbers. There seems to have been one for every occasion or circumstance. Horace Greeley brought out *The Log Cabin Song-Book* with such selections as "Tippecanoe," "Old Tippecanoe," "The Soldier of Tippecanoe," "The Flag of Tippecanoe," "Tippecanoe and Jackets of Blue," and "A Tip-Top Song About Tippecanoe," most of them set to familiar tunes. There was the New Jersey Whig song "Keep the Ball Rolling," and there was "The National Whig Song," to the tune of "La Marseillaise." By far the favorite, however, was "Tippecanoe and Tyler Too," to the tune of "The Little Pig's Tail":

> *What's the cause of this commotion, motion, motion,*
> *Our country through?*
> *It is the ball a-rolling on*
> *For Tippecanoe and Tyler too.*
> *And with them we'll beat little Van, Van, Van,*
> *Van is a used up man.*
> *And with them we'll beat little Van.*

Alexander Coffman Ross, a jeweler from Zanesville, Ohio, composed the song and introduced it at a Whig rally in that Ohio River town. Ross wrote eleven more verses to develop every possible nuance of the song's theme.

Nor was that all. The Whigs unleashed a veritable blizzard of creativity and savvy marketing, 1840-style, in support of their candidate. A dozen or so campaign biographies sang Harrison's praises, including one book geared for children and two published in German. Then there were log-cabin-shaped liquor bottles brought out by the E. G. Booz distillery of Philadelphia. There were canes with miniature log cabins for heads, and of course there were more giant parade balls rolled along by eager cider-fueled volunteers, more log cabin floats and canoe floats of various sizes and descriptions, as well as an amazing plethora of merchandise aimed at reminding citizens of log cabins, hard cider, or both. Attendees at one Whig rally were even treated to the sight of the aristocratic South Carolina planter and Whig politician Hugh S. Legaré sporting a coonskin cap.

Coons and coonskins figured prominently in Whig electioneering, usually in the form of a coonskin nailed to the wall of the candidate's imaginary log cabin, as depicted in innumerable pictures and floats. As a result, the raccoon became one of the symbols of the Whig Party from that time forth, though somewhat incongruously it was Henry Clay, rather than Harrison, who came to be called the Old Coon or the Chief Coon. Of course, Old Tippecanoe already had his nickname.[40]

When all the campaign's bedlam failed in its purpose, other forms of persuasion could be used to motivate voters to back Tippecanoe. Some Whig employers dismissed workers who refused to sign testimonials for Harrison. Some Whig editors and politicians spoke darkly of a possible resort to violence if their side did not win the coming election. Former New York mayor Philip Hone wrote, "Men's minds are wrought up to a pitch of frenzy, and like tinder a spark of opposition sets them on fire. Riot and violence stalk unchecked through the streets, and lying is no longer considered a crime."[41]

The Democrats seemed to have little to offer in reply. Attempts to address the issues before the country could not really compete, in the eyes of a great many voters, with the Whigs' circuslike entertainment, and yet the Democrats did continue to direct most of their energies into earnest attempts to persuade voters, by such outmoded means as logic and evidence, that their party's principles were the true ones. Beyond that, they made at least a feeble reply to the Whigs' focus on personalities by criticizing Harrison's military record, pointing to the fact that he had resigned from the army before the end of the War of 1812, and suggesting that he was too old to be president, a point they tried to emphasize by referring to him occasionally as Granny. They also set up O.K. clubs in many localities, with "O.K." standing for "Old Kinderhook," one of Van Buren's nicknames. The practice may have introduced the word "OK" into the English language, or it may merely have reinvigorated its use. Accounts vary as to when and how the term originated.

Surprisingly, Richard M. Johnson, campaigning vigorously in the western states, proved to be one of the party's strongest assets. By contrast, the Whigs sternly admonished their vice-presidential candidate, John Tyler, to make no statements at all, lest his decidedly un-Whiggish opinions should come out. Another of the seemingly endless Whig rhymes intoned, "We will vote for Tyler therefore, without a why or wherefore." In the end, neither party would carry the home state of its vice-presidential candidate.[42]

While the two major parties thus did battle for the hearts and minds of American voters, a little-noticed third party was also in the lists. James G. Birney was the candidate of the tiny Liberty Party. The party was a creature of the abolitionist movement, which was committed to ending the institution of slavery. Abolitionists had been disappointed when neither major party had nominated a candidate with a clean escutcheon on the slavery issue, and they had decided that a third party was their only option. The new party held its first convention, billed the National Convention of the Friends of Immediate Emancipation, in Albany, New York, in April 1840 and nominated Birney, a Kentuckian and former slaveholder turned abolitionist, on a platform that called for abolishing slavery in the District of Columbia and ending the interstate slave trade. Birney's transition to champion of freedom had involved a slow pilgrimage from advocacy of colonization to gradual emancipation to a conversion to full-blown abolitionism in 1833. He had freed his slaves, moved to Cincinnati, and in 1836 founded the weekly *Philanthropist,* by which he spread his abolitionist ideas.[43]

Neither Birney nor his supporters had any illusions about their chances of success in the 1840 election. Theirs would be protest votes. They saw the issue of slavery as a straightforward moral challenge. The two major parties were dodging that challenge, giving the voters no morally acceptable choice in the election. All that remained to men of awakened conscience was to take their lonely stand for truth, let the consequences be what they may. Whether they won or lost was less important than knowing they had stood for what was right. Their votes would be wasted only if they voted against their own principles.

The Liberty Party could not claim the support of all abolitionists, not to speak of more moderate opponents of slavery. Most of them adhered to the Whig Party. Nothing in the antislavery creed required support for the Whigs' policies of government intervention in the economy through tariffs, internal improvements, and a central bank, but the Whigs also tended to be the party of moral reform, while the Democrats were more likely to carry their laissez-faire tendencies from economics into other areas as well. In addition, the parts of the country in which economic self-interest brought many adherents to the Whig Party happened to be the same parts in which many abolitionists lived, although economic Whigs and abolitionists were not necessarily always the same people.[44]

The Whig Party endeavored to make the most of the abolitionists' natural and regional affinities by presenting itself in the North as the true party of at least moderate antislavery convictions. If those who opposed slavery wanted to make a practical difference in favor of their cause, Whigs exhorted, they should vote Whig. What northern Whig advocates did not add was that their counterparts in the South were simultaneously assuring voters in that region that slavery would be safer in the hands of the Whig Party than in those of their Democratic rivals.

There was no national election day during the first half of the nineteenth century. The various states set their own election days, so that the voting straggled along from when Ohio and Pennsylvania led off on October 30 to when the South Carolina legislature met on November 23 and allocated the state's electors without reference to the voters (South Carolina was the only state still retaining that custom). When all the votes were counted, the result was surprising only in the closeness of the popular vote. Harrison garnered 1,275,016 votes to Van Buren's 1,129,102, a fairly competitive margin of about 53 percent to 47 percent. The electoral vote was not nearly as close. Moderate margins of victory in nineteen states gave Harrison a total of 234 electoral votes to Van Buren's 60, including 11 cast by the South Carolina legislature.[45]

Interestingly enough, all of the mindless electioneering jollification the Whigs brought to the campaign was effective in getting a much larger than usual percentage of eligible voters to the polls that year. Participation had been running in the 55 to 58 percent range during the 1830s, but in 1840 it shot up to 80 percent. Apparently, large numbers of Americans were willing to flock to the polls so long as they were not asked to do any thinking about their votes or to consider issues and policies. It was more fun to chant slogans, roll big leather balls, and drink hard cider.[46]

The Liberty Party drew only 7,069 popular votes, one-fourth of a percent, and, of course, did not carry—or even affect the outcome in—a single state. Whig newspapers sneered at the Liberty Party's ineffectiveness, but *The Oberlin Evangelist*, voice of much of the evangelical segment of the population, was undaunted. "Where is the man in this 'glorious minority,' who regrets his vote?" asked its editor. "We have heard of none." He went on to assert his confidence that the Liberty Party faithful would remain just that and that their numbers would increase as more men reflected on the rights and wrongs of slavery.[47]

In the resounding, if entirely expected, defeat of the Liberty Party lay a sort of victory for Martin Van Buren, even in the midst of his own defeat for reelection to the presidency. The explosive issue of slavery had remained largely submerged. Only seven thousand out of nearly two and a half million voters had seen fit to decide their choice solely on that issue. The two major parties had ignored it, and both of them had drawn their support from every section of the country. True, the Whigs were a bit stronger in the Northeast, and the Democrats in the South and West, but both were truly national parties. The very electoral landslide that made Van Buren's defeat seem much more resounding in the electoral college than it was in the popular vote was an indication of the nationwide appeal of the parties. In state after state Harrison had won by similar moderate margins. The voters of Massachusetts had chosen Old Tippecanoe by about the same margin as those of Louisiana, and Indiana had gone Whig by about the same percentage as had Georgia. As long as these trends persisted, Van Buren's two-party system would continue to direct national disagreements into safe channels—and suppress disagreements on issues, such as slavery, that seemed unsafe in any channel.

Of course, the Whigs had achieved their result by consciously and diligently distracting Americans from the issues facing the country. They might have been able to win the election solely on the basis of the nation's economic misery in the wake of the Panic of 1837, without their carnival campaign. Still, the election of 1840 was not a statement about what the country wanted, other than that it wanted a return to prosperity. The election revealed no consensus on how that prosperity was to be brought about; nor did it show what the majority wanted in any of the other pressing questions that stood before the country at the start of the decade.

CHAPTER TWO

Tyler, Clay, and the Durability of the Two-Party System

THE WHIGS HAD elected their president, the aged and amiable General William Henry Harrison. What remained now was to see which Whigs would control the old cipher. Several had ideas. Former Second Bank of the United States president Nicholas Biddle wrote to his political ally Daniel Webster, "The impression I have is that the coming administration will be in fact your administration."[1] Biddle and Webster certainly hoped so. Webster, one of the dominant figures of the Senate, had for some time been on Biddle's payroll to represent the interests of the national bank and its director. Later generations would refer to such arrangements as bribes. Early signs seemed to indicate that Harrison would pay a great deal of attention to Webster's advice.

The dignified Webster and the scheming Biddle were not the only Whigs with plans to pull the strings that would make Harrison dance. Henry Clay was still bitter at having been passed over for the nomination, and he was determined to dominate this first Whig administration. Harrison was not eager to meet with Clay after the election lest it appear that Clay was exercising undue influence, but when in November 1840 the president-elect visited Kentucky with no plans to meet Clay, the latter headed him off in Frankfort and pressed him into spending a week at Clay's plantation, Ashland, near Lexington.[2]

Clay was soon exercising considerable influence over Harrison. Old Tippecanoe sometimes bucked at Clay's attempts to saddle and ride him. "Mr. Clay," he burst out on one occasion when the Kentuckian had goaded him a bit too far, "you forget that I am the President." But on many issues and appointments Harrison followed Clay's advice. He even offered Clay the post of secretary of state, though Clay declined the position as beneath his dignity. Besides, Whig doctrine said that Congress was to be supreme and the president subservient, and Clay preferred to run things from the Senate—if he could not do so from the White House. Meanwhile, Harrison continued to take advice from Clay's Whig rival

Daniel Webster, who accepted the appointment as secretary of state and suggested a number of Harrison's other appointments.[3]

One of these that particularly annoyed Clay was the appointment of Ohioan Thomas Ewing as secretary of the Treasury. Clay had wanted John Clayton of Delaware for the post, because Clayton was a strong bank man and a new Bank of the United States was one thing Clay definitely intended to accomplish in the administration that he planned on being only nominally Harrison's. Ewing himself was moderately pro-bank, but that was not good enough for the Old Coon, who also suspected that Webster's influence lay behind the appointment and felt deep jealousy as a result. Clay went to Ewing and told him peremptorily that "the people everywhere" wanted him to be postmaster general, adding, "You had better conform to that indication." Ewing thought otherwise.[4]

Clay was in an unpleasant frame of mind these days, despite his considerable—though not complete—influence with the president-elect. Arrogant and dictatorial during the lame-duck session of Congress that began in December 1840, Clay taunted Democrats about the recent Whig victory and their coming exile from power, and he boasted of how he was going to repeal all of their pet programs and pass his own legislation instead. "Clay's insolence is insufferable," wrote a Democrat, "and it will not be borne. Never have I seen power so tyrannically used as the new Senate are now using it." So intemperate did Clay's language become on the Senate floor that he provoked a challenge to a duel with an Alabama senator. Fortunately the authorities got wind of the matter, and the sergeant at arms arrested both men and bound them over to keep the peace.[5]

Harrison arrived in the national capital on his sixty-eighth birthday, February 9, 1841, in the midst of a snowstorm. He was no sooner established in his temporary quarters at Gadsby's Hotel than he was besieged by office seekers and others, particularly a succession of senators, who hoped to influence the incoming administration. Leading the parade was Henry Clay, who demanded that Harrison ditch Ewing and appoint Clayton to the Treasury Department. The president-elect again declined as tactfully as he could. Then Harrison was herded through a nonstop whirl of social engagements. It was tiring, but Old Tippecanoe seemed to enjoy it. He called on Van Buren, who was, for a defeated president, unusually warm and hospitable, and the two were soon on friendly terms. "The President is the most extraordinary man I ever saw," wrote Van Buren. "He does not seem to realize the vast importance of his elevation. . . . He is as tickled with the Presidency as is a young woman with a new bonnet."[6]

Harrison got away to Virginia for a few days in hopes of finding seclusion to write his inaugural address. Before he could do that, however, he had to meet the demands for public appearances in the state. He attended various parades and banquets and made a visit to the log cabin that the Richmond Tippecanoe Club had set up on that city's square. In a speech in Richmond he denied that he was or ever had been an abolitionist. He at last found some peace at his birthplace, old Berkeley Plantation, and there composed the address. It was learned, replete with allusions to classical antiquity, and remarkably long. On returning to Washington, Harrison had Daniel Webster edit it. Finding it a bit lengthy, Webster made cuts. That evening at dinner the great Massachusetts orator looked weary, and when a lady asked why, he replied, "I have killed seventeen Roman proconsuls as dead as smelts, every one of them!" Harrison accepted Webster's changes and then had Clay read the text as well.[7]

Inauguration day, March 4, 1841, was damp, cold, and cloudy. Cannon salutes began at sunrise, though no one could see the sun through the solid overcast. The inaugural parade was an echo of the campaign's showmanship. Harrison rode down Pennsylvania Avenue on his favorite horse, accompanied by two men who had served as his military aides at Tippecanoe and the Thames. Behind him marched veterans and Tippecanoe clubs with the usual assortment of floats. Then came regular army troops, volunteer militia companies, and students from Georgetown College. In all, the procession stretched nearly two miles.[8]

Harrison wore neither hat nor overcoat, demonstrating his robust constitution despite his advanced age. At sixty-eight he was the oldest man, up to that time, to take the oath of office as president of the United States. Along with the usual array of dignitaries, he took his place on the outdoor platform in front of the Capitol. The day had warmed little, and a sharp northwest wind made it feel colder still. Despite the chill wind, Harrison droned on for one hour and forty-five minutes, a record for inaugural addresses that still stands and is not likely to be surpassed. Harrison made all the correct Whig points. Congress should be preeminent. He as president would play a restrained role, using the veto very sparingly, if at all. He also mentioned his commitment to the Whig principle of the single-term presidency, no doubt much to Clay's satisfaction. Harrison added a condemnation of all antislavery activity. Congress, he said, had no power to abolish slavery in the District of Columbia or, presumably, anywhere else. Clearly, at the highest levels, Whigs were no more willing than Democrats to open the door to sectional strife that might split their party and perhaps even the nation.[9]

The press of office seekers resumed as soon as the inaugural festivities were over. Their importunities kept Harrison exhausted most of the time. For a party that had made much ado of denouncing its opponent's alleged practice of rewarding political supporters with government jobs, the Whigs had a very large number of political supporters who seemed to think that government jobs were exactly the appropriate reward for their adherence to the party. Clay even demanded the dismissal of a number of federal employees so that more of his own friends could be accommodated. Harrison could not possibly have satisfied all those clamoring for appointments, especially since rival factions of Whigs petitioned him with multiple claimants for the same posts. Among those dissatisfied in the scramble was Clay, who sponsored an unsuccessful candidate for the lucrative position of collector of customs for the port of New York.[10]

Clay's most intense dispute with the president pertained to the question of whether to call a special session of Congress. Under normal procedures in the mid-nineteenth century, Congress was scheduled to adjourn shortly after the inauguration in March and not reconvene until December. For several reasons this schedule did not suit Clay that year. For one thing, the ongoing depression had put the government on unsound financial footing, requiring Congress to make adjustments to keep the government solvent, and these would probably be necessary before December. More important, though, Clay was eager to get on with the business of passing all of the programs he had been waiting more than a decade and a half to have a president sign into law. The sooner Congress met, the sooner it could pass Clay's legislative agenda and the sooner Clay, who planned to dominate Congress, would once again have a platform from which to address the nation and gain the attention that would assure his presidential election in 1844.[11]

Harrison was reluctant to call such a session. It was unusual, and the cabinet was evenly split on the matter. The party would be more unified, he thought, and his administration more comfortable in office if they waited until the normal time. The president's reluctance drove Clay into a towering rage, and the angry Kentuckian dashed off a rather intemperate letter, disavowing any desire to dictate to the president but warning him that if he did not do exactly what Clay wanted he would look weak and vacillating. He also included a draft of a proclamation calling for a special session, ready for Harrison to sign and issue.

This was going too far, and the president wrote back accusing Clay of lecturing him. "You are too impetuous," he admonished the Kentuckian. At this Clay flew into another of his trademark towering rages. He wrote Harrison that he was "mortified" at the suggestion that he had been dictatorial and complained that enemies must be poisoning Harrison's mind against him. With that, Clay left town and headed back to Kentucky. Ultimately, it was not Clay's bombast that persuaded Harrison, but rather the secretary of the Treasury's notification that the federal government's coffers were likely to be empty before December if Congress did not take action first. On March 17, the president issued a call for a special session of Congress to convene on May 31.[12]

Ten days after Harrison issued that call, physicians diagnosed him as having pneumonia and several other maladies. He had had a cold for some time. His contemporaries pointed to his exposure to the chill and damp on inauguration day, as well as to an occasion a couple of weeks later when he had been caught out in the rain. It was also true that Harrison seemed to be wearing down under the presidential workload, especially the constant harassment of job seekers. Despite, or perhaps because of, the ministrations of his physicians, his fever rose and symptoms of pneumonia appeared, along with intestinal inflammation. The doctors diagnosed his malady as "bilious pleurisy." His condition seemed critical, but several days later he rallied. On March 31 *The National Intelligencer*, a Washington newspaper, reported him much improved. He quickly relapsed, however, and the next day *The Washington Globe* gave a gloomy account of his condition. By the evening of April 3, doctors pronounced his case hopeless. The president sank into delirium, and attendants recorded such mutterings as "It is wrong—I won't consent—'tis unjust. . . . These applications, will they never cease?" He died shortly after midnight on April 4, slightly more than thirty days and twelve hours into his presidential term, making his the shortest presidency in U.S. history.[13]

The funeral took place amid presidential pomp on April 7. Cannon salutes boomed, bands played more solemn tunes than they had five weeks before, and the casket lay in state in the Capitol. Pennsylvania Avenue was festooned with black streamers, and most private dwellings displayed crape on their knockers or bell handles. The warhorse Harrison had ridden in the inaugural parade thirty-four days earlier now walked riderless in the funeral procession, boots reversed in the stirrups. The funeral was held in St. John's Episcopal Church, with a large array of dignitaries in attendance, including a visibly moved John Tyler, hastily summoned from Williamsburg, Virginia, where he had been at the time of the president's demise.[14]

For the first time a U.S. president had died in office. Constitutional scholars had recognized for a number of years prior to Harrison's death that the nation's fundamental law was ambiguous as to what was to happen in the event of a president's death in office. Was the vice president merely to act as president, or was he actually to assume the office and title of president as well? Harrison's cabinet at first thought the former, but John Tyler held strongly to the latter. He had had some occasion to think about the possibility of Harrison's demise simply because of the ninth president's advanced age, and he had had time for more focused thought on the subject during Harrison's final illness. By the time of the president's death, Tyler had a concerted plan for establishing his own claim to be a full-fledged president. He took the oath of office as president, though his previous oath as vice president would have been sufficient had he only meant to function as an acting president. Then he issued an inaugural address.[15]

Under his persuasion the cabinet came around and agreed that he should become president rather than simply act in the dead president's place, even though the latter was more consistent with the Whigs' cant of the previous decade. When Congress later met in the session Harrison had summoned, it also acquiesced in Tyler's ascension to the presidency, although somewhat more reluctantly and with some dissenting votes. Tyler's political allies—Virginian Henry Wise in the House and Mississippian Robert J. Walker in the Senate—vigorously advocated passage of the resolutions recognizing Tyler as president. The point of all this contention represented a significant difference. As a mere acting president, a sort of temporary caretaker, Tyler would have been in a much weaker position relative to the powerful Whig Congress under the leadership of the ambitious and domineering Henry Clay. Indeed, considering the stakes, and the lack of clarity on the subject in the Constitution, Tyler's assumption of the presidency had gone remarkably smoothly.[16]

At fifty-one, John Tyler was the youngest man to have assumed the presidency. Born in Charles City County, Virginia, on March 29, 1790, he was the first U.S. president born after the ratification of the Constitution, and he saw himself as the torchbearer for strict Jeffersonian constitutionalism. He was the scion of one of the First Families of Virginia. Tyler attended the College of William and Mary, where a generation before his father had been Thomas Jefferson's roommate. After graduation, young John studied law with his father, who was governor of Virginia from 1808 to 1811. The family lived at Greenway, a genteel mansion house on a sprawling twelve hundred acres of prime land in the Virginia Tidewater. After practicing law, young Tyler once again followed in his father's footsteps by entering politics, serving in the Virginia legislature and the U.S. House of Representatives and as governor of Virginia before entering the U.S. Senate, where he was serving when the Whigs tapped him to provide the "Tyler too" to Old Tippecanoe.

Tall and thin, Tyler presented a strikingly aristocratic appearance. His most notable feature was a prominent Roman nose. The story was told that during his administration two Americans happened to be present in Naples when an excavation unearthed a bust of Cicero, prompting both to exclaim, "President Tyler!" He was quiet, reserved, dignified, intelligent, and principled—according to his lights. In 1813 he wed Letitia Christian, who suffered a stroke in 1839 that left her largely an invalid.[17]

Tyler had only recently joined the Whig Party and so did not have much of a power base within it. Nor was he a heroic figure like Andrew Jackson, whose prior accomplishments in wartime and natural force of character drew men to rally around him. Those facts meant it would be difficult for Tyler to be a strong president, which was exactly what Henry Clay wanted. If he had planned to dominate the Harrison administration, he intended all the more to control the course and actions of Tyler's presidency. The two had been friends for twenty years, and Clay expected no difficulty from the new president, nor did he intend to tolerate any.[18]

With the special session of Congress approaching rapidly, Tyler wrote a friendly letter to Clay, in reply to one from him. The president urged that any bill for the creation of a new Bank of the United States be left for the December session, when it could be given more careful consideration. Such legislation would not be simple, Tyler warned, and he would have to be satisfied that it was constitutional in every particular, or else it would be his duty to veto it. Besides, the president argued, recent revelations of gross financial corruption in the old Second Bank of the United States, for the time being operating under a Pennsylvania charter but soon to be defunct, made it an especially bad time politically to try to set up another institution just like it. The special session, he urged, should be reserved for legislation to meet the government's immediate fiscal crisis, and the bank should be left for later.[19]

Clay was undeterred. To his friends he announced that the election of 1840 had been a referendum on the Bank of the United States, as if that or any other issue had actually been placed before the voters in the midst of all the log cabin and hard cider tomfoolery. Indeed, Clay had a lengthy list of what he wanted—not only a national bank but also repeal of the Democrats' cherished subtreasury system and higher tariffs on more items, just for starters—and he claimed it was Tyler's duty to support his legislation in fulfillment of "promises" made by Harrison. Clay contended that his policies and his alone could restore prosperity, and he was determined to ram his measures through Congress—and down Tyler's throat if necessary.[20]

Clay arrived in Washington early for the special session, eager to get to work. He called on the president, who received him with his accustomed Virginia courtesy. As their discussion progressed, however, it came to have a distinct edge. Tyler reiterated that he thought the special session was no time to push for the establishment of a central bank. Clay insisted that he would have a bank and have it now. The conversation became heated, and Tyler concluded it by stating, "Go you now, then, Mr. Clay, to your end of the avenue, where stands the Capitol, and there perform your duty to the country as you shall think proper. So help me God, I shall do mine at this end of it as I shall think proper."[21]

The special session opened on May 31, 1841. Clay intended to run it, and it immediately became clear that he had the votes, the will, and the administrative and political skill to do so. "Mr. Clay is carrying every thing by storm," wrote a dismayed Democrat. "His will is the law of Congress." Clay had close political allies elected Speaker of the House and president pro tem of the Senate and dictated the leadership and even the membership of nearly every committee, and he forced his legislation through both houses, permitting only minimal debate. It was all rather ironic for a man who had for more than a decade complained about the overassertiveness of former president Andrew Jackson. Now a sympathetic Whig newspaper wrote of Clay, "He predominates over the Whig Party with despotic sway. Old Hickory himself never lorded it over his followers with authority more undisputed, or more supreme."[22]

The Kentuckian made abundant use of his characteristic charm, which few men—and, it seems, still fewer women—could resist. When crossed, however, the Old Coon snarled with rage. A Virginia Whig who went to him privately to urge him not to push the bank issue to a showdown with the president found Clay's reaction "very violent." "Tyler dares not resist," the senator raged. "I will drive him before me." On the Senate floor he was on a number of occasions rude, belittling, and insulting, and some of the other senators began referring to him as the Dictator. In reply, Clay referred mockingly to the slave who served as his personal servant: "Ask Charles if I am not a kind master."[23]

Proceeding full tilt toward his goal of reestablishing a national bank, Clay had the Senate call on the secretary of the Treasury to submit a plan for a new central bank. The plan Secretary Thomas Ewing submitted was a compromise between the desire of many Whigs, including Clay, for a reincarnation of the old Second Bank of the United States, which Jackson had killed, and the desire of others, notably states' rights purists like Tyler, for one that would show more respect for constitutional scruples. This proposed bank would operate in the District of Columbia rather than Philadelphia, would be controlled by Congress rather than a private board of directors wielding quasi-governmental powers, and would not open branches in states that denied it the permission to do so. Tyler liked the idea and urged Clay to accept it.[24]

Clay was not about to do so. He and other strong bank advocates wanted a powerful institution unfettered by any restraints of the Constitution or states' rights, but for Clay the matter went deeper than that. The issue seems to have become personal for him. He had been the chief advocate of the central bank ever since unveiling his American System more than twenty years before. He had been the bank's champion in the great Bank War against Andrew Jackson and had represented the bank's interests as a presidential candidate in the election of 1832. That election really was as close as the country had ever come to a straightforward referendum on the bank, and the bank—and Clay—had lost resoundingly. Even though the Whigs had deliberately obscured the bank issue in order to win the election of 1840, Clay was determined to see in it—and to make of it—his own vindication and that of the bank. To accept any substantive compromises on the bank issue would be to admit that his previous proposals had been wrong. Clay was determined to drive through Congress a bill to create a bank in the image of the one Jackson had killed.[25]

Clay behaved accordingly. "He is much more imperious and arrogant with his friends than I have ever known him," a Democratic senator wrote of Clay in a letter to a fellow Democrat, "and *that* you know is saying a great deal." Determined to ride down all opposition, through eight sweltering weeks of humid Tidewater summer, Clay cajoled, threatened, instructed, and intimidated his fellow members of Congress and used every legislative trick and sleight of hand he had perfected in thirty years of national politics. Finally, with much figurative groaning and straining, he pushed his own version of the bank bill through both houses by razor-thin margins. That, he assumed, was decisive. No Whig president would dare veto a bill passed by a Whig majority—not after a decade of Whig railing against Andrew Jackson for his "executive usurpation" in vetoing Whig legislation.[26]

Tyler dared. Despite the unified remonstrance of his cabinet in a five-hour meeting, he vetoed the bank bill. In his August 16 veto message Tyler explained that his conscience bound him to kill the legislation because he considered the bank, as set up by Clay's bill, to be unconstitutional. An attempt to override failed.[27]

Clay was spoiling for a fight and would not let this one pass. While other Whigs applied all their cunning to devise a version of the bank bill that would satisfy Tyler's objections while still, in effect, doing all the things to which the president had objected, Clay prepared and delivered in the Senate a lengthy address dissecting and denouncing Tyler's veto message in every detail and ridiculing Tyler himself. Again Clay made the patently false assertion that the election of 1840 had been a referendum on the bank. Since the country wanted the bank, he raged, why could Tyler not set aside his conscience and allow the bill to become law anyway? Not bothered by an overly active conscience himself, Clay always had difficulty understanding men who let theirs get in the way of his purposes. That being the case, Clay went on to suggest that if Tyler's conscience prevented him from doing what Clay said was best for the country, Tyler should resign the presidency in order to allow someone else to do what Tyler's conscience forbade.[28]

The speech was not at all diplomatic, and Clay was far from finished with his denunciations of Tyler. In a speech to the Whig congressional caucus, Clay likened Tyler to the famous traitor Benedict Arnold and suggested that the new president would go over to the Democratic Party, which would assign him to "some outhouse" as a "monument of his perfidy and disgrace." Clay almost seemed to be pushing the president into opposing him—and perhaps that was exactly what he was trying to do. Unlike Harrison, Tyler had never pledged not to seek the presidency in the election of 1844. Clay was determined that no one should stand in his way for that office again. Eager to sideline Tyler, Clay may have been trying to drive him out of the Whig Party by goading him into vetoing a second bank bill.[29]

Indeed, the stakes were higher than that. If Tyler were to veto a second bill, Clay would probably be able to exert enough pressure on Tyler's cabinet to get all or most of them to resign. Not only would that further alienate Tyler from the Whig Party's activist core, but it would also place the president in an unusual bind. The custom of the time was that a president had to fill cabinet vacancies during the term of Congress in which those vacancies occurred. If he did not offer nominations before Congress adjourned, he could not make recess appointments and the cabinet posts would remain empty for months, until Congress reconvened in December. The government would virtually grind to a halt. In that case, Tyler might actually be induced to resign, which, under the laws and customs then prevailing, would lead to a special election. Clay planned on winning that election as well as the one in 1844. The single-term principle, which Whigs had been touting as the antidote for alleged Jacksonian cryptomonarchy, was for other politicians, not Henry Clay. Clay knew the difference between propaganda and policy.[30]

Up to a certain point, events played out much as Clay had planned. Congress passed another bank bill with more or less cosmetic differences from its predecessor. Whether Tyler could have been brought around to see it as having addressed his objections will never be known, for Clay recklessly rammed it through Congress and virtually threw it at the president as if it had been a challenge to single combat. In a lengthy speech preceding the Senate's vote on the bill, Clay ridiculed individual Democratic senators and implied that by vetoing the bill Tyler would be, in effect, joining the Democratic Party. This, he professed to believe, the president would not do. "The soil of Virginia is too pure to produce traitors. Small, indeed, is the number of those who have proved false to their principles and to their party." Turning to the Democratic members of the Senate, Clay intoned, "No gentlemen, the President never will disgrace himself, disgrace his blood, disgrace his State, disgrace his country, disgrace his children, by abandoning his party, and joining with you. Never, never!"[31]

Predictably, Tyler vetoed the bill. Clay reacted immediately by swinging his political forces into action. He met with the members of the cabinet and applied pressure to resign. All of them did except for Secretary of State Daniel Webster. He had enough political stature to resist Clay's arm-twisting, and he was also unwilling to fall into line as a faithful lackey of the imperious Kentuckian. The others turned in their resignations two days before Congress was scheduled to adjourn.

Meanwhile, Clay supporters staged dozens of rallies around the country, at which angry demonstrators burned effigies of the president, and Whig newspapers loyal to Clay virtually shrieked with rage at Tyler, heaping all manner of abuse on him. Many letters arriving at the White

House threatened assassination. Outside the White House, demonstrators, apparently fortified with generous amounts of hard cider, nightly rattled the nerves of the Tyler family with a cacophony of horns and bugles jumbled together with shouts of "A bank!," "Huzza for Clay!," and "Down with the Veto!"[32]

On the floor of the House of Representatives, a Clay Whig made insulting comments to a Tyler supporter, and the two waded into each other with their fists. Other congressmen crowded around, a second scuffle broke out, and a free-for-all was narrowly averted when the clerk ran through the crush of legislators waving the mace of the sergeant at arms and shouting, "Order, gentlemen, order!"[33]

Yet not quite everything went as Clay had wished. Tyler proved remarkably quick in turning in his list of nominees to fill the cabinet vacancies, beating the deadline of Congress's adjournment and thus dodging the trap Clay had set for him. The onus of confirming or rejecting the nominations now lay with the Senate, and if it adjourned without doing so, Tyler would be free to fill the vacancies with recess appointments. In the end, the Senate approved them before going home.[34]

Worse for Clay, in some ways, was the fact that, beyond his circle of political operatives and party activists and the local crowds they could temporarily gin up by means of inflammatory rhetoric or free liquor, the American people were apathetic about the issue of the bank. They had never particularly wanted a central bank and had voted against it whenever the issue had been put to them plainly. Most of them were not waiting for the government to get them out of their financial distress—through a central bank or any other kind of high financial maneuverings or bailouts—but were working hard to take care of themselves and their families, as Americans had always done. They could not have cared less whether Tyler vetoed any number of bank bills.[35]

Still, within the world of politics, Clay ruled the Whig Party with an iron fist, and every Whig elected official knew that the powerful Kentuckian could and would wreck his political career if he stepped out of line. Few dared to do so. Clay organized a caucus of most of the Whig congressmen and senators and had it vote to expel Tyler from the party. To accompany this unprecedented act, the caucus adopted a manifesto that all but denounced the U.S. Constitution for placing too much power in the hands of the executive. It advocated amending the Constitution so as to allow Congress to override presidential vetoes by simple majorities rather than the two-thirds votes specified by the founders. Congress should be preeminent in the government, it boldly announced, the president subservient. The Clay Whigs printed up twenty thousand copies of the manifesto and distributed them around the country.[36]

The war between Clay and Tyler was just beginning. The special session of Congress adjourned as scheduled on September 13, 1841, with none of Clay's cherished legislation having passed into law. Then the senators and representatives returned three months later for the next regular session and took up just where they left off. Over the next three years Clay continued to fight tooth and nail to thwart everything Tyler tried to do, and the Kentucky Machiavelli was usually successful, much to the president's chagrin. Tyler strove to take a middle ground between Clay's acolytes and the hard-line states' righters at the Whig Party's opposite extreme, making every concession he felt he could to those who desired high tariffs and a national bank. Clay was not interested in Tyler's concessions but only in his defeat. He continued to demand the national bank without modifications and to obstruct every move toward compromise.

By 1842 Clay's health was not robust, and in March of that year, just under three weeks short of his sixty-fifth birthday, he may have suffered a mild heart attack. Yet even after resigning from the Senate one week later in order to rest and prepare for the 1844 presidential campaign, Clay continued to direct his partisans in blocking Tyler's efforts, and he watched with satisfaction as the federal government lurched from one fiscal crisis to the next, sometimes unable to pay its employees. Whigs worked themselves into a froth over Tyler's use of the veto, with a Baltimore Whig newspaper raging that Tyler was "fully as much a dictator and a despot as the Autocrat of Russia." By August 1842 congressional Whigs reached the point of actually attempting to impeach Tyler for vetoing a tariff bill.[37]

To an observer focused on national politics, the bitter disputes might have seemed to bode ill for the nation's survival. British emissary Alexander Baring, Lord Ashburton, wrote his government that it seemed "impossible that with so much disorganization and violence, the system could hold together."[38] But Ashburton was wrong. The system was more than robust enough to endure this level of political conflict. Martin Van Buren, watching from what he hoped would be his temporary political exile in New York, could perhaps take some satisfaction that the two-party system he had helped to create had succeeded in coping with even such intense political conflict in ways that did not endanger the survival of the Republic. Politicians might get angry enough about the bank or the tariff to punch one another's noses, but no one was going to try to split the country, or go to war, or shed any significant amount of blood over these questions. These were national, not sectional, concerns. Both parties drew their support from all regions of the country. The same disputes that put Whigs at odds with Democrats and pitted Tyler Whigs against Clay Whigs also served to draw the various regions of the country together. A Mississippi Whig had something important in common with a fellow Whig from Maine, and an Illinois Democrat could feel camaraderie with a Democrat from Georgia.

Even more important, the issues at stake in these conflicts did not reach deep enough into the hearts and lives of the American people or the fundamental principles on which the Republic was based. Some people might be enraged over questions of banks and tariffs, but those issues simply did not have the power to stir the great majority of Americans to their depths.

But other issues clamored for the attention of Americans in the 1840s.

CHAPTER THREE

Abolitionism

THE ABOLITIONIST MOVEMENT had its roots in Britain. Quakers had opposed slavery, and some of them had brought their convictions with them to colonial Pennsylvania. In the eighteenth century, the Methodist revival produced wide-ranging effects on society. One of these was the movement against slavery, which came to be led by evangelical Christians like William Wilberforce. The British abolitionists were successful in bringing about the eradication of slavery throughout the British Empire in 1833. By that time the concept had made the jump to the United States, absorbing earlier, more moderate opposition to slavery.

Genteel critics of the institution of slavery had previously advocated the colonization of African-Americans—that is, their resettlement somewhere outside the United States, perhaps in Africa. They planned to start with free blacks, and thereby convince slaveholders that it was socially safe to release their slaves, since the freedmen would at once emigrate. Thus members of the American Colonization Society, including Henry Clay, hoped to find a gradual and painless way to rid the nation of slavery. A few free blacks did migrate to Liberia. Most were not interested, having been born and raised in the United States. In fact, the American Colonization Society never freed a single slave, and by 1830 it was plain to clear-thinking Americans that it never would.

Abolitionists had no interest in the sort of ineffective temporizing that made the American Colonization Society a tame and harmless opponent to slavery to which even a Kentucky planter with dozens of slaves himself could complacently belong with no thought that it would ever disturb his or anyone else's "property." Instead, abolitionism called for the immediate, uncompensated termination of the institution of slavery throughout the United States: no phasing out, no deportation of blacks, but simply the freeing of every last bond servant in the country—now. This was not genteel. It was not even respectable. Most Americans considered it radical, dangerous, and far outside the mainstream. American abolitionists faced a much more difficult task than did their British brethren. The

United States had several million slaves not in a far-flung empire but throughout the southern states. Thus the rawest nerve the abolitionists touched was not the potential economic dislocation of emancipation, though that was enormous, but rather the specter of freed slaves living together with whites in a racially integrated society on a basis of social equality. A large majority of Americans found that concept positively shocking.

As in Britain, most American abolitionists were evangelical Christians. Evangelical ministers such as Charles G. Finney championed the cause. Finney's popularity as a revivalist gave his antislavery views wide circulation. To evangelicals, slaveholding was a blatant violation of God's command to love one's neighbor. Therefore, it was a sin, and sin could and must be renounced completely and immediately. Neither compromise nor gradualism could be acceptable responses to the sin of slavery, nor could it ever be valid to weigh the virtue of emancipation against the possible social and economic dislocation that might follow. Benjamin Lundy, editor of the abolitionist newspaper *Genius of Universal Emancipation,* placed on the paper's masthead the motto "Let Justice Be Done Though the Heavens Should Fall."[1]

Publishing an abolitionist newspaper was no easy task, as subscriptions were few and support was scant, but Lundy doggedly persevered. In 1829 he brought on board as an assistant twenty-four-year-old William Lloyd Garrison. Born in Newburyport, Massachusetts, Garrison had grown up in a poor family, had apprenticed as a compositor at his hometown newspaper at age fourteen, and from there had launched his own career as an independent journalist, founding a newspaper called *The Free Press,* which failed after two years. During most of the 1820s Garrison had been an advocate of colonization and a supporter of the American Colonization Society, but near the end of the decade he had had a conversion to immediate emancipation, a cause to which he would henceforth bring a proselyte's zeal.[2]

The partnership proved of brief duration, though not from any disagreement between Lundy and Garrison. A slave ship owner from Massachusetts took one of Garrison's statements personally and sued him for libel in a Maryland court. Convicted and lacking money to pay the fine, the young abolitionist found himself in the Baltimore jail. Sadly, Lundy and Garrison decided they would have to dissolve their partnership while Lundy tried to keep *The Genius* alive on a smaller scale and a reduced publishing schedule.[3]

Garrison was destined for greater things. The New York philanthropist Arthur Tappan learned of his plight. Tappan and his brother Lewis were wealthy businessmen and devout Christians. They believed that God enabled them to gain wealth so that they might use it for His purposes, and they soon became ardent advocates of abolitionism. Arthur paid Garrison's fine, securing his freedom. Garrison moved to Boston, and there, with the financial support of the Tappans and a few others, and with very few subscribers, he founded an abolitionist newspaper of his own and called it *The Liberator*. In its first edition, which appeared on January 1, 1831, Garrison made his position plain. After expressing his allegiance to the "self-evident" truth of the statement in the Declaration of Independence that "all men are created equal" and "are endowed by their Creator with certain unalienable rights," he boldly asserted that this must be applied to slaves. "I am aware," he wrote,

> that many object to the severity of my language; but is there not cause for severity? I *will* be as harsh as truth, and as uncompromising as justice. On this subject, I do not wish to think, or speak, or write, with moderation. . . . I am in earnest, I will not equivocate, I will not excuse, I will not retreat a single inch, and I will be heard.

Over the years that followed, Garrison continued his uncompromising attack on the institution of slavery in the columns of *The Liberator*.

The struggles of Garrison, Lundy, and other public advocates of abolitionism stemmed from the fact that abolitionists were a minority, even in the North, where abolitionist orators could sometimes be the targets of mob action. In that respect, North and South had differed little until this point. In the late 1820s and early 1830s, however, the South, even such Upper South states as Maryland and Virginia, was becoming increasingly and intensely hostile to any criticism of slavery. A transformation in southern attitudes was nearing its completion, driven largely by the high profits on Deep South cotton plantations and the correspondingly ever-rising price of slaves. Whereas most southerners a generation before had admitted that slavery was an evil, albeit a supposedly necessary one, the predominant view in the South of the 1830s was that slavery was a positive good, something that should not be criticized but rather expanded. The new and harsher attitude toward criticism of slavery lay behind the intense opposition to the efforts of Lundy, Garrison, and others to spread the antislavery message in the Upper South. It was no accident that Garrison published *The Liberator* in Boston or that Lundy would shortly be compelled to move *The Genius* to Lowell, Illinois.[4]

Even after being forced out of the slave states, the abolitionists still hoped to get their message to southerners and persuade them to abandon slavery. They based their appeal on a belief in the Bible and Christian moral principles, which most Americans, including southerners, professed to share. If abolitionists could convince their fellow citizens that slavery was immoral and displeasing to God, then the battle would be won, theoretically at least. In order to carry out this "moral suasion," as they called it, the abolitionists tried to get their message before the eyes of southerners. Southern white leaders immediately threatened that any northerner found carrying abolitionist literature in the South would be lynched. A vigilance committee in Columbia, South Carolina, offered a reward of $1,500 to anyone who would give information identifying a distributor of *The Liberator.*

So the abolitionists resorted to mailing their literature—until southern congressmen persuaded the Jackson administration to ban abolitionist materials from the U.S. Mail. To justify this, white southerners asserted that their happy and contented slaves would, if exposed to any criticism of the institution, immediately revolt and slaughter every white man, woman, and child within reach. Slave contentment was apparently of a very ephemeral nature.[5]

Thus thwarted from presenting their case directly to southerners, abolitionists tried petitioning Congress to take what few steps it constitutionally could against slavery—banning slavery in the District of Columbia would be a start. In response, proslavery congressmen in 1836 passed a "Gag Rule," stipulating that any petition on the subject of slavery would automatically be tabled and neither read nor debated at all. South Carolina senator John C. Calhoun, champion of what he called the South's "peculiar institution," worked out something very similar in order to prevent any discussion of abolitionist petitions in the Senate. The idea was not only to prevent any debate of slavery in Congress but also to treat the petitions in the most insulting manner possible, sending the message that Congress viewed such pleas for the freedom of bondmen as vile, unbecoming documents that it was beneath congressional dignity to accept.

The insult was duly received, but the result was hardly to quell the growth of antislavery feeling in the North. The harder the proslavery forces worked to squelch the petitions, the more zealously the abolitionists worked to circulate them and the more northerners joined the cause, stirred by the infringement of the time-honored right of petition even if they had not at first been moved by the bondage of slaves they had never seen. Petitions flooded into the Capitol by the scores and hundreds year after year, more than one hundred thousand signatures in a single year. A small coterie of sympathetic congressmen led by former president John Quincy Adams, now a Massachusetts congressman, fought tenaciously with every device known to parliamentary procedure to have the people's petitions read and debated by the House, often leaving his proslavery opponents in the House frantic with rage. The southerners fought back with every artifice fear and malice could suggest.

Despite the southern politicians' considerable parliamentary skills and almost demoniac fury against Adams and anyone else who would support the abolitionists in any way, they could not have kept the United States Congress gagged on the subject of slavery had it not been for the support of northern congressmen from both parties, and that in turn was the product mostly of party discipline. If each party was to survive, it would have to maintain a nationwide appeal, and since feeling on the issue of slavery was much more intense in the South than it was among the northern electorate as a whole, most northern congressmen were willing to go to considerable lengths to placate their southern party colleagues. This was the two-party system functioning as Van Buren had envisioned, suppressing, or at least trying to suppress, sectional differences to maintain national unity, albeit at the cost of some rather strained consciences among northern representatives.[6]

The Liberty Party had been the result of an attempt by some of the most determined abolitionists to make an end run around Congress's stubborn suppression of their political expression. Its very modest vote total was an indication that in 1840 the vast majority of northerners either were indifferent to slavery or else still considered it merely one issue among many. Even among those who did consider slavery the most important issue at that time, a large majority still believed, rather naïvely, that the Whig Party actually opposed slavery and that voting for a Whig was the most practical way of opposing the peculiar institution. As long as they held that view, the lid was likely to remain firmly in place atop the boiling kettle of discontent over slavery, at least as far as national politics was concerned.

In their use of the Gag Rule, as well as in the mob actions against abolitionist speakers and editors that took place in both the North and the South during the 1830s, the defenders of slavery did their own cause more harm than good. Each time a proslavery mob whipped, beat, hanged, or shot an abolitionist—and each time a congressional majority put U.S. citizens on notice that they were not to petition their government on certain subjects—more of the complacent citizens who made up the bulk of the northern population were awakened to the tyranny that lay behind the slave system. In that respect, the proslavery mobs and their more genteel cousins in Congress were the best publicists and recruiters the abolitionist movement could possibly have had.

Another area in which proslavery aggression helped build the abolition movement pertained to the Fugitive Slave Law. Article IV, Section 2 of the U.S. Constitution stated in part:

> No Person held to Service or Labour in one State, under the Laws thereof, escaping into another, shall, in Consequence of any Law or Regulation therein, be discharged from such Service or Labour, but shall be delivered up on Claim of the Party to whom such Service or Labour may be due.

This capitulation by the founders to the demands of delegates from the slaveholding states opened the door for the federal government's greatest offense against states' rights prior to the twentieth century. By means of it, and the Fugitive Slave Act of 1793 passed pursuant to it, slave-state law routinely reached across into free states to snatch those who had escaped from slavery to where the peculiar institution supposedly did not exist.

The Fugitive Slave Law brought slavery home to northerners who might otherwise have thought of the plight of the bondmen as something far away that need not concern them. Sometimes desperate escaped slaves along with free blacks and even some sympathetic whites did their best to obstruct the slave catchers, and sometimes the fugitives were captured anyway, and their northern friends were tried, convicted, and jailed for violating a federal law. In 1842 and 1843 several high-profile fugitive slave cases in Illinois prompted the Prairie State abolitionist Owen Lovejoy, whose brother had been killed by a proslavery mob in the 1830s, to question how far a citizen was obligated to obey a government that acted so unjustly. "Is the individual swallowed up in the citizen?" he wrote. "Is there, must there not be, an ultimate appeal to conscience and the Supreme Court, not of the nation, but of the Universe?" Lovejoy clearly believed there was, and he became active in illegally aiding the escape of slaves through the loose network known as the Underground Railroad.[7]

Others agreed with Lovejoy. In 1842 an abolitionist meeting in Adams County, Illinois, in the west-central part of the state, passed resolutions asserting that human laws contrary to divine law were not binding. Citizens might bear with such evil laws patiently, the resolutions explained,

provided there appeared to be some hope of removing the evil by political action. The implication was clear that the Adams County abolitionists were near the end of their patience. The following year the
membership of First Presbyterian Church of Chicago formally resolved
to "obey God rather than men, when human and divine legislation come
into conflict." Everyone knew what human legislation they had in mind.
The same sorts of events were under way in many other northern states
as well.[8]

Not surprisingly, the Supreme Court took a dim view of all this. In
1842 the justices handed down their decision in the case of *Prigg v. Pennsylvania*, asserting that only Congress had the right to legislate on the issue
of fugitive slaves. All state legislation on the matter was unconstitutional.
In response, seven northern states had, by 1848, passed personal liberty
laws, stipulating that no state personnel or facilities were to be used in
aiding the capture or return of any fugitive slaves. If the federal government was determined to drag people away into slavery, it would have to
provide for the matter on its own, at least in those seven states.[9]

Meanwhile, more and more abolitionists began to take an active part
in aiding fugitive slaves who were trying to move across the free states to
reach final legal freedom in Canada. During the 1840s newspapers first
began using the term "Underground Railroad" to refer to this loosely
organized network of those who helped slaves flee. There were fixed
routes with regularly established safe houses along the way. Such places
as Ripley and Mechanicsburg, in Ohio, became "stations" where runaways could receive help, shelter, and advice for the next leg of their trip.
Free blacks or white abolitionists might also serve as "conductors," leading the escapees northward by safe routes. Christian institutions were
especially active. In Oberlin, Ohio, Finney's own Oberlin College was a
stop on the Underground Railroad. So was Cincinnati's Lane Theologi-
cal Seminary. In Quincy, Illinois, students at the Mission Institute helped
blacks escaping from bondage in Missouri, across the Mississippi. In 1844
Free Will Baptists, a strongly abolitionist denomination, founded Michigan Central College, the first American college to prohibit all racial discrimination. It too was soon serving as a station on "the Road."[10]

Though the struggle over fugitive slaves would continue throughout
the decade of the 1840s and the next, there was no escaping the fact that
even such slave power provocations as the Fugitive Slave Law, with their
tendency to make more abolitionists, were still far from turning the
movement into anything more than a small minority. The awareness of
their weakness and the seeming hopelessness of ever breaking the power

of slavery within the United States led some of the most radical abolitionists in the 1840s to begin to advocate secession by the northern states in order to escape the tyrannical yoke of southern slavery. Most of those who adopted the slogan "No Union with Slaveholders" were outside of politics. Among elected officials only the most extremely radical, like Ohio congressmen Joshua Giddings, would countenance such pronouncements. Nevertheless, the idea had some resonance with a minority of the staunchest opponents of slavery. In a poem published in *The Liberator* in the mid-1840s, John Greenleaf Whittier wrote:

> *Make our Union-bond a chain,*
> *We will snap its links in twain,*
> *We will stand erect again.*[11]

By 1843 Garrison and a few of his most zealous acolytes were denouncing the United States Constitution as a covenant with hell.[12]

Most abolitionists, especially evangelical Christians, disagreed. While yielding nothing to Garrison in their hatred of the system of slavery, they could see the good as well as the bad in the Constitution and American society. They still had hopes of achieving results through the political process, hopes that eventually gave birth to the Liberty Party. They also found Garrison's extremism and impracticality, as well as his tendency to embrace every offbeat idea that came along, unnerving. One particular area of disagreement was Garrison's desire to place women in positions of leadership within the American Anti-Slavery Society, which was strongly opposed by the evangelicals. The differences between the two groups became intense enough in 1840 to bring about a split in the society. Garrison seized control of it, though with a tiny fraction of its former membership. Most abolitionists followed Lewis Tappan in forming a separate organization, the American and Foreign Anti-Slavery Society. Whereas Garrison and his followers saw the Constitution as a proslavery document, Tappan's faction saw it as fundamentally antislavery, with only a few glaring proslavery points in need of correction. Their approach would be more practical and political than that of the Garrisonians.[13]

Another way in which Tappan and his followers differed from the Garrisonians was that they continued to hope that American churches might be the catalysts for changing society's views on slavery. The churches were enormously important institutions within American society in the 1840s. The largest religious organization in the country at that time was the Methodist denomination—officially the American Methodist Episcopal Church. It numbered more than one million members, and could count on a regular attendance of two to three times that many. Thus on any given Sunday, about one in every five Americans would be sitting in a Methodist church.

The Methodist movement had from its inception taken a strong stand against slavery. John Wesley referred to it as an evil, "the vilest that ever saw the sun," and the slave trade as the "execrable sum of all villainies." Early Methodist rules forbade slavery. Francis Asbury, the father of American Methodism, hated slavery. "O Lord," he wrote in his journal in 1780, "banish the infernal spirit of slavery from Thy dear Zion." Twenty years later he wrote in disgust of efforts to present slavery as acceptable for Christians: "If the Gospel will tolerate slavery, what will it not authorize?" Asbury had once petitioned President George Washington for the abolition of slavery. In 1800 the General Conference of the Methodist Church required its member conferences in states where slavery still existed to petition their legislatures for its gradual abolition. Methodist pastors were to help gather signatures on such petitions, and the submitting of petitions was to continue in each state "from year to year till the desired end be accomplished."

That stance was to change. Methodism faced constant pressure in the southern states, where both pastors and lay members began to agitate against the denomination's forbidding Methodists to own slaves. Around the beginning of the nineteenth century, a number of state governments adopted laws either banning or greatly hindering the practice of manumission, the voluntary freeing of slaves by their owners. Allowing man's law to trump God's, southern Methodists pled with the denominational leadership to set aside Methodist teaching on this subject or at least to suspend it within their states. Reluctantly, the national Methodist leadership gave in. Even Asbury felt compelled to acquiesce in special rules within some slave states, permitting Methodists to buy and sell slaves as long as they did not do so "unjustly, or inhumanely, or covetously."

In the years that followed, Methodist denominational leadership had become much more comfortable with slavery, even as slavery was becoming more and more entrenched in southern culture as the means by which fortunes were being made in the cultivation of the newly discovered short-staple cotton plant, which would grow throughout the Deep South. Keeping pace with the degeneration in society, Methodist leadership at the national level was soon asserting that slavery was at worst a societal evil rather than an individual one. Since the individual could not, in this way of thinking, be held responsible for participating in societal evils, he was welcome in the church, evils and all. Over the next three decades the rapid influx of many unrepentant slaveholders as members in good standing of Methodist churches in the South largely muted most of the denomination's remaining witness on the issue of slavery. Only a tepid and generally ignored rule against clergy slaveholding remained.[14]

Worse, Methodists who still held to the old ways were increasingly disturbed to find that those now in power in the denominational hierarchy were not only unconcerned about the evils of slavery but were actually hostile to those who found fault with human bondage. By the 1820s Methodist periodicals were urging the faithful not to be so judgmental as to criticize slavery. In 1836 the Methodist General Conference met in Cincinnati, and some of the delegates raised the issue of two ministers who had recently given antislavery speeches in that city. It rapidly became apparent that Methodism was now as unequivocal in condemning slavery's critics as it had once been in condemning the institution itself. By a large majority the General Conference adopted a resolution disapproving of those ministers' conduct and expressing the General Conference's opinion as "decidedly opposed to modern abolitionism" and disclaiming "any right, wish, or intention, to interfere in the civil or political relation between master and slave, as it exists in the slaveholding States of the Union." The bishops jointly announced that they had "come to the conviction that the only safe, scriptural, and prudent way for us, both as ministers and as people, is wholly to refrain from this agitating subject." Thereafter, Methodist ministers who chose to obey God rather than man and condemn slavery anyway were defrocked. Tolerance for the slaveholders meant intolerance for abolitionists.[15]

The opposition to abolitionism in the Methodist Church had as much to do with the desire of northern delegates and bishops to avoid turmoil as it did with that of their southern counterparts to champion the cause of slavery. Denominational hierarchies are notoriously averse to boat rocking and far more concerned with stability than with spiritual fervor, doctrinal correctness, or religious zeal. If ministers were allowed to speak out plainly against slavery, they would upset the southern brethren, whose numbers and well-established belligerence on the subject demanded respect. It was far easier to hush the abolitionists than to deal with an enraged proslavery lobby within the denomination—easier, that is, if one could sufficiently sublimate his conscience.[16]

Chief among those who did not wish to see the Methodist boat rocked were the denomination's bishops. The highest officials within Methodist polity, the bishops presided as a group over the quadrennial meeting of the General Conference, and individual bishops traveled throughout the country to conduct yearly meetings of Methodism's district assemblies, known as annual conferences. In the latter capacity, several of the bishops used their power to squelch any expression of disapproval of slavery, ruling proposed antislavery resolutions out of order before they could be taken up for debate. Not that the bishops were opposed to any expression of opinion on the subject of slavery. When in 1838 the Georgia Annual Conference passed a resolution stating that slavery was "not a moral evil," that the church should have nothing to say about it, and that the conference strongly approved of the bishops who had muzzled northern Methodist condemnation of the peculiar institution, the presiding bishop made no objection. The following year the South Carolina Annual Conference followed suit. Apparently discussion of the "agitating subject" was acceptable as long as that discussion was favorable to slavery.[17]

The 1840 General Conference met in Baltimore on May 1 and continued in session throughout the month, while the Democratic National Convention met elsewhere in town, nominated Van Buren, and adjourned, and rowdy hordes of hard-cider-drinking Harrison supporters marched through the streets to the strains of "Tippecanoe and Tyler Too" as part of their Whig "young men's" convention. The Methodists took no notice. They had serious business on hand. The seven bishops issued a joint address to the delegates, applauding the general unity of the denomination but deploring the persistence of some Methodists in bringing up the issue of slavery, which was divisive. It certainly proved to be so at that year's conference. New England delegates introduced antislavery petitions, which southern delegates roundly denounced. Southerners called for the full approval of the institution of slavery, which outraged northerners. In the end, the conference refused to take any action against slavery and instead approved the resolutions of Georgia and South Carolina while condemning the abolitionist tendencies of the northern conferences.[18]

This state of affairs certainly did not reflect majority opinion in the pews or even the pulpits of Methodist churches in the North. Seven out of every eight abolitionists in the country were evangelical Christians, and a large share of those were Methodists. Beyond the out-and-out abolitionists were many northern Methodists who were more or less uncomfortable with slavery. How could a Christian claim to love his neighbor as he did himself, as the Bible commanded, when he held that neighbor in bondage as a slave? The great majority of northern Methodists did not believe this was possible, and therefore many of them held that a church member should not own slaves. Even more northern Methodists were convinced that a clergyman should not be a slaveholder. Dissatisfaction over the denomination's growing acquiescence on the issue of slavery led a trickle of members to separate from the Methodist Episcopal Church during the late 1830s and early 1840s.[19]

The rumblings of dissatisfaction within the denomination rose to the level of open revolt in late 1842. After much urging from abolitionists within the denomination, the Massachusetts Methodist minister Orange Scott agreed to lead a group of antislavery Methodists in seceding and forming a new denomination, "a new anti-slavery, anti-intemperance, anti–everything wrong church organization." In the "everything wrong" category, he included the entire structure of the Methodist episcopacy, foreign as it was both to the Bible and to American ideas of polity. Scott was a prominent revivalist and the editor of an abolitionist Methodist weekly, *The True Wesleyan*. He hoped that within a year the new group might number as many as two thousand. In May 1843 the come-outers held an organizing convention in Utica, New York, and officially set up the Wesleyan Methodist Connection, with more than six thousand members throughout the northern states. The new antislavery denomination more than doubled in the next year, to fifteen thousand, men and women from all walks of life, a veritable cross section of northern society, though perhaps a bit younger than average. Together they made up somewhat more than 1 percent of the total Methodist community. Though still relatively small in numbers, the Wesleyans represented a rapidly growing answer to the Methodist leadership's determination to squelch criticism of slavery.[20]

The Methodists' troubles did not end with the Wesleyan secession. Despite the exodus of some fifteen thousand abolitionists within the space of a year, the fact was that of those Methodists who considered slavery a sin, the majority had remained in the Methodist Church, and there the issue of slavery came back with a vengeance at the 1844 General Conference. Bishop James O. Andrew of Georgia owned slaves. It is not entirely clear how many he owned or for how long. Some accounts say he had gained his first slave with his first wife, who died in 1842, and additional slaves with his second wife, whom he married in 1844. Other evidence suggests that Andrew already owned a number of slaves in his bachelorhood.[21]

His marriage in 1842 to his second wife, and his acquisition through her of several more slaves, triggered intense scrutiny of his status as a slaveholder. At the 1844 General Conference, northern delegates demanded that Andrew refrain from exercising the office of bishop until he divested himself of his slaves. It was simply too much for annual conferences in the North to submit to the religious authority of a man who actually owned fellow human beings. Andrew was by all accounts a gentle soul, and he offered to step down as bishop. At this point southern delegates intervened. Ministers from twelve slave states, including Emory College president Augustus Baldwin Longstreet, met and drew up a resolution urging Andrew to defy the northerners. They demanded that he stick to his position and force northerners to accept his episcopacy and his slaveholding. Their argument was that slavery was not a moral issue and therefore the church should not take sides on it. The delegates from the northern conferences would not bend this time, and the General Conference voted by a large majority to remove Andrew as bishop. Outraged southerners then split from the Methodist Episcopal Church (MEC) and the following year formally organized themselves as the Methodist Episcopal Church, South (MECS). With that the nation's largest Christian denomination had fractured into separate entities, the strongly proslavery MECS and the moderately antislavery MEC, as well as the staunchly abolitionist Wesleyan Methodists.[22]

The year after the Methodists completed their split, their Baptist brethren faced a similar crisis. Like Methodists, Baptists in the eighteenth century had taken a strong stand against slavery and in favor of the equality of man, but as the denomination had become more respectable, it had penetrated the slaveholding class in the South—and the slaveholding class had penetrated it. The denomination began to take an official position of neutrality with regard to slavery. A few small Baptist congregations on the frontier in Kentucky and Missouri had formally broken fellowship with the rest of their brethren rather than accept the denomination's newfound acceptance of slavery.[23]

By 1845, southern Baptists had come to believe that their denomination was not neutral enough on the slavery issue. They were discontented because they believed the denomination's Home Missions Board was sending more missionaries into the northern states than into the southern. They were right. The board was unwilling to appoint as missionaries men who owned slaves, and thus fewer eligible candidates were available in the South. A showdown in that year led to a split similar to the one the Methodists had undergone, with the denomination separating into independent northern and southern wings. Southern Baptists asserted that they would not cooperate with the national denomination "on any terms implying their inferiority." In short, they were not going to give up slavery, and they were not going to tolerate anyone saying that they ought to.[24]

The story was much the same among Presbyterians, though a preexisting fault line channeled differences about slavery into two separate branches of the denomination. In 1818 the General Assembly of the Presbyterian Church had passed a resolution condemning slavery and exhorting all Christians to labor for its eradication, but by 1845 the Old School branch of Presbyterianism could blandly assert that slavery was a Christian institution. The New School Presbyterians, on the other hand, maintained their communion's witness against the South's peculiar institution. Thus an earlier division stemming from opposing attitudes toward revivals became infused with the slavery issue as well, so that among Presbyterians, as among the nation's other two largest denominations, rival branches differed starkly on the issue.[25]

The various schisms within the Methodist, Baptist, and Presbyterian denominations during the mid-1840s had a significance beyond mere ecclesiastical history. For a people as strongly religious as nineteenth-century Americans, such matters carried more weight in many ways than the doings of Congress. Religion touched on people's most deeply held convictions about fundamental questions of right and wrong. Americans had always been divided in matters of religion—Methodists and Baptists coexisted with Presbyterians, Episcopalians, Lutherans, Catholics, and others—but the differences had mostly involved theology rather than day-to-day questions of morality, and those differences had extended more or less throughout the whole country. Now slavery had divided the nation's three largest denominations along strict North-South lines. Any social force that could tear apart the churches of that day could do the same to the rest of society under the right circumstances. Henry Clay, no churchgoing man himself, wrote of this development, "Scarcely any public occurrence has happened for a long time that gave me so much real concern and pain as the menaced separation of the church, by a line throwing all the Free States on one side, and all the Slave States on the other."[26]

All of this makes sense of the concerns of men like Martin Van Buren that slavery had to be kept out of national politics. Though from a moral standpoint one could take an entirely different view of the matter, from the perspective of politics, the slavery issue was too powerful, too dangerous, too likely to tear the nation apart. So far the two-party system had proven more durable than the structures of the major denominations, partially because the stresses on political institutions were not as great as those on religious institutions when the point in question was one of straightforward morality. Prospects were fair that the political system might continue to hold, provided nothing happened to change the country's political landscape. Prudent men, with tolerant consciences, could hope that the issue of slavery would somehow, someday, lose its dangerous force, and until that day came, they could try to keep the issue firmly outside of the nation's politics. Yet the fundamental inconsistency of slavery struck at the very core of the nation's identity. In a country based on the principle that all men are created equal and endowed by their Creator with certain inalienable rights, an entire group of human beings was systematically denied those rights and that equality. It remained to be seen how far the nation could go toward fulfilling its self-conscious destiny of spreading its free ideals across a continent while still harboring within itself an institution that was the negation of those ideals.

And meanwhile, the course of events in the 1840s was about to change the country's political landscape.

PART TWO

Westward Expansion

CHAPTER FOUR

The Oregon Trail

SINCE THE FIRST English colonists arrived in North America, the opportunity to find new land and a new start, economically and perhaps socially, just beyond the western horizon had been important to Americans. The westward march of settlement had seemed as inexorable as the progress of an alpine glacier down a mountain valley, but instead of ice this was a river of people, each seeking a new start on new land—one farm just west of the last, a new village springing up on the next likely-looking riverside bluff or at the fording of the next stream by a rude frontier trail. So the frontier had crept westward to the Mississippi during the first four decades after independence, crossed the Father of Waters without skipping a beat, and reached the western portions of Missouri and the eastern regions of Iowa by the 1830s.[1]

West of Missouri and Iowa lay the Great Plains, which an army exploratory expedition in the 1820s had labeled the Great American Desert. Beyond the plains were the Rockies, and beyond them—and even a real desert or two—lay the well-watered Pacific slope of the continent, but it had long seemed out of reach. British and American ships had visited a coast they called Oregon since the late eighteenth century and engaged in fur trade with the Indians there. Lewis and Clark reached that coast by land in 1805, having crossed the continent from the Mississippi in the preceding nineteen months, but their experience could have created no illusions that the trip to the Pacific coast would be an easy one. The expedition had been an epic journey for a military party of hand-picked soldiers and guides. It was hard to see how the course of commerce could ever take the route across the interior of the North American continent.[2]

In the three decades that followed, American trappers roved the Far West, but no settlers. As with the first colonization of America's eastern coast, when commercial interests no longer sufficed to propel settlers into new territory, religious motives provided the additional drive. In the case of Oregon, religious motivation entered the story in a roundabout way and played the role of initial catalyst.

In 1831 several northwestern Indians arrived in St. Louis with the returning annual fur-trading caravan. They had been curious about the white man's country, and while in St. Louis they enjoyed the hospitality of U.S. Superintendent of Indian Affairs William Clark, who had visited their homeland in Oregon a quarter century before. Also in St. Louis that fall was a visiting member of the Wyandot tribe from the East, an educated man named William Walker. Walker apparently did not meet the northwestern Indians while they were in town, but a little more than a year later, in January 1833, he wrote an account of their visit to G. P. Disosway, an Indian agent to the Wyandots in Ohio. In this account, Walker related that the northwestern Indians had asked that the white man's "Book of Heaven" be sent to them, along with suitable instructors. Perhaps Walker had heard second- or thirdhand reports of the Indians' discussions with Clark, or perhaps he wrote what he thought they should have said. In any case, Disosway believed him and forwarded his letter to a Methodist periodical called the *Christian Advocate and Journal,* which published it in March 1833.[3]

The letter was a powerful appeal for the large segment of the American population who were devout evangelical Christians. A number of men began preparing to go to Oregon as missionaries. One of the first to step forward was thirty-year-old Methodist pastor and schoolteacher Jason Lee. Lee traveled the overland route with an expedition of American fur traders, and on the advice of officials of the British Hudson's Bay Company in Oregon, he established his mission in the Willamette Valley.[4]

More missionaries followed, among them Marcus Whitman. Whitman, a physician, visited Oregon in 1835 and on the way made a reputation for himself by successfully removing from the back of the famous mountain man Jim Bridger an arrowhead that had been embedded there for three years. Late that summer Whitman returned to the East to gather helpers for mission work in Oregon. One of them, Narcissa Prentiss, he married. Marcus and Narcissa, along with their friends and fellow Presbyterian missionaries Henry and Eliza Spalding, then prepared for the journey to Oregon, now under the auspices of the American Board of Commissioners for Foreign Missions.[5]

The Whitmans planted their mission station in eastern Oregon at Waiilatpu, just west of modern-day Walla Walla, Washington, to minister to the Cayuse. Narcissa and Eliza were the first white women to cross the Rockies, and their letters home, along with those of other missionaries, including several missionary wives who arrived a short time later, painted an enticing picture of a lush green land of fertile soil and mild climate in the Willamette Valley and, perhaps more important, related accounts of a cross-country journey that, though strenuous, was possible even for families. "It is astonishing how well we get along with our wagons where there are no roads," wrote Narcissa Whitman from the plains during their crossing. "I think I may say it is easier traveling here than on any turnpike in the States."[6]

Thus, from missionaries as well as from businessmen and fur traders, knowledge of the Oregon Country grew, and with it grew interest, as the territory on the Pacific slope became the focus of the nation's well-developed westering habit. The steady pressure of American westward expansion had briefly gathered itself behind the barrier of the Great Plains, and now it was about to burst out with a surge unlike any that had gone before.

Officially, the Oregon Country comprised that part of the North American continent lying west of the crest of the Rockies, north of the northern boundary of Mexican California (latitude 42° north), and south of the southern tip of Russian Alaska (latitude 54°40' north). Those boundaries encompassed all of the modern-day Canadian province of British Columbia and the U.S. states of Washington, Oregon, and Idaho, as well as small parts of Wyoming and Montana. The United States claimed the area because of an American sea captain's 1792 discovery of the mouth of the Columbia River and because of Lewis and Clark's 1805 arrival in the territory. The British staked their claim on the presence of their Hudson's Bay Company's trading posts in the region, especially the one at Fort Vancouver on the Columbia. Spain and Russia had also once made vague claims to the region, but Spain had renounced its interest in 1819, and Russia had done the same in 1824 and 1825. Meanwhile, in 1818 Britain and the United States had reached an agreement by which the two nations would exercise "joint occupancy" of the Oregon Country, but that arrangement clearly could last only as long as the region remained largely unoccupied. As soon as people began flowing into Oregon, the question of its ownership would come due.[7]

Among the first Americans to take up the implied challenge and set out with the specific purpose of wresting Oregon away from the British was a group of seventeen men from Peoria, Illinois. In the fall of 1838

Jason Lee made a speaking tour in the East, and his descriptions of Oregon fired many an imagination. One of his stops was the Main Street Presbyterian Church of Peoria, where he spoke on September 30. Five boys belonging to the Calapooya (or Kalapuya) tribe were traveling with Lee, and one of them took ill in Peoria and had to stay there several weeks to recover. Lee's lecture was powerful, and over the weeks that followed the young man told glowing tales of his homeland, where the Columbia River teemed with salmon. Several local men began to take an interest.

Under the encouragement of a thirty-five-year-old Peoria lawyer named Thomas J. Farnham, they organized themselves as the Oregon Dragoons and elected Farnham as their leader. Over the winter Farnham's wife sewed them a flag bearing the motto "Oregon or the Grave," and the following May they set out, proudly bearing their new banner. The Oregon Dragoons, often called the Peoria Party, were part of the filibustering tradition that had over the previous three decades prompted small groups of Americans to venture on equally quixotic private expeditions into Spanish or Mexican territories with the goal of winning those lands for the United States. The stated purpose of the Peoria Party was to drive British fur traders out of the Oregon Country and secure it for the United States. Then they hoped to pickle and ship a great deal of salmon.[8]

After gathering on Peoria's courthouse square on May 1, 1839, and solemnly pledging to stand by one another come what may, the seventeen Oregon Dragoons, who ranged in age from those in their early twenties to a man of fifty-four, started off on their journey, cheered by their townsmen and following their "Oregon or the Grave" flag.[9]

The Oregon Dragoons planned to follow the by now tried and proven route across the continent blazed by the fur-trading caravans. That route started near Independence, Missouri, on the Missouri River, and from there led across the Kansas prairie to the Platte River in what is today Nebraska, then along the banks of the Platte to its forks in the western part of the state, up the North Platte into central Wyoming, southwest along the valley of the Sweetwater River, across the Continental Divide via the remarkably gentle South Pass, down the valley of the Snake River to the Columbia, and down the valley of the Columbia to the Willamette River. The route, which came to be known as the Oregon Trail, balanced directness with easy travel.

The journey west did not turn out to be an easy trip for the Peorians. After three weeks of travel and almost incessant bickering among themselves, the Dragoons reached Independence. There the mountain man Andrew Sublette advised them to follow the Santa Fe Trail instead of the more direct route to Oregon. Used by traders carrying goods from the Missouri River to sell in New Mexico, the Santa Fe Trail angled southwest. It may be that Sublette reckoned the more heavily traveled Santa Fe Trail was a more appropriate route for such a bunch of obvious greenhorns, who he might have hoped would turn back before they got themselves into trouble. At any rate, Farnham planned to follow the Santa Fe Trail to what is now eastern Colorado, then cut north and pick up the Oregon Trail somewhere in present-day Utah.[10]

The Peoria Party struck out over the seemingly endless plains, traveling day after day across the gently rolling grasslands under an enormous sky that reminded a man just how small he was. Like many travelers who came before and after, they were astonished by the violence and majesty of Great Plains thunderstorms. "Peal upon peal of thunder rolled around, and up and down the heavens," wrote Farnham of a storm that struck their camp one night, "and the burning bolts appeared to leap from cloud to cloud and from heaven to earth, in such fearful rapidity, that the lurid glare of one had scarcely fallen on the sight, when another of still greater intensity." The animals huddled together in terror, and neither whip nor spur could move them. "Hail and rain came down in torrents," Farnham recalled, and the almost constant flashes of lightning revealed broad sheets of water forming across the lower places of the prairie.[11]

The heavy rains during the journey across the Kansas and Nebraska prairies made camping miserable and traveling a continual struggle with mud and swollen streams. Food supplies ran low. Farnham had counted on the party shooting enough game to feed itself along the way, but game was scarce at first, and the men's flintlock rifles would not work properly in the wet weather. They had to go on short rations—a quarter cup of flour per day. They mixed the flour with water, of which they had no shortage, fried up the batter in bacon fat, and choked down the resulting johnnycakes as best they could. Three members of the party quit and turned back. The Dragoons eventually reached lands where buffalo were thick, sometimes so thick the party could hardly move forward through the dense herd. By this time their flour was gone, and they had nothing but meat to eat.[12]

All the while they quarreled among themselves, the disputes becoming increasingly intense. One day two of the more hot-tempered members were arguing in their tent when one of them became so enraged that he grabbed for his rifle but took it by the muzzle. The hammer caught on the fabric of the tent, and the gun went off, badly wounding its owner in the side. Since the party had brought no medical supplies, they had to borrow some, along with a wagon to carry the wounded man, from a passing train of Santa Fe traders. Thereafter, they made slower progress, and their bickering became so intense that they voted to depose Farnham and elect another man as their leader. Meanwhile, Sioux raiders stole two of their horses, and three more members of the Oregon Dragoons decided to leave the group and set out on their own.[13]

On July 5 the party reached Bent's Fort, a private trading post set up by the fur traders Charles and William Bent in what is today eastern Colorado. There the strife among the Peorians came to a head, and they voted Farnham and two others, including the wounded man, out of the party. Two more chose to join Farnham's faction. The two separate groups continued on toward Oregon, eventually further disintegrating into ones and twos and one large group of four men. They faced snow, ice, and periods of near starvation. One group was happy to purchase and eat two dogs from the Indians.[14]

Eventually nine of the men made it to Oregon, though as ordinary settlers rather than would-be conquerors. Those who did make Oregon were thin from starvation and hardship and sported shaggy hair and beards and ragged clothes. Their grueling journey across the continent hardly seemed to predict any significant future American migration in that direction. Nonetheless, when Farnham visited the mission stations and associated settlements in Oregon, sixty-seven U.S. citizens asked him to use his legal training to help them draw up a petition, which they then asked him to take to Washington, begging the United States government to exercise sovereignty and protect the rights of Americans in the region.[15]

By the time Farnham and his fellow Peorians reached Oregon in late 1839, at least ten different towns back in the Mississippi Valley had "Oregon Societies," dedicated not to conquering Oregon but to settling it. Ownership would follow settlement. And despite the hardships of the journey, a handful of other Americans made their way to Oregon in the late 1830s and early 1840s. These included another forty Methodist missionaries who traveled to Oregon by ship, led by Jason Lee on his return journey after a visit to the East. Others came the hard way, across the continent.

Appeals continued to come from Oregon settlers to the U.S. government to provide them with some oversight. They resented the local influence of the Hudson's Bay Company, which they believed overcharged them for supplies and provisions. Of course, with no competition, the Hudson's Bay Company price was the real market value. Still, the settlers wished for some U.S. governmental presence in the territory. Indeed, carrying a petition from the settlers to the government in Washington, D.C., was the chief errand that had brought Jason Lee east in 1838. Other appeals followed.[16]

President Tyler was an enthusiastic advocate of the westward expansion of the United States. In his first formal address to Congress, in the summer of 1841, he had written in glowing terms of the glories and benefits of territorial growth and had hinted that the United States was destined to spread all the way to the Pacific. He saw this growth as an expansion of an empire of liberty, providing sufficient room to offer freedom to the oppressed peoples of Europe. "We hold out to the people of other countries an invitation to come and settle among us as members of our rapidly growing family," he had written, "and for the blessings which we offer them we require of them to look upon our country as their country and to unite with us in the great task of preserving our institutions and thereby perpetuating our liberties."[17]

Eager as he may have been to add Oregon to the domain of free and orderly government provided by the United States Constitution, Tyler had to tread lightly in responding to the requests of Americans there for a U.S. government presence lest it upset the arrangement with England. This was especially undesirable given that the two countries were in the midst of negotiating what would become the Webster-Ashburton Treaty, fixing the U.S.-Canadian boundary east of the Rockies. Nonetheless, with the strong encouragement of expansion-minded senators, Tyler could and did take some modest steps toward facilitating the flow of American settlers into Oregon. One step was to explore the route, at least as far as the Continental Divide, and so he ordered the army to send a small expedition to scout the Oregon Trail as far as South Pass. The commander of the expedition was Lieutenant John C. Frémont of the U.S. Army's Corps of Topographical Engineers.[18]

Born in Savannah, Georgia, in 1813, Frémont had received his army commission in 1838 after attending the College of Charleston and serving as a civilian mathematics instructor to midshipmen on a U.S. Navy warship. In 1841, the twenty-eight-year-old Frémont had significantly enhanced his career prospects by wooing, winning, and wedding the seventeen-year-old favorite daughter of the powerful Missouri senator Thomas Hart Benton. It could have been a disaster for Frémont, since the senator at first was enraged that Frémont had eloped with his daughter, Jessie, but Benton's wrath proved transient, and he soon became a booster of his son-in-law's career.[19]

After learning the trade of a topographical engineer under the tutelage of Joseph Nicollet in explorations of the upper Mississippi Valley, Frémont, with Benton's powerful support, won the assignment to lead the expedition to South Pass. While in St. Louis that summer preparing for the expedition and looking for a guide, Frémont had chanced to encounter the mountain man Kit Carson on a Missouri River steamboat. He hired Carson on the spot, and the doughty frontiersman became the mainstay of all Frémont's explorations from that day forth. Frémont, with Carson and twenty-two other members of the expedition, set out from Chouteau's Landing, where the Kansas River joined the Missouri, on June 10.[20]

A man who met Frémont just before he left Washington for his expedition described him as "about the medium height, spare of flesh, but strong in bone and muscle; hair black and parted in the center, falling carelessly in folds over his large head to the shoulders; eyes and eyebrows black, complexion dark and swarthy, large square forehead, wide mouth." Most people found the young officer striking. Some considered him a man of destiny, and none held that opinion more strongly than did John C. Frémont himself.[21]

While Frémont led the expedition to scout the Oregon Trail, Tyler, urged on by both of Missouri's senators, made other arrangements to extend U.S. influence into the territory itself. The British were already exercising an indirect government interest there through the Hudson's Bay Company. Tyler decided to counter by appointing a sub–Indian agent, a fairly low-ranking official. The man he selected was Elijah White, a physician. It was perhaps not the most judicious selection. White had traveled to Oregon by sea and joined Jason Lee at his Willamette Valley mission. In 1841, under suspicion of immoral conduct, White had left Oregon and by another sea voyage returned to the States. Still, men who had been to Oregon, even by ship, were not all that common in Washington, and Tyler did not have many from which to choose. In appointing White, Tyler also encouraged him to take as many emigrants with him as he could when he went back to Oregon, this time overland.[22]

By May 14, 1842, the industrious White had collected eighteen wagons, with 112 emigrants, of whom 52 were adult men, all set to accompany him on his trek to Oregon to become sub–Indian agent there.

Economic pressures had begun to augment the lure of Oregon and the call of religious duty as motivations for heading west. Hard times had lingered after the Panic of 1837, prompting some farmers in the Ohio and Mississippi valleys to look to greener fields in Oregon. They were eager to take advantage of White's supposed familiarity with the trail to guide them through the nineteen hundred miles of wilderness that lay between them and their new farms. Indeed, some five hundred people had expressed their intention of joining White's party, but most had been unable to sell their farms in the depressed real-estate market of the time.[23]

Those who joined White's party formed the first organized wagon train to set out with the specific purpose of establishing new homes in Oregon. The party's wagons rolled out of Independence, Missouri, on May 16, 1842, almost a full month ahead of Frémont's party. Their trip west was much easier than that of the Peoria Party three years before, but not without its difficulties. They followed the main Oregon Trail and made good time, but bickering broke out when White decreed that all the party's dogs should be killed at once so as to prevent noise that might give away their position to the Indians, or perhaps to avoid a plague of rabies—accounts differ. Twenty-two dogs were killed and matters had reached a complete impasse, with the remaining dog owners ready for violence, before White and his supporters finally backed down and repealed the odious decree of canicide.[24]

Along the Platte River the wagon train encountered great herds of bison. "No adequate conception can be formed of the immensity of the numerous herds, which here abound," wrote one of the travelers. "The entire plains and prairies are densely covered and completely blackened with them, as far as the most acute vision extends." The wagon train halted for a few days to feast on the finest cuts of buffalo meat. "I think I can truly say I saw in that region in one day more buffaloes than I have seen of cattle in all my life," wrote another of the emigrants. "They seemed to be coming northward continually from the distant plains to the Platte to get water and would plunge in and swim across by the thousands." The vast herd splashing through the river "changed not only the color of the water, but its taste, until it was unfit to drink; but we had to use it," recalled the pioneer ruefully. "We could hear them thundering all night long. The ground fairly trembled with vast approaching bands, and if they had not been diverted, wagons, animals, and emigrants would have been trodden under their feet." The men kept up bonfires around

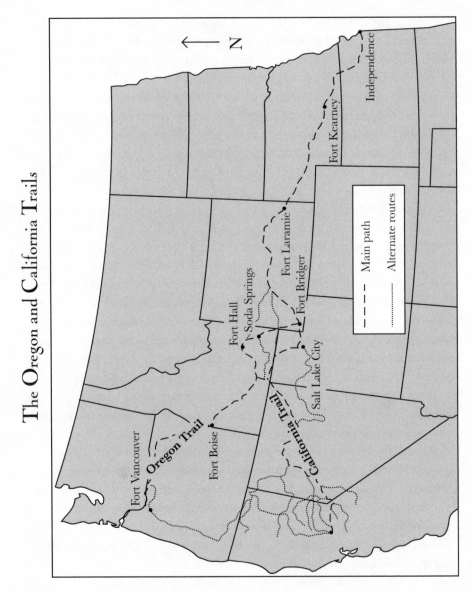

The Oregon and California Trails

the camp at night and periodically fired their rifles into the air to ward off the tide of beasts.[25]

Following a few weeks behind the emigrants, Frémont with his army expedition reached the Platte as well, but Frémont called the river by a form of its Otoe Indian name, Nebraska, from a word meaning "flat water." It was the first use of the name of the future state in a written document.[26]

By that time White's wagon train was moving through the western part of what is today the state of Nebraska, past the stony landmarks of Courthouse Rock and Scotts Bluff. The majority of the emigrants had become seriously dissatisfied with White's leadership. They held another election and replaced him as captain with a handsome and ambitious twenty-three-year-old guitar maker from Mount Vernon, Ohio, Lansford W. Hastings. White and his followers remained disaffected for a number of days and traveled in a separate group a little ahead of the main wagon train.[27]

At Fort Laramie, a traders' stockade on the Laramie River in eastern Wyoming, White hired the mountain man Thomas Fitzpatrick to serve as a guide, paying him with $500 in government funds. This proved such a good decision that it somewhat restored White's reputation in the wagon train. Hastings remained captain, but a more amiable mood prevailed in the party. While they camped near Fort Laramie, some of the emigrants repaired rickety wagons by cutting them down into carts, while others sold spavined oxen for a pittance and purchased a few supplies and fresh horses. Before they pressed on, trappers warned them that the Sioux, through whose range they were about to pass, were in a surly mood.[28]

Mid-July found the wagon train in central Wyoming, toiling along the valley of the Sweetwater River, near which they encountered the 120-foot-high exposed granite pluton that a group of trappers had named Independence Rock some years before after celebrating the Fourth of July there. Hastings and his second-in-command, Asa Lovejoy, decided to ride away from the train and carve their names in the tough granite, confident that two men on horseback could easily overtake the plodding oxen after they finished their sightseeing.[29]

The train had proceeded several miles, or most of a day's journey, and was approaching another rock formation, this one called Devil's Gate, where the Sweetwater River—but not the trail—passed through a narrow cut in a granite ridge, when the emigrants were startled from their contemplation of the rocks by the approach of a large party of Sioux. To the amazement of the whites, the Sioux were bringing in Hastings and Lovejoy. The two had had quite an unpleasant day, having been captured that morning and treated roughly until they had managed to convince the Indians, through the interpretation of one of them who spoke English, that the wagon train was not, in fact, on its way to join the tribe's enemies, the Blackfoot. Finally, with apparent reluctance on the part of some in the band, the Indians decided to return the two men to the wagon train, along with most of their property—horses, guns, saddles, and bridles—in exchange for some tobacco.[30]

Throughout the rest of the journey along the Sweetwater, relations with the Sioux remained tenuous, and men who roved out from the train to hunt buffalo were often robbed of their meat as well as their horses. A member of the party estimated that at one point he could see several thousand Sioux camped within sight of the wagon train. Fitzpatrick's savvy with Indians was a key factor in preventing an attack and perhaps a massacre. Still traveling several weeks behind the emigrants, Frémont's heavily armed party, including the redoubtable Carson, had serious concerns about proceeding any farther into Sioux country in the present agitated state of the tribe but finally went ahead, thanks in part to Frémont's unquenchable ambition and the skillful guidance of the fur trader Joseph Bissonette.[31]

The emigrants, as well as Frémont's army explorers, still a couple of weeks behind, reached South Pass without a major clash with the Sioux. The pass itself was so gradual as to be almost disappointing, more of a broad sloping plain than anything that looked like the imagination's picture of a mountain pass. Frémont and Carson actually had to spend some time looking for the summit, and Frémont wrote that the ascent was as gentle as the slope of Capitol Hill in Washington, D.C. Frémont's report of his explorations along the trail and in the vicinity of South Pass reads very much like a guide to future emigrants, which is exactly what he and his sponsors, Senator Benton and President Tyler, intended it to be. After scouting about in the Wind River Range—that "savage sublimity of naked rock," as he would call it in his report—Frémont headed for home to publish his findings. Frémont's wife, Jessie—Senator Benton's daughter—applied her considerable literary skills to the report, and Frémont himself had a flair for the dramatic. Their collaboration helped build excitement for westward migration and began to establish the reputation that would eventually win for Frémont the sobriquet the Pathfinder.[32]

By the first of August, Hastings, White, and company had reached the Green River in southwestern Wyoming. Rougher trail lay ahead, the season was getting late, and the party's draft animals were badly fatigued. They needed to make better time, and the only way to do that was to lighten the loads. Prized possessions taken from eastern homes and hauled with much labor across the plains now had to be abandoned beside the trail. The women lamented the loss of feather beds, chairs, dishes, and cooking utensils. The men had to part with items they had hoped to use in Oregon, including even wagons and harnesses. The party's wagons were abandoned, sold at Fort Hall, or else disassembled and the pieces used to build pack saddles so that the teams could haul the necessary supplies on their backs rather than on wheels.[33]

Thus unencumbered, the party pressed on more rapidly. They made stops of a day or two at the Hudson's Bay Company outposts of Fort Hall, where the last of the wagons were sold, and Fort Boise. Ahead of them loomed the Blue Mountains, and their towering appearance "struck us with terror," wrote emigrant Medorem Crawford. "Their lofty peaks seemed a resting place for clouds." Yet once the party got among them, the mountains proved more of an inconvenience than a threat. Crawford thought the trail through them was "very sidling and uncomfortable rocky." Having safely cleared the mountains before snow flew, the party's next stop was Whitman's mission at Waiilatpu; they enjoyed the hospitality of each outpost in turn and took the opportunity to purchase supplies or horses as needed. At Waiilatpu they listened with fascination as Whitman preached to the Indians in their own language and with more comprehension as he preached to them and to his family in English.[34]

From Waiilatpu they pressed on another 150 miles to the Methodist mission at The Dalles, where they again rested and refitted for a few days. Resuming their journey, they arrived at the settlements in the Willamette Valley on October 5. One of the participants, looking back on the experience many years later, thought that the last three weeks of travel through Oregon before reaching the Willamette Valley were the hardest part of the entire journey, exhausted as man and beast were by this time. The rest stops at Waiilatpu and The Dalles had been much needed.[35]

Despite the hardship and occasional squabbles, the first organized wagon train had reached Oregon. True, it arrived minus its wagons, but overall the venture had been a splendid success and the harbinger of other expeditions to follow. The settlers found the Willamette Valley all that they had hoped, though their enjoyment of it was sometimes tempered by their annoyance with White, who was soon claiming to hold all government power in Oregon. He turned out to be a petty if more or less benevolent would-be dictator, and people generally ignored him as much as possible. At any rate, one eccentric and power-hungry bureaucrat was not going to stem the coming tide of American immigration to Oregon.[36]

In February 1843 Marcus Whitman rode into St. Louis, his face and hands scarred by frostbite. He had crossed the continent in the dead of winter, having left his mission station at Waiilatpu on October 3, just after Hastings's party passed through on its way to the Willamette Valley. With him was the second-in-command of the party—and Hastings's companion in brief captivity to the Sioux—Asa Lovejoy, who had agreed to turn back and accompany Whitman on his winter journey. When they reached Fort Hall, they learned that the Sioux were still as hostile as they had been that summer. To avoid them, Whitman and Lovejoy detoured to the south, following the course of the Bear River. Working their way around the snowbound Uinta Mountains, they picked up a trapper for a guide at a dreary trading post in western Colorado. At Fort Uncompahgre, another trappers' trading post, they exchanged their guide for another, but when a blizzard caught them in the valley of the Gunnison River, their new guide panicked. Whitman left Lovejoy in camp for a week while he took the guide back to Fort Uncompahgre and exchanged him for another, presumably made of sterner stuff.[37]

The journey became a seemingly endless misery of cold and hunger. To stave off starvation, they ate their dog and one mule. In the mountains of southern Colorado, the fur trader Charles Bent provided them new animals and equipment, and they set off for Bent's Fort, the trading post Bent and his brother William had established on the Arkansas River east of the Rockies. Some miles from the fort, they met William Bent, who informed them that a party of trappers was about to depart for the East. Eager to join them, Whitman decided, for the first time on the trip, that it would be permissible to travel on Sunday, and he pressed on ahead of Lovejoy and their guide to reach the fort before the trappers left. As it turned out, Whitman got lost, and Lovejoy and the guide beat him to the fort, a fact he remorsefully attributed to his wrongdoing in traveling on the Sabbath. A messenger sent galloping ahead bid the trappers wait, and Whitman was able to join them for the final leg of his journey, while the exhausted Lovejoy remained at Bent's Fort until summer.[38]

Whitman's arrival in St. Louis created a minor sensation, not only because of the amazing feat he had just completed but also because he brought the first news of the Hastings wagon train's safe arrival in Oregon. Whitman was pleased to see the growing enthusiasm for Oregon and the prospects of large-scale migration, but had no desire to tarry in Missouri. He had come east with a purpose—two purposes, actually, which both required him to continue his journey all the way to the Atlantic coast.

One of Whitman's reasons for making his epic winter trek was his concern about the future status of Oregon. He was deeply worried that the Oregon Country was falling further under the sway of the Hudson's Bay Company and thus of the British Crown. The arrival of Hastings's party, along with the overinflated Sub–Indian Agent White, may have given Whitman hope that the territory could be brought into the United States. Part of his purpose in undertaking his winter crossing of the continent seems to have been to encourage more settlers to go to Oregon and to urge the U.S. government to take steps to secure the territory. His first destination on the East Coast was Washington, D.C., where he arrived still sporting his travel-worn buckskins and a buffalo robe. There he talked with President Tyler, Secretary of State Daniel Webster, and other members of the cabinet, urging that the federal government take steps to aid and support emigrants bound for Oregon.[39]

Whitman's other and much more pressing concern involved the future of his mission station at Waiilatpu. The American Board of Commissioners for Foreign Missions had decided to close the stations at Waiilatpu and Lapwai, retaining only the one among the Spokane tribe near the Hudson's Bay Company's Fort Colville. Mission work among the Indians was discouraging. Their native religions had a strong hold on them, one not easily broken. The wife of a missionary at the Spokane station would write in 1847, "We have been here almost nine years and have not yet been permitted to hear the cries of one penitent or the songs of one redeemed soul." To make matters worse, some of the board's missionaries in the Oregon Country did not get along. Disheartened by this situation, the board had decided early in 1842 that its limited resources could be more profitably invested elsewhere. Elijah White had delivered the board's letter to Whitman when he reached Waiilatpu just ahead of the rest of Hastings's party. Whitman was eager to urge the board to maintain the Waiilatpu and Lapwai stations, and thus he arrived at the board's Boston headquarters on March 30, 1843.

If Whitman thought his winter journey in the mountains had been cold, he found it was nothing compared with the icy reception he received from the dour Presbyterians of the American Board of Commissioners for Foreign Missions. The members were shocked by Whitman's rough-hewn appearance—he wore the same buckskins and buffalo robe he had in the nation's capital—and immediately gave him money to buy a respectable suit of clothes. They were not inclined to give him anything else. They reproached him for having abandoned his post without permission and wasted money on the cross-country journey, and they were not eager to hear his arguments against their decision. Grudgingly they listened and finally agreed to allow the stations at Waiilatpu and

Lapwai a new lease on life. Whitman and the other missionaries would have the board's permission to stay in the Oregon Country, but they would not have any more of the board's money. The members even declined to pay the expense of Whitman's return journey.[40]

Undaunted, Whitman made plans to travel back to the Oregon Country the following spring, and he let it be known to all and sundry, including the influential *New-York Tribune* editor Horace Greeley, that he would do what he could to help guide another wagon train through the difficult western part of the journey. He placed notices in newspapers and in a pamphlet that he had printed, not only repeating his offer to guide a wagon train west of Fort Hall but also describing the beauty and desirability of Oregon.[41]

Whitman's efforts, along with the news that the previous year's party had reached Oregon safely, did much to encourage additional emigration, and 1843 saw a migration on a much larger scale than in previous years. In fact, emigrants prepared to go in such numbers as to create a bit of a sensation. "This migration of more than a thousand persons in one body to Oregon," wrote Greeley, "wears an aspect of insanity." Greeley may have been particularly well qualified to pronounce on the issue of insanity, as he was none too stable himself. On the issue of westward migration, however, he would come around in time. For now he expostulated about wilderness, deserts, storms, hunger, and "the savage, snowy precipices of the Rocky Mountains."[42]

Still farther east, on the other side of the Atlantic, *The Edinburgh Review* was inclined to Greeley's present view of westward migration. The interior of the continent was "a howling wilderness of snow and tempests," the editor opined, a desert "of hopeless sterility," inhabited by Indians of "more than Scythian savageness and endurance, who cannot be tracked, overtaken, or conciliated." In short, the British had little to fear from American efforts to settle the Pacific Northwest: "Oregon will never be colonized overland from the United States." Other newspapers in Britain and the United States took much the same tone.[43]

By the spring of 1843 the pattern for travel to Oregon was set, at least to a certain degree, and the experience of that year's emigrants taught additional refinements. Those wishing to make the trip gathered in northwestern Missouri, near Independence, in the spring of 1843. A number of them held an organizational meeting on May 20, just west of Independence, and elected Peter H. Burnett as captain of that year's wagon train. The experience of previous emigrants had demonstrated clearly the superiority of oxen to horses or mules for pulling the wagons across the continent. "The ox is a most noble animal," wrote a grateful Burnett after his crossing, "patient, thrifty, durable, gentle, and does not run off." He predicted that future Oregon emigrants would "be in love with their oxen. The ox will plunge through mud, swim over streams, dive into thickets, and he will eat almost anything."[44]

By May 21 some 120 wagons were on hand, accompanied by perhaps 875 emigrants. In addition to the oxen (and a few mules) that would pull the wagons, another three thousand cattle and horses would accompany the party. The emigrants hired a former mountain man as a guide, and the first of the wagons rolled out of Elm Grove on May 22.[45]

Naturally, there were disagreements. This time the chief strife early in the journey pitted those who were bringing large numbers of cattle, which were scarce in Oregon, against those who had few if any besides their draft oxen. The latter wished to push on more rapidly and leave the herds behind, exposing them to possible danger during the crossing of the plains. Burnett finally despaired of reconciling the difference and resigned as captain. The families without cattle, about half the party, elected William Martin their captain and pressed on ahead. The cattle-owning families elected Jesse Applegate as their captain and followed behind, though to everyone's surprise, including their own, they were able to keep pace with the supposedly faster noncattle wagon train.[46]

A day on the trail began at 4:00 a.m. with a volley of shots from the wagon train's sentinels to awaken the emigrants. Amid much bustle they hurried to strike their tents, catch and hitch their teams, and take their places in the column. The emigrants were divided into platoons of four wagons, often groups of friends, neighbors, or extended family. To share equally the dust-eating misery of the rear reaches of the column, each platoon moved up one spot in the march order each day until it got its turn crossing the fresh grass and breathing the clean air at the head of the column. The next day that platoon rotated to the rear, and the progression began again. If one of a platoon's wagons was not ready to take its place at the appointed time for departure, the whole platoon lost its place in line, creating considerable pressure on laggards not to let their friends down.[47]

During the day, the guide would ride ahead to choose the best route, as well as the best places for nooning and for camping that evening. With him would ride a party of men detailed to make whatever improvements the route might need, digging down the steep banks of a creek or filling in some buffalo path that lay athwart the trail. Despite their efforts, the wagons still came in for an occasional jostling, dislodging carelessly packed cargo or breaking an axletree—with attendant frustration and delay. Men not driving wagons or working on the road detail often rode abroad to hunt game. Women and children might ride in the wagons, but more often walked along beside them across the open prairie. Nooning was an hour-long halt, during which man and beast could feed and rest and teamsters led their oxen to water. Bugles summoned the wagon train to renew the march, and an afternoon of trekking across the grasslands followed.[48]

Near sunset, the guide directed the head of the column to the camping place he had selected and had the teamsters circle the wagons. When the wagon corral was complete, ox chains bound the tongue of each wagon to the axle of the next, securing the draft animals inside and providing a defensive barrier against whatever dangers might lie without, chiefly Indians. Evenings were busy, at least at first, with men tending to their stock or digging shallow wells near the riverbank in order to secure clearer water than its turbid stream provided. Women went about cooking the evening meal while children gathered buffalo chips for fuel. With the next morning's 4:00 a.m. wake-up guns in prospect, travelers—or at least those who had not pulled sentinel duty—would seek sleep not long after chores and mealtime were over, though some fiddle or banjo music might round out the evening.[49]

The wagon train covered an average of fifteen or twenty miles per day across the prairies, a brisk pace for a mostly ox-drawn caravan. The emigrants found that the lowly ox was more durable than the horse and less desirable to the Indians, who always lurked close by, ready to steal livestock, especially horses. Many families soon realized that their wagons were far too heavily loaded, and the first hundred miles or so of trail were dotted with pieces of furniture and equipment, some quite valuable, abandoned to ease the loads on straining oxen.[50]

Whitman rode along. In eastern Kansas, just before the wagons had reached the Platte River, he visited the nearby camp of another army exploring expedition, led once again, as had been the case the previous summer, by Lieutenant John C. Frémont. Frémont had forty men and a twelve-pounder mountain howitzer this year, and his goal was to proceed due west from the upper Missouri towns of Independence and St. Joseph and try to find a pass through the Rockies in what is today Colorado. Then his orders called for him to scout the headwaters of whatever rivers flowed into the Gulf of California and from there to proceed northwest to Oregon. Whitman and Frémont discussed Oregon and the trails leading to it for several hours before the missionary returned to the wagon train.[51]

The high plains rivers were swollen with the runoff of melting snows in the Rockies, and crossings were perilous. The south fork of the Platte River required a makeshift ferrying operation that took several days. At the Laramie, by some accounts, Whitman was the only man willing to swim his mule across the swirling waters carrying the towline for yet another improvised ferrying operation, this one managed by stretching uncured buffalo hides over the wagon boxes and allowing them to dry, thus turning each wagon box into a watertight vessel that could be floated across the river.

The trail brought many other dangers. A mule died after being hit by a stray shot during the fording of the North Platte, a child some days later after falling under the wheels of a wagon. Some dangers were those common to nineteenth-century life. A man died of illness, and a few days later a second did as well. A woman successfully gave birth to a healthy child.[52]

On they plodded at the pace of walking oxen, across the high plains, along the valley of the Sweetwater. At Independence Rock one of them left a record of their passing: "THE OREGON CO. arrived July 26, 1843." On August 3 the emigrants sighted the snowcapped peaks of the Rockies. Forage grew scarcer as they entered increasingly arid climate zones, and despite continued worry about the threat of Indian attack, the emigrants split up into smaller wagon groups so as not to strain local supplies of grass and water. They passed the Laramie Range on the south side of the trail, and then the Wind River Range loomed even more impressively to their right, its snowcapped peaks trailing out of sight to the northwestern horizon. In the broad valley between the Wind River Range to the north and the Antelope Hills to the south, the wagons rolled through South Pass, though if any of the emigrants noticed it, he left no record. For the weary travelers it was apparently just one more long, gradual slope covered with sagebrush and thin, sere grass in a succession of such prairie swells as they had been toiling over for what seemed a very long time. Now, however, their trend was ever so gently downhill, and the streams, when they came to them, would be flowing toward the Pacific. The emigrants were officially outside the territory of the United States.[53]

Whitman found a better route for the next section of trail, avoiding a dry stretch he remembered from his 1836 crossing, and led the wagon train by a southward detour to Fort Bridger, a trappers' trading post at the foot of the towering Uintas in what is today southwestern Wyoming. The leading elements of the migration paused at Fort Hall on the Snake River, the easternmost outpost of the Hudson's Bay Company in Oregon. The company's chief official there, the highly experienced Richard Grant, told the emigrants that it was impossible to take wagons any farther west. Whitman had been traveling near the tail of the column, and at this point he came up and assured the leaders that he could take them through, wagons and all. He knew of a couple of fur trappers who had brought wagons through to Oregon two years before. The emigrants took his advice instead of Grant's and pressed on.[54]

By October 1, they had reached the valley of the Grande Ronde, a tributary of the Snake, and a light snowfall the next morning warned them that time was short. Ahead lay the rugged Blue Mountains. Unlike the preceding year's party, this group of emigrants had enough manpower to clear a road and so was able to take all its wagons across to the valley of the Columbia, the men often going ahead with axes while the women drove the wagons. A much heavier snowstorm hit them in the mountains, but they were able to press on and reach Whitman's mission station, where supplies awaited them. Whitman had been as good as his word, working hard not only to guide the wagon train but to provide advice, assistance, and medical attention up and down the column as needed. During the entire migration, three men had died of disease, and another had drowned. The column's numbers had increased, however, as more than that many babies had been born along the way.

Having brought the party through to his station as promised, Whitman could lead them no farther. It was now too late in the season to cross the Cascade Range, so most of the travelers left their wagons at Whitman's station for the winter, and building rafts from the abundant timber that clad the hills, they pressed on via the Columbia River, passing through its gorge to reach the west side of the Cascades, though with much difficulty and hardship. The Oregon winter had set in by then, and rain was incessant. The officials of the Hudson's Bay Company, though not at all eager to encourage American settlement in Oregon, nevertheless would not let the new arrivals starve and kindly provided supplies to help them get through that first winter.[55]

The new arrivals represented an enormous addition to the population of Oregon. Earlier in 1843, before the arrival of Whitman's wagon train, settlers already living in Oregon had voted 52–50 to establish a provisional government. The new arrivals increased the number of American settlers in Oregon fivefold. Their letters home brought enticing news of Oregon to more eastern communities than ever before. The fact that the 1843 migration had been able to take its wagons all the way through to Oregon was especially impressive and encouraging.[56]

The year 1844 brought an even larger migration across the plains and mountains, and in 1845 another three thousand pioneers flocked into Oregon, almost doubling the region's population. The floodgates of American migration to the Pacific Northwest were open, and wagon trains continued to make their way across the plains and mountains in each of the remaining years of the 1840s, rapidly populating the Oregon Country with American settlers.[57]

CHAPTER FIVE

The Allure and the Danger of California

SOUTH OF OREGON was California. A distant and semiautonomous province of Mexico, California had drifted along in pleasant indolence for decades before gaining the notice of substantial numbers of Americans. Yankee trading ships called regularly there during the first half of the nineteenth century, trafficking in sea otter pelts and then conducting the even more extensive hide and tallow trade. A sprinkling of Americans began to stay and settle along the California coast, some of them as agents of the hide and tallow traders. These, along with others who did not choose to remain in the province, wrote glowing accounts of the region's potential, calling the attention of their eastern compatriots to this delightful part of the western coast of their continent.[1]

The most famous of these was published in 1840—the year of the log cabin and hard cider campaign—by Richard Henry Dana. Entitled *Two Years Before the Mast,* Dana's book recounts his journey to California on the brig *Pilgrim.* A scion of an old Massachusetts family and a recent graduate of Harvard, Dana had thought an ocean voyage advisable for his health, but rather than taking passage to Europe and back in the comfort of a passenger cabin, as any normal young man of his class would have done, Dana had shipped "before the mast" as a common sailor on the *Pilgrim,* a vessel bound around Cape Horn for California in the hide and tallow trade. Dana waxed enthusiastic about the glories of California— forests, mountains, streams teeming with beaver and fish, valleys covered with immense herds of cattle, rich soil that yielded bumper crops, and the finest climate in the world. Yet he felt the inhabitants were too lazy to take advantage of their good fortune. "In the hands of an enterprising people," he wrote, "what a country this might be!"[2]

The United States had plenty of enterprising people, and some of them were soon making plans for California. Organized migration to California began more or less simultaneously with that to Oregon, though it was never as large. The first party of overland emigrants for California came from Platte County, in western Missouri. The sixty-nine men, women, and children who left their homes for the westward trek were those who had heeded the exhortations of the returned trapper Antoine Robidoux, who praised California. The emigrants had resisted the warnings of those local merchants who slandered the distant shore because they did not want to lose business. The band of pioneers set out in May 1841, the year before Elijah White and Lansford Hastings and their party made their own westward migration to Oregon. The California emigrants were fortunate enough to encounter the mountain man Thomas Fitzpatrick, who would skillfully guide White and Hastings the following year. Fitzpatrick was on his way to Oregon and readily agreed to hire on as guide for the California-bound group until their ways parted. They followed the route of the Oregon Trail up the valley of the Platte, past Fort Laramie and Independence Rock, along the Sweetwater, and through South Pass.[3]

By the time they reached Soda Springs, near modern-day Pocatello, Idaho, nearly half of the emigrants had decided to divert to Oregon instead, since that would allow them to follow an experienced guide on a well-blazed trail. Thirty-four hardy souls, including one woman and one child, exchanged their wagons for pack saddles and set out southwestward toward California, knowing only that they must bear west from the Great Salt Lake. They were delighted to find a westward-flowing river, Nevada's Humboldt, on September 23. This curious stream rose in the mountains of northern Nevada and trended generally west-southwest across the Great Basin, dodging mountain ranges and providing the ideal corridor through this washboard of horst and graben topography.[4]

If the pioneers of this first party knew any name for the river, it would probably have been Ogden's River, after its discoverer, Hudson's Bay Company explorer Peter Skene Ogden. It went by several monikers until it received its modern name in 1848. Finding this highway between the ranges must have seemed too good to be true for the small band of emigrants, and so it turned out to be. As they followed it downstream, the river seemed to grow smaller, in defiance of all their experience with rivers, if not of the laws of nature itself. Rivers certainly did nothing like that in Missouri. Then, to what must have been their unspeakable dismay, this semialkaline remnant of a river flowed into a marshy lake—and stopped. The Humboldt is the largest North American river whose waters naturally fail to reach the sea. Sinking into the ground and evaporating into the air, the river simply ends at the intermittent lake known as the Humboldt Sink.

There was nothing to do now but strike southwestward across the desert toward the Sierra Nevada, still some fifty miles away. By October 16 the mountains loomed before them, and their scouts reported them "barely passable." Some advocated backtracking to Fort Hall in Idaho before winter snows cut off that way of escape, but they were almost certainly already too late for that. They pressed on into the mountains, and on the next-to-last day of October, they discovered a river flowing west, the Stanislaus, and followed it to the Central Valley of California, arriving exhausted and almost unable to believe they had finally reached the promised land.[5]

Thirty-four Americans were not exactly going to populate the province, even followed as they were by two other small bands of Americans who in the months to come made their way into California from New Mexico and Oregon. The latter party, forty members in all, came in 1843 and was led by Lansford Hastings, captain of the 1842 Oregon wagon train. Like others before him, Hastings, by then twenty-four years old, became quite enamored of California and enthusiastic about his own prospects there, especially if many more Americans should migrate there and elect him to office within whatever political entity their presence might engender.

To boost migration to California, Hastings published his *Emigrants' Guide to Oregon and California*, telling the story of his 1842 trip to Oregon and his journey down to California the next year, and giving suggestions about the trail. One tip involved a possible shortcut. Hastings had noticed, as anyone could who studied a map of the route to California, that the trail bent first northwest for a couple of hundred miles and then southwest. A future wagon train could, at least in theory, save a considerable distance by cutting across this bend in the trail. If the emigrants broke away from the Oregon Trail a bit sooner, cut across what is today northern Utah, and rejoined the established California Trail in modern-day Nevada, the trip would be shortened and thus the danger of being caught in the late autumn snows of the Sierra Nevada would be diminished.[6]

Another party of Americans had come to California, temporarily, in 1842, but not by the usual route or for the purposes of settlement. In September of that year, Commodore Thomas ap Catesby Jones, commanding the United States Navy's Pacific Squadron, was cruising off Peru when he received a report that the United States and Mexico had gone to war and that Great Britain intended to make the most of the occasion by seizing California. After consulting with his ship captains, he decided that it was his duty to seize California first and immediately made sail for Monterey. On October 19 his flagship, the frigate *United States,* entered the harbor and dropped anchor in front of the dilapidated castle that passed for a seaward defense of the town. Jones trained his guns on the crumbling fort and demanded its surrender, and the nonplussed Mexican commander complied. Occupying the castle and town with his sailors and marines, Jones had his men raise the Stars and Stripes and announced that all of California was now annexed to the United States.

Two days later he was dismayed to learn that in fact no state of war had existed. The whole thing had been a false rumor. With elaborate apologies, Jones gave California back to Mexico. The locals were impressed with the courtesy and good discipline of the American sailors and marines, but the incident tended to excite Mexican suspicions, not entirely unfounded, that the United States had designs on California. Not long thereafter, Jones rotated stateside according to the routine succession of commanders, but Secretary of the Navy Abel P. Upshur declined to inflict any punishment "on an able and well-intentioned commander." Still, Jones's embarrassing blunder gave future American commanders on the Pacific coast a cautionary tale to ponder.[7]

John C. Frémont visited California in the spring of 1844. After meeting with Whitman in May 1843 on the prairies of eastern Kansas near the eastern end of the Oregon Trail, Frémont had led his party of forty men of the U.S. Army's Corps of Topographical Engineers westward across the plains. Failing to find a practical pass through the Rockies in what is today Colorado, Frémont turned north into Wyoming and along the eastern foot of the Laramie Range to strike the Oregon Trail in the Sweetwater Valley. Already the passage of the 1841 California-Oregon Party, the White-Hastings Party of the following year, and that summer's large Burnett Party, along with the occasional fur trader's wagon, had worn away the grass and in some places a little of the rocky soil as well to make the trail an unmistakable path across the plains.[8]

Frémont and his men followed the Oregon Trail through South Pass and into the valley of the Green River on the western slope of the Rockies. There he could not resist the temptation to detour to the south and see the Great Salt Lake, of which trappers had told him. The expedition left the trail and followed the Green River downstream, then swung west through the rugged Wasatch Range to enter the valley of the Great Salt Lake through Weber Canyon. Their first glimpse of the lake made understandable the fact that upon encountering it some mountain men had thought they had reached the Pacific. Frémont was determined to explore the lake and at least one of its islands using a canoe-shaped eighteen-foot, six-man inflatable rubber boat he had brought along.[9]

When they reached the lake, Frémont, Carson, and several of their men climbed into the frail craft and paddled through the whitecaps to the nearest of the islands, a five-mile-long hump of land that now bears Frémont's name. Carson's skepticism about the patent boat proved well founded when the flimsy vessel nearly swamped and two of its air chambers began to separate from each other. Somehow it held together well enough to carry them to the island and back, with one member of the party constantly pumping a handheld bellows to maintain sufficient air pressure. The view from the island's high point revealed the amazing expanse of the lake, from its turquoise shallows to the wine-dark waters where the shadows of clouds or islands cloaked its deeper reaches. Rimming the lake and seeming scarcely to rise above its surface were wide, flat salt-white beaches that finally gave way to dun-colored, almost treeless slopes rolling upward from the shore. Scoring the hillsides a few hundred feet above the surface of the lake was the scar of a previous shoreline, from a time when a much larger lake had occupied the entire valley and several adjoining ones, a remnant of the earth's catastrophic geologic past. Beyond the grassy hills that surrounded the lake rose the great majestic wall of the Wasatch front to the east, while lower but still impressive ranges marked the horizon to the north and south.[10]

Reluctantly, Frémont resisted the temptation to make further explorations of the lake in his frail boat this late in the season, and having rejoined the main body of his expedition, he turned their course toward Oregon. Working their way north again, Frémont and his explorers cut back onto the Oregon Trail at Fort Hall and pressed west, crossing the Blue Mountains in October and visiting Whitman's mission at Waiilatpu, though missing the good doctor himself, who was making his rounds to the mission station at The Dalles. Frémont's expedition continued on to the Willamette Valley. Though his orders specified that he should return to the States at this point, Frémont decided to enter California. He first led his party south into what is today northwestern Nevada and then, incredibly, proposed that they cross the Sierra Nevada in mid-January. Fortunately for Frémont and his men, it was a mild winter in the Sierras, yet the band of tough explorers and mountain men barely survived the crossing. Most of their horses and mules did not. Nearing starvation and suffering from frostbite and snow blindness, the men staggered into the valley of the Sacramento River in early March and were all but overwhelmed by the lushness of the enormous valley after the barren wastes through which they had come.[11]

Where the American River joined the Sacramento, they found the settlement of Johann Augustus Sutter. Sutter had emigrated from Switzerland to escape bad debts and perhaps the wife and children he abandoned when he left. Coming to California in 1839, he had gained favor with the local government by exaggerating his importance in the old country, particularly his role in the Swiss army reserve. In talking to his new hosts, Sutter promoted himself from first underlieutenant to captain. The Mexican rulers of California granted him fifty thousand acres and local authority that he boasted extended to "the power of life and death over everyone in his district." Sutter even possessed his own fort, a stronghold with adobe walls eighteen feet high and from two and a half to five feet thick. Two-story corner bastions mounted more than ten cannon. Inside, the fort bustled with all manner of artisans—from blacksmiths to carpenters to coopers—who maintained the Swiss emigrant's extensive domains. Sutter received the haggard Americans hospitably, commenting, "The starvation and fatigue they had endured rendered them truly deplorable objects."[12]

Frémont and his men camped outside the walls of the fort for sixteen days, partaking of Sutter's sumptuous fare for most of their meals. California was exerting its charm on the trail-weary explorers, and three of Frémont's men sought and received their discharges and took service under Sutter. Frémont reoutfitted his expedition, including new animals, by purchase from Sutter. Then in late March he led his men down the Central Valley of California. From the locals he had learned that the best way out of California would be south into the San Joaquín Valley, which he and his men found teeming with game and with herds of wild horses, then east over a much lower pass than he had traversed when entering the Central Valley that winter. From there, a route called the Old Spanish Trail would lead him to Santa Fe and allow further exploration of the region between the Rockies and the Sierras, a region Frémont was starting to call the Great Basin. Once again Frémont returned to civilization after an expedition that won him further renown as the Pathfinder.[13]

Ordinary Americans continued to flock westward along the trails toward both Oregon and California, spurred and instructed by the guidebooks of Frémont and Hastings. Most arrived safely, but in 1846 one group of emigrants demonstrated just how much could go wrong along the trail and how much it could cost an unwary or unlucky band of travelers.

During the winter of 1845–46, the brothers George and Jacob Donner made plans to emigrate from their home in Sangamon County, Illinois, to California. The Donners were substantial farmers living in the middle of the best farming country on the face of the globe, but they hoped for better things in California. Sixty-two-year-old George Donner, the younger of the brothers, epitomized the population of America's western states in that era with his readiness to believe that better land was to be found somewhere farther on. He had migrated from his native North Carolina to Kentucky, Indiana, and Illinois before trying a stint in Texas, then returning to Illinois. As sketched in Frémont's glowing reports, Hastings's *Emigrants' Guide,* and the editorial page of the local *Springfield Journal,* California sounded like just the place for George Donner.[14]

With their families, their hired hands, and several of their neighbors, the Donners formed a party of thirty-three and pushed off with nine wagons from the town square in Springfield, Illinois, in mid-April 1846. Following the customary route, they traveled through Independence, Missouri, and set out from there onto the open prairie on May 12. A week later they joined a larger wagon train led by William H. Russell. The addition of the Donners' party brought the group's total to about two hundred men, women, and children. By one count, more than five hundred wagons were on the overland trail that spring, with the Donners' wagon train being near the tail end of an intermittent procession that stretched for more than 150 miles.[15]

The journey across the plains went well, despite the occasional violent thunderstorm. George's wife, Tamsen, wrote from the trail along the Platte River a letter addressed to a friend who had stayed back in Illinois, telling her how pleasant and easy the journey had been thus far. Even cooking over a fire of buffalo chips had proven no hardship, and Tamsen pronounced the new fuel as good as hickory chips. The Indians were friendly, the prairie "beautiful beyond description." "Indeed," she added, "if I do not experience something far worse than I have yet done, I shall say the trouble is all in getting started."[16]

When the party celebrated Independence Day at Fort Laramie, it was a bit behind the ideal pace for crossing the continent, but not dangerously so. Two weeks later, however, near the Little Sandy River in what is today Wyoming, the wagon train reorganized into several smaller parties. Part of the reason for the reorganization was an "open letter" to California-bound emigrants from Lansford Hastings. From the headwaters of the Sweetwater River, Hastings sent his missive back down the trail in the hands of a messenger on horseback. The letter was addressed to anyone making for California and urged the virtues of the proposed shortcut he had suggested in his recently published *Emigrants' Guide to Oregon and California.* Hastings claimed that his new route, the Hastings Cutoff, would shorten the journey to California by some two hundred miles.

In his letter, Hastings promised to wait at Fort Bridger and guide the travelers over the new route. Despite the offer, most of the wagon trains chose to stick with the proven route. Among those facing a decision at the fort was A. J. Grayson, traveling with his young wife. The news of Hastings's proposal "created some excitement among the emigrants," Grayson recalled. "Some were for going the new route without reflecting, whilst the more prudent were for going by the old trail via Fort Hall." Grayson asked an experienced mountain man at Fort Bridger for his opinion, and got emphatic advice to stick with the old trail. He did.[17]

The Donners chose the cutoff. With that route in mind, they and several other families formed a new wagon train and on July 20 elected George Donner its captain. The newly formed party numbered eighty-seven people and twenty-three wagons. Spirits were high at the prospect of a better route that would save them hundreds of miles of weary travel. The only exception was Tamsen Donner, who thought they were foolish to leave the established trail on the word of a man they did not know and who might turn out to be merely a "selfish adventurer."[18]

Five days after breaking camp on the Little Sandy, the Donner Party, as it was now called, reached Fort Bridger, the beginning of the Hastings Cutoff. There they found that Hastings had recently departed, leading a party of sixty-six wagons bound for California via the south shore of the Great Salt Lake. Nonetheless, Hastings had left word at the fort that any California-bound emigrants should follow behind him. They would find the road "smooth, level, and hard" under their wagon wheels, leading through country with plenty of wood and water, good pasturage for their stock—except in a single forty-mile dry stretch—and no canyons to traverse.[19]

For the first few days out of Fort Bridger, the new trail lived up to its billing as it took them steadily southwest, directly toward the looming mass of the Wasatch Range. On August 3 the Donner Party reached the mouth of Weber Canyon, leading into the Wasatch, and at the first crossing of the Weber River, they found a piece of paper held aloft in the split end of a stick. It was a note from Hastings informing any emigrants who might be following behind him that Weber Canyon was all but impassable to wagons and that he had little hope of getting through with the wagons he was then guiding. He recommended instead a different course through the mountains, which he sketched out vaguely in his note. Three men of the Donner Party rode ahead to overtake Hastings, gain more information, and, if possible, persuade him to come back and guide them through. Catching up with him near the southern end of the Great Salt Lake after a hard ride, they prevailed on him to come back as far as the Wasatch and point out the route he thought they should take, but then he felt obliged to hurry back to the other wagon train, which had gotten through Weber Canyon only by dint of backbreaking labor.[20]

Hoping to avoid a similar difficult passage and a loss of time they now could ill afford, the emigrants of the Donner Party decided to take Hastings's advice again and try the alternate route through the Wasatch, with the goal of reaching the Great Salt Lake in one week. The trail immediately proved difficult, sometimes requiring a full day's work by all the men to make a short stretch passable for the wagons. Eight days of work completed an eight-mile wagon road into a gulch the emigrants thought would lead them through the mountains but which instead turned out to be a box canyon. When they learned they would have to backtrack the whole eight miles, the party nearly dissolved in panic, with individual families striking out on their own in the desperate quest for a way through the mountains. Cooler heads prevailed, and the men were soon back at work on a new trail.[21]

The gorge they now took, since known as Emigration Canyon, proved to be little if any improvement on the Weber Canyon route. More labor made it just passable, and even then they had to harness six or eight yoke of oxen to drag each wagon up some of the steeper slopes. Finally, a full month after entering the Wasatch, with man and beast exhausted, wagons in need of repair, and supplies dwindling, they finally sighted the salt-white shores of the lake and congratulated themselves that they now had the most strenuous part of the journey behind them and could look forward to good roads and pleasant travel the rest of the way to California.[22]

Early September found them plodding along the southern shores of the Great Salt Lake while behind them the advancing season was already painting the slopes of the Wasatch gold, orange, and crimson with the turning leaves of maples and aspens. It was a beauty the emigrants likely could not enjoy, laden as it was with ominous portent. Another note from Hastings stuck in a forked stick by the trail promised them they would reach the next water after two days and two nights of hard driving. Ahead of them lay the Great Salt Lake Desert, not forty miles, as they supposed on the basis of Hastings's note, but rather eighty. The travel would be as flat as any they could have longed for during the journey through the Wasatch, but utterly devoid of water. Hour after hour the wagons creaked and groaned over the whitish sandy floor of the desert, raising clouds of alkaline dust from the evaporite deposits of the massive lake that had once covered these salt flats. With only brief halts they pressed on day and night.

Humans and animals began to falter on the fourth day. Men unhitched the oxen and took them ahead to water, then brought them back for the wagons and the women and children. The first oxen reached water on the evening of the fourth day, and by the following morning, all of the wagon train had done so as well, leaving behind several dozen cattle that had died along the trail and others that had stampeded toward the water and been lost. When a weeklong search failed to recover the missing animals, some of the wagons and possessions had to be left behind as the party limped forward. The first snow of the journey fell on them at their desert oasis before they departed for another twenty-two-hour dry pull across a western arm of the desert.[23]

By this time it was clear that their provisions would run out well before they could hope to reach the settlements of California, so after discussing the matter the emigrants decided that two men should ride ahead to Sutter's Fort and bring back supplies for the rest of the party. While the two rode on, the situation of the wagon train continued to deteriorate. They struck the main track of the California Trail in what is today eastern Nevada at least three weeks later than they would have if they had not taken the cutoff. On September 24, they reached the Humboldt, which they still called Ogden's River.

Their progress down the Humboldt was a procession of misery. Cattle and horses began to die from exhaustion and the alkaline water. Local Indians, sensing the weakness of the party, began to steal cattle or shoot arrows into oxen that strayed within range of their coverts. They shot at men who ventured out from the caravan too, but hit none. By October 5 tempers had frayed to the point that one of the more popular members of the party became enraged and attacked a fellow emigrant—who killed him in self-defense. The killer, though one of the most capable men in the party and entirely innocent in the affair, was banished from the wagon train and forced to ride on to California alone.[24]

The wagon train reached the Humboldt Sink at midnight on October 12, and the next morning, while they were eating breakfast, Indians stole twenty-one head of their oxen. This left them with scarcely enough to pull the remaining wagons, and to lighten the loads on the emaciated beasts, everyone now had to walk all the time, many of them with heavy loads. Parents carried their children. One old man, traveling alone, lay down beside the trail and died. No one had the time or strength to go back and bury him. Two days later another emigrant, a wealthy man, went missing, and suspicion rested on several other members of the party. With the wagon train strung out over a dozen miles of trail, there was plenty of solitude for a lonely murder. The party halted and several of the young men went back and recovered his wagon and oxen, but the man himself was never found.[25]

At this desperate juncture, Charles Stanton, one of the two men sent ahead to fetch supplies, returned with five mules loaded with flour and dried beef, all courtesy of Johann Augustus Sutter. Accompanying Stanton were two of Sutter's Indian employees, sent along to help with the mules and guide the party over the Sierras. With their hunger assuaged, the emigrants decided to halt for a few days at the foot of the Sierras at a place called Truckee Meadows, near the site of modern-day Reno, Nevada, so that their remaining oxen could gain strength for the hard pull over the mountains. The snowcapped peaks of the Sierras stood before them a mute threat, but the first heavy snowstorms usually did not descend on these mountains until mid- to late November. October was scarcely more than half over, so the emigrants figured they had time. After a four-day pause, however, they became alarmed as dark clouds piled up on the summits above them. Fearing this might mean early snow, they decided to push on into the mountains immediately, and on October 23 they left the meadows.[26]

Five days later they were still toiling up the trail well short of the summit when swirling snow engulfed them and began to accumulate—six inches down at Prosser Creek, as much as five feet near the summit of the range. The snows of the Sierra Nevada had come almost a full month earlier than normal. In a state verging on panic, most of the travelers pressed on up Cold Stream Canyon toward the summit of the pass at the best speed they could, individual families or small groups desperately struggling to complete their crossing before winter fully took hold in the lofty mountains whose name meant snow. It was no use. The snows had piled up in the pass to such a depth as to block transit until spring. They were trapped.[27]

Unwilling to accept their plight, the emigrants paused a day or two to gather their strength and then made a concerted effort to break through. Leaving all but a few of the wagons, they strapped the most essential supplies and equipment to the backs of the oxen and mules and fought their way upward through the drifts. Again they failed to make the summit. In desperation they agreed to butcher all the animals the next day—since their other provisions were nearly gone—and, taking the meat, press on over the mountains on foot. That night, however, a powerful blizzard struck and continued to blow for the next several days. Abandoning for the time all hope of escape, the emigrants settled in for the winter as best they could in makeshift shelters of brush and saplings and a cabin or two. Most of them camped near a long, narrow mountain lake, now called Donner Lake, within sight of the summit of the pass, about six miles away, and, at just under six thousand feet, a little more than one thousand feet below it. The two Donner families camped at Alder Creek, several miles back down the trail.[28]

Over the next six weeks several small parties, composed mostly of young, unmarried men, tried to make their way over the mountains but were forced back. Finally, in mid-December, fifteen men and women, including parents who left their small children with relatives at the camp, set out in a desperate effort to reach the settlements and summon help. One of the men, a native of Vermont, had fashioned snowshoes for the fifteen, and some of them reckoned that even if they died on the trail, their absence from the camp would leave more of the rapidly shrinking food supply for those they left behind. They took scant rations for six days and had been out nine when, on Christmas Day, another powerful blizzard struck. One member of the party had already died, and as the storm raged, others succumbed one by one. Faced with starvation, the survivors resorted to cannibalism. On such fare, and a single deer that they succeeded in shooting, the steadily dwindling party struggled on. Seven were still alive when they reached a village of Indians, who fed them and led them to the white settlements.[29]

It took a few days to organize a relief expedition, which set out into the mountains on February 22, 1847. A total of four expeditions were needed to extricate all of the stranded emigrants from the Sierra snows, and by the time they arrived, some of the survivors at the Donner Lake camps had also engaged in cannibalism, though none at the Donner families' camps at Alder Creek. Finally, amid much continued hardship and several more deaths, the rescue was completed. It was April 29 before the last survivor reached Sutter's Fort. Of the eighty-seven travelers who started down the Hastings Cutoff back at Fort Bridger, forty-eight reached the California settlements. Thirty-nine of the pioneers had died along the way, including George Donner and his wife, Tamsen. Also dead were the two Indian vaqueros Sutter had sent along with the provision-laden mules the previous October. Lansford Hastings himself had arrived in California the previous autumn together with the wagon train he had guided. After their backbreaking struggle through Weber Canyon, the party had made the rest of the journey to California with no more than the usual vicissitudes of overland travel and had crossed the Sierras well ahead of the snows.[30]

CHAPTER SIX

The Mormons and Their Migration

ANOTHER GROUP OF American emigrants was traveling west during 1846, though its destination was neither Oregon nor California. This group was composed of adherents of a religious faith that called itself the Church of Jesus Christ of Latter-day Saints and that everyone else called Mormonism. The father of the movement was Joseph Smith, who as a young man living in Palmyra, New York, in the 1820s had claimed to receive special divine revelations. Smith had been born in Vermont in 1805. The region of upstate New York to which Joseph moved with his family as a boy continued to be swept by so many highly emotional revivals in the Second Great Awakening that it was referred to as the Burned-Over District. Those who had become addicted to the emotion without being genuinely changed by the orthodox Christianity behind it were ready to embrace all manner of strange new beliefs, including a curious mania for treasure hunting by means of occult divination.[1]

Smith claimed special powers for finding treasure—powers he exercised by peering at a "peep stone," or "seer stone," placed in a stovepipe hat he held upside down in front of him. He would gaze into the hat, and the stone would supposedly reveal to him the location of treasure. He was convincing enough to persuade some of the locals to pay for his services, though an unfulfilled contract to find a Spanish silver mine near the town of Harmony, in the Susquehanna River valley of Pennsylvania, led to his being charged in court as a "disorderly person and an impostor." He was convicted, but the record is unclear as to what punishment he received. Thereafter, he stayed in the area and married a local girl, to the outrage of her father, who considered him a charlatan and a ne'er-do-well.[2]

Smith also claimed to have special knowledge gained by visions he said were from God. Among the information conveyed by these visions was the news that all religious denominations were in error—they were abominations, in fact. In 1827, Smith told several neighbors and family members that an angel named Moroni had come to him in Palmyra and shown him where to find a number of golden plates, inscribed with strange writing in a language Smith called "Reformed Egyptian," as well as two special seer stones affixed to a golden breastplate. Smith kept these treasures carefully hidden, explaining that he was not permitted to show them to anyone, though he did offer to let his highly skeptical father-in-law feel the weight of the locked chest in which he said they were hidden.[3]

While Smith's wife, Emma, or occasionally a friendly and credulous neighbor took dictation, Smith sat concealed behind a curtain and recited what he said was the English translation of the text, revealed at first by the use of the special seer stones that came with the plates and later with an ordinary seer stone. The curtain was necessary to keep any mere mortal save Joseph Smith from seeing the sacred plates he said were present. Later he covered the plates with a cloth and dispensed with the curtain. Later still, it was possible to dispense with the plates themselves. Since any of the seer stones—the special pair the angel gave him or his own old reliable peep stone—allowed vision of objects at a distance, the presence of the plates was not necessary for their translation, and they could remain hidden in some place known only to Joseph. While Emma or one of the others busily scribbled away, Smith sat hunched over with his face in his hat, reading, as he claimed, through the seer stones the translation of the strange writing.[4]

The result was the Book of Mormon, first published in Palmyra in 1830, purporting to be the story of Israelite people who had lived in pre-Columbian America. Smith got two of his friends and nine others, members of his own and one other family, to attest that they too had seen the golden plates—or at least a vision of them, since the angel had reclaimed them at or before the end of the translation process. Smith, having moved back to upstate New York, began making converts, whom he organized as the Church of Christ (the name later changed). Initially the growth of Mormonism was slow, as the Smith family had a well-known reputation in the immediate vicinity, and not a good one. Nevertheless, Joseph Smith was a man of immense personal magnetism and charisma, and he successfully won over two highly persuasive Campbellite ministers from Ohio, Parley Pratt and Sidney Rigdon. Their united efforts, reaching beyond the locality in which the Smith family was known, were soon drawing substantial numbers of followers to the new and distinctly different gospel.[5]

As numbers grew, so did the resentment of neighbors, who distrusted the strange new cult. Smith decided to move the headquarters of his religion to Kirtland, Ohio. On arriving at the new center of Mormonism, a few miles from Lake Erie, Smith declared that his religious group should become a commune, but like many other communal experiments before and since, it proved a failure. Smith had to give up his communitarian beliefs after about two years. He continued to announce new revelations, which were no longer received with seer stones and a hat but, as he alleged, by direct communication from God, and he succeeded in overcoming the claims of some of his senior followers—who, after all, had seer stones of their own—that they had received rival revelations from the Almighty. He also dealt with his wife's dissatisfaction by communicating a conveniently timed revelation directed specifically to her: "Murmur not because of the things which thou hast not seen, for they are withheld from thee and from the world. . . . The office of thy calling shall be for a comfort unto my servant, Joseph Smith, Jun., thy husband, in his afflictions, with consoling words, in the spirit of meekness." Meanwhile, Smith took what additional comfort he could by carrying on an affair with his seventeen-year-old housekeeper.[6]

The presence of Smith's now more than one thousand devoted followers in the little Ohio town that had previously had scarcely that many inhabitants aroused alarm and resentment. Smith's seemingly total control over his followers unnerved non-Mormons. Opposition grew and in 1832 led to the tarring and feathering of Smith and one of his chief lieutenants. Smith had announced at the time of leaving New York that the Mormons should eventually set up their City of Zion in western Missouri and had sent an advance party to begin preparations for the arrival of the entire community at a site a few miles west of Independence. There too the reaction to the Mormon presence progressed from attempts to buy the Mormons out to panic and violence—more tar and feathers, and the burning of some of the Mormons' houses—as local residents became increasingly desperate to get rid of this strange cult.[7]

Back in Kirtland, Smith announced a new revelation. "The redemption of Zion must needs come by power," he proclaimed, and set about raising a Mormon army. He marched on Missouri at the head of two hundred armed men, stirring considerable alarm among non-Mormons. He reached the state and attempted to open negotiations, but when this failed to produce any sort of agreement for the Mormons to return to the Independence area, Smith disbanded his force and went back to Ohio, much to the disgust of some of his more warlike followers. The Missouri Mormons, who would soon be more numerous than their Ohio brethren, moved to a more sparsely settled part of Missouri, well north of Independence.[8]

Having returned to Kirtland, Smith had his followers build a lavish stone temple. There the Mormons worshiped enthusiastically, shouting (sometimes curses against the people of Missouri), babbling in "unknown tongues" (purported languages understood by no one on earth, including the speaker), and rolling on the floor. They had swung from the rafters in their previous house of worship, but Smith had discouraged this, and the new temple's size did not lend itself to such expressions of religious ecstasy. The expensive temple consumed much of the Mormon community's resources and ran Smith deeply into debt. Smith announced revelations that the Mormons were to build two more lavish structures beside the temple, one to house the movement's printing effort and the other "a house . . . wholly dedicated unto the Lord for the work of the presidency." In search of the needed funds, Smith and a handful of associates traveled to Salem, Massachusetts, where a revelation had told him "much treasure" was to be found, but the seer stones proved ineffective, and his party returned none the richer.[9]

Smith turned next to a more popular frontier method of acquiring treasure and set up a wildcat—that is, unchartered—bank, which he called the Kirtland Safety Society. He did so at the worst of times, however, on the eve of the Panic of 1837. The venture promptly failed. Local authorities cited Smith for running an illegal bank and issued a warrant for his arrest, and many holders of his now-worthless banknotes obtained legal writs against him. A number of Mormons, including some high-ranking ones, turned on Smith and denounced him as a charlatan. Smith and the other top Mormon leaders left Kirtland just ahead of a lynch mob.[10]

Clearly the time had come to carry out Smith's long-expressed intention of relocating to Missouri. They journeyed west during the weeks that followed, Smith sometimes traveling hidden in the back of a wagon. Thousands of their devoted adherents followed that summer, 1838, in a mile-long wagon train. Despite the recent defections of some of his followers, his movement continued to attract converts, both within the United States and, soon, from Britain as well, to which Smith had dispatched missionaries. With thousands of his followers settled around him in a northwest Missouri town he christened Far West, Smith established the new headquarters of his religion and had his people start work on another temple.[11]

Trouble was not far behind. The Mormons formed their own militia, which Smith called the Danites, both for self-defense and for suppressing dissent among the Mormons themselves. Smith's chief lieutenant, Sidney Rigdon, hinted at one of the militia's intended purposes in a couple of orations, one advocating the hanging of those who left the Mormon faith and the other announcing that any further incident of mob violence against the Mormons would result in a "war of extermination," in which the Mormons would carry the war into the homes of their enemies until all were dead. Newspapers across the state subsequently published the speech, and the reaction was horror and outrage. When the state elections were held the following month, a large number of Mormon men marched en masse to the polls at the county seat in Gallatin to vote as a bloc, fanning the fears of non-Mormon Missourians that the cult was about to take over their society. A riot ensued, with numerous injuries. Smith marched on Gallatin with a force of more than one hundred Danites and extorted from the local justice of the peace a promise to take no action against the Mormons.[12]

The situation rapidly escalated. Missourians eager to drive out the Mormons raided their settlements and farms, burning houses. Smith retaliated, sending a force of Danites to burn much of the hamlet of Gallatin as well as Missourians' cabins in outlying areas. Mormons and Missourians skirmished, with deaths on both sides. Missouri governor Lilburn Boggs responded by mobilizing the state militia and announcing that because of their "open and avowed defiance of the laws, and of having made war upon the people of this State . . . the Mormons must be treated as enemies and must be exterminated or driven from the state, if necessary for the public good." The so-called extermination order became infamous in Mormon history, but Boggs had not been the first to raise the subject.[13]

What followed became known as the Mormon War, with both vigilantes and the Missouri militia burning Mormons' barns and houses, taking their goods and livestock, and occasionally killing some of them, including seventeen men and boys under gruesome circumstances at the hamlet of Haun's Mill. Smith wanted no bloody Götterdämmerung and, along with some of the other Mormon leaders, agreed to surrender for trial in order to bring an end to hostilities. The local commander of the Missouri militia promptly ordered him shot after a drumhead court-martial, but another militia general, Alexander Doniphan, refused to carry out the order. Instead, after several months' incarceration, Smith and his cohorts escaped, apparently with the full collusion of Missouri authorities, who did not want the embarrassment of putting them on trial. Meanwhile, one of the remaining senior leaders, Brigham Young, had led the Mormons, bereft of most of their property, to safety in Illinois during the winter of 1838–39.[14]

Reunited with his followers, now fourteen thousand strong, in friendly and tolerant Quincy, Illinois, Smith decided to build his new Zion about fifty miles upstream at the tiny Mississippi River settlement of Commerce, Illinois. He renamed the place Nauvoo (which he said was Hebrew for "beautiful plantation"), and virtually overnight it became the second-largest city in Illinois. Obtaining a charter for the town from the Illinois legislature was not difficult. Smith played Whigs against Democrats, tantalizing both parties with the prospect of the Mormon bloc voting in their favor, and Illinois politicians fell over themselves in catering to the prophet's demands.

The new charter made Nauvoo a virtual state within a state, in which the mayor—Smith, of course, seconded by a few thoroughly compliant aldermen—was supreme ruler and judge. The town was authorized to operate its own militia. So Smith built up a five-thousand-man private army he called the Nauvoo Legion and appointed himself lieutenant general, a rank higher than any then existing in the United States Army. He outfitted himself in a gaudy uniform complete with gold-braided epaulets and a hat with an ostrich feather plume.[15]

He continued to promulgate new revelations from God, including orders for a new temple to replace the one left behind in Kirtland and the one planned but never built in Far West. The new structure, begun in the fall of 1840, would be built of wood and stone at a cost of more than a million dollars, donated by Smith's followers, many of whom also contributed immense amounts of volunteer labor to the project over several years. In 1841 Smith revealed that the Almighty also wanted His people to build a large luxury hotel and call it the Nauvoo House, adding, "My servant Joseph and his seed after him have place in that house, from generation to generation, forever and ever, saith the Lord," despite the fact that Joseph and his family lived in a commodious mansion house elsewhere in Nauvoo.[16]

Another alleged revelation that same year was even more startling, though Smith did not announce it publicly. To a select circle Smith vouchsafed that God demanded—and was very insistent—that Smith, and perhaps some other Mormon men, take multiple additional wives. Smith said he knew that it would create controversy but claimed to care only about absolute obedience to God. To his first wife he passed on God's personal admonition: "Let my handmaid, Emma Smith, receive all those that have been given unto my servant Joseph." With impressive alacrity in obeying the divine command, Smith on April 5, 1841, wed Louisa Beaman, his official second wife (not counting the maid back in Kirtland). Over the next two years he married a number of other women, variously estimated at up to eighty-seven in number and ranging in age all the way down to fourteen. Smith kept the secret of the new doctrine to the inner circle of Mormon leaders, some of whom also felt commanded to indulge in plural marriages, while others hotly objected to the practice.[17]

Smith was riding high—prophet, seer, "first president" of the Church of Jesus Christ of Latter-day Saints, mayor of Nauvoo, lieutenant general of his own private army, wealthy businessman, and now master of a large and growing harem. The object of intense fear and loathing among the surrounding non-Mormon population, heightened by persistent rumors of the prophet's strange teachings on marriage, Smith enjoyed the adulation of his thousands of adoring followers. In 1844 he had his people nominate him for president of the United States, and he expressly dispatched a new wave of Mormon missionaries, fanning out across North America in their hundreds, to stump for his campaign.[18]

In May 1842 someone attempted to assassinate Smith's old nemesis Lilburn Boggs, shooting the former Missouri governor through the window of his house and badly wounding him. Suspicion rested on Orrin Porter Rockwell, an associate of Smith's. John C. Bennett, a former high-ranking Mormon who had broken with Smith over the issue of polygamy, claimed that Smith had admitted to putting a price on Boggs's head and to knowing that Rockwell had been the triggerman. The state of Missouri issued a warrant for Smith's extradition as a conspirator in the crime, renewing with more vigor its previous desultory efforts to have Smith extradited for his part in that state's Mormon War. Smith protested his innocence and, for a time, stayed out of sight. When the Illinois governor issued orders for his extradition and a sheriff arrived in Nauvoo with a warrant, the Nauvoo municipal court announced that it had the authority to quash any writ it chose to, and it chose to quash this one. Later, after the election of a more amenable Illinois governor, Smith agreed to come to Springfield to have the warrant officially dismissed, and this he accomplished. Rockwell was tried in Missouri but acquitted in 1843.[19]

Further trouble arose when Smith selected as his next bride the wife of one of the Nauvoo Mormons. She apparently objected, and Smith backed off, but in June 1844 her angry husband and several other disaffected Mormons banded together to start a newspaper called the *Nauvoo Expositor*. Its first issue, published on June 7, was filled with criticism of Smith. Most damaging, it announced to the reading public what had been only the subject of rumor up to that time: Joseph Smith was preaching—and practicing—polygamy. On June 10 Smith ordered the city marshal of Nauvoo to destroy the *Expositor*'s printing press. This might be Mormon Nauvoo, but it was also Hancock County, Illinois, and such a deed had legal repercussions. From the county seat at Carthage, twenty miles away, came the sheriff with a warrant for Smith's arrest. The Nauvoo court, over which Smith presided, quashed the warrant and sent the sheriff back to Carthage empty-handed. Smith called out the Nauvoo Legion and put Nauvoo under martial law. The smaller and less well-equipped Illinois militia responded by mobilizing in turn.[20]

With the turmoil in the western part of the state threatening to explode into war, Illinois governor Thomas Ford visited Carthage and sent Smith a note asking him to surrender to face charges in a lawful court. Smith and several cohorts fled across the Mississippi River, but on hearing that his people had fallen into panic at the absence of their prophet, and that some were accusing him of cowardice, he turned back and surrendered. He also consented to an order of the governor officially disbanding the Nauvoo Legion. In Carthage, Smith and several other Mormon leaders were charged with riot, for the destruction of the press, and Smith and his brother Hyrum were also slapped with the much more serious charge of treason, for calling out the legion and placing Nauvoo under martial law. The two were confined in the small jail in Carthage. Governor Ford disbanded the militia and left town. Three days later a mob, possibly of members of the disbanded Hancock County militia, broke into the jail and killed the Smith brothers.[21]

In the wake of Smith's death, Brigham Young outmaneuvered several rivals, including the charismatic Sidney Rigdon, for leadership of the Latter-day Saints. Meanwhile, he also acquired eight of the late prophet's widows, boosting his harem to twelve wives. Young proved an even stronger leader than Smith had been. Under his direction work continued not only on the great Mormon temple at Nauvoo but also on the Nauvoo House and several other building projects.[22]

Still, it was becoming increasingly clear that the Mormons would have to leave Illinois. In January 1845 the Illinois legislature revoked Nauvoo's charter and mandated the disbandment of the Nauvoo Legion, but Young continued to operate both a city government and a military force on an extralegal basis. Governor Ford wrote to Young that California

The Mormons: From Palmyra to Nauvoo

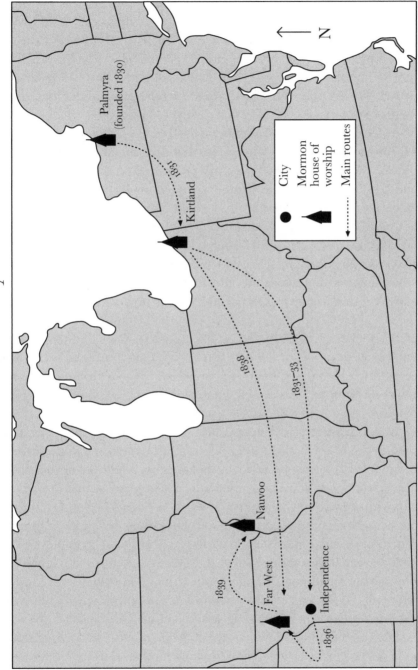

would be a very suitable place for the Mormons. It was outside the boundaries of the United States, was largely empty, and could easily be wrested from the weak grasp of Mexico. There, Ford suggested, the Mormons could "establish an independent government of your own subject only to the laws of nations. You would remain there a long time," he added, "before you would be disturbed by the proximity of other settlements."[23]

Young agreed about the ultimate need to leave Illinois, but before the Mormons went, he was determined that they should complete the temple at Nauvoo. While the final work proceeded on that structure, Young and his lieutenants made plans for the coming mass migration. They gathered all the information they could about the West, and from the accounts of trappers and other explorers they learned of the valley of the Great Salt Lake. Lansford Hastings stopped by Nauvoo in the spring of 1845, plugging for California settlers as he was doing elsewhere and providing information about the intermontane region as well. Young read with interest Frémont's report of his 1843 excursion through the valley of the Great Salt Lake and noted the explorer's quite accurate assessment of the region's fertile soil and, as Young would later find to his dismay, quite inaccurate claim that the Great Salt Lake possessed a freshwater arm. Other features of the region appealed to the Mormons even more. It was far from any substantial settlements, and it was outside the United States.[24]

In September 1845, Young issued orders for a scouting party to proceed to the valley of the Great Salt Lake. That same month skirmishes began taking place between local vigilantes and elements of the (theoretically disbanded) Nauvoo Legion in the countryside around the Mormon city, with at least one fatality. Anti-Mormon raiders burned a number of outlying Mormon-owned houses and businesses, triggering a stream of Mormon refugees into Nauvoo. Governor Ford explained that he could do little to halt the violence when the entire non-Mormon population of Illinois was unanimous in a fierce determination to have the Mormons out of the state, dead or alive. In an October 1 meeting with representatives of the governor, including Judge Stephen A. Douglas, Young formally agreed that the Mormons would begin their westward migration as soon as the grass was green and growing on the prairies of Iowa the following spring.[25]

By November 30 the temple was complete enough to hold a dedication ceremony, and ten days later Young and other Mormon leaders began conducting rites there. This was important, since in Mormon belief, as Smith had taught, many spiritual benefits were to be obtained only by means of such ceremonies conducted in a proper temple. Thereafter, rites went on in the appropriate special chambers of the temple "almost night and day."[26]

Young and the Mormon leadership possessed a strong enough control over their people to impose on them a high degree of regimentation and discipline. The move west was no exception, being entirely centrally planned and extremely well-organized. Using a semimilitary organization paired with Old Testament terminology, Young divided the emigrants into companies, each commanded by a captain and equipped and supplied according to a detailed schedule issued from Young's headquarters, the outfit to be purchased by individual families if they could afford it or provided for them by the church if they could not. He referred to the whole as the Camp of Israel.[27]

The plan had been for the migration to begin in April 1846, but events prompted Young to start it several months earlier. That winter Young narrowly evaded government officials trying to serve him and eight other Mormon officials with warrants stemming from an indictment for allegedly running a counterfeiting ring in Nauvoo. Then word reached them that U.S. troops stationed in St. Louis would attempt to block the Mormons' escape to the West. This was patently untrue. Someone was apparently spreading the rumor for the very purpose of spurring the Mormon departure. It worked. The first group, composed of Mormon leaders and their families, crossed the Mississippi and started out across Iowa on February 4. In the days that followed, the tightly organized companies set out one after another. A cold spell near the end of the month froze the Mississippi solid, allowing many additional companies and their wagons to roll across the ice. After the ice broke up in the spring, the ferrying process resumed, and by mid-May more than ten thousand Mormons were making their way across Iowa.[28]

Winter travel was slow, and the early spring rains brought deep mud. The journey was a struggle, and Young and his lead party did not reach the Missouri River until mid-June. Other parties of Latter-day Saints were strung out behind them all the way back to Nauvoo, where another six thousand or so still had not yet departed. Reluctantly, Young decided that it would not be practical even for an advance party to push on through to the Great Salt Lake that year. Instead, they would camp on the west bank of the Missouri near the site of modern-day Omaha, Nebraska, which the Mormons would call Winter Quarters, with plans to press on as early as possible in the spring of 1847.[29]

The Mormons: From Nauvoo to the Great Salt Lake

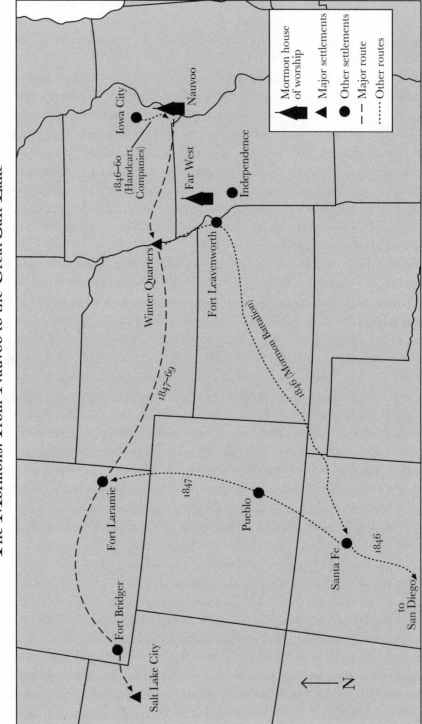

So it was that the Mormons became part of the westward migration in 1846. While the Donner families and their friends met during the late winter months of that year in Springfield, scarcely 130 miles east of Nauvoo, to organize their own journey to California, groups of Mormons were already crossing the Mississippi and beginning their snowy trek across Iowa. While the Latter-day Saints continued on their trail across Iowa that May and June, the Donners and other California- and Oregon-bound emigrants, including the Mormons' old nemesis former governor Lilburn Boggs of Missouri, toiled up the Platte and across the high plains of Wyoming. When the ways parted at Fort Hall and the Donners set out on their fateful journey over the Hastings Cutoff, Boggs stuck with the party following the established trail and reached California without incident. The Latter-day Saints had much different motivations from those of thousands of other Americans streaming across the continent that summer, and they had a different goal in view. Yet they too were part of the great migration that was, virtually overnight, putting the stamp of American culture, in all its sometimes curious permutations, on the western half of the continent.

In the summer of 1845, a newspaper editor named John L. O'Sullivan, far off in New York, had written an editorial in the *Democratic Review* claiming that it was the United States' "manifest destiny to overspread the continent allotted by Providence for the free development of our yearly multiplying millions." In December of that year O'Sullivan had written in *The New York Morning News* of "the right of our manifest destiny to overspread and to possess the whole of the continent which Providence has given us for the development of the great experiment of liberty and federated self-government entrusted to us." O'Sullivan was arguing that the United States had a divinely appointed mission to spread across the entire North American continent, not only as an outlet for the nation's rapidly growing population, but also because God had entrusted this nation with the task of spreading the domain of freedom. Since liberty followed the flag, U.S. expansion was a blessing for all concerned and should be pressed forward aggressively.

Americans seized eagerly on O'Sullivan's term "manifest destiny" as the perfect expression of how they had for some time seen their drive for westward expansion. Though the words might have been new, the concept certainly was not. Indeed, O'Sullivan had been talking that way for a number of years. As far back as 1839 he had advocated westward expansion with the term "divine destiny," and all along he had been expressing the thoughts of his fellow citizens that nothing could be more obvious than that God intended the United States to spread liberty across North America and in turn enjoy the blessings of the whole continent. By the mid-1840s, with Americans flocking to Oregon in steadily growing numbers, with continuing clamor for the annexation of Texas, and with some Americans beginning to take notice of the previously almost empty Mexican province of California, the concept of Manifest Destiny seemed more urgent than ever. O'Sullivan's words conjured such great power because the nation seemed to be rushing toward the fulfillment of its destiny with a speed and strength that dazzled even those who were carrying out the expansion.

Still, the question remained, for any who cared to take note of it at the time, as to whether and how much the institution of slavery should spread while the nation was overspreading the continent—or, for that matter, when the liberty America was spreading across the continent should spread to those parts of America where slavery prevailed. For most Americans in the mid-1840s, these were still side issues, secondary points to be settled at some future time, preferably as distant as possible. Yet the very surge of westward expansion that was even then hurrying the nation toward the realization of its long-cherished destiny would force Americans to confront such questions far sooner than most of them imagined or desired.

PART THREE

The Politics of Expansion

CHAPTER SEVEN

Tyler and Texas

BACK IN THE NATION's capital, John Tyler—His Accidency, as angry Whigs called him—had kept up efforts to conduct his administration without the support of a political party and in the face of bitter opposition from Congress. Despite his virtual expulsion from the Whig Party and the attempts of congressional Whigs to impeach him for using the veto power, Tyler continued to hope that he might win election to the presidency in his own right in 1844. The first and greatest obstacle to that ambition was the fact that he had no political party. "I must have a party," he told his close friend Nathaniel Beverley Tucker, a University of Virginia professor. "Make one!" Tucker exhorted. But the president replied, "I have not time. I must have one ready made."[1]

Perhaps, Tyler thought, the Democrats would adopt him, but that proved a vain hope. He had made enemies on that side of the aisle over the years, and besides, the Democrats had their own contenders for the nomination and had no need of giving their nod to a Whig reject. Tyler clung tenaciously to the faint prospect that the Democrats might change their minds about him, but in the meantime he began to think that perhaps he could, after all, generate a party of his own, destined to supplant one of the other two. That was not as far-fetched as it would be in the twenty-first century, since the two major parties at the time were scarcely fifteen years old, and their founders were still alive and mostly still active in politics. If Tyler was to accomplish such a feat in the teeth of the political opposition he had already aroused, his administration would need a landmark accomplishment that would give him a powerful issue on which to run in 1844.

The issue Tyler chose was Texas, taking a firm new grip on an old nettle. As a devoted follower of Thomas Jefferson and James Madison who believed that republican institutions worked better in a bigger country and also that those institutions would be an inestimable blessing throughout the realm over which they extended, Tyler was an enthusiastic backer of U.S. territorial expansion, and he had had his eye on the Lone Star

Republic since first coming into the presidency. Where better to extend the territory of the United States than in that vast republic on its southwestern border peopled overwhelmingly with Americans who ardently wished for union with their native land? In his first address to Congress after the death of Harrison, Tyler had mentioned his desire for the annexation of Texas.[2]

A considerable portion of the land west of the Sabine River and south of the Red—known to its erstwhile Spanish and Mexican overlords as the province of Tejas—was to have been part of the Louisiana Purchase back in 1803, but Spain had subsequently claimed it, and the United States government had accepted that claim in the 1819 Adams-Onís Treaty. Many Americans, including Thomas Jefferson, continued to hope for the acquisition of Tejas by future treaty or purchase. Others simply did not see that acceptance as valid or binding on them and viewed the land on the far side of the Adams-Onís line as rightfully American and thus fair game for private expeditions aimed at making it such—and offering wealth and adventure. Various groups of such filibusters—so named from a Spanish transmutation of a Dutch word meaning "freebooters"—staged several forays into Spanish Tejas during the first two decades of the nineteenth century, with uniform lack of success and usually fatal consequences to themselves. The Spaniards were ferocious with those they saw as interlopers on their lands, and their customary response was a mass execution.[3]

In the early 1820s the Spanish colonial authorities adopted a policy of encouraging Americans to settle in the largely empty province of Tejas, but to do so as good Spanish colonists under the auspices of contracted land agents called *empresarios*. The first empresario was Connecticut-born Moses Austin, quickly succeeded on his death by his son Stephen. In similar fashion, other empresarios took up large government land grants in Tejas with the commitment to populate them with dutiful citizens. Hardly had Stephen Austin received his authorization, however, than the people of Mexico successfully revolted and threw off the Spanish yoke. After some confusion, Austin received confirmation of his grant from the new government of an independent Mexico and over the years that followed strove conscientiously to people his land grant with settlers who would be good Mexicans.[4]

That was no easy task. The new nation proved chronically—spectacularly—unstable. The junta of generals who had secured independence elevated one of their number, Agustín de Iturbide, as Emperor Agustín I, but ten months later popular discontent drove him from power and from the country. Thereafter, three factions struggled for control in Mexico. The monarchists and centralists were authoritarian and traditionalist and could count on the support of the major landowners and the Roman Catholic Church. The federalists valued freedom and admired the U.S. system of government. In 1824 the federalists succeeded in establishing a Mexican constitution modeled after that of the United States and influenced by the Spanish constitution of 1812. But during the years that followed, the splendid new frame of government was honored mostly in the breach, as the factions struggled for power and the monarchists and centralists strove to eliminate the constitution entirely or to alter it beyond recognition.[5]

Over the course of the next decade, the Anglo settlers of Tejas came to feel increasingly alienated from turbulent Mexico and its procession of short-lived governments. The friction had multiple sources. Many of the settlers had migrated from the southern states and had brought slaves with them, contrary to Mexican law. Occasional Mexican attempts to crack down on the practice created hostility, but it was only one source of difficulty and far from the largest. A few of the empresarios and somewhat more of the settlers could be fractious and inclined to flout Mexican law in various ways. On the other hand, some of the local Mexican garrison commanders could be harsh and provocative in their use of power. When the centralists held sway in far-off Mexico City, they pursued policies inimical to the freedom-loving Americans, making unfavorable changes in tax law, imposing ruinous tariffs, curtailing local self-government, and otherwise infringing the rights promised by the 1824 constitution.[6]

The breaking point came with the rise to power of Antonio López de Santa Anna. A general who had championed the cause of the federalists in the coups and revolutions of the 1820s, Santa Anna was in fact an unprincipled opportunist who, in Mexico's upheavals of the past twenty years, had frequently betrayed his comrades and changed sides when treachery seemed to offer the best path to personal ease, wealth, and power. Elected president as a federalist in 1833, Santa Anna several months later dismissed the legislature, suspended the constitution, and began to rule as a dictator. Several Mexican provinces rose in revolt against this shocking usurpation, Tejas among them. At the head of his army, Santa Anna brutally crushed the uprising in the province of Zacatecas and then turned his attention to Tejas, a border province whose Anglo population, Santa Anna believed, had long been in need of humbling.[7]

Leading his army into Tejas, Santa Anna declared that he would take no prisoners. After victories at Goliad and at San Antonio de Béxar, where the defenders had taken shelter in an old mission called the Alamo, he was as good (or as bad) as his word, insisting on the slaughter of wounded Texians (as the residents of Texas called themselves) and others who had been taken prisoner. Then he pursued what was left of the Texian army eastward across most of the province. Representatives of the citizens of Tejas had just finished drafting a declaration of independence as the Republic of Texas, claiming the territory all the way south and west to the Rio Grande, well beyond the old provincial boundary. But it appeared that all who defied Santa Anna would soon have to take refuge east of the Sabine—within the United States.

A dramatic turn of fortune intervened on April 6, 1836, when the Texian army, led by Sam Houston and heavily reinforced by volunteers from the United States, turned at bay near the confluence of Buffalo Bayou and the San Jacinto River. Catching Santa Anna unprepared, the Texian army administered a devastating defeat, killing 630 Mexican *soldados* and capturing all of the remaining 730 who were part of the force under Santa Anna's immediate local command. They would have killed Santa Anna had he not hastily disguised himself in a private soldier's uniform. By the time his identity was discovered, the initial killing frenzy had passed, and Houston was able to make a deal. Santa Anna, as the supreme authority in the Mexican government, would, in exchange for his life and early release from captivity, recognize the independence of the Republic of Texas and order his remaining, as yet undefeated, troop columns to withdraw from its borders.[8]

It was an undemocratic solution on both sides. Those in government back in Mexico City had no intention of heeding Santa Anna; they quickly declared him deposed and his agreement with Texas null and void. The people of Texas, for their part, longed to see justice done to the captive despot, and on one occasion during Santa Anna's captivity some two hundred of them, armed and seething, very nearly succeeded in carrying it out. With the utmost difficulty the government of Texas managed to keep Santa Anna out of the hands of its own outraged populace until it could spirit him out of the republic, sending him into the United States because public clamor made it impractical to ship him directly to Mexico. After visiting Washington and conversing with President Andrew Jackson, Santa Anna made his way back to Mexico, where he announced that his agreement with Texas had been coerced and was therefore void. Nonetheless, after the debacle of San Jacinto and the effective loss of Tejas, even Santa Anna's remarkable charisma and complete freedom from scruples of any sort were, for the moment, insufficient to restore him to power, and the victor of the Alamo had to content himself for the time being with retirement on his hacienda near Jalapa.[9]

Many people in both the United States and Mexico—and nearly everyone in Texas—had assumed that once Texas broke away from the latter, it would quickly find a home in the former. It did not. Despite a 97 percent vote in favor of annexation in a fall 1836 Texas referendum, the republic was to remain independent, not by its own choice but by that of the United States, owing to two reasons. First, Mexico loudly asserted its continued ownership of all of Texas and openly threatened war with the United States in the event of annexation, which was enough to make some senators and representatives question whether Texas was worth the potential price in blood and treasure.

The second reason was far more important. Texans had practiced slavery more or less surreptitiously under Mexican rule, and now they did so openly, since the institution was fully legal under the laws of the republic. Adding Texas to the Union would therefore add a slave state, one of such immense size as to pose the threat of subdivision into even more slave states. The addition of even a single slave state would upset the balance of the Senate, where slave and free states had possessed equal numbers ever since such distinctions had mattered. It would also increase the voting strength of slave states in the House, where southern whites were already overrepresented by credit for three-fifths of their slaves, though of course the slaves could not vote.[10]

The fundamental question in determining many an American's reaction to the possibility of Texas annexation was, How important was slavery now? Was it only one issue among many, perhaps to be outweighed by the significance of such a vast expansion of the American empire of liberty, the onward march of the fulfillment of America's God-given purpose of extending the realm of self-government? Or was slavery—even slavery in a far-off corner of the continent—so important as to counterbalance every other consideration? Specifically, should the potential annexation of Texas be seen primarily as a gain for the United States, or a gain for slavery? That was the question that American voters and their elected representatives had to answer, and for some of them, particularly in the free-state North, the answer was that slavery amounted to the negation of America's promise of freedom, and therefore no gain for slavery could also be a gain for the United States.

Chief among those who opposed annexation were the abolitionists.

So completely did the issue of slavery dominate their point of view that many of them came to believe that the entire story of the settlement of Texas and its subsequent revolt against Mexico had been nothing but a gigantic proslavery plot from start to finish. The first effort to annex Texas had fallen right into the middle of the fierce ongoing battle over the Gag Rule and incurred the bitter opposition of Adams and his devoted band of congressional abolitionist sympathizers. An indication of the significance of slavery in this dispute was to be seen in the fact that Adams, while president, had sought to purchase Texas from Mexico, but now that it was an avowedly slaveholding republic, he would not accept it gratis. In the face of such determined opposition, Jackson had given up the attempt to secure annexation, and Van Buren had not pursued it.[11]

By early 1843 rumors had reached the United States, and the White House, that Great Britain had its own designs on Texas. This was a disturbing prospect to Americans since it threatened to foreclose any hopes of future expansion in that direction and also raised the specter of the United States being threatened both north and south by the powerful British Empire. The scuttlebutt also had it that British abolitionists were working on some sort of scheme by which their government would compensate Texas financially for the emancipation of all of the republic's slaves. This was alarming to U.S. slaveholders, who imagined that a non-slaveholding Texas would become a refuge for slaves escaping from the southern states. One also gets the sense that American slaveholders simply hated to see any retreat of slavery, any move that would make them more isolated and would emphasize the opinion of the rest of the civilized world that their "way of life" was evil.[12]

Both the vague prospect of British annexation of Texas and the possibility that the British, short of annexation, might find a way to rid Texas of slavery tended to move Americans, and especially southerners, toward quick action of their own on the Texas question. This is exactly what Texas president Sam Houston had meant to accomplish by entering into a diplomatic flirtation with Britain in the first place. He had no intention of adding Texas to the British Empire, but he did want to provoke enough American jealousy to get his republic absorbed into the United States.[13]

Tyler needed little prodding. Already eager to annex Texas but concerned that the matter be pursued in such a way as to avoid stirring up sectional conflict, Tyler in November 1843 gave his secretary of state, Abel P. Upshur, permission to pursue the matter. Upshur, who had already served Tyler as secretary of the navy, had recently moved over to replace Daniel Webster, the last of the old Harrison cabinet members to resign. Upshur had been a capable and innovative secretary of the navy, and for some years Tyler had considered him a friend. The president could be rather naïve about his friends.

Upshur, like Tyler a Virginian, was an even more doctrinaire disciple of John C. Calhoun. Indeed, unbeknownst to Tyler, Upshur was quietly backing the South Carolinian for the presidency in 1844. For men like Upshur and Calhoun, the principle of states' rights was merely a handmaiden to their real passion, the rights of the South and of slaveholders. Upshur was a sectionalist whose chief goal was to advance the interests of the South, which he saw as being synonymous with the interests of the slaveholding class. Slavery, Upshur maintained, was "a great positive good, to be carefully maintained and preserved." He strongly agreed with Tyler that the annexation of Texas was desirable, but their reasons were different. Tyler saw Texas annexation as something that would benefit the entire United States, but for Upshur it was desirable chiefly as something that would strengthen slavery and the South within the United States.[14]

Upshur, who confided to friends that he despised the president he worked for, was even more eager for annexation than was Tyler and had already quietly entered into negotiations with Texas without the president's permission. The secretary of state had no interest in Tyler's desire to settle the Oregon boundary question with Britain, and he pursued such negotiations less than halfheartedly. Adding Texas to the Union was Upshur's supreme goal and, as he explained to friends, the only reason he was willing to associate himself with what he called "the odium" of the Tyler administration.[15]

Over the next few months, while Upshur and a cabal of Calhounites in Tyler's administration schemed for the electoral downfall of their chief and the triumphant election of their idol, Upshur carried out zealous secret annexation diplomacy with Texas and less energetic exchanges with Great Britain on the subject of Oregon. Calhoun's presidential aspirations fared poorly, as various state and local Democratic Party organizations showed little interest in the fiery South Carolinian, but Upshur's other endeavors prospered surprisingly well.

Texas was willing, having been made more so by recent military setbacks. A Texian expedition to Santa Fe in 1841 had ended in ignominious failure with the capture of the whole force. The Mexicans had then brutally mistreated the prisoners while marching them south to Mexico City. The following year another Texian expedition, this one to the Rio

Grande Valley, had become a similar debacle after a promising start, and its survivors had surrendered at the Mexican town of Mier. The captors had decimated the Texas prisoners, making the men draw straws to determine which man in ten would be shot. Then twice during that year, Mexican military forays had resulted in brief occupations of San Antonio. It was a good time for Texas leaders to listen attentively to U.S. overtures of annexation. On the other hand, Texians were somewhat reluctant to show further interest if the Senate was likely to shoot down an annexation treaty. In such a case, Texas would have provoked Mexico to renewed efforts in the ongoing hostilities, hurt its diplomatic standing with Britain and France, and failed to win U.S. protection.[16]

Still, Upshur and the Texas negotiator Isaac Van Zandt were able to make progress on a treaty. Even Upshur's less zealous efforts with Britain seemed promising, largely because Britain was eager to compromise on the issue and Upshur, as a southerner, felt no burning need to hold out for the maximum possible amount of territory on the country's northern boundary. On February 27, 1844, Upshur and the Texas emissaries completed the negotiation of an annexation treaty. The document lacked only the necessary signatures. Meanwhile, prospects for an agreement with Great Britain looked good.[17]

At this point matters took a surprising turn, as Tyler found himself compelled to reorganize his cabinet, courtesy of the United States Navy. While Upshur had been secretary of the navy, his favorite project had been the navy's new state-of-the-art warship, *Princeton*. Designed by Swedish-born inventor John Ericsson, *Princeton* featured a number of innovative features including a marine screw in place of paddle wheels, giving the vessel more speed and power from its steam engine. The ship's sponsor and first commanding officer was Captain Robert F. Stockton, a very senior naval officer who belonged to a politically powerful family from Princeton, New Jersey. In 1841 Tyler had offered him the position of secretary of the navy, but the captain had chosen instead to remain on active duty, oversee *Princeton*'s construction, and become first commander of what would be the pride of the fleet. Stockton's political influence had secured congressional funding for the new vessel, and he had persuaded Ericsson, who had previously been working in Britain, to come to the United States to design her.[18]

Among *Princeton*'s startling innovations was her main battery, which consisted of two enormous guns—much larger than previous naval ordnance—mounted in such a way that they could pivot to fire on either beam. One of the guns, like the ship's many other ingenious novelties, was designed by Ericsson. Made of wrought iron, the new cannon was fifteen feet long, and its bore was twelve inches in diameter. It featured a breech reinforced with another band of wrought iron, shrunk in place and thus prestressed so as to secure the breech against bursting when large powder charges were used to propel the heavy 228-pound shot that the cannon could hurl out to ranges of as much as five miles. The gun was nicknamed Oregon, and after an extensive program of more than one hundred test firings, it was certified as sound.

Ericsson was a genuine inventive genius. Stockton considered himself a genius. To finish out *Princeton*'s main battery, the captain designed his own imitation of Ericsson's Oregon, another wrought iron twelve-incher. Not understanding how Ericsson's gun worked, Stockton decided to reinforce the breech of his gun by simply adding more wrought iron, forgoing the cumbersome business of shrinking a hot iron band onto the tube, but making the breech some twelve inches thicker. The resulting thirteen-and-a-half-ton monster gun was dubbed Peacemaker. Confident in the strength of his massive piece of wrought iron, Stockton certified it after scarcely half a dozen test firings. Ericsson expressed reservations about both the construction and the certification process of the gun, but Stockton was tired of the brainy Swede wanting to design every system on the *Princeton* and dismissed the inventor's concerns.[19]

Constructed at Philadelphia, *Princeton* slid down the builder's ways and into the Delaware River on September 5, 1843. Although torrential rains dampened the festivities, a large crowd was nevertheless on hand, along with a brass band, and the launching went off without a hitch, accompanied by the booming of a cannon salute. A rapturous newspaperman described the sleek new vessel as looking as graceful as a swan as it rode easily on the quiet waters of the river. In celebration of the launching, Stockton, who loved conviviality, that evening threw an enormous banquet, inviting some four hundred of the nation's most influential personages and their guests. It was said to rival a previous banquet Stockton had given for Tyler at which no fewer than two thousand bottles of champagne were consumed.[20]

Six weeks later the famously speedy British paddle wheeler *Great Western* was in port at Philadelphia, and Stockton arranged for a race to be held when the powerful steamship was ready to put to sea. On October 19, as scheduled, the British ship swept down the Delaware toward *Princeton*'s berth with sails set and a full head of steam. *Princeton* allowed her a quarter-mile lead and then gave chase. After overhauling and passing far ahead of the swift British ship, the American warship dropped back alongside. Stockton hailed his counterpart and wished him a happy voyage. *Princeton*'s crew gave three cheers. Then, putting on steam again, the speedy warship "walked away" from the laboring paddle wheeler, finally leaving her out of sight astern.[21]

With his ship the admiration of the nation, Stockton enjoyed more than ever playing the proud and gracious host. In December he invited much of the high society of Philadelphia to come aboard *Princeton* for a gala celebration and tour of the vessel, complete with cannon salutes. Gentlemen and ladies in their finery strolled about the decks and marveled at the enormous guns. In January 1844 New Yorkers were treated to similar shipboard hospitality, complete with an excursion up the North River and a demonstration firing of the great Peacemaker. Despite the cannon's enormous size, an amazed onlooker noted, "the recoil of the gun was very slight, and the shock was scarcely felt."[22]

The next month the navy's new sensation arrived at the national capital. On February 17, President Tyler, Secretary of War William Wilkins, the newly installed secretary of the navy, Thomas Gilmer (in place of Upshur, recently elevated to secretary of state), several members of the army and navy brass, various congressmen, and a number of others took a pleasure excursion in *Princeton* down the Potomac. The sleek and powerful warship easily cut through the thin rime of ice on the river, and the guests were amazed by her seemingly effortless motion through the water—no splashing paddle wheels or straining sails and stays, only a slight smudge of smoke from the high-grade anthracite coal that fired *Princeton*'s boilers. Eager to make an especially strong impression on his VIP guests, Stockton had his men demonstrate one of the big guns. Though both were the same caliber and performance, Peacemaker, with its massive breech, looked far more impressive. Besides, it was Stockton's own design. So he selected it for the demonstration firing. The president, members of the cabinet and of Congress, assorted brass, and other dignitaries trooped forward to gather around the mammoth cannon. On command, the gunner triggered the firing mechanism and the Peacemaker spoke with a deep boom. The 228-pound cannonball struck the water two or three miles from the ship and skipped along the surface for another mile or so, tossing up fountains of spray to the delight of the onlookers. Pleased with the impression he had made, Stockton had his men fire another round, to similar applause.[23]

The event had been a success, but Stockton had bigger plans. He scheduled a grand gala demonstration cruise for February 28 for all the Washington elite. Tyler would be there, of course, as well as most of the cabinet, including Secretary of State Upshur, who had just the day before completed work on the Texas annexation treaty and who viewed the *Princeton* with particular pride since its development and construction had taken place on his watch as secretary of the navy. Most of Congress would be there too, as well as a virtual who's who of Washington society, including seventy-five-year-old former first lady Dolley Madison. Also along was twenty-three-year-old Julia Gardiner, daughter of New York state senator David Gardiner. The Gardiner family had come to the capital for the winter social season, as they had done the year before when the lovely and vivacious Julia had taken the Washington salons by storm. The fifty-three-year-old president, a widower since September 1842, was smitten and had been courting her assiduously for several months. On this outing Julia was accompanied by her father and sister. Absent from the Potomac excursion was *Princeton*'s designer, John Ericsson, who was still at odds with Stockton since their disagreement over the Peacemaker. Fine carriages deposited some four hundred elegantly attired men and women at the Washington waterfront, where steam launches ferried them out to the waiting *Princeton,* which rode gracefully at anchor, decorated with the flags of every nation represented in Washington.[24]

Resplendent in full uniform, Stockton greeted his guests as they were piped aboard. As they got under way, *Princeton*'s secondary battery of forty-two-pounder carronades fired a twenty-six-gun salute, one for each state in the Union, and the marine band played "The Star-Spangled Banner." The day was beautiful, unseasonably warm, and the civilians enjoyed their cruise down the river. When they reached the broad waters of the lower Potomac, Stockton ordered another demonstration firing of the Peacemaker. Gentlemen in beaver hats and ladies in hoopskirts crowded forward for an up close look at the spectacle. With its customary roar, the Peacemaker sent its 228-pound ball several miles across the estuary. To the delight of the crowd, Stockton had his men fire a second shot, which brought renewed gasps and expressions of awe from the spectators.

For the afternoon, Stockton had laid on a sumptuous luncheon of roast fowl and ham to be washed down with fine wine. Seating at the dining tables was inadequate for the crowds, but most of the ladies as well as the president and cabinet members got to eat in the first shift while the others waited their turn. The ship had steamed down the river past Mount Vernon, turned, and was on her return journey, still about fourteen or fifteen miles below Washington, and the winter sun was nearing the western horizon by the time the first set of diners finished their repast and the many champagne toasts that followed. Tyler proposed three toasts, then Stockton proposed another to the president, and more toasts followed. At last the first shift of diners rose, perhaps somewhat unsteadily, to make room for others. Stockton paused as one of his officers leaned over to tell him that a guest had requested another firing of the Peacemaker. "No," the captain replied, "no more guns tonight." The officer added that the request had come from the secretary of the navy, Thomas Gilmer, and Stockton decided it amounted to an order.[25]

The big gun was always a crowd-pleaser, and the announcement that the sailors were going to fire it again hastened the general movement of VIPs up to the main deck. The cabinet members were emerging into the late-afternoon sunlight, and Tyler was just stepping onto the ladder to follow them when back in the dining area his son-in-law, William Waller, struck up a patriotic air, and the president stopped to listen.[26]

Up on deck the dignitaries crowded around the Peacemaker to get a good view of the firing and in hopes of being able to see the flight of the shot. Secretary of War Wilkins joked that despite the warlike office he had held for almost two weeks, he found the discharge of the cannon disturbing, and he stepped farther away from the gun. Senator Thomas Hart Benton of Missouri had been chatting with Gilmer as they had come up from below, and the two of them took a position next to Upshur just to the left of the gun. A lieutenant suggested to Benton that he would be able to see the flight of the shot better from a particular vantage point at the right rear of the piece, so he walked around the Peacemaker's massive breech, leaving the cabinet secretaries on the other side.[27]

Once again the spectators were impressed at the ease, smoothness, and precision with which the Peacemaker's thirteen and a half tons of wrought iron could be swung into line for firing. Watching with interest as the gunner reached for the firing mechanism, Senator Benton opened his mouth to help relieve the anticipated pressure on his ears from the gun's firing. Next to him a woman, in the excitement of the moment, took hold of his arm. The firing hammer drew back and then fell with a sharp, metallic tap. Then Benton saw a flash, and everything went blank.[28]

Others standing farther away thought for an instant they saw a ring of bright red fire suddenly appear just in front of the Peacemaker's breech before the entire scene was blotted out in a dense, roiling cloud of white powder smoke and *Princeton* shuddered perceptibly beneath their feet. The smoke gradually drifted away to reveal a scene of carnage. The rear third of the Peacemaker was missing, and the deck around it was a bloody shambles. One of the fragments of the gun, a two-ton chunk of wrought iron, had traveled back across the ship and torn a gaping hole in the opposite bulwark.

Strewn across the deck were the dead, some of them horribly mangled. The secretary of state was eviscerated, the secretary of the navy nearly decapitated. Both were dead on the spot. So too were the navy's chief of construction, Commodore Beverly Kennon; the U.S. diplomat Virgil Maxcy; and David Gardiner, as well as President Tyler's black servant, Armistead, and several sailors. As Senator Benton regained consciousness, he saw two more bloodied sailors picking themselves up from the deck and a stunned Captain Stockton, hat gone, hair singed off, face blackened, standing gaping at what was left of the Peacemaker. The captain had suffered powder burns and soon had to be led to his bunk below in a state of hysteria. The woman who had been holding Benton's arm had been knocked down, but miraculously neither she nor any other woman had been seriously injured by the explosion, though several had been splattered with gore and one had been hit in the head by a severed arm.[29]

Belowdecks, the sound of the terrific crash had interrupted William Waller's song. Many of the women were eager to rush on deck to learn the fate of their male relations, but the men present in the dining area thought it best to prevent them from viewing the scene above, especially as reports reached them of the carnage. Dolley Madison was among those who had remained belowdecks. In the five years of life that were left to her, she would never speak of that day. When Julia Gardiner received the news of her father's death, she fainted into the president's arms. The ship returned to Washington that evening, depositing its surviving VIP passengers where they had embarked that morning. The bodies were removed the next day. In the investigation that followed, Stockton was able to save himself by maintaining that the whole debacle had been Ericsson's fault.[30]

The explosion of Stockton's poorly designed cannon had created serious problems for Tyler's plan to annex Texas. Despite Upshur's gross disloyalty to the president, replacing him with someone more suitable was not going to be easy. Tyler's choice would, first of all, need to be someone who would accept a position in his pariah administration, loathed by the Whigs and not fully accepted by the Democrats. Beyond that, Tyler wanted someone who would support the annexation of Texas and who would do so on the same basis that Tyler favored, as something that would be good for the whole country and not just one section. The president did not want to make Texas an issue in the controversy over slavery. The abolitionists were bound to bring up the connection, but Tyler hoped to dodge that as much as he could and keep Texas a national issue.[31]

Considering this, Tyler's choice of John C. Calhoun as Upshur's replacement was amazingly inept, so much so as to prompt latter-day historians to enter into a lengthy debate as to what Tyler might have been thinking. Some serious students of the era believe that Calhoun's partisans in key political positions in Washington maneuvered the president into a position in which he felt compelled to make the offer to Calhoun, and some of the evidence definitely points in that direction. Other historians maintain that Tyler's hand was forced by an inept and unauthorized offer of the job to Calhoun by an underling. Still others claim that Tyler wanted Calhoun because of his stature as a senior statesman and argue that it was the president who cleverly maneuvered the South Carolinian into a position in which he felt compelled to accept the office. At any rate, Calhoun, who had by this time abandoned his presidential hopes for 1844 and publicly announced his noncandidacy, did accept Tyler's perhaps reluctant offer of the position of secretary of state.[32]

Tyler may not have been completely comfortable putting the Texas affair in Calhoun's hands. On March 6 he formally sent his nomination of Calhoun to the Senate for confirmation, and that same day he met with Texas chargé d'affaires Isaac Van Zandt to urge that the annexation be finished up quickly. Tyler had appointed Attorney General John Nelson as acting secretary of state pending Calhoun's confirmation, and he told Van Zandt that he would rather Nelson negotiated the treaty. Unfortunately, the signing of the treaty had to await the arrival in Washington of Texas's special envoy, James P. Henderson, and he did not arrive until the end of March, by which time Calhoun was just taking over the State Department.[33]

By this time the negotiations over Texas annexation, which Tyler had hoped to keep as quiet as possible until he could present a treaty to the Senate, had become a matter of national notoriety, widely discussed in the newspapers amid rumors that a Texas annexation treaty had already been ratified by the Senate or perhaps was awaiting only the necessary signatures at the time of Upshur's death.[34]

Public opinion was divided on the issue of Texas annexation. The abolitionists, of course, were dead set against it, led as before by John Quincy Adams, who saw in the movement for annexation only "slave-envenomed motives" and the work of "the great slave-power conspiracy." Party loyalists of both the Whigs and the Democrats were almost as hostile to annexation, fearing that it would break up their parties into contentious northern and southern factions. And there were some who feared that the issue could produce that divisive effect on the country as a whole. Still, there was a great deal of expansionist feeling in the country at large, and many Americans saw in Texas annexation merely one more step in the fulfillment of the nation's God-given destiny of overspreading the continent with its free—if, perhaps for the moment, imperfect— institutions. Even some of these were hesitant, however. Might annexation lead to war with Mexico? Or even Britain and France? And then of course there was the issue of slavery. Many a nonabolitionist found reason for pause in the contemplation of whether annexation would truly mean spreading America's free institutions or merely spreading the "peculiar" one within America.[35]

To satisfy this last group of would-be expansionists bothered by slavery, Mississippi senator Robert J. Walker wrote a letter to the general public and had it printed in *The Washington Globe*. Walker had been born and raised in Pennsylvania and then as a young lawyer had migrated to Mississippi, where he continued the practice of law and, like many southern professionals who became well-to-do, became a slaveholding planter. Elected to the U.S. Senate in 1836 as a Democrat, Walker was a strong advocate of Texas annexation and expansion in general. Later he became a supporter of Tyler and had urged fellow senators to endorse Tyler's assumption of the presidency in 1841.[36]

Walker's 1844 open letter strove to allay the qualms of northern expansionists about the South's peculiar institution. Slavery, Walker explained, was inefficient. It lent itself to the cultivation of staple crops, and these exhausted the soil. This had happened in Virginia and Maryland, and planters there had stopped growing tobacco and begun selling off surplus slaves to the Deep South. If the United States acquired Texas, the same trend would continue. More and more slaves would be sold from the older slave states into Texas, and then as Texas soil became exhausted, the forces of economics would compel slaveholders to free their slaves, and the freed slaves would naturally migrate across the Rio Grande and into Latin America. Thus Texas would become the means by which both the institution of slavery and the enslaved African-Americans would somehow vanish from the country. This belief that slavery expansion would sap the virulence of the institution was very much in accordance with Tyler's own thinking.[37]

The idea of ridding the country of the moral guilt of slavery without having to face the perplexing problem of living in a multiracial society afterward was a very appealing one to many Americans. Racism was by no means limited to the boundaries of the slave states, and even much antislavery feeling, except among the staunchest abolitionists, was tainted with at least a hint of the idea that blacks were inferior and could not live with whites on equal terms. Those who felt this way eagerly seized on Walker's arguments. Many newspapers reprinted Walker's letter, and he had a large number of copies printed as pamphlets and distributed as widely as possible. When the supply of pamphlets began to run low, a paper in Natchez, Mississippi, in early March brought out its own edition of Walker's letter, also in pamphlet form, to meet the wide demand.[38]

With a growing groundswell of popular support for annexation, Calhoun took over the final negotiations that were to accomplish it. During the interval caused by Upshur's death, the Texians had grown more concerned about the issue of security. Upshur had given them a verbal guarantee that the United States would defend Texas after annexation, but now that Upshur was dead, they wanted that assurance in writing. Calhoun provided it. On April 12 he and Henderson signed the treaty, but before submitting it to the Senate for ratification, Calhoun hoped to reach some sort of understanding with Mexico, and so he held several discussions with the Mexican minister in Washington, in hopes that Mexico might be persuaded to accept a financial settlement in exchange for dropping its claims to Texas. Such an assurance would have made Senate ratification easier, but nothing came of Calhoun's overtures.[39]

The new secretary of state was much less conciliatory with Great Britain, and that was all the more remarkable since Britain had recently sent a mollifying message to the United States. In a letter written the previous December, British foreign secretary Lord Aberdeen had sought to reassure the United States that although Britain did favor the universal abolition of slavery, it did not seek this end by nefarious or threatening means. "We shall counsel," Aberdeen had written of the United States and Texas, "but we shall not seek to compel, or unduly control." By this Aberdeen hoped to answer recent concerns about possible British machinations in Texas.[40]

Calhoun chose not to interpret it that way. The mention of Britain's preference for the abolition of slavery affected the South Carolinian like a red cape in front of a bull, and he responded by writing a combative letter to Britain's minister to the United States, Richard Pakenham. Launching into a lengthy defense of slavery as a humane and beneficial institution, Calhoun forcefully asserted that the U.S. government would take whatever steps necessary to secure slavery from every possible threat, including annexing Texas if that was necessary to save the domain of the Lone Star Republic from the evils of abolitionism. The nonplussed Pakenham made no response beyond acknowledging receipt of the letter and assuring that it would be transmitted to Her Majesty's government.[41]

Then Calhoun included a copy of his letter along with the documents relating to the treaty and sent the whole batch—treaty, letter, and all— over to the Senate for ratification. Tyler's own letter to the Senate accompanying the treaty called for annexation as a benefit to the whole country, but Calhoun's letter to Pakenham made the issue entirely sectional. As the new secretary of state presented the matter, the chief reason for annexing Texas was to assure that it could never become a nonslaveholding area and thus pose an indirect threat to slavery in the southern states.

If Calhoun wanted the Senate to ratify the treaty, presenting it in such terms seems downright counterproductive, but Calhoun saw the whole matter as a test. As far as he was concerned, Aberdeen's mere statement that Britain would like to see the emancipation of all slaves everywhere was not only an insult but a threat. The very suggestion of a nonslave Texas was a frightening specter to slaveholders like Calhoun, conjuring up as it did vague ideas of a haven for runaways and a virtual petri dish for the incubation of horrifying plots of slave uprisings in the southern states. If the North declined to support the cause of slavery by doing its part to banish forever the specter of a nonslave Texas, it would show itself to be unconcerned about the welfare of the South, Calhoun asserted, and that would be "not a little ominous to the duration of our system."[42]

Some who knew Calhoun and had watched his political career over the years believed his actions with regard to the treaty had a far more sinister motive than merely finding out to what lengths the North would go in support of southern slavery. Missouri senator Thomas Hart Benton believed that since Calhoun had realized he could not be president of the United States, he was now trying to bring about the breakup of the country so that he could become president of a new union to be formed by the slaveholding states. Another longtime observer who agreed with Benton was *Washington Globe* editor Francis Preston Blair. He too thought Calhoun had made Texas annexation a sectional rather than a national issue in order to split the Union. "I sincerely believe," Blair wrote in a private letter, "that Calhoun and his old Junto of conspirators are more than ever anxious to separate the south from the north. They want Texas only as a bone of contention."[43]

In his own private letters, Calhoun maintained staunchly that he wanted the Senate to ratify the treaty, but this he wanted only if it was an explicit affirmation of slavery and of the whole nation's duty to protect and perpetuate slavery. If the Senate would not ratify the treaty and do it as a statement of support for slavery, Calhoun wrote in a letter to his daughter, then "the South will be lost, if some prompt and decisive measures be not adopted to save us." If Benton and Blair could have read that letter, they would immediately have recognized Calhoun's "prompt and decisive measures" as disunion, and they almost certainly would have been right. Calhoun had come to hold the position that the North must bow to the South and make the United States a uniformly proslavery nation or else the South must break up the country and go its own way.[44]

The result for the Texas annexation treaty was utterly predictable. When the treaty came to a vote in the Senate, the nays numbered thirty-five, the yeas only sixteen. The treaty had needed a two-thirds majority for ratification. Instead, more than two-thirds of the senators present had voted against it. With the matter made into a straightforward bid for the endorsement of slavery, few northern senators could vote for it. Between the distaste for slavery in Texas and the fear that annexation would lead to war with Mexico that would cost more than the Lone Star Republic would be worth, the move found little support. What remained to be seen was how Tyler, Calhoun, and the American people would react to this development. To complicate matters, the election campaign of 1844 was already in full swing.[45]

CHAPTER EIGHT

The Election of 1844

HENRY CLAY FELT certain that his time to win the presidency had come at last. Defeat in two major presidential campaigns, and disappointment in his quest for a party nomination in other presidential election years, had only sharpened Clay's hunger for the office. In the four years since his bitter disappointment in 1840, he had ruthlessly whipped the Whig Party into line, ramming his policies down the throats of its politicians and purging everyone who thwarted his will. Now the party was unified, disciplined, and ready to march in lockstep under the banner of Clay's American System. It was just the vehicle to carry the proud Kentuckian all the way to the White House, and he anticipated the coming victory with a relish whetted by previous failure and long-deferred ambition.

Texas threatened to ruin all that. Clay had nothing against annexation, as long as it did not interfere with his political ambitions, but that was exactly what it seemed likely to do. Clay had previously been a supporter of annexation, but he had laid the groundwork for the coming presidential campaign on the foundation of his American System, especially his call for high protective tariffs, as well as his refrain about the evils of "executive usurpation," by which he meant any presidential action, especially a veto, that thwarted the will of Henry Clay. He had laboriously united the Whig Party on these issues. If Texas became the central issue of the campaign, all that work would be lost. The Whigs would be divided on Texas, and bringing them together for his campaign would require onerous compromises and shaky coalitions. Clay's chief wish for the Texas issue was that it would go away.[1]

In hopes of making it do so, Clay, in April 1844, a few days after the signing of the treaty, wrote a letter to the general public explaining his position with regard to Texas. He had been traveling in the South in recent weeks, and he had gained the impression that southern Whigs were not enthusiastic about annexation. Convinced, as he usually was, that his opinions were those of the American people, Clay felt confident that his letter would have a good effect, despite the misgivings of some of his political friends. In the letter Clay explained that he thought annexation would be worthy of consideration if it could be done without excessive expense, or the risk of foreign war, or divided public opinion within the United States, or the threat of disunion within the United States, and he made it very clear that these conditions had not been met. Therefore, Clay went on to state, he opposed annexation "at this time." That last statement could be interpreted to mean that Clay might consider annexation at some future time, but since the fulfillment of his conditions was about as likely as a heavy snowfall in south Texas, the letter could also be taken as an assurance that the likely Whig standard-bearer for 1844 was solidly and permanently opposed to annexation. As Clay intended, that is exactly how northern antislavery Whigs interpreted it. Since Clay presumed that his Democratic opponent would take a similar stand, opposition to annexation could not possibly bring any political cost. The letter first appeared in the morning edition of Washington's *National Intelligencer* for April 27.[2]

That same evening *The Washington Globe* printed a letter from the presumptive Democratic presidential candidate, Martin Van Buren. With pledges of support from three-fourths of the Democratic state delegations, Van Buren was as confident of the Democratic nomination as Clay was of beating him after he got it. Like Clay, Van Buren felt the need to tell the public what he thought about Texas. A number of political leaders had written to him asking him to state his position. So while the Kentuckian was drawing up his letter, the Little Magician was writing one of his own. In a long and rather labored composition, Van Buren explained that Texas annexation was not necessary at the moment. The bruited machinations of Britain and France posed no threat, and passing up the opportunity for annexation now would not close off the chances of gaining Texas at some vague time in the future. On the other hand, immediate annexation would involve trouble and expense, and some might see it as hurting America's reputation. In brief, Van Buren was against annexation for the present, but was at least theoretically open to it in the distant future.[3]

One candidate who did favor annexation was running not for president but for vice president. Former Tennessee governor James K. Polk was an ambitious and, at age forty-eight, still relatively youthful politician (compared with the sixty-seven-year-old Clay and sixty-one-year-old Van Buren) who was a rising star in the Democratic Party. A staunch political ally of Andrew Jackson's since before Old Hickory claimed the White House, Polk had gone on to serve as Speaker of the House of Representatives before leaving Congress to pursue the campaign that had put him in the Tennessee governor's mansion from 1839 to 1841. He now hoped to win the Democratic vice-presidential nomination. In response to an inquiry about his position, Polk stated his strong support for "immediate re-annexation" of Texas—"reannexation" because Polk, like many other Americans, held that Texas had been included in the Louisiana Purchase and had been foolishly surrendered to Spain in the 1819 Adams-Onís Treaty.[4]

The Whigs' 1844 national convention met in Baltimore on May 1, four days after the publication of Clay's and Van Buren's letters. That was not enough time for the country to digest the politicians' statements or for any reaction, pro or con, to develop and grow political legs. The convention nominated Clay by acclamation, and added as his running mate New York University president Theodore Frelinghuysen. A former U.S. senator from New Jersey, the fifty-seven-year-old Frelinghuysen was sometimes called the Christian Statesman and had been criticized for letting his fervent evangelical faith influence his politics. An antislavery man even before the birth of the abolitionist movement, Frelinghuysen had been a leader in the well-meaning but ineffective American Colonization Society.

His presence on the Whig ticket in 1844 was the party's nod to its large evangelical constituency. The alliance was not always a natural one—the earnestly moral and fervently antislavery evangelicals yoked together with the sharp-eyed bank-and-tariff men who itched to use the government to harness other people's money for the more efficient pursuit of mammon. The scarcely noticed incongruity of the situation was personified in a national ticket that paired the devout Frelinghuysen and the considerably less pious Henry Clay, but it would not be the last time an American political party would woo evangelical voters with vague promises of respect for their moral concerns and a token representative in the number two spot on the ticket. Jubilation prevailed among the Whigs as Clay's march to the White House seemed unstoppable.[5]

The Democratic convention was scheduled to meet in the same city only twenty-six days later, but in political terms those twenty-six days turned out to be a very long time, especially for Martin Van Buren. In response to his antiannexationist stance, a roar of disapproval rose and grew steadily in volume. Proslavery partisans in the South and expansionists throughout the country were outraged. Letters poured into local Democratic headquarters demanding that state delegations be released from their commitments to Van Buren, and some were. Political associates wrote the New Yorker hinting that he should withdraw from the race, since his presence on the ticket would make it impossible to carry a number of key states and might even split the party, as proannexationists bolted to form a party of their own. Even Van Buren's old friend and patron Andrew Jackson had to break with him on this point. The doughty former president released a public statement saying that the United States needed to annex Texas at once to forestall British designs on the Lone Star Republic. Now that Van Buren had come out against immediate annexation, Jackson announced, he was not acceptable as the Democratic Party's nominee.[6]

Van Buren still hoped the party would rally behind him as the only alternative to a Whig victory in the fall, but many Democrats now perceived the race for the nomination as wide open, and half a dozen eager aspirants quickly plunged into the fray. John C. Calhoun was one, and his hard-line southern supporters hurriedly began organizing to get him the nomination. Another was the somewhat scandalous former vice president Richard M. Johnson. Also angling for the nomination was Johnson's fellow veteran of the Battle of the Thames, sixty-one-year-old Lewis Cass. A native of New Hampshire, Cass had served for seventeen years as governor of the Michigan Territory, then as secretary of war under Andrew Jackson and ambassador to France under Van Buren. He was an ardent advocate of Texas annexation. Several other ambitious politicians jumped into the short and sudden race for the nomination.[7]

Another candidate who was running hard for the presidency in 1844 was the accidental incumbent, John Tyler. Though he was not necessarily a contender for the Democratic nomination, Tyler was definitely a bidder for the votes of those who favored territorial expansion. He had had his eye on this election at least since the day Harrison's death propelled him into the White House. In the spring of 1843, Tyler had been well received in a political tour up the East Coast to Boston, raising his presidential hopes still higher. The president had also been diligently using federal patronage to try to build up a party apparatus of his own. With gusto he sacked federal appointees who did not actively favor his cause, filling their places with his faithful supporters, notwithstanding his earlier strictures against Andrew Jackson for allegedly doing the same thing. He commissioned journalist Alexander G. Abell to write the almost obligatory fawning campaign biography, and let postmasters and other appointees know that if they wanted to keep their jobs they would undoubtedly purchase and distribute large numbers of copies.[8]

Tyler experienced a slight political surge during the spring of 1844, probably less from his hardball political tactics than from the inherent power of the Texas issue that he had broached. A handful of his supporters held a small convention in Baltimore, simultaneous with the Democratic event, to give him an independent nomination and hope that a deadlocked Democratic convention would look in his direction. If he stayed in the race, Tyler could only draw votes away from the Democrats. His presence on the political scene could only be a distraction for the Democratic Party as it strove to select a nominee of its own.[9]

Clay was in ecstasies. It was not every day that a Whig got to see anything as entertaining or as downright funny as the present Democratic political train wreck. "I do not think I ever witnessed such a state of utter disorder, confusion, and decomposition as that which the Democratic Party now presents," he wrote gleefully to a political associate. His election, which had seemed assured even against a Democratic Party united behind the formidable political skills of Van Buren, now appeared more certain than ever. Indeed, it was not clear how the Democrats would even mount a respectable challenge, and Clay envisioned himself gliding past a divided and bickering opposition to enter the White House with ease.[10]

The Democrats held their convention on May 27, and the anti–Van Buren forces gained an immediate tactical advantage when Robert J. Walker, the Pennsylvania-born Mississippi senator and author of the widely distributed proannexation pamphlet, moved that the convention adopt a rule requiring that a candidate receive the votes of two-thirds of the delegates in order to receive the party's nomination. The Democrats had used this rule before in 1832 and 1836, and in the former year it had boosted Van Buren's bid for the vice presidency. Now it was sure to work against him. Despite recent defections, the Little Magician still had the support of a majority of delegates—but not the necessary two-thirds.[11]

Van Buren's loyalists, led by former U.S. attorney general Benjamin Butler, bitterly opposed the measure. Butler was a longtime member of Van Buren's so-called Albany Regency organization that had at times dominated New York's Democratic Party. After serving in the Jackson and Van Buren administrations, Butler had become U.S. attorney for the Southern District of New York. As Van Buren's floor leader at the convention, Butler flung himself into the fight against the two-thirds rule. With a face described by one onlooker as white with anger, he loosed an hour-long tirade, jumping up and down in his fiery passion. The intense performance drew applause, but failed in its purpose of persuading the convention to reject the rule. It passed; ominously, a number of delegates who were committed to Van Buren nevertheless voted for the rule. The clear implication was that, although they were obligated to vote for Van Buren on the first ballot, they did not want him to take the nomination.[12]

On the first ballot Van Buren won a clear majority, with 146 out of 266 votes cast. That left him 32 votes short of the 178 required by the two-thirds rule. Cass was the second-highest vote getter with 83, Johnson was a distant third with 24, and a handful of others, including Calhoun, divided the other 13. Van Buren's lead was large, but his enemies were determined and resolutely held out against him in ballot after ballot. As foreshadowed by the vote on the two-thirds rule, Van Buren delegates began deserting after having fulfilled their commitments on the first ballot. The Little Magician's vote strength started to erode immediately, and it gradually sank over the next six ballots, until on the seventh ballot—the last of the convention's second day—the former president drew only 99 votes.[13]

As Van Buren's support waned, Cass's gradually grew, but his tide crested at 123 on the seventh ballot, far short of the necessary two-thirds. Johnson's support remained about level through the seven ballots, while fifty-three-year-old Pennsylvania senator James Buchanan experienced a miniature surge that raised his support from 4 votes on the first ballot to 26 votes on the fifth. Then he too began a gradual decline. It was clear after the seventh ballot that something needed to change or else the convention would face a prolonged deadlock.

When the delegates met the next morning for the third day of the convention, heads were already hot after the previous two days of futility. Insults flew between Van Buren and anti–Van Buren delegates and tempers frayed. At times the delegates appeared ready to wade into one another with their fists. Meanwhile, Gideon J. Pillow of Tennessee and George Bancroft of Massachusetts were doing some behind-the-scenes maneuvering, with the result that the supporters of Johnson and Buchanan shifted their votes to a surprise candidate. James Polk had been angling for the vice-presidential nomination and had yet to receive a single vote for president. Now, on the eighth ballot, he shot into third place, with 44 votes. Cass and Van Buren each registered more than 100 votes on that ballot, but the momentum in Polk's favor was unmistakable. Supporters of Van Buren considered Polk, who was, like Van Buren, a steadfast Jacksonian, preferable to Cass, whose ambitions they saw as being the fountainhead of the opposition to the former president. One state delegation after another shifted its votes to the Tennessean, and on the ninth ballot Polk won in a landslide, with a total of 231 votes. The nation had its first dark-horse presidential candidate.[14]

The Democratic platform reflected the enthusiastic expansionism that had won Polk the nomination. It boldly called for the reannexation of Texas and the reoccupation of Oregon. Again the suggestion was that this was territory that had once rightfully been American but had been fumbled away by inept diplomacy. The Democratic Party asserted that the United States should now claim as its own the entire Oregon Country, all the way up to the southern boundary claimed by Russian Alaska at latitude 54°40' north. Democrats were soon expressing their determination to have the whole territory with the slogan "Fifty-four Forty or Fight!" Here was spread-eagle expansionism for both North and South, with the implied but thunderous message that expansion was not about spreading slavery but about extending the domain of American constitutional liberty, not a policy for one narrow sectional interest but for the whole country.

Two other presidential nominations rounded out the field for the 1844 election. Simultaneous with the Democratic convention, Tyler's little band of supporters met elsewhere in Baltimore to nominate him. Notified of his selection, Tyler enthusiastically accepted, but few thought he had much of a chance to win. The widower president was in an expansive mood these days. On June 26 he married Julia Gardiner, the young woman, thirty years his junior, who had collapsed into his arms upon the death of her father in the dreadful accident on the *Princeton* that February. Tyler would spend most of the summer honeymooning in his new bride's home state of New York. When the couple returned to Washington, young Julia became quite a hit in Washington social circles. She brought her own special style to the White House and originated the custom of having the U.S. Marine Band play "Hail to the Chief" on the president's arrival at social events. Win or lose in November, Tyler would enjoy the summer and fall.[15]

A final presidential nomination came from the Liberty Party. Once again that small band of determined abolitionists nominated James G. Birney as their candidate. Their message was that men should vote according to their conscience, regardless of the consequences, and not be taken in by the major parties' distractions or vague claims to stand against slavery. They knew they had no chance of winning, but they hoped for more than the ten thousand or so votes they had garnered last time out.

Henry Clay and the Whigs were having a truly delightful summer. First there had been the Democratic disarray over Texas, then the Democratic convention had dumped its party's foremost active politician in favor of a man who was anything but a household name. "Are our Democratic friends serious in the nominations which they have made in Balti-more?" smirked Clay. The despised Tyler's leap into the race further warmed the hearts of Whigs, since the incumbent president had no chance of winning but would draw off some of Polk's expansionist votes. As for the Liberty Party, its continued futility seemed guaranteed. How could it possibly become a threat to Clay? Gleeful Whigs looked forward to the election, derisively asking, "Who is James K. Polk?"[16]

The parties waged their campaigns throughout the summer of 1844, while the issues facing the country continued to develop. The Senate's formal rejection of the Texas annexation treaty came on June 8. Tyler reacted by hinting to Congress that annexation could be accomplished by a joint resolution of both houses admitting Texas as a state, since that was the usual method for admitting states. For the time being, however, Congress declined to act. In Texas, President Sam Houston was furious at having his republic once again hung out to dry by the United States. In Mexico City, President Antonio López de Santa Anna, now back in power, raged against Texas and threatened destruction to the upstart republic and any nation that might give it aid and comfort.[17]

The election campaign became somewhat simpler when John Tyler decided to bow out of the race. His summer spent honeymooning in New York had shown him that his support among the American people simply was not sufficient to give him a realistic bid for returning to the White House. Democrats urged him to withdraw rather than divide the proannexation vote, and Tyler finally decided they were right. On August 20 he wrote a lengthy letter for publication addressed to "My friends throughout the Union," defending his actions in office and explaining his reasons for withdrawing.[18]

The controversy over the annexation of Texas and Oregon continued to consume all of the electorate's attention, much to the chagrin of Henry Clay. Along with others in the Whig leadership, he grew nervous. Whigs in his hometown of Lexington, Kentucky, held a mass meeting to deplore all the attention given to Texas. It was a plot, they asserted, by underhanded politicians who wanted to distract the American people from the truly important issues of banks, tariffs, and presidential usurpers who vetoed Whig legislation. Those were the questions that should decide the current campaign, according to the Lexington Whigs. But elsewhere across the South more and more voices were calling for annex-ation and criticizing Clay's April letter in the *National Intelligencer* repudi-ating it.[19]

Poor Henry Clay. He was at heart a modern politician without modern tools. Firm in the unshakable belief that he should be president, Clay had no public opinion polls to tell him what else he ought to believe. Apparently his April letter had not been quite accurate in expressing his unalterable core values. So he took another guess. On July 1 *The Tuscaloosa Monitor* printed a letter from Clay clarifying his position on Texas annexation. "Personally," he wrote, "I could have no objection to the annexation of Texas." But he did not want to take any course that would threaten a possible breakup of the Union. Here he pointed out that some people in South Carolina—obviously Calhoun's faction—were angling for just that outcome and using Texas for the purpose. As long as this threat remained, Clay implied, he would continue to oppose annexation. The whole business, he maintained in closing, had been nothing but "a bubble, blown up by Mr. Tyler, in a most exceptionable manner, for sinister purposes, and its bursting has injured nobody but Mr. Van Buren."[20]

This second effort by Clay proved at least as unfortunate as the first. Instead of striking a note that would please everyone, it seemed to offer something to outrage almost everyone. Southerners were furious that he would mention those unnamed South Carolinians as the potential source of disunion. This mention, huffed *The New-Orleans Commercial Bulletin*, "for Mr. Clay's own sake, had better been omitted, as it is certainly uncalled for." Why did Clay not mention the New England abolitionists who had made statements that seemed to imply the threat of disunion if the United States admitted Texas? And for that matter, if New Englanders were justified in making vague threats of disunion if Texas was annexed, what was wrong with South Carolinians making similar threats if it was not?[21]

Abolitionists and other antislavery northerners reacted to Clay's letter with equal outrage. Many of them had already been critical of Clay. Earlier that summer *The Green-Mountain Freeman* had blasted Clay as a collaborator with the slave power and had similarly lambasted as dupes those antislavery Whigs who planned to vote for him. It was folly to vote for Clay in hopes thereby of preventing Texas annexation. Clay owned sixty slaves and approved of the institution. He had on many occasions during his career in government helped to spread the peculiar institution. Regardless of what he might say during an election campaign, he could not be trusted. "Who," asked the editor, "can so far divest himself of his reason and common sense as to believe for a moment that *Henry Clay* will lend himself to the support of any measure that will tend in the least to curtail the Slave Power of this nation and advance the interests of Impartial Liberty?"[22]

With the appearance of Clay's July 1 letter in *The Tuscaloosa Monitor*, many abolitionists saw their long-held worries about Clay's reliability fully confirmed. "How many faces has Mr. Clay got?" demanded *The Weekly Ohio Statesman*. The editor was scandalized by Clay's assertion that he personally had no objection to annexation, and he thought Clay's talk of the danger of disunion was really nothing but a subterfuge to cover his impending sellout to the slave power. Again and again the abolitionist press hammered home the argument that Clay was not to be trusted on the issue of slavery.[23]

The complaints of the abolitionists made little impression on Clay. He was accustomed to their criticism, and he despised them, even while he expected to carry some of the northern states on the strength of antislavery votes. Where else could antislavery voters turn? The alternative was Polk, who openly favored Texas annexation, and since abolitionists had convinced themselves that annexation represented an increase in the power of slavery, that was no option at all. How many people, even abolitionists, would want to waste their votes on the hopeless Liberty Party and thereby give up all say in such exciting issues as the bank, the tariffs, and the evils of "executive usurpation"? Clay felt he had little to fear from the abolitionists and their more moderate antislavery brethren, rage though they might. When election day came and presented its obnoxious alternative, they would hold their noses and vote Whig as they had always done before.

What did worry Clay was the continued dissatisfaction of expansionists, especially southerners. Polk could make real inroads with Whig supporters if voters decided that Texas was too good to pass up, with or without slavery. Since southerners already embraced slavery, they were the most likely to defect to the Democrats. The danger for Clay seemed to lie in the growing groundswell of proannexation feeling, especially in the South.

To head off the threat in that quarter, Clay in late July decided to write another letter. Dated July 27, and paired with his letter published in Tuscaloosa at the beginning of the month, it became known as his second Alabama letter. In it Clay expressed regret that his previous letter had been misunderstood and said he thought it had been quite clear. He reiterated that he had no personal objection to annexation, but that he did not favor such a course at this time because it might lead to war with

Mexico and because of the opposition of some states—but certainly not because of the opposition of the abolitionists. In fact, so far was Clay from agreement with the abolitionists that he believed the issue of slavery should not be considered at all in the decision of whether to annex Texas. Slavery, he asserted, was "destined to become extinct at some distant day" as a result of the "inevitable laws of population." It made no sense, therefore, for northerners to "refuse a permanent acquisition, which will exist as long as the globe remains, on account of a temporary institution."[24]

The purpose of the letter was twofold: to assure moderate northerners that they need not worry about slavery in Texas—either because slavery was not a problem or because Clay would not annex Texas—and to give a wink and a nod to proannexation southerners, signaling them that once in the White House he would be able to finesse the threats of foreign war and domestic unrest and achieve the peaceful annexation of Texas. Clay hoped his slyly worded letter would draw support from each group. Instead, it drew fire from both. Southerners complained about Clay's characterization of slavery as a "temporary institution," while the abolitionist press seized on the letter as further proof of Clay's true desire to annex Texas. Loyal Whigs in the North tried to maintain either that Clay was still really holding the same position he had always held and had only clarified his steadfast opposition to annexation or else that the letter was a forgery. Friends and political associates hinted to Clay that it might be best not to write any more letters. "Your letter on the Texas question has given the rascals a new impulse," wrote a correspondent from Ohio. "The public mind is excited."[25]

Democrats in both North and South crowed that the Kentuckian had flip-flopped. "For Texas; against Texas; for slavery, yet it is an institution which the inevitable laws of population will abolish!" complained a southern editor. Meanwhile, *The New York Herald* sneered, "Mr. Clay saw the tide setting against him, and he shifted his sails accordingly." "He wires in and wires out," rhymed another gleeful Democratic editor, "And leaves the people still in doubt / Whether the snake that made the track / Was going South or coming back."[26] Clay was trying desperately to straddle the issues of slavery and Texas, but the more he tried, the worse his situation became.

Clay's fellow Kentuckian and distant relative Cassius M. Clay was a Lexington newspaper editor. He was also that rarest of creatures, an abolitionist south of the Ohio River. Sensing that their candidate was in danger of hemorrhaging antislavery support in the North, Whig politicians in Ohio brought Cassius Clay to their state to campaign for his kinsman and reassure northern voters that Henry Clay was sound on slavery. Word of this leaked out and created a minor furor in strongly proslavery Kentucky, which the presidential candidate felt compelled to try to calm, despite the fact that his friends were by now begging him to quit writing letters. In a September 2 letter to *The Lexington Observer and Reporter,* Henry Clay repudiated his relative's views and strongly denied that he was, or ever had been, an abolitionist.[27]

Meanwhile, Polk had received a boost in August when John Tyler withdrew from the race. The Virginian would have garnered few votes in any case, but this election was shaping up to be close enough to make every one count. As for Tyler, he remained ebullient, rejoicing with his new wife and consoling himself that his efforts as president during the preceding four years and his presence as a candidate during the preceding three months had helped prod the Democrats into adopting the Texas issue as their own. Amused at Clay's obvious discomfort with the issue and betrayed in the Kentuckian's repeated epistolary attempts to dodge it, Tyler gave his endorsement to Polk and grimly hoped for revenge on the implacable enemy who had dogged his every action as president.[28]

When election day came, the national tally was 1,337,243 popular votes for Polk, or about 50 percent of the total number of ballots cast. Clay received 1,299,062 votes, or about 48 percent, with the remainder going to minor-party candidates. In the electoral college, where votes really counted, the election was more complex. Polk had 170 electoral votes to Clay's 105, but the outcome had hung in a finer balance than the margin of victory suggested. Clay had not been able to convince southerners that he was truly in favor of Texas annexation, and the entire Deep South had gone in a bloc for Polk, even though Louisiana, Mississippi, and Georgia had been in the Whig column four years before, and Whigs had had hopes of wooing Alabama away from its Democratic allegiance. Thus Clay's waffling on Texas annexation had brought him no significant dividends among proslavery voters. Yet even if Clay's coy flirtation with Texas annexation had won him all four of the southern states in which Whigs had believed they had a chance, he would still have been two votes short of victory in the electoral college.[29]

At the other end of the political spectrum and almost the other end of the country, New York presented a much different case. There Clay's equivocation had convinced many antislavery Whigs that he could not be trusted on the issue that mattered most to them. Their response was to bolt to the Liberty Party, which polled 62,300 votes nationwide, an almost ninefold increase from the 7,069 votes it had garnered in 1840. The Liberty Party voters in New York were by all odds the most significant of that party's electorate: 15,800 New Yorkers cast their votes for James G. Birney, while Polk carried the state by only 5,100 votes. If even one-third, much less eight-ninths, of the Liberty Party voters in New York had opted to stay with the Whigs instead, Clay would have carried the state, and New York's 36 electoral votes would, all by themselves, have given Clay an electoral college majority of 141 to 134, even with the Deep South remaining solidly in Polk's camp. Clay's waffling had cost him the election.

The Whigs were in shock. Clay believed his defeat had been the result of "a most extraordinary combination of adverse circumstances." Throughout the country, Whigs lamented that their great man—the great statesman of the age—had been defeated by a mere political nobody. It was a devastating setback. "For the present," as one Whig leader put it, the Whig party in his part of the country was "dispersed, and we cannot know our position until the heat and smoke of the conflict have passed away."[30]

From New York, Clay's running mate, Theodore Frelinghuysen, wrote to console him on the defeat. "The Abolitionists were inimicably obstinate," Frelinghuysen lamented, noting that he had been denounced as an abolitionist himself in the South but condemned by the full-fledged abolitionists for sharing the ticket with the compromising Clay. Frelinghuysen was not in the depths of despair, however, partially because he had never partaken of Clay's overweening ambition and partially because he had a larger perspective and a confident expectation of future good that did not rest on any election by the American people. With a change of subject that seemed obvious to him but might well have surprised Clay, he urged his disappointed fellow candidate to look to "better prospects, and surer hopes, in the promises and consolations of the Gospel of our Savior. As sinners who have rebelled against our Maker," Frelinghuysen continued,

> we need a Saviour or we must perish, and this Redeemer has been provided for us. . . . "Come unto me," cries this exalted Saviour, "come unto me, all ye that are weary and heavy laden, and I will give you rest." Let us, then, repair to Him. He will never fail us in the hour of peril and trial. . . . I pray, my honored friend, that your heart

may seek this blessed refuge, stable as the everlasting hills, and let this be the occasion to prompt an earnest, prayerful, and the Lord grant it may be a joyful, search after truth as it is in Jesus Christ.[31]

Clay apparently gave the matter serious thought.

Meanwhile, on the national political scene, the momentum now lay with the Democrats, the annexationists, and, curiously, with John Tyler.

CHAPTER NINE

Texas Annexation

W ITH P OLK ELECTED, the lame-duck Tyler still managed to pull off a major expansionist coup of his own in the waning days of his administration. Between election day in November and inauguration day in March was a full four months—time for Tyler to accomplish something toward Texas annexation, or time for the opportunity to slip by, perhaps, if the Virginian did nothing. British authorities, always eager to keep the United States, their chief transatlantic rival, as weak as possible, were striving to throw such obstacles as they could in the way of U.S. annexation of Texas. Lord Aberdeen had been encouraged by the Senate's rejection of the annexation treaty the previous summer and was working on a formal diplomatic agreement involving Britain, France, Mexico, and Texas, guaranteeing Texas independence and giving Britain and France the right to intervene to prevent any future American attempt at annexation. The British had sat on their hands during the election campaign, fearful that any maneuvering on their part might jeopardize the election of Clay, whom they very much wanted to see in the White House. With the American electorate having refused to fulfill Europe's wishes, British diplomatic machinations could resume with full vigor.[1]

Texas leaders, irked at the rejection of the treaty, were in no mood to rebuff British overtures and were flirting brazenly with the idea of an arrangement of some sort, especially since Santa Anna, who had by now returned to power in Mexico, was once again threatening to invade the Lone Star Republic. The negotiations between Texas and Britain certainly appeared serious when viewed from the vantage point of Washington, and the prospect seemed real that, whatever agreement would be reached, Texas might continue nominally independent but in reality become a British protectorate and possibly even its ally against the United States in the event of war. That prospect was intolerable to Tyler, Polk, and the American people, and preventing it seemed to require immediate action. The occasion was by no means to be the last time during the turbulent events of the 1840s that British activities, or the tacit threat of them, helped force the hand of U.S. policy.[2]

So Tyler pushed aggressively for annexation. This time he possessed both enhanced public support, thanks to the mandate for Texas annexation provided by the recent election, and a less heavy-handed legislative strategy. Rather than attempt to gain ratification of a treaty by two-thirds of the Whig-controlled Senate, Tyler would now rely on ordinary legislation to get the job done, despite complaints by some that annexing new territory in this manner was unconstitutional. Tyler, himself a stickler for the Constitution, was unconcerned, since that document said nothing at all on the subject. The House of Representatives acted first, though only after weeks of debate. Whig congressman Milton Brown introduced and the House adopted a bill authorizing the admission of Texas as a state and stipulating only that no slavery should exist in the portions of the Lone Star Republic that extended north of the 36°30' Missouri Compromise line. The Senate responded with a much different bill. Sponsored by old Jackson ally Thomas Hart Benton, the Senate legislation merely provided for the appropriation of funds for negotiations now aimed at producing an annexation with Texas. Some thought Benton, who had never been an advocate of annexation, was merely stalling.[3]

As the prospect loomed of a long and contentious showdown between the houses, President-elect Polk, who had arrived in Washington a few weeks early for his inauguration and was eager to see the matter settled before he took office, quietly suggested that each house pass both versions and let the president choose which to sign. The idea caught on sufficiently to garner a narrow 27–25 victory in the Senate on February 27. Aware that the president who had been meant to choose between the two options was his successor, Tyler was not sure whether he ought to sign the bill or leave that to Polk. He was understandably tired of being called a usurper and so on Sunday, March 2, dispatched Secretary of State Calhoun to Polk's lodgings to obtain his final blessing on the act. Polk declined comment. Like most Americans, Young Hickory avoided business on the Lord's Day, and besides, Tyler was still president. The decision was his. The next evening, his last in office, Tyler made his decision to offer the Lone Star Republic statehood under the terms of Brown's bill.[4]

Meanwhile, a related political development had occurred during that same lame-duck winter. More or less simultaneous with the debate over Texas annexation, John Quincy Adams had launched yet another effort to have the odious Gag Rule repealed. With southerners openly pushing annexation on the grounds that it was necessary for the preservation of slavery, northern representatives no longer felt bound to support the Gag Rule as a way of preventing the discussion of slavery. If southerners could discuss what ought to be done in support of slavery, surely the House could at least receive the petitions of northern citizens in opposition to the peculiar institution. Adams's motion for repeal passed on December 3 by a vote of 180–80, with representatives voting mostly along strict sectional lines. Every northern Whig and most northern Democrats voted for repeal, while their southern colleagues of both parties overwhelmingly opposed it. On this issue, at least, sectional loyalty had overridden party discipline. Nevertheless, this was the same Congress that would vote to annex Texas, demonstrating that although southerners supported annexation as a proslavery measure, many northerners favored the move as one of national expansion, without regard to slavery. For now, Manifest Destiny still reached across the sectional divide.[5]

While Congress debated and finally approved Texas annexation that winter, Tyler approached the end of his administration with equanimity. He felt vindicated by the widespread public support for annexation, even if many in Congress were still bitter against him. On February 18 he and Julia held a final presidential ball with three thousand guests in attendance. A marine band was on hand to play cotillions and the more daring waltzes and polkas the Tylers had introduced to Washington society. "Wine and champagne flowed like water," commented a delighted guest. Congratulated on hosting such a gala event, Tyler joked, "Yes, they cannot say *now* that I am a President *without a party*."[6]

On a rainy March 4, 1845, James K. Polk took the oath of office as the eleventh president of the United States. Already one of his chief campaign promises was well on its way to fulfillment. What remained to be seen was how Texas and Mexico would react to Tyler's last major act in office. Polk took steps immediately to try to influence both reactions. He replaced Tyler's rather undiplomatic emissary to Mexico with one who promised to be more congenial to his hosts, suggesting that the new president wished to improve relations with the United States' southern neighbor.

He also dispatched Commodore Robert F. Stockton, sponsor of the *Princeton* and designer of the infamous Peacemaker, to carry the U.S. offer of annexation to Texas. Arriving at Galveston with his flagship (*Princeton*, of course) leading a U.S. naval squadron, the headstrong and mercurial Stockton not only delivered his message but also contacted Major General Sidney Sherman of the Texas army. The two launched a curious scheme to raise and equip an army of Texans and launch them against the Mexican Rio Grande port of Matamoros, apparently under the supposition that the Mexicans were preparing an advance into Texas. It was not an implausible claim—the Mexicans had made several forays into the republic and had threatened war with the United States should it annex Texas—but it was not the case this time. The U.S. minister to Texas succeeded in quashing the scheme. Historians still wonder whether Polk knew anything about his commodore's adventure, though it seems doubtful. Polk was a secretive president, always playing his cards very close to the vest, leaving those who came after to speculate on his purposes and intent in this matter as in others.[7]

The Texans' response to the offer of U.S. annexation was not as uncertain as their recent flirtation with Britain might have suggested it would be. The overwhelming majority of the republic's citizens were only too eager for annexation, and their preponderance left little choice to those few Texas officials who might have dreamed of a great empire of their own. The Texas congress accepted the U.S. offer by unanimous vote, and a convention called for the purpose quickly ratified the decision. By June 1845 word of the acceptance was on its way to Washington, and Stockton and *Princeton* were back in American waters with the good news in time for Fourth of July festivities.[8]

Meanwhile, Polk was dealing with the other half of his dual campaign pledge on westward expansion, the part that pertained to the Oregon Country—or, as Polk put it in his inaugural address, "that portion of our territory which lies beyond the Rocky Mountains." Continuing, the new president had announced, "Our title to the country of Oregon is 'clear and unquestionable.' " From Lewis and Clark some forty years before to the more recent presence of mountain men, Jason Lee and the Whitmans, and the current steady stream of emigrants on the Oregon Trail, the United States had indeed a long-standing and strong claim to the Northwest. Predictably, however, the British did not see it that way and reacted belligerently to Polk's assertion. Prime Minister Sir Robert Peel dispatched one of Her Majesty's frigates to the disputed coast, and other prominent voices in the sceptered isle announced that the crisis could well lead to war.[9]

Polk didn't blink. To his political mentor Andrew Jackson, Young Hickory wrote that he would hold his ground "firmly, boldly, but prudently" and would "not recede." That suited the aging former president, who had fought the British in two wars and still carried the scar of a British officer's saber. He pointed out astutely in his reply to Polk that economic considerations would make it all but impossible for the British to wage war at this time. Polk had but to make a bold stand, and John Bull would back down.[10]

Yet while Old and Young Hickory exchanged assurances of the need for an unflinching position, British and American diplomats continued their negotiations without hindrance from Polk. A long-standing U.S. proposal was still on the table, offering to extend the borderline that now ran westward from the Lake of the Woods in Minnesota, along the forty-ninth parallel, across the mountains, and all the way west through the Oregon Country until it struck salt water on the eastern shore of the Strait of Juan de Fuca. On the far side of that strait, Vancouver Island remained a particular issue of dispute. It extended some distance south of the forty-ninth parallel, but the British were dogged in their unwillingness to relinquish their claims to any part of the island.[11]

American negotiators were inclined to indulge their counterparts in this and cede the island to Britain, and with that the diplomats might have laid the matter to rest, had not one of their number, Lord Pakenham, the British ambassador to Washington, intervened to scotch the proposed settlement. Without consulting London, where negotiations seemed about to produce an agreement, Pakenham rejected the proposal out of hand, adding a few choice comments in his note to Polk's secretary of state, James Buchanan. Polk responded by ordering Buchanan to withdraw the offer to place the boundary on the forty-ninth parallel and to revert to the position on which he had campaigned, U.S. occupation of all of Oregon all the way up to 54°40'. This president was not going to be bullied. "If we do have war," he remarked grimly, "it will not be our fault."[12]

While tensions continued to rise in the dispute over Oregon, Texas took its place in the Union, and the nation extended its protection to the twenty-eighth state. Prior to annexation, Tyler had posted Colonel (Brevet Brigadier General) Zachary Taylor with some two thousand troops—about a quarter of the total strength of the U.S. Army at the time—at Fort Jesup, Louisiana, not far from the Sabine River. Dubbed the Army of Observation, Taylor's force had the duty of monitoring events in Texas and, should the Lone Star Republic agree to annexation, moving into the new state to provide the "defence and protection from foreign invasion and Indian incursion" to which it would then be entitled. In June 1845, Polk ordered Taylor to advance into the new state. On the advice of Andrew Jackson Donelson, the senior U.S. diplomat in Texas, Taylor made his destination the Gulf Coast town of Corpus Christi, at the mouth of the Nueces River. Transporting some of his troops by sea while others marched overland, Taylor had his little army in place by the end of August. Over the next couple of months the War Department reinforced his command to a strength of just over thirty-five hundred men. It now constituted almost half of the U.S. Army and was the largest force the nation had brought together in one place since the War of 1812. The army's presence was an unprecedented boost to the local economy, and the sleepy hamlet of Corpus Christi enjoyed six months of boom times.[13]

Napoleon Jackson Tecumseh Dana, a young lieutenant in the Seventh U.S. Infantry Regiment, was part of Taylor's army and wrote of his experiences in many long letters to his wife. He found the trip to Corpus Christi unpleasant in a small schooner bucking wildly on the rough Gulf of Mexico, but the camp on the beach near the mouth of the Nueces was much more enjoyable. "There is always a very strong sea breeze blowing here," he explained, "which renders the land very pleasant and Corpus Christi Bay the roughest piece of water for its size I have ever seen." Fellow officer Captain Ephraim Kirby Smith of the Fifth Infantry fully agreed. "The climate here is perfectly delicious and healthy," he wrote to his wife, "and so cool from the trade wind, which blows steadily, that our cloth clothing is very comfortable." Somewhat less pleasant were the rattlesnakes that occasionally crawled into the men's blankets at night. One of Dana's comrades awoke to find himself sharing his bed with an especially large specimen. After killing the reptile, the officer counted nine rattles on its tail.[14]

Though small, Taylor's army was tough and efficient. Its field-grade officers were not professionally trained, but long years of frontier service had made them doughty, aggressive, and fairly competent in handling small units. Most would readily get the hang of commanding larger ones when the opportunity arose. The company-grade officers were the army's strongest element. Most of them, like Dana, were West Point graduates, bright, highly trained, and professional, and many, including Dana, would be heard from again in much higher rank when the Civil War came: Ulysses S. Grant, Robert E. Lee, George G. Meade, Pierre G. T. Beauregard, John Sedgwick, and Braxton Bragg among them. In all, well over three hundred veterans of the Mexican War would reach general officer rank in the Civil War.[15]

The rank and file were not exactly the best and brightest of American society. The booming civilian economy, strong labor market, open frontier, and fierce cultural emphasis on personal freedom would have made the life of a soldier in the regular army unappealing to most Americans, even if hardship, danger, sickness, boredom, and bad food had not done so already. Joining the enlisted ranks of the army was generally the resort of men who had no other options, and the average soldier was prone to binge drinking, brawling, and desertion when not closely supervised. Yet they were thoroughly drilled, hardened by their rough life, and disciplined by the army's harsh methods. Like soldiers of any time or place, they required good leadership, but with it they were the equals of any troops in the world. During the months the army spent at Corpus Christi, training and drills took up much of the soldiers' time, and Taylor's force became even more proficient.[16]

As if Texas and Oregon did not present foreign policy problems enough for the Polk administration, California seemed a likely third flash point, one that could touch off war with Mexico, Britain, or both. Polk shared the long-standing desire of many Americans to acquire California and was eager to purchase it from Mexico. The recent influx of Americans into the region gave added grounds to hope that the Pacific slope of the Sierra Nevada would someday belong to the United States. In the fall of 1845, it became apparent that the British were at work there as well. British agents were urging the Mexican government to march an army into California to crush the American settlers and forestall any possibility that they might someday demand the region's annexation by the United States. The British were showing enough additional interest in the region to make it clear that they desired, at best, to annex California to their own empire or, at worst, to deny it to the United States.[17]

Polk responded in kind. If the British could use agents, so could he. He chose First Lieutenant Archibald H. Gillespie, of the U.S. Marine Corps. On the next-to-last evening of October, the president dispatched the officer to travel across the continent and make contact with Frémont, who was leading yet another exploring expedition, this one through the mountains of Oregon. As Gillespie understood his orders, he was to cooperate with Frémont in instigating an uprising on the part of the largely American population of California against the distant government in Mexico City. This was to be very much an undercover operation, not least because the quickest and most practical route to California led through Mexico itself. In the guise of a businessman, Gillespie took passage on a merchant vessel from New York to Veracruz, traveled across Mexico to Mazatlán, on the Pacific coast, and from there took ship again for Monterey, California.[18]

Nevertheless, Polk preferred to settle all the outstanding questions by negotiation, as long as that did not involve a sellout of U.S. interests or honor. Even before Gillespie left New York, the president signed a commission for John Slidell of Louisiana to serve as "Minister Extraordinary and Plenipotentiary" to Mexico. Slidell had grown up in New York but had moved to Louisiana in 1819, at age twenty-six, after a duel. He became a lawyer in New Orleans and by 1845 was a Louisiana congressman. He spoke fluent Spanish.[19]

It was by no means clear, however, that the Mexicans would receive him. The U.S. consul in Veracruz had been trying for months to get an answer to that question. The reply he finally received from Mexico's foreign minister was that the government in Mexico City wanted a say in both the selection of the American envoy and his title, as well as U.S. naval deployments in the Gulf of Mexico. Foreign minister José Manuel de la Peña y Peña stated that the envoy should be a commissioner, not a minister, and hinted that it should be someone the Mexicans liked. He added a pointed reference to former U.S. agent to Mexico William S. Parrott, whom they definitely did not. He further demanded that U.S. naval vessels should not cruise in international waters off the port of Veracruz. Polk had conceded to the Mexican demands in appointing Slidell, rather than Parrott, as his envoy, but he had still availed himself of Parrott's knowledge and experience by appointing him as secretary of Slidell's legation. Since the importance of Slidell's mission and the results Polk hoped he would achieve merited the more important title of minister, that is what Polk had called him, and the president apparently felt that the whereabouts of U.S. warships in international waters were none of Mexico's business.[20]

Polk had authorized Slidell to offer a variety of solutions to the outstanding difficulties between the United States and Mexico. Chief among the difficulties was the disputed southwestern border of Texas as well as the issue of Mexican debt to U.S. creditors, variously estimated at from $2 million to $10 million. Slidell was to offer that the United States would pay the whole sum in exchange for Mexico's acceptance of the border Texas had been claiming since 1836, the Rio Grande from its mouth to its source. If Mexico would also grant the rest of New Mexico, Slidell was authorized to add a $5 million cash payment to the American assumption of loans. For a boundary line that ran to the coast and included San Francisco in U.S. territory, Slidell could make the cash bonus a whopping $20 million, and should the new boundary include Monterey, California, the final sum paid to Mexico would be $25 million in addition to the debt assumption.[21]

Polk's December 2 State of the Union message reviewed the situation the country faced in regard to Britain and the status of Oregon, as well as the long-brewing difficulties with Mexico. He explained that he was sending a minister to Mexico. This was Slidell, though Polk did not mention his name. With Britain, Polk took a hard line. "Oregon is part of the North American continent, to which, it is confidently affirmed, the title of the United States is the best now in existence," the president stated, and he was not going to entertain any compromise about its possession. The public welcomed the address with enthusiasm. "Jackson is alive again" was the response of jubilant crowds after news of the address reached New York, and other cities were equally exultant.[22]

Back in Mexico, John Slidell was anything but exultant. He arrived in the capital on December 6, to the consternation of the Mexican government, which had expected the United States to take considerable time in selecting and sending an envoy. On learning of Slidell's approach, Peña y Peña even sent a message imploring the U.S. consul in Veracruz to stop the Louisianan there, but it was too late. The Mexican government ignored Slidell for his first two weeks in the capital while the acting president of Mexico, General José Joaquín de Herrera, and the Council of Government tried to figure out what to do with him. At length, they decided that Mexico would not receive him because his title was that of minister.[23]

An increasingly impatient Slidell, meanwhile, sent several increasingly testy notes to Peña y Peña, protesting his shabby treatment. Late in December, still ignored by the Mexican government, Slidell decided that his own dignity and that of the United States forbade him any longer playing the role of supplicant would-be minister in Mexico City, so he departed the capital during the last week of 1845 and traveled to the town of Jalapa, whence he sent his report to Washington and awaited instructions.[24]

Herrera and Peña y Peña had reasons for their hesitation. Perennially unstable Mexico was tormented by demagogues and racked by rebellion. Ambitious men had pointed to the yanquis as the source of problems that stemmed mostly from within their own society. Texas annexation further inflamed the Mexican people to the point that any leader who showed even reasonable courtesy to the United States or its representatives was in danger of being overthrown by another who convinced the people that he would take a harder line against the gringos. This threat became reality for the Herrera regime when, a week after Slidell's departure from Mexico City, a rebellious general, Mariano Paredes y Arrillaga, arrived in the capital at the head of seven thousand of the Mexican army's best troops—troops that Herrera had ordered him to use for the defense of the northern frontier—and on January 1, 1846, took over the national government, thus demonstrating the fate of Mexican leaders who would so far countenance U.S. overtures as to allow the northern neighbor's minister to remain, ignored, for three weeks in the Mexican capital.[25]

While impasse gave way to coup in Mexico City, back in Washington, President Polk seemed to think better of his truculent stance toward Great Britain in the matter of the Oregon Country and placed back on the table, near the end of the year, the previous U.S. proposal for the extension of the boundary along the forty-ninth parallel to the Strait of Juan de Fuca. The wisdom of this step became all the more apparent when the new year brought word from Slidell of Mexico's almost helpless intransigence and the probable need for firmer measures in the Southwest. For Polk the decision to negotiate with Britain and stand firm against Mexico was largely determined by the fact that Britain would negotiate and Mexico would not.[26]

Hence on January 13 he dispatched orders to Zachary Taylor to move his little army from Corpus Christi to a position on the Texas side of the Rio Grande. As was necessary for the commander of a military force far from the national capital in those days of slow communication, Taylor was to have broad discretion. Mexico was not to be treated as an enemy, but if the Mexicans declared war, attacked Taylor's force, or simply moved an army north of the Rio Grande, the general was free to maneuver both defensively and offensively in response. He could also call on Texas for the aid of its militia, should that force be needed to help repel a Mexican invasion.[27]

Polk was taking a momentous but measured step. As long as he had allowed the Mexicans to hold the disputed ground between the Nueces and the Rio Grande, the southern republic had had little motivation to negotiate or even to take notice of American overtures. Now the shoe would be on the other foot, so to speak. United States troops would occupy the land Texas claimed all the way to the north bank of the Rio Grande. The next move would belong to the Mexicans, who could opt either to open negotiations or to take up the gage of war Polk had thus thrown down.

PART FOUR

War with Mexico

CHAPTER TEN

Armies Along the Rio Grande

TAYLOR WAS HAPPY to receive the order to advance to the Rio Grande. He had suggested such a movement several months earlier, because the camps around Corpus Christi were growing unpleasant and his men bored. The army was eager to move, and Captain Kirby Smith wrote his wife that the move to the Rio Grande would likely occasion no conflict with the Mexicans. Instead, the army would simply wait in the new camp "until all difficulty is settled by negotiation between the two governments." Despite everyone's desire to be off, logistical difficulties dictated that it would be March before Taylor could get his army, now numbering some 3,550 officers and enlisted men, into motion.[1]

The early stages of the march were uneventful, with the only opposition coming from occasional scorpions and snakes, and from the climate itself, as the men endured hot and sometimes waterless marches. Kirby Smith nevertheless admired the scenery. He was charmed by the sight of the Nueces "winding through the prairie like a blue ribbon carelessly thrown on a green robe" and gave his wife a list of the different kinds of wildflowers he had seen. He had to admit, though, that the march was fatiguing.[2]

General Taylor suspected that he might encounter Mexican forces anywhere beyond a stream called the Arroyo Colorado, and he was proven right when late on the evening of March 19 a party of U.S. dragoons, scouting ahead of the army, reached the arroyo and saw Mexican cavalry on the other side. Neither party fired, but here were Mexican troops on land claimed by Texas—and now the United States—in hostile array that obviously portended an attempt to prevent the U.S. forces from crossing. Two Mexican cavalry officers appeared and announced through an interpreter that any U.S. crossing of the Arroyo Colorado would be viewed as a hostile act by the Mexicans.[3]

Taylor ordered the tail end of his column, some miles behind, to press on as rapidly as possible and move up to support the van in preparation for a battle. Contemplating what the morrow might bring, some of Taylor's men wrote farewell letters to their families that night, just in case. The following day, with his whole force on hand, Taylor deployed his army for battle. Then, at around 10:30 a.m., he sent the lead formation splashing through the shallow waters—about four feet deep and eighty yards wide. Four companies of infantry under the command of Captain C. F. Smith led the way, joined by General William J. Worth himself. A squadron of dragoons followed, and behind them the rest of the army. The Americans were keyed up in anticipation of a fight and, according to Kirby Smith, "eager for the game to begin." As the lead troops neared mid-stream, their comrades watching from the northern bank held their breath in silent anticipation of the first shot.[4]

It never came. The Mexican cavalry, clearly lacking heavier support, galloped a hasty retreat. Muttered curses registered the disappointment in the American ranks, but the men soon recovered their high spirits. As the head of the column arrived on the far bank of the arroyo, the men broke out in cheers and a band struck up "Yankee Doodle" and then "Garry Owen." The march went on, traversing a countryside covered with luxuriant grass, dotted with abundant wildflowers, interspersed with dense thickets of chaparral, and teeming with wildlife, including large herds of wild horses. An American officer noted that the fauna also included tarantulas, centipedes, and "uncommonly large" rattlesnakes.[5]

On March 28 Taylor's small army arrived on the north bank of the Rio Grande opposite the Mexican town of Matamoros. The river there was about one hundred yards wide, and on the far bank the Americans could see numerous sentinels and Mexican flags as well as the many civilians who had turned out for the arrival of the American army. Taylor had his men splice together several wagon tongues to form a makeshift flagpole, and on it they raised the Stars and Stripes while the army cheered and its bands played "Hail, Columbia" and "The Star-Spangled Banner." The Mexicans, soldier and civilian alike, watched silently from across the river.[6]

Taylor sent General Worth under flag of truce to confer with the local Mexican commander, General Francisco Mejia, but Mejia decided it was beneath his dignity to speak with one of Taylor's subordinates and instead had Worth meet with his own subordinate, General Rómulo Díaz de la Vega, at a location about twenty yards from the river, on the Mexican side, since he did not want any American officer to enter the town of Matamoros. The meeting was polite, but each side made clear that it considered the land between the Rio Grande and the Nueces to be its own. Worth demanded to see the U.S. consul in Matamoros, fearing for that official's freedom and safety. Díaz de la Vega refused, and Worth said he considered the refusal a belligerent act. He went on to state that Taylor would take any appearance of Mexican troops on the north bank of the Rio Grande as a hostile act, and with that the meeting ended.[7]

No hostile action followed in the immediate wake of the parley, but both sides went to work strengthening their positions. The Mexicans, who numbered some three thousand regular troops with twenty pieces of artillery, dug an emplacement for a heavy twelve-pounder cannon sited so that it could "rake the front face of the American camp" across the river. Taylor responded by positioning Captain James H. Duncan's battery of light six-pounders so that they could bombard Mejia's headquarters, and both sides busied themselves building redoubts and breastworks for their infantry. Taylor named the American earthwork Fort Texas, and kept about one thousand men busy working on it for three weeks. Meanwhile, he established a supply base at Point Isabel, near the mouth of the Rio Grande, naming it Fort Polk. The mood in Taylor's camp was one of supreme confidence and even eagerness to go ahead and attack Matamoros. "No one seems to think a disaster to our Army a thing possible," wrote an American officer in his diary.[8]

On April 11 the uneasy peace along the Rio Grande was shaken by the arrival in the Mexican camp of a new commander, General Pedro de Ampudia. The Mexican army at Matamoros received him with much "beating of drums and blowing of trumpets," an American officer recalled, and with a twenty-one-gun salute. A cruel man who had two years earlier had a man's head cut off and then fried in oil so as to preserve it for public display, Ampudia was eager for a showdown with the Americans. He began preparing his army for an April 15 assault on the U.S. position, and immediately dispatched a note to Taylor with an ultimatum: take his army back across the Nueces, starting within twenty-four hours, or suffer the consequences. Taylor politely refused to budge. Many junior officers in the U.S. force were delighted at the direction events were taking, eager as they were to trounce the Mexicans. A slightly more senior Kirby Smith noted soberly in a letter to his wife, "We are here neither in a state of Peace nor war."[9]

The day before Ampudia's planned assault, word reached the Mexican camp that Mexico City had dispatched General Mariano Arista to supersede Ampudia at Matamoros. The citizens of the Mexican town had sent an appeal to President Paredes, asking that the brutal Ampudia not be left in supreme command of their district, and the president had complied. Hearing that Arista was on his way, Ampudia tried to persuade

Taylor's Army of Occupation

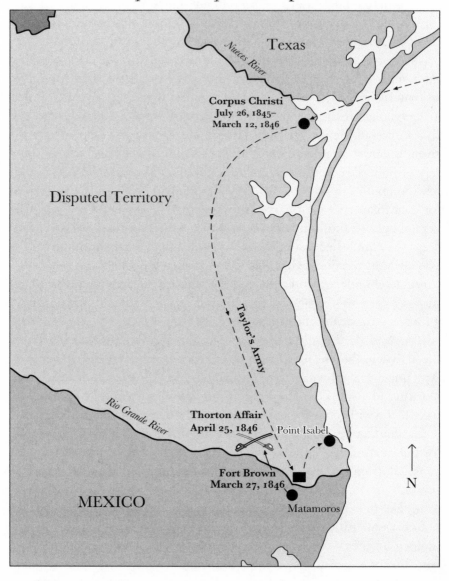

his subordinate officers at Matamoros to agree to attack the Americans without authorization from Mexico City, but the Mexican officers refused. Thwarted, Ampudia had to wait peacefully for Arista's arrival and then serve under his orders.[10]

Yet all was not quite peaceful along the lower Rio Grande. On April 9, Taylor's quartermaster officer Colonel Truman Cross had gone missing. Cross had last been seen riding his horse out of camp on routine business that would have taken him about three miles away. When he did not return by nightfall, his comrades became alarmed. Mexican guerrillas, known as *rancheros,* had been seen lurking in the area, and the Americans suspected the worst. Taylor sent a note across the river to Ampudia, asking if his men had knowledge of the American officer's fate, but the Mexican general, who, according to one account, was at that moment wearing Cross's watch, claimed to know nothing of the matter. A few days later *rancheros* ambushed a U.S. patrol that was searching for Cross, killing its commander, Lieutenant Theodoric Porter, after a sharp fight in which Porter succeeded in downing three of his assailants. Two other Americans died in the engagement. Another patrol found Cross's remains, about four miles from the American camp. His wounds indicated that he had been killed with a lance, a favorite weapon of mounted Mexicans. The U.S. camp seethed with desire to avenge the deaths.[11]

Arista himself was no more inclined to accept the status quo along the Rio Grande than Ampudia had been. On April 23 he ordered General Anastacio Torrejón with sixteen hundred cavalry to cross the Rio Grande upstream from Taylor's camp, implicitly threatening the U.S. line of communications. To monitor this menacing movement, Taylor dispatched Captain Seth Thornton with a patrol of sixty-three dragoons. U.S. Army dragoons may have been fairly tough characters, but they were not quite equal to 24 to 1 odds. Nor was Thornton, as it turned out, equal to his Mexican opponent in cunning. He rode into an ambush that got sixteen of his men killed or wounded and the rest, including himself, captured. On April 26, Taylor wrote to Washington, "Hostilities may now be considered as commenced."[12]

Back in Washington, Polk had already been contemplating asking Congress for a declaration of war as a response to Mexico's complete rebuff of Slidell. Some newspapers were clamoring that the national honor be upheld in the matter. An example was *The St. Louis Republican,* which urged the country "not to suffer so open an insult to her representative to pass unnoticed." Other newspapers, such as the Whig *Washington Daily National Intelligencer,* criticized Polk for sending Taylor's force into too much danger along the Rio Grande. The *Intelligencer* pointed out that Mexico's regular army was larger than that of the United States and, with the southern republic's turbulent recent past, its soldiers were more experienced in combat. "The danger of our little army is confessed," wrote the Whig editor, who went on to complain that Taylor's force was "almost a forlorn hope."[13]

Polk was undeterred and increasingly convinced that he would have to take firm measures with Mexico. On May 5 he learned of Ampudia's ultimatum, and three days later Slidell arrived back in Washington, affirming that it was no use attempting to negotiate with the Mexicans and suggesting that war was the only remedy. Tense days followed in Washington. The next day, Saturday, May 9, Polk and his cabinet held an earnest consultation. All agreed that any act of Mexican aggression would be immediate cause for war. The president and all but one member of the cabinet believed the present situation was intolerable, that the country already had ample grounds for war against Mexico, and that the president ought to call on Congress for a declaration. Polk contemplated sending such a message to the other end of Pennsylvania Avenue the following Tuesday, and before the cabinet meeting adjourned at two o'clock that afternoon, he directed the secretaries of state and war to assemble and have copied all of the documents pertinent to U.S. attempts to bring about a peaceful settlement with Mexico, so that the president could transmit the copies to Congress along with his war message.[14]

At six o'clock that evening the adjutant general of the army stopped by the White House with Taylor's April 26 dispatch notifying the government of the commencement of hostilities with the attack on Thornton's reconnaissance. "American blood has been shed on American soil!" trumpeted the evening edition of the Democratic *Washington Union*. Around the country other papers were spreading the news. *The New Orleans Commercial Bulletin* had already run a report of the Mexican attack, along with word of Taylor's appeal to the governor of Texas for the aid of volunteers from that state. By May 12 *The Raleigh Register* was proclaiming in the capital of North Carolina, "War Actually Commenced with Mexico."[15]

Polk's choice had been made for him. On Monday, May 11, Polk sent his war message to Congress. It recounted the "grievous wrongs perpetrated upon our citizens throughout a long period of years," noted Mexico's complete intransigence against any possibility of a negotiated settlement, formally announced to the two houses the recent news of the outbreak of fighting on the U.S. side of the Rio Grande, and asked for a declaration of war. After brief debate the House adopted such a declaration by a vote of 173–14. The Senate, as was its wont, took somewhat more time for bloviation, and then concurred with the House by an even more lopsided vote of 40–2. Congress also appropriated $10 million for the war and authorized the president to augment the regular army by calling on the states for fifty thousand volunteers. The American people received the news, by and large, with enthusiasm. War rallies in major cities drew huge crowds—twenty thousand in Philadelphia, more in New

York—while *The New York Herald* exulted that the conflict now beginning would "lay the foundation of a new age, a new destiny, affecting both this continent and the old continent of Europe."[16]

Recruitment surged all across the country. On May 7 the citizens of Natchez, Mississippi, held a meeting for the purpose of raising a company of volunteers for the war and quickly had the necessary recruits. Other companies organized elsewhere around the state. Mississippi congressman Jefferson Davis, a West Point graduate and veteran of seven years in the regular army, let it be known that he would be willing to accept the colonelcy of the Mississippi regiment if its soldiers should elect him to that post. Meanwhile, New Orleans had a company ready to go by May 3 and soon had a full regiment of volunteers, then several more. The Louisiana legislature passed an appropriation of $100,000 for raising volunteers in the state, and one thousand miles away the Michigan legislature did the same. Even the thoroughly Whiggish and antiannexationist *Cleveland Herald* urged its readers, "Now that war is begun . . . every American citizen must stand by his country and hold himself ready to fight its battles." By May 19 enlistment had gone so well that the secretary of war was obliged to turn down the offer of an eager Pennsylvania company, the Duquesne Grays, because that state's quota had been filled.[17]

Back on the Rio Grande, Taylor worried about the obvious threat to his supply lines posed by Torrejón's presence on the American side of the river. The Mexican cavalry was across the Rio Grande; the Mexican infantry might not be far behind. Taylor's supply base at Point Isabel, on the Gulf, was not secure against such threats, and the American general determined to make it so. Leaving the Seventh Infantry and two batteries of artillery—about five hundred men in all—with supplies enough to stand a two-week siege in Fort Texas under the command of Major Jacob Brown, Taylor took the rest of his army and on May 1 set out for Point Isabel.[18]

Old Rough and Ready's hunch proved sound, for on that same day Arista left General Mejia with a garrison at Matamoros and set out with the rest of his own army, now reinforced to about six thousand men, for a downstream crossing of the Rio Grande, whence he hoped to link up with Torrejón in Taylor's rear, completely severing the U.S. line of supply. All he had to do was get his main body in between Taylor and the coast.[19]

Arista's bid failed. His river crossing was a clumsy affair, with insufficient boats available. Meanwhile, Taylor's tough regulars legged it almost thirty miles over rough country in less than twenty-four hours to reach Point Isabel about midday, May 2. Learning that he had missed his quarry, Arista revised his plan. He would now take position between Taylor and Fort Texas. The sound of Mejia's guns bombarding the U.S. garrison there would bring Taylor hurrying back from the coast—and into the path of Arista's army. With twofold numerical superiority, the Mexican general felt confident of victory.[20]

Back at Fort Texas all had been quiet until the evening of May 2, when the garrison had heard the church bells of Matamoros ringing and had looked over their parapets to see a procession of priests and monks making the rounds of the Mexican works, blessing each cannon in turn. This ominous portent was fulfilled the next morning when those guns opened fire on the American fort. The bombardment did not prove very lethal. The chief engineer, Captain Joseph K. F. Mansfield, himself a member of the garrison, had designed the earthen ramparts skillfully, and they stood up well to the Mexican twelve-pounders. Still, the thumping of cannon aimed at them tried the men's nerves. No one could have been better suited to hold them to their task than the Seventh's commanding officer, Major Jacob Brown, a thirty-four-year veteran who had enlisted as a private in the Eleventh U.S. Infantry at the outbreak of the War of 1812. By the end of that conflict he had risen to the rank of second lieutenant, and shortly thereafter he transferred to the Seventh, which had recently won its proud nickname, the Cotton Balers, by its stubborn defense of Andrew Jackson's cotton-bale ramparts at the 1815 Battle of New Orleans. Now he would command the Seventh in its defense of the earthen ramparts of Fort Texas, though his men generally did not know the name of the fort.[21]

From where Taylor was with the main army at Point Isabel, the sound of the guns at Matamoros was clearly audible, but the general was in no hurry. Confident that Brown and the Seventh could hold Fort Texas, he put his army to work loading every supply wagon it had as well as strengthening Fort Polk. "We continue to hear the cannonading," wrote Major Philip Barbour of the Third Infantry, "which is the best proof that the Fort has not fallen."[22]

To check on the state of affairs back on the Rio Grande, Taylor turned to the only volunteer unit in his army, Captain Samuel Walker's company of Texas Rangers. Walker had fought Mexicans before, as part of a Texas expedition against the Mexican town of Mier in 1842. Captured along with all of his comrades in that ill-fated expedition, Walker had escaped from his prison near Mexico City and walked to the coast at

Tampico, whence he escaped by ship back to Texas. To Walker and his men, who had recently been tangling with the *rancheros,* went the assignment of finding a way through Mexican lines into Fort Texas and then returning through the same dangers to bring word to Taylor. Taking only a few handpicked members of his company, Walker successfully penetrated the Mexican encirclement, killing five Mexican pickets in doing so. He reached Fort Texas, and returned to Point Isabel on May 5 with mail from the garrison and word for Taylor that the fort was holding well. Only one man had been killed by the Mexican bombardment, and the U.S. artillerists had silenced the two Mexican twelve-pounders, the enemy's heaviest guns.[23]

Inside the fort spirits were high. The only casualty had come on Sunday morning, May 3, about half an hour after the bombardment had started. A piece of shell had struck a soldier in the head, killing him instantly and sending his body toppling down the slope of the fortifications. A sergeant in the dead man's company, recognizing on the corpse the auburn hair of one of his men, called out to the captain, "Shea is killed, sir." Whereupon the reply came from another direction, "No, sir, I ain't." The unfortunate soldier was in fact a Sergeant Weigart. Comrades carried his body to the hospital tent inside the fort, and about an hour later another Mexican shell found the tent, entirely removing poor Weigart's head but doing no injury to anyone else—"as if they had a special spite against that particular man," one of the officers of the Seventh later recalled.[24]

As bombardment continued from that day into a second—the day Walker had arrived—and then into a third, the men were amazed and delighted by the absence of casualties. On the third day, May 5, the shelling was the heaviest yet. On that morning a shell struck Major Brown, tearing off his leg below the knee. Surgeons performed a proper amputation, and the major clung to life. Since the hospital tent was clearly no safe place, his men took him to the fort's magazine bunker, but the heat in that enclosed chamber aggravated his raging fever, and on May 9 he died. His regiment would miss him. "He was a perfect bulldog for the fight," lamented one of his officers.[25]

On the afternoon of the day Brown was wounded, the Mexicans sent in a demand for the fort's surrender. Captain Edgar S. Hawkins, now in command, called a council of his officers; the unanimous decision was to refuse, and some of the officers were contemptuous of Hawkins for even putting such a question to them. That night the Americans expected a Mexican assault. The troops were excited—feeling insulted at the suggestion of surrender and eager to come to grips with the Mexicans. They rested on their arms throughout the night, but daylight came on May 6 without any Mexican attack.[26]

On May 7 the Mexican shelling was even heavier and much more accurate than the previous three days' relatively ineffective fire. Shells scoured the inside of the fort. One burst at the feet of a corporal, another rolled over a soldier's back before bursting, while yet another rolled between the legs of a soldier seated to eat his dinner and exploded. All three men were unharmed. So too were several clusters of soldiers into which shells fell and exploded. So was Captain Hawkins when a shell passed through his tent just above his head while he was eating breakfast. Several more tents were holed, and fifteen horses killed. A shell scored a direct hit on the trunk containing the equipment of the regimental band, sending broken instruments flying in all directions, but not a single man was hurt. "A kind Providence kept us safe," wrote Lieutenant Dana.[27]

That same day, at three o'clock in the afternoon, Taylor's army left Point Isabel, marching to the relief of Fort Texas. His general orders to the army anticipated the likelihood of battle and "enjoin[ed] upon the battalions of Infantry that their main dependence must be in the bayonet." They covered seven miles of difficult sandy road before camping for the night, and the next day they had plodded another eleven across the monotonous plain before encountering what they had been expecting ever since leaving the coast. Near a pond named Palo Alto, Arista's army was arrayed in line of battle a mile long, squarely across their path.[28]

In the coming fight the onus of attacking would rest on Taylor, who had to relieve his garrison at Fort Texas. Arista had the luxury of being able to stand on ground of his own choosing and make the Americans come to him, enjoying the age-old advantage that a defender always holds over an attacker—as well as a twofold superiority in numbers. Indeed, this had been a key consideration for Arista in deciding to attack Fort Texas. Such a situation would all but compel Taylor to do exactly what he was now doing—rush back to the relief of his garrison—and the flat plain around Palo Alto offered just the sort of strong defensive position from which Arista's army could halt and defeat Taylor. As Taylor's army advanced toward Arista's position, the American officers had to admire the skill with which the Mexican army was deployed, its flanks solidly anchored on dense woods.[29]

The U.S. forces deployed quickly through the thick chaparral on either side of the road, forming a line of battle opposite the Mexicans. Taylor placed his flying batteries (the U.S. Army's mobile light field

The Battle of Palo Alto, May 8, 1846

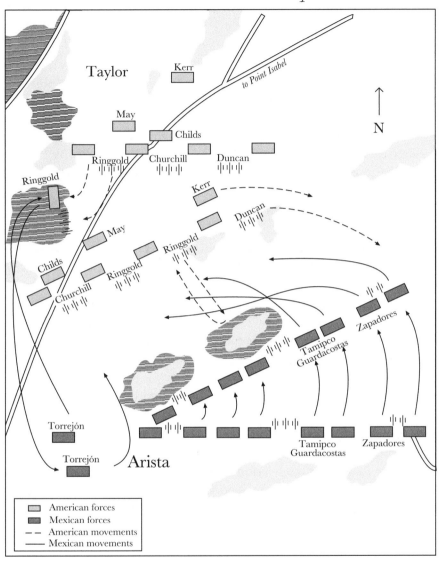

artillery) at either end of his line and his heavy eighteen-pounders on the road in the center. At a range of seven hundred yards, the Mexican artillery opened fire, their round shot bouncing and rolling across the field, kicking up dust but doing little execution in U.S. ranks, where Taylor's soldiers were sometimes able to spot the oncoming cannonballs and dodge out of their path. The well-drilled U.S. troops continued their deployment without confusion despite the incoming artillery fire. In reply, Taylor advanced his artillery in front of the line, and the U.S. guns opened a steady, methodical bombardment. Unlike their Mexican counterparts, the American gunners had exploding shells. The U.S. artillery officers were highly trained professionals, all having graduated in the upper half of their West Point classes. The U.S. batteries were also highly mobile, their personnel all mounted, so that they could move rapidly from point to point on the battlefield. The American gunners pounded the Mexican lines mercilessly.[30]

Now it was Arista who faced a predicament. His army was steadily taking casualties while his own artillery's attempts to reply were proving ineffective. An advance by his infantry through the thick brush of the chaparral would likely result in his troops becoming disorganized and ineffective, the very problem that he had hoped to pose for Taylor in choosing this ground. So Arista opted for a cavalry charge instead. He sent Torrejón's horsemen galloping toward the U.S. left, bent on taking some of the cannon that had been tormenting them.[31]

The guns tore into the charging column, and the supporting infantry on the American left, the Fifth U.S. Infantry Regiment, stood firm in support. As the Mexican lancers bore down on them, the well-drilled foot soldiers, following smartly their officers' commands, changed their formation to a hollow square, the standard infantry response to a cavalry charge. On all four of the square's faces, each front-rank soldier dropped to one knee, holding his musket with its butt on the ground at his side and its bayonet extending up and out at an angle of about forty-five degrees. Behind this bristling row of bayonets, the second rank volleyed into the faces of the oncoming horsemen, and nearby artillerists could dash into the square for shelter after loosing their final blasts of canister into the attackers. As long as they remained steadfast, infantrymen in a square were all but immune to the finest cavalry on the planet, and the Fifth Infantry proved very steadfast on this day. The bloodied Mexican cavalry streamed back toward their own lines in retreat.[32]

After a brief pause, Arista ordered them forward again. American cannon and muskets emptied more saddles. Again the U.S. line proved solid, and the mounted soldiers made their retreat even more quickly than they had before. Then the chaparral caught fire, the dry grass under the brush burning fast. Smoke blinded both armies, and flames killed some of the wounded Mexicans lying between the lines. As soon as visibility permitted, Taylor sent some of his dragoons on a ride to reach the Mexican wagon train, but Mexican cavalry intercepted them and drove them back.[33]

Stepping up the pressure still more, Taylor moved the right wing of his line forward. Mexican artillery struck at the troops. In the ranks of the Fourth U.S. Infantry, a cannonball decapitated a soldier before slamming into the jaw of Captain John Page, and the explosion of gore knocked down several men standing nearby. Still, the American line held steady, and the pressure on Arista's ranks mounted. Finally, with his soldiers' morale beginning to crumble under the daylong punishment of the American guns, Arista ordered a retreat, and his army withdrew in good order.[34]

The Americans held the field. Their casualties totaled four dead and forty-two wounded, while the Mexicans had left more than five hundred of their dead on the field. Yet Arista, who had pulled back only a short distance, still blocked Taylor's route to Fort Texas. Among the American dead was Major Samuel Ringgold, shot just as the fighting was coming to a close. Ringgold was the father of the U.S. Army's mobile light field artillery—the "flying artillery," as it was called—which had been the major factor in the victory at Palo Alto.[35]

In Fort Texas, between blasts of the Mexican guns on the south bank of the river, the garrison heard in the distance that day the sounds of artillery. The men of the garrison knew that Taylor's army was engaged, and they guessed that it must be taking place about six miles away. As night fell and the army did not appear, they wondered why Taylor waited, and some whispered of the possibility that he might have been defeated and turned back.[36]

The next morning, May 9, Taylor called a council of war of his senior officers. Of the ten senior officers present, seven advised that the army should stay where it was, entrench, and await reinforcements, leaving the garrison of Fort Texas to hold out as best it could. Taylor was unmoved. "Gentlemen," he concluded, "you will prepare your commands to move forward."[37]

They advanced along the road toward Fort Texas and found Arista and his army another six miles closer to Matamoros. The Mexican general had chosen an even stronger defensive position—a deep but dry meander scar of the Rio Grande called Resaca de la Palma. Here the chaparral was much thicker than at Palo Alto, dense and high enough to deprive the deadly American gunners of a useful field of fire. Arista's line was long, but the important sector was in the center, flanking the Matamoros road, and there Arista placed his best troops. With the artillery's effectiveness reduced, the battle degenerated into a confused brawl.

Taylor deployed the Eighth and Fifth Infantry regiments to the left of

The Battle of Resaca de la Palma, May 9, 1846

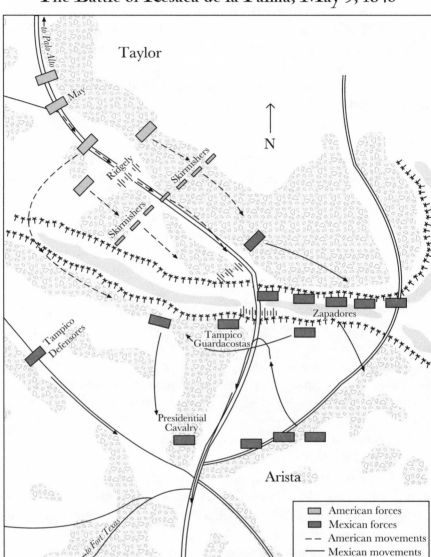

the road and perpendicular to it, with the Third and Fourth Infantry regiments extending the same line to the right. Then he ordered the line to advance. The two regiments on the left quickly became engaged in an ugly close-range battle among the thick foliage.[38]

Small parties of Americans and Mexicans stumbled into each other in the chaparral. The Fifth Infantry's commander, Lieutenant Colonel James S. McIntosh, another of the army's doughty veterans of the War of 1812 and one of the three senior officers who had favored action in the council of war that morning, emerged from some brush to find himself in the midst of six Mexicans, who immediately lunged at him. Two of them thrust their bayonets toward his mouth. The sixty-two-year-old McIntosh was able to shove one of the weapons back, but the other broke several of his teeth and drove through his mouth and out the back of his neck. Leaving the bleeding officer on the ground for dead, the Mexicans turned to a U.S. soldier who emerged from the brush thirty feet away. After shooting him, they beat his head in with the butt of a musket. McIntosh played possum until the Mexicans moved on, then made his escape. Another U.S. officer met him and asked what he could do for him. "Give me some water and show me my regiment," growled the indomitable McIntosh.[39]

Taylor advanced a battery of his artillery to soften up the enemy center. Mexican lancers burst out of the chaparral so near that the battery appeared doomed, and the artillerymen prepared to fight for their guns with handspikes and rammer staffs. Before it came to that, a final blast from their cannon, delivered at point-blank range, turned the horsemen back.[40]

Taylor quickly went over to the offensive, launching a mounted charge of his own. He sent Captain Charles May and a company of dragoons galloping straight up the road in column-of-fours. They got in among the guns but, with Mexican troops converging on them from all sides, could not stay there and had to return as quickly as they had advanced.[41]

Taylor then turned to Colonel Belknap of the Eighth Infantry and ordered him to take those guns and keep them. The foot soldiers did so, and in the bargain they also broke the center of the Mexican line, capturing the Mexican artillery and General Rómulo Díaz de la Vega at the same time. In a desperate attempt to recoup the rapidly deteriorating situation, Arista personally led a last charge by his lancers, but the battle was now lost for him beyond remedy. He shortly recognized that fact and broke off his doomed attack. As the lancers began to fall back, the American troops grasped that the day was theirs. "A deafening shout of triumph went up from the whole of our line," wrote an American officer.[42]

When Arista's troops on either wing witnessed the defeat of the center, their already shaky morale collapsed. The army disintegrated into a mass of individuals fleeing for life and freedom. "The pursuit now commenced," recalled Captain Philip Barbour, "and on we went, Dragoons, Artillery and Infantry in one mass at full run, yelling at every step." In

Fort Texas, about three miles from the battlefield, the American defenders who had listened to the sounds of the distant battle this day and the previous one now saw swarms of fleeing Mexican soldiers emerging from the chaparral at a run, having thrown away their weapons to speed their escape. The fort's guns opened up on the fugitives, and from the chaparral behind them U.S. dragoons and "flying artillery," having outpaced the infantry, soon emerged in pursuit.[43]

The defeated Mexicans' flight carried them all the way to the Rio Grande, where, rather than await the tiny ferry boat, thousands plunged into the river and attempted to swim to the Mexican shore. One officer in the pursuing U.S. forces estimated that as many as three hundred drowned. Taylor reported that his men later buried two hundred Mexicans on the battlefield and estimated that another one hundred escaped burial, lost in the chaparral. Approximately one hundred prisoners remained in U.S. hands, including the hapless General Díaz de la Vega, while hundreds of Mexican soldiers melted away into the chaparral to find their way home as best they could. Taylor's troops also captured seven cannon and three stands of colors, numerous small arms, and all of the Mexican baggage and ammunition wagons. U.S. casualties for Resaca de la Palma totaled thirty dead and seventy-one wounded.[44]

As the last of the Mexicans made their way across the river, the American dragoons rode up to Fort Texas, swinging their caps over their heads in triumph. The five hundred men of the garrison had heard the sounds of cannon again at about three o'clock that afternoon, and this time they also heard the crackle of musketry. Best of all, the noise of battle was steadily drawing perceptibly closer. Off-duty men left their bomb shelters and lined the parapet, ignoring the Mexican guns that still boomed in Matamoros. As the dragoons galloped up to the walls, the garrison broke out in wild cheers, tossing their caps into the air. "You might have heard the cheers two miles," thought Lieutenant Dana.[45]

Major Brown and Sergeant Weigart were the only American fatalities of the nine-day siege. Two more soldiers had been wounded in the last two days before their relief, but American officers were amazed at the lightness of their casualties. Taylor ordered the fort renamed Fort Brown, in honor of its fallen commander. In later years a town would grow up around the old fort and take the name Brownsville. Meanwhile, on the evening of the day of Resaca de la Palma and the fort's relief, Taylor wrote his report to the authorities back in Washington: "Our victory has been complete."[46]

CHAPTER ELEVEN

The Monterrey Campaign

EVEN BEFORE THE NEWS of Palo Alto and Resaca de la Palma arrived, the rest of the country, with a few exceptions, rallied enthusiastically to the American cause. Tens of thousands hurried to enlist in the new volunteer regiments being raised in most states, while Congress with surprisingly little debate authorized the raising of more than twice as many troops as Polk had originally envisioned, some fifty thousand in all.

A few voices were raised in opposition to the war, and these mostly belonged to abolitionists, who saw in the conflict a conspiracy of the slave power to add more territory to the southern states and thus to spread the domain and increase the power of slavery. Henry David Thoreau refused to pay his taxes that summer, because he said he disagreed with slavery and the war with Mexico. After a night in the Concord jail, Thoreau went free when his aunt paid his taxes. Other abolitionists forbore such quixotic action but denounced the war as an unjust expansion of slavery.

Still, even people who opposed slavery could see in the war with Mexico not a campaign to spread slavery but a fulfillment of America's Manifest Destiny to overspread the continent and increase the domain of ordered, constitutional liberty. If the American system of government was not yet perfect, if, for example, it countenanced slavery in some places, it could be improved at some future date. At this point, vocal opposition to the war tended to be limited to those for whom immediate abolition of slavery had become the only political issue of import. The vast majority of Americans enthusiastically supported the war.

The public mood being what it most obviously was, even the Whigs were, for the moment, a truly loyal opposition, and only a few of them ventured an occasional potshot at the Polk administration on the way to supporting, willingly or expediently, the war appropriation. Some Whigs might have harbored quiet objections to the war—or might have said later that they had done so—but for the time being the path of political expediency suggested caution in such matters.[1]

One Whig who was not so easy for Polk to get along with even during these early days of the war was the ranking general of the U.S. Army, Winfield Scott. Already a legend, the sixty-year-old Scott had been a general since 1812. He had led troops brilliantly in the bloodiest battles of the war that began in that year and in virtually every one of the army's operations since. Six feet five inches tall and of hulking frame, Scott had a commanding presence. By personality he was bombastic, overbearing, and, like many great generals, self-confident to the point of conceit. He was also a Whig. That party's authoritarian, antidemocratic strain seemed to appeal to men who wore shoulder straps, including Zachary Taylor and most of the other senior generals in the U.S. Army. Unlike Taylor and many of his brother officers, Scott was fairly openly nursing presidential ambitions. If anything else was needed to assure tense relations with Polk, Scott supplied it regularly with his tactless criticisms of the president and his party, some of which naturally found their way to Polk.[2]

At the outbreak of war, Polk had thought that he would not be able to escape the necessity of giving Scott field command of the army, of which he had been the ranking general for the past five years, and he directed Scott to assume that position. Then circumstances conspired to open another opportunity. Scott was slow to leave Washington, and while the general lingered, Polk learned of another of his insulting comments. Then in late May news reached Washington of Taylor's victories at Palo Alto and Resaca de la Palma. It would hardly do now to replace the newly victorious general in the field, who was also the obvious candidate for the one additional opening Congress had lately authorized at the rank of major general—the same rank Scott held. Accordingly, Taylor got the promotion and kept the field command, and Scott received orders to remain in the capital handling rear-echelon duties.[3]

While such decisions were being made in Washington, Taylor proceeded to occupy the town of Matamoros without resistance. He maintained strict discipline among his troops and insisted that they refrain from robbing or mistreating Mexican civilians. Indeed, U.S. quartermasters paid top prices for local Mexican produce. But while Taylor's orders strictly protected private property, public property was another matter. In keeping with the laws of war, all public property in Matamoros was the rightful spoil of the American conquerors. Much to the delight of Taylor's soldiers, public property included all large stocks of tobacco, since that commodity was by Mexican law a government monopoly. The Americans cheerfully confiscated all they found. Both tobacco stockpiles and large amounts of weapons and ammunition turned out to be hidden in private buildings and churches throughout the town, and, as an American officer noted, "wherever public property is found secreted in a house, the house and all in it is condemned."[4]

Taylor was soon to discover that, at least during this interlude of the war, his chief problem was not the Mexicans but the volunteer troops who were beginning to arrive in south Texas in large numbers—larger numbers, in fact, than Taylor had wanted or could conveniently accommodate for the time being. The volunteers were poorly disciplined and contained at least a leavening of riffraff—or men who were prepared to become all manner of criminals if they thought they saw the opportunity, which they did in the docile civilian population around them. The problem was exacerbated by the fact that supplies were scarce, and the men sometimes had at least the excuse of hunger for their plundering. Some of their acts, however, were crimes against persons, for which there could be no shadow of an excuse. Taylor had to use his regulars to police the bad tendencies of the citizen-soldiers.[5]

A further problem with the volunteers was the length of their enlistments. Some had signed up before Congress had authorized one-year enlistments and thus could be held only to the constitutional standard ninety-day terms. This was scarcely time to organize them and ship them to the mouth of the Rio Grande, leaving no time at all for useful service. Yet most of them, having tasted the inconveniences of army life as well as the heat of south Texas, would not reenlist. They were pure deadweight to the army, so much baggage that had to be hauled from New Orleans to Point Isabel and back—and fed and watched all the while.[6]

The Texas volunteers presented their own set of problems, in some ways the same and in others quite different from those posed by the volunteers from the older states. They had been in a state of war with Mexico, of varying intensity, for the past decade. The Mexicans had introduced the concept of giving no quarter into the conflict at the outset with the massacres at the Alamo and Goliad. The Texans had not been especially eager to take prisoners at San Jacinto, and since then the level of humanity in the contest had remained low to nonexistent. In the 1842 Mier Expedition 176 hapless Texans surrendered in that Rio Grande Valley town after an unsuccessful raid across the river. Santa Anna wanted to have them all killed but gave in to international pressure and had only every tenth man shot and the others put to hard labor for a year and a half.

In unnumbered smaller encounters and raids on both sides of the Rio

Grande, Texans and Mexicans had met in almost primal combat in which the taking of prisoners was exceptional. Even as Taylor had waited for the Mexican response to his presence on the Rio Grande, his Texas scouts had been engaged in a low-grade conflict with the Mexican *rancheros,* as small parties met, skirmished, and occasionally died at a distance from the main armies. Quarter was neither asked nor given. As the Texans advanced with the army into Mexico proper, they had a propensity to think in terms of settling scores, both with individual Mexicans whom they chanced to recognize from previous unpleasant encounters and sometimes with the whole Mexican nation. Taylor and his regulars would do what they could to restrain them.[7]

Polk's strategy was to seize those parts of northern Mexico that seemed most desirable for annexation to the United States and to pressure the Mexican government to an agreement by occupying the next tier of provinces as bargaining chips. In pursuit of these goals, at the outset of the war he ordered Brigadier General Stephen W. Kearny to lead an expedition from Fort Leavenworth, Kansas, along the Santa Fe Trail to the town of that name, taking control of New Mexico. Then, if possible, Kearny was to continue westward to California. Meanwhile, Commodore John D. Sloat's Pacific Squadron of the U.S. Navy would seize the ports of California and be ready to cooperate with Kearny in completing the acquisition of that province. Polk assigned Brigadier General John E. Wool to put together an army of volunteers at San Antonio, Texas, and, with Taylor's approval, march into Mexico and occupy the town of Chihuahua, a provincial capital and trading center.[8]

Kearny was a savvy and experienced officer. Born in New Jersey in 1794, he had served as a young officer in the War of 1812, alongside fellow officers John Wool and Winfield Scott, and had been wounded and recognized for conspicuous gallantry. After the war he participated in exploring expeditions on the Yellowstone River and served at various frontier posts and in the army's periodic clashes with the American Indians. He had become executive officer of the First U.S. Dragoon Regiment upon its organization in 1833 and had taken a leading role in the training and development of the regular army's first regiment of horse soldiers. In 1836 Kearny had succeeded to the colonelcy of the First Dragoons, a position he had held for a decade by the time the Mexican War broke out. Along with his orders for the cross-plains expedition had come a promotion to brevet brigadier general.[9]

Kearny would take 420 men of his own First U.S. Dragoons, a battalion of artillery numbering 220, another small battalion of volunteer Missouri infantry counting just over 150 in its ranks, and more than 800 men of Colonel Alexander Doniphan's First Missouri Mounted Volunteers. Kearny's dragoons were hardened professionals, but the Missourians were completely unaccustomed to military discipline and accepted little. Still, they were tough and resourceful frontiersmen who respected both Kearny and Doniphan. The latter was himself a strong man—perhaps six feet six inches in height and weighing more than 240 pounds. More important, he was a strong leader, though without military training. Kearny would have preferred that the Missourians serve as infantry rather than as horse soldiers, both because infantry usually fought harder than cavalry and because foot soldiers were easier to supply. But most Missourians preferred to ride than to walk—though they found it a great nuisance to have to carry sabers—and Kearny had to take what he could get.[10]

In all, Kearny's force would include 1,659 men, sixteen pieces of artillery, more than four thousand horses and mules, and fifteen thousand cattle and oxen. Kearny was familiar with the plains from his previous service as colonel of the First Dragoons and realized that neither the grass nor the water sources along the Santa Fe Trail could support a mass of this size. So he moved his force in a series of small detachments until it reached the ample sources of water and grass at Bent's Fort, on the Arkansas River near the modern-day site of La Junta, in southeastern Colorado.[11]

Kearny's men made the 650-mile trip to Bent's Fort during the early summer of 1846. They left Fort Leavenworth in late June, following the Santa Fe Trail and finding it as clear and easy to follow as any dirt road in America. Many of the men thought the plains had a charm all their own. "We passed through the most beautiful country I ever beheld," one of them wrote. "The tall grass would be ruffled by the gentle breeze until you imagine it was the rising waves of the ocean." Others also commented on the beauty of this great ocean of grass, and lest the endless prairie should grow monotonous, the Great Plains weather provided plenty of variety. Blazing sunshine and parching heat could sometimes give way to violent thunderstorms almost as quickly as the cloud shadows chased one another across the prairie swells.[12]

The Missourians of Doniphan's regiment, most of them on the plains for the first time in their lives, marveled at the enormous herds of buffalo they passed, and dined on buffalo steak as a welcome relief from their steady diet of salt pork and hardtack. Prairie dog towns were also fascinating, and some of the soldiers tried unsuccessfully to shoot or catch the elusive but seemingly innumerable rodents. Less welcome were the swarms of mosquitoes that plagued the men day and night. One officer noted that at times the mosquitoes were so numerous "as to make it almost impracticable for a horseman to travel alone"; another officer recorded in his journal that at night the bothersome insects were "literally swarming in our tents." The men also shuddered at their first experience of cooking over fires made of buffalo chips, when they could find no wood. "The smell of the smoke is not agreeable," wrote a Missourian, and some of the men decided they preferred to go without cook fires.[13]

As many Santa Fe traders before them had done, some of the soldiers stopped to carve their names in the soft sandstone of thirty-foot-high Pawnee Rock, a prominent landmark along the trail about three hundred miles from Fort Leavenworth. Others just admired the outcrop as they marched by. By the time they reached Bent's Fort in late July, the long trip across the plains had helped put at least a modicum of discipline into the raw Missouri recruits. They needed it. One regular officer wrote to his wife, "But for the example set by the regulars I verily believe the volunteers would not reach Santa Fe."[14]

From Bent's Fort, Kearny sent messages ahead summoning New Mexico governor Manuel Armijo to surrender, but Armijo refused. Word had it that he was mustering his forces for the defense of the province. Kearny proceeded on. As his men marched and rode southwestward from Bent's Fort, they could see the twin volcanic mountains known as the Spanish Peaks, outliers of the Sangre de Cristo Mountains, away off on the right. Beyond those rose what one of Kearny's men referred to as "the blue ridges and peaks of the Rocky Mountains." Ahead was a spur of the Rockies through which Kearny's army had to pass, laboring through the difficult Raton Pass and sometimes having to haul their supply wagons up the steep slopes by long ropes and lower them down the other side in the same manner. The men were not too preoccupied with the toils of their journey or the prospect of battle to fail to note the wonders of the country through which they were marching. "The whole range of the Rocky Mountains with their snow clad summits [is] in full view," enthused one of the Missourians, who noted a few days later herds of seventy or eighty antelope "skimming across the prairie."[15]

After descending into New Mexico, Kearny's troops covered the final reaches of the Santa Fe Trail. At settlements along the way Kearny made lengthy speeches to the inhabitants, announcing that they would be respected in their religion and their peaceful vocations and would even be accorded citizenship. His goal was to gain New Mexico without bloodshed, and in that he was successful. Armijo, though possessing more or less comparable numbers and significant advantages of terrain, apparently strove to live up to his motto, "It is better to be thought brave than to be so." The Americans had to traverse narrow mountain passes where a few determined men could have stood off an army, and at one such defile they anxiously anticipated a fight, but Armijo never made a stand.[16]

Kearny's troops marched and rode into Santa Fe unopposed on August 18, 1846, having covered another 250 miles since leaving Bent's Fort. They raised the Stars and Stripes over the governor's house and fired a thirteen-gun salute. Kearny issued a general order, formally annexing New Mexico to the United States. And so, noted one of the Missourians in his journal, "after a journey of 1,000 miles we still find ourselves inside the limits of our widely extended Union."[17]

The inhabited portion of New Mexico consisted of a narrow strip of settlements centered on the capital of Santa Fe and extending up and down the Rio Grande. The region's population was some forty thousand, of whom perhaps a quarter were Indians. Texas claimed all lands to the east of the Rio Grande, including Santa Fe itself, on the basis of the 1836 Treaty of Velasco, which Santa Anna had signed soon after his atrocities at the Alamo and Goliad and the Mexican government had refused to ratify. Yet the Texans had had difficulty in making good their claims. An 1841 foray into New Mexico ended with the capture of more than two hundred Texans, who were brutally treated while in Mexican captivity. Nevertheless, the New Mexico settlements were commercially dependent on trade with the United States via the Santa Fe Trail. American merchants crossed the plains by wagon train to carry on a profitable trade of U.S. manufactured goods for New Mexican furs and gold.[18]

The New Mexicans received Kearny's men readily enough, and relations between citizens and soldiers were generally friendly. The Missourians were fascinated and sometimes charmed with the curious customs of the locals. Some thought the town rather dirty and regarded its adobe houses with pity, but one Missourian had to admit that "they are remarkably neat and clean" on the inside. A grand ball was held a few days after the arrival of the American troops, and although one of Kearny's officers noted that the music by the local musicians was "execrable," relations between Americans and Mexicans were "harmonious." Somewhat to the surprise of the Americans, all the locals at the ball, both men and

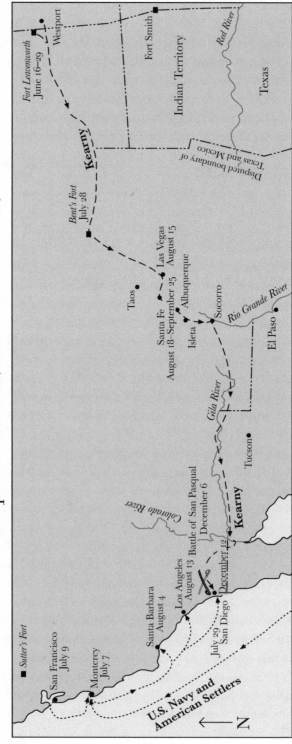

The Conquest of California, June 16 – December 12, 1846

women, smoked tobacco profusely, and the atmosphere became so rank that Kearny himself began to feel ill and had to retire.[19]

Kearny did his best to make sure that his men treated the citizens well, reimbursing them for any fences, crops, or animals appropriated or damaged by his troops. He established Fort Marcy, overlooking Santa Fe, and had Doniphan, who was a lawyer in civilian life, draw up a constitution for the new U.S. territory of New Mexico, complete with a bill of rights. Kearny sent a copy of the new frame of government back to Washington for approval. Then he turned his attention to scouting possible routes farther west, toward California.[20]

Despite the success of Kearny and of other peripheral operations, President Polk still intended that the main U.S. effort would ride on the shoulders of Zachary Taylor and his army—by far the largest force the United States had available at that time. Polk's orders to Taylor were discretionary, but, communicating through the secretary of war, he suggested that Taylor might occupy the city of Monterrey, capital of the province of Nuevo León and strategically located on the high road to the capital of Mexico. Taylor sensibly concluded that the thousand-mile advance to Mexico City, across mountains and deserts, was impractical. He did, however, believe that his army could take Monterrey and then perhaps the capital of the province of Coahuila, Saltillo, another fifty miles along the high road.[21]

The question then remained as to how best to get there. Taylor ordered Ben McCulloch's company of Texas Rangers to scout the direct road from Matamoros to Monterrey. They found it unsuitable for the march of the army, lacking sufficient sources of water. Taylor therefore concluded to march on Monterrey via Camargo, a village along the Rio Grande one hundred miles west-northwest of Matamoros, though four times that far by the meanderings of the river. Taylor's reason for selecting Camargo as the jumping-off point into the Mexican interior was that it was accessible to steamboats coming up the Rio Grande. The march up the south bank of the river was a difficult one for Taylor's troops, but by moving the army in separate contingents, he was able to get them to Camargo by late summer. The men suffered considerably from the heat. Describing one stage of the march, Lieutenant Dana wrote, "The sun was getting hotter and hotter and at times was almost intolerable. The march was as really distressing as I ever hope [to see], and horses and men appeared to put forth their last energies to struggle against the debilitating effect of the hot climate and scorching sun." Insects and disease added to the suffering, especially among the volunteers, who lacked the regulars' strict discipline about camp hygiene.[22]

By the time Kearny had taken Santa Fe, Taylor was ready to begin his campaign into the Mexican interior. His advance guard, the Second Division, under the command of General William Worth, marched out of Camargo on August 19, 1846, and by early September had taken up a position at Cerralvo, about sixty-five miles to the southwest of Camargo on the road to Monterrey and only about fifty-five miles from that city. Much as they had done on the way from Matamoros, the troops marched during the early-morning hours so as to avoid being on the road during the almost unbearable heat of the day. In Cerralvo the men of Worth's division found some slight relief from the heat. At an elevation of more than eleven hundred feet, autumn was already beginning to make itself felt in what one American called "a climate of delicious temperature," as it must indeed have seemed after the sweltering valley of the Rio Grande.[23]

By September 6 the rest of Taylor's army marched out of Camargo also bound for Cerralvo and points south. Taylor took with him only 6,200 men—all of the 3,200 regulars on hand and some 3,000 of the available 7,700 volunteers. The remainder he distributed in various garrisons at Camargo, Matamoros, and other posts in the vicinity.[24]

About twenty-five miles beyond Camargo the American army passed through the town of Mier, the scene of disaster for the Texians four years before. Some of the survivors of that expedition, as well as of the subsequent imprisonment and decimation, were now among the Texas Rangers with Taylor's army. Many of them expressed their desire for revenge on General Ampudia, and a few of the Texans found someone else with whom to settle a score. At a little village just south of Mier, several Texans recognized a Mexican who had treated them cruelly while they were in captivity after the 1842 expedition. In retaliation they gave the hapless Mexican a savage beating and might well have killed him had not other U.S. troops intervened. Foiled, the Texans turned their quarry over to army headquarters as a spy.[25]

Beyond Cerralvo the road lay along the eastern foot of a spur of the Sierra Madre, making for pleasant scenery and even more delightful relief from the heat of the Rio Grande Valley. It also made travel more difficult, with rocky roads crossed by numerous mountain streams. In the distance, some fifty miles away, the Sierra Madre proper reared up, looking deceptively close through the clear air. At the foot of those mountains lay Monterrey. On September 17 Worth's division, still leading Taylor's army, followed the road through Sierra Alva Pass to the west side of the spur, opening up a vista across more than twenty-five miles of intervening valley to the slopes of the Sierra Madre. "The view came suddenly on us just as the sun was rising," wrote Dana, "and the sight was so grand, so beautiful, that all exclaimed at once. The tops of the mountains actually appeared to reach the sky, and their sides of crags and rocks appeared to be right perpendicular. Their outline is very sharp, and every peak is sharp."[26]

On September 6, the same day that the last of Taylor's field army marched out of Camargo, a curious character was far to the south, in the Mexican town of Jalapa, where he had paused on his journey from Veracruz to Mexico City. The infamous Antonio López de Santa Anna, murderer of the defenders of the Alamo and Goliad, was back in Mexico after a two-year exile. Mexico's favorite demagogue had departed office in 1844 in one of the southern republic's depressingly regular government upheavals and since that time had maintained himself abroad, always scheming for a comeback.[27]

As the trouble between Mexico and the United States had heated up, Santa Anna had sent discreet emissaries to Polk suggesting that he, Santa Anna, was the true choice of the Mexican people and that he would be reasonable in negotiating the difficulties with the United States. Specifically, he suggested, through his intermediaries, that for $30 million he would be willing to give up Mexico's claims north of the Rio Grande as well as New Mexico and part of California. Polk was impressed so far as to direct the U.S. naval officer commanding the warships patrolling the Gulf to allow Santa Anna safe passage into Mexico.[28]

In August 1846, Santa Anna arrived in Veracruz, and in the weeks that followed he plied his well-practiced charm on the populace, which was heartily tired of Paredes's regime and its recent reverses. On September 15, Santa Anna arrived at Mexico City to a hero's welcome. Gone now was any talk of a deal with the Americans. That had all been for Polk's private consumption anyway. Instead, styling himself the Soldier of the People, he took command of the Mexican army, promising to drive out the hated gringos.[29]

Pending Santa Anna's arrival at the front, the shake-up of command following the defeats at Palo Alto and Resaca de la Palma had left Pedro de Ampudia in charge of the Mexican army confronting Taylor. Ampudia felt confident. With an army now reinforced to seven thousand regulars and three thousand *rancheros*, he hoped to take the offensive and

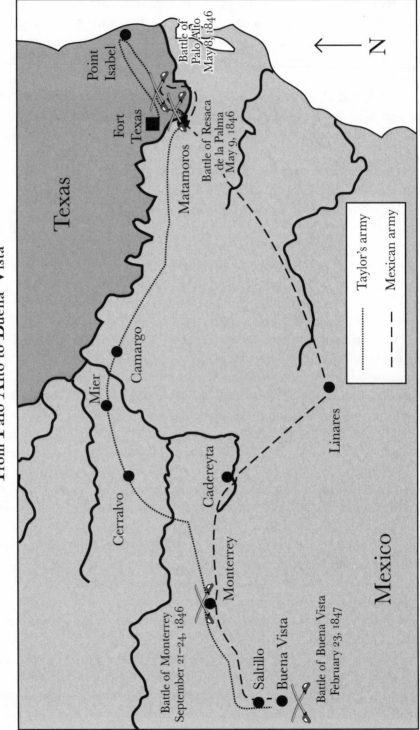

From Palo Alto to Buena Vista

defeat Taylor east of Monterrey. He had to give up the plan when his subordinate officers unanimously demurred. They were probably influenced by the overwhelming strength of Monterrey's fortifications. Why fight the enemy in the open when they could await him behind thick masonry walls?[30]

That reasoning had much to commend it. Hemmed in by the Sierra Madre and the Santa Catarina River, the city could be approached by Taylor only from the northeast, where he would have to pass the powerful strongholds known as La Tenería and El Rincón on the town's eastern edge. Backing them up from a position just beyond Monterrey's northern outskirts was an enormous stone fortress that the Mexicans called La Ciudadela (the Citadel) but which the Americans would name the Black Fort because of its dark masonry. Even the houses of the city seemed designed for defense, made as they were of stone and ranging along straight streets so that every building became a potential redoubt. West of the town—behind it relative to the direction from which the Americans would advance—rose two hills, flanking the river: Independencia on the north bank, Federación on the south. Each was crowned with an additional stronghold. The fort known as El Soldado stood atop Federación Hill, and the large, ornate, and heavily fortified Bishop's Palace on Independencia.[31]

On September 19 the American army encamped at Walnut Springs, "a beautiful grove of Lofty Timber," as one American described it, "in the center of which gushed from the rocks a delicious spring of water." The spring was three miles from Monterrey. As the U.S. column had marched toward the city that day, several Mexican civilians told Captain John Henshaw of the Eighth Infantry that he and his men were "going to a fandango at Monterrey." General Ampudia was in command there, the vaqueros said, and the Mexican force was well provided with artillery and confident of victory.[32]

Escorted by two companies of dragoons and two of Texas Rangers, Taylor rode forward to reconnoiter personally. A heavy fog concealed the city at first, then lifted when Taylor was about a mile and a half away. Even before the city came into view, Mexican and American skirmishers were already trading shots between the armies. When Taylor was fifteen hundred yards from the city, the Mexican artillery in the Black Fort opened fire on the reconnoitering party, but Old Rough and Ready was not to be hurried and retired only after he had seen what he came to see.[33]

He recognized the Bishop's Palace as the key to the city, and he conceived a daring plan to take it. Boldly dividing his army in front of a more numerous foe, he would lead the main body of his force on the direct approach against La Tenería and El Rincón while a large detachment would swing around to take the high ground on the west side of the city. It would capture Rinconada Pass, cutting off any reinforcement or supply for Ampudia and the Mexican garrison of Monterrey and also cutting off the Mexicans' retreat. Then the flanking column would capture the key forts overlooking the city. Late that afternoon Taylor dispatched an engineer officer, Captain Mansfield, along with a small party including young engineer lieutenant George G. Meade, on a risky reconnaissance to see if the route of the turning maneuver was feasible. Mansfield returned around ten o'clock that night with the report that it was. Taylor assigned that task to Worth's Second Division, which included most of the army's regulars.[34]

With the reconnaissance complete, Worth's division set out from its camps at two o'clock on the afternoon of Sunday, September 20. The volunteers of the other two divisions lined the road to see the regulars march out. Swinging far to the west, Worth's route then curved back east to approach the city from the left rear of the Mexican defenses. As the men marched along, the ground to their left sloped away very gradually in cultivated fields, bisected by irrigation ditches, while to their right a series of steep hills rose toward the great wall of the Sierra Madre. Shortly before sundown, Worth halted the column for a rest, and while the men filled their canteens at wells that served a small cluster of shacks nearby, Worth and several of his officers ascended one of the hills to the right of the road to observe the approaches to Independencia Hill.[35]

Despite Mansfield's skillfully chosen route, Mexicans in Monterrey had spotted the column and dispatched a force of infantry and cavalry to dispute its advance. When scouts notified Worth of the approach of Mexican horsemen, he sent out a party of Texas Rangers under Ben McCulloch to counter them. The Texans had a brief clash with the Mexicans, exchanging a few shots and receiving long-range artillery fire from Independencia. A Mexican shell burst in a field a few yards from the road, throwing pieces of cornstalk in all directions but injuring no one. For many of the Texans it was their first experience of shell fire. With night coming on and the enemy's advance halted, the rangers withdrew to rejoin Worth's main body.[36]

Having marched through a hard downpour of rain around sundown, the column made an uncomfortable camp that night northwest of the city—due north of their objective—with no tents or blankets and little to eat. They could light no fires, since they were within range of the guns on Independencia. "That was the most cheerless, comfortless, unhappy night I ever spent," wrote Lieutenant Dana. Captain Henshaw's thoughts were of his amazement that the Mexicans, from their hilltop position, had not yet taken Worth's main column under artillery fire.[37]

They were off again at sunrise, now drawing occasional long-range artillery fire from the Bishop's Palace and other Mexican works on Independencia Hill, but they met no serious opposition until they neared the vital Saltillo Road, Ampudia's line of supply, communication, and, if necessary, retreat. Only a few hundred yards from the road, a large body of Mexican lancers, estimated at fifteen hundred to two thousand men, appeared and immediately charged. The Texas Ranger battalion was at the front of the U.S. column and began deploying in skirmish line along a fence. Ben McCulloch's company had been scouting out in front of the rest, however, and now they were caught up with the Mexicans in a wild horseback mêlée as they galloped back to rejoin their comrades, with rifles, pistols, and shotguns blazing. The Eighth Infantry advanced as skirmishers, taking the Mexicans under fire. The other U.S. infantry regiments deployed into line, and two batteries of U.S. artillery quickly unlimbered and added their fire. The fight was over in fifteen minutes with the Mexicans in full flight. They left behind at least thirty-two dead, including their commander, Colonel Juan Najera, and a large number of wounded. U.S. losses were light. Several of the Texas Rangers had suffered lance wounds, including Walker, who had a slight wound in the neck.[38]

With the Mexican cavalry out of the way, Worth's column quickly took possession of the Saltillo Road, prompting the exultant general to fire off a dispatch to Taylor: "The town is ours." Not quite, but the position did cut off the only adequate line of supplies for the Mexican garrison. Worth still needed to take Independencia and Federación. The latter, rising from the south bank of the river, would be first.[39]

Worth dispatched a force of three companies of regular infantry and small detachments of six companies of dismounted Texas Rangers, 350 men in all, under the command of Captain Charles F. Smith of the regular army, tasked with taking Federación. Smith led his force through a cornfield and then across a ford of the Santa Catarina. From the river they proceeded up the hill through rough chaparral, aiming for a Mexican artillery position that guarded its west end. Mexican fire was intense but ineffective.[40]

Notified by Smith that the Mexicans on the hilltop had been rein-

The Battle of Monterrey, September 21-24, 1846

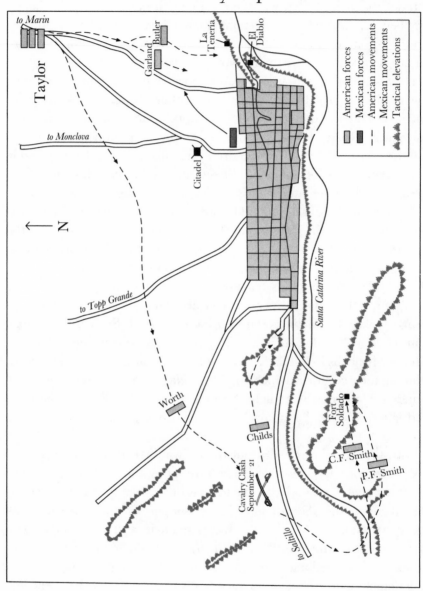

forced, Worth sent Colonel Persifor F. Smith's Second Brigade to join the attack. Together the troops of both commands fought their way uphill. Lieutenant Dana, leading his company of the Seventh Infantry, was astonished to note that not a single one of his men had been hit during the advance, despite the thousands of bullets buzzing past them.[41]

As the Americans burst out onto the summit of the hill, the Mexicans fled the position, leaving behind their lone nine-pounder gun. The Americans turned this gun against El Soldado, the Mexican fort at the other end of the ridge, and soon knocked out its only gun. Persifor Smith then ordered the men forward: "Take that other fort!" The Americans charged, and the defenders fled in disorder, leaving the entire hill to the two Smiths and their troops. The Americans sent up a tremendous cheer and raised the Stars and Stripes over the two strongholds, where the flags would be clearly visible to Taylor and the rest of the army on the other side of Monterrey.[42]

The Mexicans on Independencia were still lobbing ineffectual shots at them across the river, but the Americans on Federación Hill savored their triumph and continued to bang away in response with their captured nine-pounder. As the duel between the hilltops continued through the twilight, the reverberations of the cannon echoed back and forth from the walls of the Sierra Madre. Then, as darkness gathered, Worth's men bedded down—hungry again—for another night in the open, made more unpleasant by another nocturnal thunderstorm.[43]

One of the most important reasons for Worth's success was that while his men had been rattling the lock on the back door of Monterrey, the rest of Taylor's army had been doing its best to kick in the front door. Hoping to divert Mexican attention from Worth's turning movement, Taylor had ordered a major demonstration against the works on the east side of the city. The operation succeeded, but at a heavy cost.

Taylor placed Brigadier General David E. Twiggs's division on the left and Brigadier General William O. Butler's on the right. Twiggs himself was out of action that morning. Believing that an empty intestinal tract enhanced chances of surviving an abdominal wound, he had dosed himself so thoroughly with laxatives that he was incapacitated for duty. Command of the division fell instead to his senior brigade commander, Colonel John Garland. To Garland, Taylor gave a vague verbal order to advance and take any of the Mexican fortifications he thought he could.[44]

Uncertain as to what the order required but unwilling to bear the onus of flinching, Garland led his division into the teeth of the Mexican defenses. As they advanced toward La Tenería, his men took fire from that fort and from the roofs of the houses on the outskirts of town, as well as severe enfilading fire from the Black Fort and El Rincón. Confusion set in among the jumbled buildings and narrow streets on the edge of town. Casualties were high, and some of the troops became pinned down in the shelter of the buildings. Braxton Bragg's battery of flying artillery raced up and took position in support but could make little impression on the stout houses. Elsewhere along the front, artillery proved equally unavailing. Unwilling to accept a setback, even in a diversionary attack, Taylor fed more troops into the fight.[45]

One of the regiments Taylor committed was the Mississippi Rifles, commanded by West Point graduate and former U.S. congressman Jefferson Davis, who also had the distinction of being Taylor's son-in-law by his first marriage to Taylor's daughter, since deceased. In their red shirts, black slouch hats, and white duck pants, the Mississippians made a striking appearance, and having received their training from a former professional officer like Davis, they were better than the average regiment of volunteers. They advanced toward La Tenería alongside the First Tennessee Volunteer Regiment and successfully stormed the fort. Other U.S. troops took the small fort known as El Diablo. Elsewhere, including along the front of Butler's division, which advanced on the U.S. right, gains were small and losses high. Finally Taylor ordered all troops to pull back to their starting points except for those holding La Tenería and El Diablo, who would continue to hang on to their prizes.[46]

On September 22 the battered American forces on the east side of Monterrey rested and regrouped while Worth's column continued to press its advance from the west. At 3:00 a.m. Worth dispatched a storming party to take Independencia Hill, with its dominating Bishop's Palace. The storming party, commanded by Colonel Thomas Childs, consisted of six companies of regulars, from various regiments, and two hundred Texas Rangers. Directing the advance were Captain John Sanders and Lieutenant Meade of the Topographical Engineers.[47]

The darkness and fog, along with the heavy storm of wind and rain, covered their advance up the steep hill. Near the top, the men had to climb almost vertically, pulling themselves up by grabbing the tough vegetation or handholds in the rock. Still, with the advantage of surprise, Worth's assaulting column was able to creep well up the slope without being discovered. When the clanking of canteens gave them away, the Mexicans opened fire through the murky semidarkness. The Americans continued to clamber upward, yelling wildly and pausing occasionally to shoot. Within minutes they were on the crest. The assault quickly overran the entire hilltop except the palace itself. That towering pile of masonry proved impregnable to infantry assault, so Worth had a detachment of artillerymen take a twelve-pounder howitzer apart, haul the pieces to the top of the hill, and reassemble it there. Then they got to work on the walls of the palace, aided by long-range fire from the captured guns on Federación Hill, to the south.[48]

The palace still held out for a time under this pounding, but as the howitzer shells came over the walls and detonated inside, the Mexican commander sent messengers back to the city calling for help. A regiment of lancers moved out to attack the Americans, and the garrison of the palace sallied out to join them. The result was disastrous. Once the Mexican troops were in the open, the Americans slaughtered them. Most of the survivors fled downhill toward Monterrey, while only a few turned back into the palace. Yet so stubborn did the structure prove that even that small remnant was able to hang on until the twelve-pounder battered down the gate and additional U.S. artillery—light field pieces this time—actually unlimbered inside the enclosure to blast the last defenders out of their coverts. By 4:00 p.m. the Bishop's Palace was securely in American hands.[49]

The next morning, September 23, Taylor directed Brigadier General John A. Quitman to probe forward from La Tenería, entering the city if it seemed practicable, and to "advance carefully as far as he may deem prudent." A short time later, Quitman learned that the Mexicans had evacuated El Rincón, another of the forts on the east side of the city. So he sent Davis and the Mississippi Rifles to occupy that fort and, if possible, advance into the town. Davis and his men found that it was indeed possible and began fighting their way from house to house.[50]

Taylor reinforced the Mississippians with several more regiments of both volunteers and regulars. The streets were still swept by Mexican gunfire, but the Americans used picks and crowbars to break through the walls between adjoining houses. Then they would throw in a six-pounder artillery shell, fuse lit, and let the explosion do much of the work of clearing out the defenders. The town's civilian population was sheltering in the cathedral plaza. Once a house was cleared, American marksmen would take up positions on its flat roof to lay down covering fire for their comrades' advance to the next house.[51]

On the other side of Monterrey, Worth waited impatiently for orders from Taylor, which never came. In fact, this was a lapse on Taylor's part, but by mid-morning Worth heard the sound of gunfire from the east side of town and assumed that orders from Taylor for him to join the assault had somehow failed to reach him. He led his men forward. Captain Henshaw described how his men charged over hedges, fences, and walls, and "through beautiful gardens filled with the richest tropical fruits." As they neared the center of the city, they encountered stiff Mexican resistance. Like their comrades on the other side of town, Worth's men began fighting their way from house to house, battling from one flat rooftop to the next. Within a few hours, Worth's troops had penetrated to within one block of the cathedral plaza in the center of Monterrey, the Mexicans' last defensive position. The vanguard of Taylor's main body was by that time fighting only two blocks away on the other side of the plaza.[52]

Taylor, however, having conceived the entire day's exercise as a reconnaissance in force, pulled his troops back to La Tenería and El Rincón, on the east side of town, much to the disgust of his men, who rightly believed that victory was near. Worth, hearing the sound of firing cease on the opposite side of the plaza, halted his own troops. Throughout the night he had his men use their ten-inch mortar to lob shells into the final Mexican stronghold. This proved especially uncomfortable for the Mexicans, who had turned the cathedral into a massive ammunition magazine and feared the results of a direct hit. Meanwhile, in the American-occupied portion of the town, a U.S. officer found an abandoned bakery and quickly detailed some of his men to bring it into full production, baking loaf after loaf of fresh bread for the famished troops of Worth's division.[53]

The next morning Worth started his men forward again, but word soon reached them that surrender negotiations were under way. The guns on the east side had already fallen silent when a Mexican emissary entered Taylor's lines under flag of truce before dawn. Concluding a final agreement took a series of meetings over a period of more than twenty-four hours, and the Mexican officers proved far more adept at negotiating than they had at fighting.[54]

At first Ampudia insisted that his army be allowed to march away from the city intact, while Taylor maintained that they would have to surrender as prisoners of war. At length, Ampudia, who had little choice, sent word to Taylor that he agreed to surrender, but when the generals met to work out the details, the Mexican went back on his word and once again insisted that his army must be allowed to go on its way. In support of his demand, Ampudia glibly lied, saying he had received word that Mexico had agreed to negotiate all disagreements with the United States and that commissioners from the two countries would soon be meeting.[55]

Taylor had no way of knowing if this fiction was true, and at last he gave in to Ampudia's suggestion that each army appoint three commissioners to work out the terms of surrender. This was an obvious ploy to move decision making away from the steadfast Taylor, and it worked.

The commissioners finally agreed upon—and Taylor accepted—terms that allowed the Mexican army to keep its cavalry horses and six pieces of artillery and to retire beyond Rinconada Pass. Taylor agreed not to advance beyond that pass for eight weeks or until he heard from his government. On September 25, the Mexican garrison of Black Fort saluted its flag, lowered it, and marched out. Then the Americans marched in while a band played "Yankee Doodle." When the Stars and Stripes went up the flagpole, American artillery on Independencia Hill fired a twenty-eight-gun salute, one for every state in the Union.[56]

News of the victory at Monterrey predictably triggered rejoicing in the United States, but President Polk and his cabinet, whose business it was to think of strategic and political factors rather than twenty-eight-gun salutes and "Yankee Doodle," were not completely satisfied with the outcome. They could see how the complexion of the war might have been changed had Ampudia's army been captured, disarmed, and paroled, and they pointed out that Taylor had exceeded his instructions by agreeing to the provisional eight-week truce. He could, they believed, have accomplished much more.[57]

Perhaps, but his army was very tired and had suffered heavy casualties on the first day of the battle. Many of Taylor's subordinates were later vocal in stating that the agreement that ended the Battle of Monterrey was all that could have been achieved, and at the time of the negotiations many officers in Taylor's army had believed that since peace negotiations were under way, letting Ampudia's army go "was but following up the generous and forbearing policy of our government."[58] Many of the rank and file, on the other hand, believed they had been cheated out of a complete victory. The Texans especially doubted the wisdom of the move, remembering how a similarly generous agreement at San Antonio in 1835 had ended with the Mexican army breaking its parole. Taylor's position with his own government, however, was secure. With the country singing the praises of Old Rough and Ready, Polk could not censure him, but he could, and did, order a suspension of the truce and a resumption of active operations.[59]

In the opposing capital, Santa Anna used popular enmity toward the United States to solidify his grasp on power, installed a puppet president to administer the government in his absence, and set out to take command of Mexican forces in the northern part of the country. He acted energetically to draw together the largest army he possibly could, with which he hoped to destroy Taylor's army. For this purpose Santa Anna ruthlessly stripped northern Mexico of all garrisons, turning a deaf ear to the complaints of the populace. The Soldier of the People was not going to let their fears stand in the way of his glory. He worked hard at training, organization, and—his greatest problem—funding, and by January 1847 he had an army of more than twenty thousand encamped at San Luis Potosí.[60]

While Taylor's army rested at Monterrey and Santa Anna's gathered its strength some miles to the south, U.S. forces continued to act on other fronts. Naval forces under Commodore David E. Conner seized the Mexican Gulf port of Tampico, and Brigadier General John E. Wool led a small army totaling about thirty-four hundred men—mostly volunteers—out of San Antonio on September 23 and then southward across the Rio Grande at Eagle Pass and thence to the Mexican town of Monclova. Since the road to Chihuahua, his original objective, was impracticable for an army due to rough terrain and lack of water, Wool, after consulting by courier with Taylor, marched to join the latter's force near Monterrey.[61]

CHAPTER TWELVE

New Mexico, Chihuahua, and California

MEANWHILE, ANOTHER AMERICAN force was advancing south from Santa Fe, New Mexico, with plans to join Wool at Chihuahua: the First Regiment of Missouri Mounted Volunteers, commanded by Colonel Doniphan. Alexander William Doniphan—Will to his friends—was an American original. When Abraham Lincoln met Doniphan fifteen years later, he would comment, "You are the only man connected with any great military enterprise who ever came up in his looks to my expectations." In fact, Doniphan and Lincoln had a number of things in common. The future colonel was born seven months earlier than the future president and about 150 miles northeast of the birthplace of Lincoln, who at the time of the Mexican War was serving as a member of Congress.[1]

Doniphan started his life on the Kentucky side of the Ohio River about seventy-five miles southeast of Cincinnati. After graduating from Augusta College, he read law and gained admittance to the Kentucky bar. Seeking new opportunities, he moved to St. Louis and then settled in the little town of Liberty, Missouri, in the western part of the state, where he continued to practice law and also served as a Whig in the state legislature and as a brigadier general in the Missouri militia. During the Mormon War in the late 1830s, Doniphan was among those Missourians who counseled and sometimes compelled restraint in dealing with that group, and it was he who had refused an order to execute Joseph Smith.[2]

Doniphan had had no hesitation about enlisting for the present war, despite the fact that he had recently married. Like most Americans, he was a strong believer in Manifest Destiny, convinced that God intended the United States to spread the domain of representative self-government across the continent. For Doniphan the institution of slavery, and the possibility that it might spread into the new lands, were no flies in the ointment, for he owned slaves himself. As soon as war had broken out, Doniphan had volunteered for service, and the governor of Missouri, eager to have the support of a prominent Whig, tasked him with raising the First Regiment of Missouri Mounted Volunteers.[3]

The regiment organized at Fort Leavenworth, and to no one's surprise, the troops promptly elected Doniphan their colonel. For the training of his regiment Doniphan had the services of First Lieutenant Andrew Jackson Smith, a tough, dour, no-nonsense regular (West Point class of 1838), borrowed for that purpose from the First Dragoons. He was highly competent, and the men took well to their training, though they were far from being regulars. Indeed, though they might pick up a smattering of drill, the Missourians would never acquire more than the vaguest rudiments of military discipline.[4]

Doniphan and his men had crossed the plains and occupied New Mexico with Kearny, then had remained behind as garrison while Kearny had headed west with his handful of dragoons to enter California. Having established a territorial government in New Mexico and left a small garrison there, Doniphan proceeded to the next step of his instructions and marched south along the Rio Grande for Chihuahua and a planned rendezvous with Wool.[5]

Meanwhile, back in New Mexico, trouble flared up, and the truth is that Kearny had badly overestimated the friendliness of the locals. In fact, many of them were only as friendly as Kearny's apparently overwhelming military force made it seem expedient to be. Now that Kearny and most of his troops were gone, having departed either westward for California or southward for Chihuahua, the mood was changing. At first the difference remained below the surface.[6]

Charles Bent, whom Kearny had appointed as the new U.S. governor of New Mexico, was a longtime resident of Taos, eighty miles north of Santa Fe. Born in Charleston, Virginia (now West Virginia), in 1799, Bent had grown up in St. Louis and gone into the overland trade with New Mexico via the Santa Fe Trail. Along with his younger brother William and partner Ceran St. Vrain, he had in 1830 organized Bent, St. Vrain and Company. They traded with whites, Indians, and Mexicans for the benefit of all and were an influence for peace on the southern plains, especially since William Bent was married to a Cheyenne. Charles settled in Taos, where he became successful in business and married a local woman. Well liked and active in the town's affairs, Bent had become one of the leading citizens of Taos.[7]

None of that could save him when on the night—actually in the predawn hours—of January 19, 1847, the Indians of the Taos pueblo, together with area Mexicans, staged an uprising against American rule.

They first killed the town sheriff and another official and then headed for Bent's house, shouting and banging on his door. Bent met them at the door and asked what they wanted. He had always been on good terms with these people, and so the reply came as a shock.

"We want your head, gringo," shouted someone in the crowd. "We do not want for any of you gringos to govern us, and we have come to kill you."

Bent protested that he had always been kind to them, but the response was "Yes, but you have to die now so that no American is going to govern us." With that, members of the mob shot Bent in the chin and stomach, pushed him aside, and stormed into the house. Other members shot several arrows into Bent's face and slashed at him with knives as he lay gasping on the floor. Bent's wife, her sister (the wife of Kit Carson), the Bent children, and two other women in the house managed to escape by hacking their way through the adobe wall of a back room to reach the courtyard. A few minutes later Bent followed, and soon the attackers also found their way into the courtyard. There they scalped the still-living Bent and finally beheaded him; they left his family physically unharmed, though destitute. Thereafter, the rebellious Indians and Mexicans continued their killing spree, slaughtering more than a dozen Americans in the surrounding area, as well as Mexicans who had cooperated with American rule.[8]

Colonel Sterling Price had brought his Second Missouri Mounted Volunteer Regiment out on the Santa Fe Trail the preceding September and remained in charge at Santa Fe while Doniphan was combating Apaches and Mexicans to the south. On January 20 Price learned of the previous day's massacre at Taos and elsewhere around the province. "It appeared to be the object of the insurrectionists," Price commented, "to put to death every American and every Mexican who had accepted office under the American government."[9]

To combat the uprising, Price scraped together such force as could be spared from the Santa Fe area—somewhat fewer than five hundred men, including six companies of his own Second Missouri, along with a company of regular dragoons and another of New Mexico volunteers led by Bent's old partner St. Vrain. They struggled through snows in the mountains and fought and won two battles against larger forces of Indians and Mexicans before reaching Taos on February 3. The Indians holed up within the stout outer walls of the pueblo, and for a day those walls successfully defied the fire of Price's several small mountain howitzers. On the second day, however, Price's men stormed the enclosure and after heavy fighting succeeded in stamping out resistance. Price's casualties numbered seven killed and forty-five wounded, of whom many later succumbed. The Indians and Mexicans in the pueblo suffered 154 deaths during the fighting and an unknown number of wounded. Not long after that, Price and the insurrectionists reached a peace agreement, providing that the rebels hand over the ringleaders of the massacre. Ultimately seven Mexicans and four Indians were convicted in the matter and hanged in the plaza of Taos.[10]

While Price finished with affairs in New Mexico, Doniphan continued on his southward journey with the First Missouri on the campaign into Chihuahua as Kearny had ordered before departing for California. The Missourians' route led down the valley of the Rio Grande, or roughly parallel to it, though they were sometimes far from the river. None of the way was easy, but the two-hundred-mile stretch from Valverde to near El Paso was some of the hardest. With its rough and rocky terrain and severe scarcity of wood and water, the region was already known as La Jornada del Muerto—the Journey of Death. Temperatures dropped well below freezing at night, and an early snowfall had given notice of the approach of winter. For days the men struggled through thirst, cold, and fatigue. "Our men are shooting every crow or hawk or every other wild thing they can to eat," wrote one of the Missourians in his diary, and the next morning he noted that the men had awakened beneath a blanket of two inches of fresh snow. By December 23, they were near El Paso and coming into better country closer to the river, with grass for the horses and water and timber readily available.[11]

On Christmas Day, Doniphan called a halt at 2:00 p.m., after having covered eighteen miles, and the lead contingent of the regiment encamped near an old channel of the Rio Grande called El Brazito, about nine miles south of present-day Las Cruces, New Mexico. About half of the regiment was still a number of miles back the trail. In honor of the holiday, Doniphan gave his men the rest of the day off. Although his scouts had in recent days detected signs that a large Mexican force might be hovering near the column, Doniphan allowed his men to unsaddle their horses and then scatter in all directions, gathering firewood, hauling water from the river, or hunting rabbits. Those who chose to stay in camp lounged about playing cards—the colonel's game was three-card loo—or firing their rifles into the air by way of celebration. Doniphan posted no sentinels, but he did dispatch a few mounted scouts to ride farther along the trail.[12]

Martin Van Buren

William Henry Harrison

Henry Clay

John J. Crittenden

John Tyler

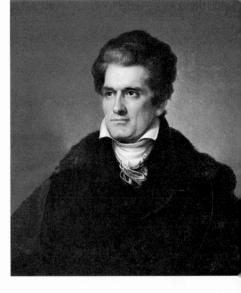

John C. Calhoun

Daniel Webster

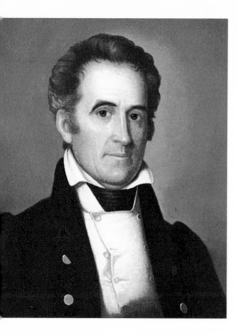

Richard Mentor Johnson

Jason Lee

William Lloyd Garrison

An 1852 William S. Jewett portrait
of John C. Frémont

Kit Carson

Independence Rock

Portrait of Joseph Smith by an
unknown artist, circa 1842.
The original is on display at the
Community of Christ headquarters,
Independence, Missouri.

The Mormon temple in Kirtland,
Ohio, as it appears today

Brigham Young

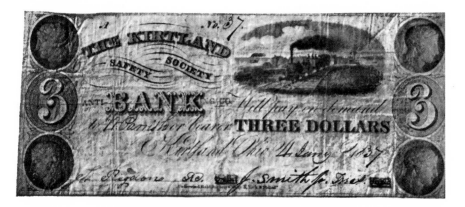

A Kirtland Safety Society three-dollar bill

The reconstructed Mormon
temple in Nauvoo, Illinois,
an almost exact replica of the
original, as it appears today

James K. Polk

John Slidell

Zachary Taylor

Winfield Scott

Nicholas Trist

Lewis Cass

Robert E. Lee

Abraham Lincoln in 1846

One of Doniphan's officers called his attention to a large dust cloud to the east. It extended several hundred yards from side to side. The Missouri officers paused and gazed at it, and Doniphan commented, "That does look suspicious." He played out the rest of his hand, then stood and glanced up at the dust cloud again and noticed that it was significantly closer. "By God, that does look forked!" he exclaimed, by which he meant it appeared dangerous. Picking up his saber, he began shouting orders to his officers to get their men into line and ready for battle. The camp was soon a scene of pandemonium. Various bugles sounded assembly, and men dropped their armloads of firewood and scrambled for their rifles and sabers and into line while officers shouted, "Fall into line," "Get your horses," "Fall in on foot here." Presently the scouts Doniphan had dispatched came galloping back into camp confirming that the Mexicans were present in force, and they were advancing.[13]

Mexican Lieutenant Colonel Antonio Ponce de Leon had advanced with between eleven hundred and thirteen hundred men of his El Paso garrison, deployed them to attack the Americans, and was now leading them into battle. About five hundred Missourians were present, and almost all of them would fight dismounted. Once they had formed a semblance of a line of battle, the Missourians awaited the onset of their more numerous foes with considerable nonchalance. As one of them recalled, laughing, talking, and jesting were common in the ranks. Still, the sight of the Mexican force approaching, infantry and artillery in the center, cavalry, with their red jackets, brass helmets with bearskin plumes, and wicked-looking lances, drawn up on the flanks—was a sobering one, and a Missourian admitted that it made his "blood flow chill."[14]

The Mexicans halted several hundred yards in front of the Missourians' line, and a single rider galloped forward carrying a black swallow-tailed flag decorated with images of skulls and crossbones. As he approached, it was clear he had some message for the Americans, so Doniphan sent his adjutant, Lieutenant DeCourcy, along with Thomas Caldwell, a merchant fluent in Spanish, to go out and talk to him. They met about one hundred yards in front of the American lines. The Mexican was Lieutenant Manuel Lara, and he brought from Colonel Ponce de Leon a demand that Doniphan come into Mexican lines at once to agree to the surrender of his force. If he would not, Lara warned, the Mexicans would give no quarter. Caldwell said Doniphan would not, and Lara, flourishing his black skull-and-bones flag, replied, "We shall break your ranks and take him."[15]

"Come and take him," Caldwell shot back, inviting the Mexicans

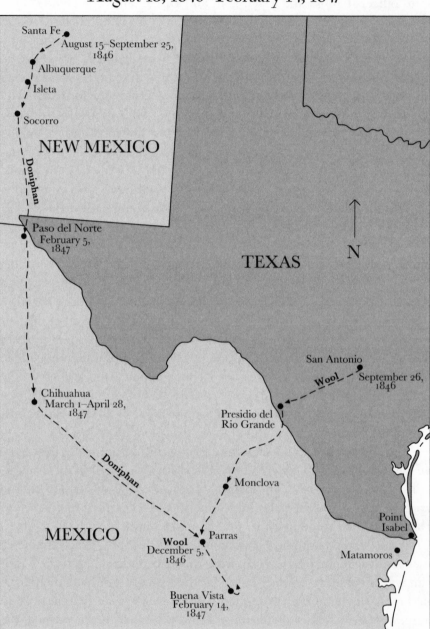

Doniphan's Campaign
August 15, 1846 – February 14, 1847

Santa Fe

August 15–September 25, 1846

Albuquerque

Isleta

Socorro

NEW MEXICO

Doniphan

Paso del Norte
February 5, 1847

TEXAS

N

San Antonio

Wool

September 26, 1846

Chihuahua
March 1–April 28, 1847

Presidio del Rio Grande

Doniphan

Monclova

MEXICO

Point Isabel

Wool
December 5, 1846

Parras

Matamoros

Buena Vista
February 14, 1847

with a curse to go ahead and make their charge. Caldwell and DeCourcy galloped back to American lines and told the Missourians that they were in a fight for their lives.[16]

The Missourians had their backs to the Rio Grande, about half a mile to their rear. In front of them, the Mexicans launched their charge across a roughly level plain covered with grass and low chaparral. Although the Mexican infantry carried smoothbore muskets with a maximum effective range of under one hundred yards, their commander had them halt and deliver a volley at four hundred yards, then reload, advance to three hundred yards, and deliver another. Their fire was harmless to the Missourians, but each time the Mexicans fired, Doniphan ordered some of his men to lie down, out of sight in the grass, and he strictly ordered his men to hold their own fire and let the Mexicans come on. With more discipline than anyone else would have given them credit for possessing, the Missourians obeyed.[17]

Encouraged by the apparent results of his attack, Colonel Ponce de Leon continued his advance, pausing again to fire at two hundred yards. A single Mexican cannon banged away at the Americans, but the gunners' aim was high. After one discharge of the gun, Doniphan later said, he thought something like a whole bushel of copper ore passed all of ten feet over his head. Still, the Mexican artillerists were persistent, if not effective, and continued to load and fire. Doniphan continued urging his men to hold their fire. The troops later admitted that it was hard not to shoot when the Mexicans were advancing to a range less than that at which many of the Missourians had often brought down running deer, but Doniphan was pacing along the line, exhorting the men to hold their fire and then be cool and deliberate when the time came to fight. One of the Missourians remembered the officers repeating over and over, "Reserve your fire."[18]

The Mexican lancers began to move around Doniphan's left flank, so he ordered that side of his line to bend back at right angles to the rest of the line so as to face them, forming what one of his men called "an elbow." When the Mexicans saw this, they interpreted it as the beginning of an American retreat, and the Missourians could hear them excitedly shouting, *"Bueno! Bueno!"*

With cheers the lancers charged headlong toward the Missourians' lines. Doniphan shouted for his men to stand and deliver their fire, and the volley that followed decimated the attackers. A dozen or so mounted Missourians charged out and captured the Mexican cannon. Colonel

Ponce de Leon went down wounded. Confusion set in among his troops, and the entire Mexican force collapsed into disorderly flight, leaving several hundred of their number killed, wounded, or captured. Doniphan's losses were seven men wounded, leading one of his men to comment, "It seems that providence was on our side." The entire battle had lasted scarcely half an hour, and when it was over, the colonel went back to his game of loo.[19]

Having decisively won the Battle of El Brazito, Doniphan's command continued its march the next day and occupied El Paso without a fight two days later. A delegation of civic leaders met them as they approached the town, offering its surrender and begging that the American commander spare El Pasoans' lives and property. Doniphan promised to do so, and, with a few unfortunate exceptions among his sometimes undisciplined troops, the promise was faithfully kept. The citizens proved eager to please and plied the conquerors with fresh fruit, something the Americans considered an unheard-of luxury in the waning days of December.[20]

After a six-week pause in El Paso to gather supplies and reinforcements, including a scratch battalion of American traders whom Doniphan organized into a military unit, the expedition set out again, trekking south through the desert toward Chihuahua City. The little American army had had no information from the outside world—no instructions from higher headquarters or news of how the war was progressing—since before arriving in El Paso, but Doniphan remained undaunted. He would continue carrying out the last orders he had received, and those were to advance and take Chihuahua. The journey led across semidesert lands, where days were hot under a blazing sun and nights freezing. In one dry stretch of the journey, the expedition lost a number of oxen and might have had to abandon some of its wagons had not a timely rainstorm, along with hail, intervened to provide the needed water. Later a prairie fire demanded fast action by the Missourians to save their food and ammunition wagons, and on another occasion a sandstorm presented its own set of challenges.[21]

After a 250-mile journey beyond El Paso, Doniphan and his men on February 28, 1847, came face-to-face with a Mexican army of three thousand—about three times their own numbers—fifteen miles north of Chihuahua. The Mexicans, commanded by General José A. Heredia, held extensive fortifications on high ground atop a bluff on the far side of the Sacramento River. A skilled Mexican engineer officer had laid out the defensive works, and they were elaborate and carefully designed to maximize every advantage of the already advantageous terrain. One of the Missourians surveying the works uneasily from the valley floor to the north thought that "the place seemed impregnable."[22]

The Mexicans were confident. When the Americans came in sight, some two miles away, the Mexican troops waved their sabers defiantly over their heads. Two-thirds of Heredia's men were regulars, although most of those were relatively recent enlistees. The rest were *rancheros,* who planned to help ride down the fleeing Americans with lassos and machetes. The Mexican soldiers had cut short lengths of rope and also had a large number of handcuffs so as to be ready to shackle or tie up the numerous American prisoners they planned to take. Their generals were making plans to follow up their overwhelming victory on the Sacramento with an advance that would regain all that Mexico had lost in Chihuahua and New Mexico. Many citizens of Chihuahua City came out and sat down on nearby hillsides to see the slaughter of the gringos.[23]

Doniphan was confident too. He made a brief speech to his men in an offhand style, telling them he had given orders that the army should camp that evening inside the Mexican fortifications. His men responded enthusiastically with cheers and shouts of "Yes, yes, we will, Colonel." The column marched out of its encampment toward the Mexican lines to the strains of "Yankee Doodle," played by the band of the volunteer artillery battalion.[24]

After studying the Mexican position through a telescope, Doniphan led his command, complete with its 330 wagons belonging both to the Missouri regiment and the accompanying merchants, to the west around the left of the Mexican position, then up the steep slope of the escarpment and onto the plateau. From there his way toward the Mexican position was barred by a steep-sided ravine, thirty feet deep, but his men quickly built an earthen ramp that allowed the wagons, some of which weighed twelve tons, to struggle across, the reluctant mules goaded by the shouts and lashes of their drivers. Heredia responded by sending his lancers to charge the Americans, but Doniphan's artillerymen quickly unlimbered their twelve-pounder howitzers and inflicted such punishment on the advancing horsemen that they turned tail and fled in disorder.[25]

Then Doniphan's men moved up to press their attack against the Mexican fortifications. A battery of artillery rushed up to within fifty yards of the enemy works and opened fire, receiving fierce fire from the Mexicans in return. Before Doniphan could order a coordinated attack, some of his units charged without orders. Further confusion resulted when one of his staff officers, apparently intoxicated, galloped through the formation shouting nonsensical orders. Doniphan spurred his horse after him, trying his best to make clear that he wanted the regiment to charge, but the result was an uncoordinated attack, with the various companies advancing not all at once but at staggered intervals. Seeing the regiment charge in this manner, Doniphan buried his face in his hands and groaned, "They're gone! The boys will all be killed!" Quickly recovering from his shock, the colonel galloped after his men.[26]

His dismay proved unfounded. The Americans stormed over the Mexican breastworks and laid into the defenders, firing their rifles and pistols, slashing with bowie knives, and swinging their guns as clubs. Major Meriwether Lewis Clark, son of the explorer Captain William Clark, commanded Doniphan's volunteer artillery battalion. He led his artillerists over the Mexican breastworks and quickly manned several cannon the defenders had just abandoned, turning them on their erstwhile owners with deadly effect. Many of the Mexicans fought stoutly, but nothing, it seemed, could halt the Missourians' onslaught. The surviving Mexicans finally took to their heels in retreat, leaving their fortifications in the hands of Doniphan's wildly cheering Americans.[27]

In the Battle of the Sacramento, the Americans suffered casualties of 4 dead and 8 wounded while inflicting on their foes losses of 169 killed, 300 wounded, and 79 taken prisoner. The Missourians spent most of March 1 burying the dead Mexicans.[28]

The following day, March 2, 1847, Doniphan's column marched into Chihuahua, with the band of Clark's artillery battalion once again playing "Yankee Doodle" and "Hail, Columbia." The Missourians were impressed by the large and commodious city of fifteen thousand inhabitants, with its broad streets, abundant water, many cottonwood trees, and Gothic cathedral. Wool's army, however, was nowhere to be found, and Doniphan had received no word of his or any other American movements. Without any further instructions or orders, he sent messengers to carry his report back to the United States and settled down to wait in Chihuahua City. Finally, deciding to press on and join Wool at Buena Vista, Doniphan put his well-traveled command on the road yet again and joined the larger American force in May 1847, having traveled some thirty-five hundred difficult miles since leaving their home state. Their enlistments were up and there was no one left to fight against in the country around Buena Vista anyway, but Doniphan's Missourians had already won their fame and made their contribution to U.S. victory.[29]

Meanwhile, when Kearny had parted company with Doniphan back at Santa Fe, the regular officer had proceeded west to conquer California with a force of three hundred dragoons. Near Socorro, New Mexico, on October 6, 1846, he met the mountain man Kit Carson, who was passing through New Mexico on his way to Washington, D.C., with messages from John C. Frémont in California. Carson brought word that California was already in American hands, thanks to the navy, miscellaneous American settlers, and Frémont's exploring expedition, of which Carson himself had been a part. All Kearny needed to do, it appeared, was go out there and take command, as his orders directed. Kearny arranged for another courier to carry Carson's dispatches on to the capital while the redoubtable Carson, who knew the country well, joined Kearny's expedition. In order to speed his trip west and to strengthen the U.S. position in New Mexico, Kearny detached two hundred of his dragoons to stay behind in the territory while he traveled west with the remainder.[30]

Just as the population of New Mexico inhabited a string of settlements along the Rio Grande, so the population of California lived in a collection of villages extending along the Pacific coast from San Diego, in the south, to Yerba Buena, a village on San Francisco Bay, in the north. The province had a population of some ten thousand whites, five thousand semicivilized Indians, and ten thousand Indians still completely steeped in their tribal ways, and that gave it a population density of just one person for every twenty-six square miles. Its capital, an adobe pueblo called Ciudad de Los Angeles, counted fifteen hundred inhabitants.[31]

Like New Mexico, California was separated from the rest of Mexico by hundreds of miles of mountains and deserts. Communication with Mexico City was excruciatingly slow. Trade with the rest of Mexico was nonexistent. In California, even more so than in New Mexico, the population, though culturally and ethnically similar to the rest of Mexico, had become all but divorced from it in thought and attitude. Several minor revolts had established California as an autonomous province where Mexico's writ scarcely ran at all. Even the governor had difficulty asserting his authority as the province lurched along in a state of near anarchy, disorderly but sleepy and easygoing, commonly known as the "derelict on the Pacific."[32]

Among the province's five thousand non-Indian inhabitants were some twelve hundred immigrants, two-thirds of them American. Most of these lived in the extreme north of the area of settlement, along the Sacramento River in the northern part of California's Central Valley, largely because that area was closest to the mountain pass by which the California Trail crossed the Sierra Nevada into the fertile lands west of the range.[33]

The province had recently seen startling developments. For the past several months John C. Frémont, accompanied by a band of sixty hard-bitten mountain men, including Carson, had been on another expedition to the Far West. In December 1845, four months before the outbreak of the war, he had entered California, reached Sutter's Fort, and obtained permission from California's Mexican governor, General José Castro, to winter in the Sacramento Valley. In March 1846, however, Frémont had left the valley and approached the coastal town of Monterey, then California's chief port. When Castro ordered him back, Frémont raised the U.S. flag and prepared to offer battle. Castro was ready to accept it, and he had artillery; on learning this, the Pathfinder reluctantly withdrew across the mountains into Oregon.[34]

The following month, April 1846, Lieutenant Gillespie of the U.S. Marines arrived in California on the errand on which Polk had sent him at the end of the preceding October, having been delayed by the need to make his journey by a particularly roundabout route—via the Sandwich Islands (modern-day Hawaii), in fact—in order to avoid arousing suspicions among either the Mexicans or the British. A Royal Navy squadron was cruising the Pacific coasts of Mexico and California with apparent designs on the latter.[35]

Gillespie caught up with Frémont in May at Upper Klamath Lake, just inside Oregon, narrowly escaping death at the hands of Indians shortly before the meeting. Having received the message Gillespie had brought from Washington, Frémont immediately took his band back into California.[36]

Meanwhile, trouble had broken out there. In the wake of Frémont's March adventure, Castro had taken a more belligerent stance toward the large contingent of American settlers. The settlers, some of whom needed little enough prompting to undertake violence at the best of times, returned it in spades. Several hundred of them began raiding Mexican installations, capturing prisoners and weapons. Then they proclaimed the independent California Republic, based at Sonoma, and made themselves a flag—a somewhat crude affair depicting a grizzly bear and a single star. Ten days later they easily beat off the attack of fifty of Castro's troops sent to subdue them.[37]

Shortly thereafter, Frémont reached Sonoma and took charge of the incipient Bear Flag Revolt. He sent a letter to Washington resigning his army commission and proclaiming himself commander of the new California Battalion, consisting of his original band plus about 190 of the settlers. Gillespie was his adjutant.[38]

Cruising offshore, Commodore John Sloat of the U.S. Navy had been anxious for information as to whether war had indeed broken out between the United States and Mexico; he worried that the British would dash in and seize Monterey and was nervous lest he should embarrass himself—as Commodore Catesby Jones had done four years before—by seizing the town prematurely. When he heard of Frémont's involvement with the Bear Flag Revolt, he assumed that the Pathfinder was acting on orders from Washington and that war was a reality. Accordingly, he landed a force of 250 sailors and marines at Monterey and took the place without firing a shot. Castro fled, and Sloat then detached vessels from his squadron to occupy the province's other port towns.[39]

Then things got complicated. Frémont rode in at the head of his California Battalion, eager to become once again a part of the U.S. armed forces. The short-lived Bear Flag Republic came to an end in favor of a presumed impending annexation to the United States. To Sloat's consternation, however, Frémont revealed that he had not received any word of the outbreak of war between the United States and Mexico. His actions had been entirely unauthorized. Sloat had several days to envision himself as the possible goat of another Catesby Jones–style debacle. Then to Sloat's immense relief, Commodore Robert F. Stockton arrived from the States to take over command of the Pacific Squadron. Stockton was less nervous than his predecessor. If he had enough political clout to survive the Peacemaker incident on the *Princeton*, nothing he did here in far-off California—even starting a war with Mexico, if one was not indeed already under way elsewhere—was likely to hurt him. He carried on calmly with the occupation of California, transporting Frémont's battalion down the coast to help take Los Angeles.[40]

All seemed quiet in California. Then in September 1846 a major uprising broke out in Los Angeles. Gillespie had been left in charge of the town, and he had not done an especially good job of administration, ruling with undue harshness. On September 23, rebels attacked and for several days besieged Gillespie and his fifty-man garrison. An agreement made under flag of truce allowed the Americans to withdraw from Los Angeles, abandoning the town for the time being to the Californios. Gillespie's force marched to San Pedro, where one of Stockton's vessels took them aboard. In short order, during the weeks that followed, the Californios drove out the other small U.S. garrisons up and down the coast. Stockton made a bid to retake Los Angeles, but once his landing party had advanced beyond the range of naval gunfire support, it found itself hopelessly handicapped by lack of artillery and cavalry. The Californios, who were skilled horsemen, had plenty of mounts but only a single gun, yet that was enough. The landing party retreated to the ships. Frémont, who had returned with his battalion to the Sacramento Valley, refused to give his assistance, and Stockton found himself for the present unable to retake the coastal settlements.[41]

Meanwhile, Kearny had been making his way through the deserts of the Southwest, together with his small escort of two companies of dragoons, about one hundred men, along with Frémont's scout Kit Carson, who had brought the news. In any case, a larger party could scarcely have managed the difficult thousand-mile route from Santa Fe via the Gila River valley. One of Kearny's officers noted in his journal that if in future years a route were selected for a road to California, it would not be through the rugged and difficult Gila River valley.[42] After extreme hardships, the expedition had almost reached the Colorado River when, on November 22, Kearny sent out a reconnoitering party that brought in several Mexican civilians who had just come from California. They informed Kearny of the successful uprising of the Californios. Los Angeles, they said, was in their control, but U.S. forces continued to hold San Diego. Kearny therefore decided to head for San Diego, which in any case seemed the nearest and best place to make contact with the fleet.[43]

Kearny's men forded the Colorado on November 25 and continued their wearisome westward march across more deserts and rough terrain. Water was scarce and of bad quality, food the same. The horses gave out one by one. Only the weather was pleasant, but on December 1 that changed, as the new month came in cold and windy. The next day they reached Warner's Ranch, or Agua Caliente, a pleasant oasis of farmland in the California desert about seventy miles from San Diego. The proprietor was not present, but an Englishman living in the area confirmed the report they had received on the other side of the Colorado that the Mexicans had taken Los Angeles but that Stockton had several warships at San Diego and controlled the town. Kearny sent the Englishman ahead with a message notifying Stockton of his presence at Agua Caliente and of his intended arrival at San Diego.[44]

On the morning of December 5 they met a party of thirty-nine sailors and marines under Gillespie, dispatched by Stockton in response to

Kearny's message. Gillespie had with him an Indian who brought word that Andrés Pico, chief leader of the Californios, was encamped with about one hundred men not far away at San Pasqual. Kearny sent half a dozen mounted dragoons to reconnoiter Pico's camp, but the lieutenant leading the small squad blundered so as to alert the sleeping Californios to his presence. When the squad returned to camp shortly before midnight and informed Kearny that the element of surprise had been lost, Kearny decided to attack immediately. Boldness seemed the best course, and Carson assured him that the Californios would not fight well and that attacking them would be the best way to acquire better horses.[45]

A bitterly cold night had followed an evening of driving rain. Everything in camp seemed to be soaked, and most of it now frozen too. It was so cold the bugler could not blow reveille, so officers and sergeants routed the shivering soldiers out of their frozen blankets. Once on the way, however, the men were excited, eager to come to grips with the enemy.[46]

Shortly before dawn on the morning of December 6, they crested the ridge overlooking the broad, open valley of San Pasqual. The clouds had broken, and up on the heights they were above the fog. The moon, low on the western horizon, shown brightly, and Kearny gave his final orders for the attack on the Mexican camp below. The dragoons spurred their trail-weakened horses down the slope, and then everything began to go wrong. Perhaps not realizing the degree to which their long journey from New Mexico had exhausted them—and especially their horses—the command began to lose cohesion. The men on the strongest horses—generally the officers as well as noncommissioned officers and experienced privates who had taken better care of their animals—began to separate from the rest of the command. A party of about forty of these better-mounted men, Kearny among them, was soon far ahead of the others.[47]

As they reached the valley floor, Kearny, rather than pause for the remainder of his troops to close up, gave the command "Trot," but his aide, Captain Johnston, misunderstood and gave the order to charge.

"O heavens!" Kearny exclaimed. "I did not mean that!" But it was too late, and the already fragmented command became even more strung out as the troopers urged their horses to full speed and the gap widened between the stronger and the weaker animals. The command became broadly scattered.[48]

At the first onset of the handful of Americans in the lead, the Californios fired a few shots and then rode away. Most of the Americans found that their powder was wet and they could not shoot at all. The Cal-

The Battle of San Pasqual, December 6~7, 1846

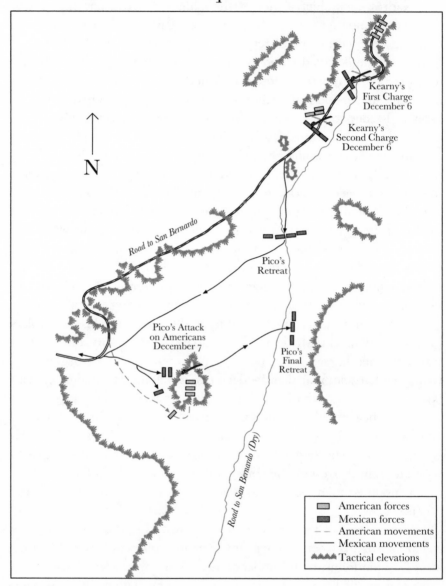

ifornios were well mounted and superb riders, and they easily stayed clear of the charging dragoons on their half-starved horses and mules. After retreating some distance, the Californios seemed to discover the weakness of the force pursuing them. It was still scarcely half-light, and the fog persisted in the valley. Turning, they charged and overran the lead group of Americans, killing or wounding virtually all of them. The Californios now used their lances exclusively and had a significant advantage over the Americans, who, with their firearms useless, were reduced to fighting with sabers.[49]

As more Americans came up from the remainder of Kearny's scattered column, the Californios easily rode around them and attacked from all sides, cutting down Kearny along with most of his command group. The mules pulling one of the two howitzers Kearny's men had laboriously brought over the mountains chose this moment to bolt, and the Californios captured the gun almost effortlessly.[50]

Finally, the Americans were able to get off a shot from the other howitzer, spraying grapeshot into the charging lancers. Gillespie's detail, though their captain himself was badly wounded, managed to fire another round with the small four-pounder cannon they had brought with them. The Californios had brought no artillery and had not bargained on riding into the teeth of cannon fire. Delighted with the capture of a howitzer, which was a victory in itself, they rode off, leaving the battlefield to the decimated Americans. Bringing along the artillery had probably saved the command from annihilation, though it still remains unclear whether that was more owing to the blasts fired by two of the guns or the distraction to the Californios provided by the capture of the third.[51]

About forty-five or, at the most, fifty Americans had actually participated in the Battle of San Pasqual. Of these, twenty-two were killed and sixteen wounded. Among the latter were both Kearny and Gillespie, who like most of the casualties had suffered multiple lance wounds. Perhaps seventy of Pico's Californios got into the fight. Their losses are harder to ascertain. Reports range from one to six killed and from twelve to eighteen wounded.[52]

Kearny's force buried their dead in unmarked graves to prevent the Californios from plundering the bodies, then crept on as best it could, carrying its many wounded on travois rigged to the few pitiful remaining mules. A painful day of travel brought them a few miles to a hilltop defended by Pico's men, blocking their route to the sea. This time the American powder was dry, and Kearny's men inflicted at least five casualties while suffering none themselves. Having taken up a defensible position on the hilltop, Kearny settled down to eat mule meat and wait for more help from Stockton.

In hopes of securing that help, he dispatched another party of couriers. They reached Stockton and were returning with a letter from him, explaining that he would not send any help, when Pico's men caught them and read the dispatch. One of the messengers who did make it to Kearny's hilltop position brought the bad news. Kearny decided to send another plea for help. The next party of three messengers was led by the renowned Carson himself. On the evening of December 8, despite the heightened vigilance of the Californios, who knew Carson was present and would probably try to get out, the couriers made good their escape and, despite great hardships—which included walking barefoot over stones and cacti—covered the twenty-nine miles of rough country to San Diego.[53]

In response to the message brought by Carson's party, Stockton finally dispatched a force of 120 sailors and 80 marines, and this command marched through the night and reached Kearny the next morning, December 10, just as he had come to the conclusion that his crippled force was going to have to fight its way through enemy lines if it was to escape. His men rejoiced at the arrival of the relieving column, and the dismayed Californios made off without waiting to try conclusions with the new force.[54]

Once united in San Diego, the Americans regrouped, recuperated, and prepared to advance against Los Angeles. Stockton and Kearny handled the question of command amicably. The higher-ranking Kearny agreed to serve under Stockton's overall command while serving as field commander of the land forces. These were composed primarily of Stockton's sailors and marines, the former sadly lacking in the intricacies of infantry drill, though doughty and well disciplined. Stockton and Kearny remedied this by training them to fight from a hollow square formation. This was the preferred formation against the ubiquitous Californio cavalry, and sticking to it at all times in the presence of the enemy would greatly simplify the training of sailors as foot soldiers.[55]

On December 29, 1846, the Americans set out from San Diego bound for Los Angeles. The band of the USS *Congress* marched at the head of the column, and behind it followed the sailors and marines, the small remaining party of dragoons (all now on foot), and a company of volunteer mounted riflemen drawn from California's Anglo population and commanded by Gillespie. In all, the column numbered 563 men and 44 officers, not counting the band.[56]

On January 8, 1847, a day that Kearny did not fail to remind his men was the anniversary of the great American victory at New Orleans in the War of 1812, the column neared Los Angeles and encountered a force of some five hundred Californios commanded by José María Flores. Flores's men had taken up a position on bluffs behind the San Gabriel River.

Commodore Stockton personally led the American artillery across the river to a position from which the guns could silence their Mexican counterparts. Then Kearny led a charge by sailors, marines, and dragoons that swept the Californios from their position and sent them reeling in headlong retreat. The Battle of San Gabriel lasted scarcely an hour and a half from first shot to last.[57]

The next day the Americans followed up their victory and met the Californios again closer to Los Angeles. After two unsuccessful charges on the Americans' square formation, the Mexicans retired, giving up the town. On January 10 Kearny's forces marched into the town with band playing and colors flying.[58]

As the fleeing Californios made their way northward, they reached the adobe farmhouse known as Campo de Cahuenga, near Cahuenga Pass in what is now North Hollywood, and there encountered Frémont and his California Battalion, who had hitherto done absolutely nothing in the fight for the province. Frémont arranged a meeting with Californio leader Andrés Pico and, in the name of the United States, negotiated a completely unauthorized treaty, granting the Californios citizenship rights without requiring an oath of allegiance, pardoning parole violators, and so on. He even took possession of the mountain howitzer Kearny's men had lost at San Pasqual. Overall, the agreement, known as the Treaty of Cahuenga, ended the conflict in California but was unduly generous considering the military situation and was a studied piece of insubordination to Frémont's superiors Kearny and Stockton, both of whom were close enough to have been consulted in the matter. It was vintage Frémont.[59]

On January 14, Frémont rode into Los Angeles in the midst of a heavy rainstorm, leading the four hundred irregular volunteers of the California Battalion. Since October 27, 1846, Frémont had once again held a commission in the U.S. Army, this time as lieutenant colonel in recognition of his having raised the California Battalion. His arrival was the immediate prelude to a major imbroglio among the U.S. brass in California. Frémont was a desperately ambitious narcissist. Stockton was headstrong and high-handed at the best of times, and the release of tension after the defeat of the Californio uprising seemed to be anything but the best of times as far as the commodore's mental stability was concerned. For reasons best known to himself—but that may have involved currying the favor of the powerful senator Thomas Hart Benton, Frémont's father-in-law—Stockton decreed that Frémont would be governor of California.[60]

This put Kearny in an impossible situation. Polk had issued him a direct order to assume the role of governor himself. Kearny did not covet the job but felt compelled to obey orders. Frémont felt no such compulsion and happily thumbed his nose at not only his immediate superior but the commander in chief's order as well. Stockton backed him, asserting that he and Frémont were entitled to ignore the president's order because they had already conquered the province before Kearny arrived and Kearny had not brought with him enough troops to do so himself. Stockton emphasized his point by sending Kearny a note stating, "You will consider yourself suspended from the command of the United States forces in this place." That took nerve, since Stockton did not outrank Kearny and could not conceivably have had the power to relieve him of command. At least some of Stockton's subordinate naval officers were embarrassed at his course of action, but could do nothing about it. Kearny and his fellow army officers were livid, but with little manpower in California they too were, for the moment, powerless to enforce the president's order against the mutinous commodore and his army accomplice. Kearny moved his small force of dragoons back to San Diego and sent word of the situation to Washington.[61]

The winds soon began to change. On January 29, 1847, Lieutenant Colonel Philip St. George Cooke arrived in California with the Mormon Battalion, one of the most unusual units in the army. The battalion had come into existence as the result of a deal made the preceding spring between the U.S. government and Mormon leader Brigham Young. After leaving their settlement at Nauvoo, Illinois, during the course of the winter of 1846, the Mormons had migrated across the state of Iowa and, crossing the Missouri River, made their winter quarters just north of what is today Omaha, Nebraska. Eager to raise money to purchase supplies to continue the migration to the Far West the following summer, Young had dispatched Mormon elder Jesse C. Little to Washington, D.C., to solicit the federal government's assistance. That in itself was an odd development, considering the hostility with which the Mormons regarded the United States and its "gentile" (i.e., non-Mormon) citizens, but Young was nothing if not pragmatic.

Little arrived in Washington in May 1846, shortly after the declaration of war with Mexico. He met with President Polk, who suggested that the best way for the Mormons to raise the necessary cash would be for at least five hundred of them to enlist as volunteers in a battalion of their own to serve the United States in the war that was commencing. They could then receive the standard pay and allowances of soldiers. When

Little got back to the Mormons' camp on the west bank of the Missouri, Young readily embraced the idea. With his forceful encouragement the battalion achieved the requisite number—five hundred—of the most reluctant recruits who ever signed up to soldier for Uncle Sam. The Mormons did not particularly want to fight for the United States, and they suspected that the recruitment of the battalion was really just another American ploy to betray and persecute them. But Young bade them go, and go they did.[62]

The Mormon Battalion, carrying U.S. government muskets and rifles but still wearing civilian clothes, since they had turned over their army-issued uniform allowance to their church, marched out of Fort Leavenworth, Kansas, in mid-September 1846, following the Santa Fe Trail in the wake of Kearny's expedition. With them went Mormon official Orson Pratt, sent by Young to make sure all the soldiers turned over the whole of their pay to the church.

The battalion's company officers were Mormons from among the ranks, but its commander was to be a regular army officer. The first to fill that role was Captain James Allen, promoted to the temporary rank of lieutenant colonel of volunteers, but he succumbed to illness shortly after the battalion left Fort Leavenworth. Learning of Allen's demise, Kearny, in New Mexico, sent the first available regular officer, First Lieutenant Andrew Jackson Smith, to take command. Smith was a tough, no-nonsense regular (West Point class of 1838) who started the real transformation of the men of the battalion into something like soldiers. The Mormons hated him and were delighted when, upon reaching Santa Fe, they met Cooke with orders from Kearny to take command of the battalion and march it to California. A captain in the First Dragoons and one of Kearny's favorite subordinates, Cooke, like Allen, would rank as lieutenant colonel of volunteers.[63]

After helping Doniphan and Price suppress Apache depredations in New Mexico, the battalion set out on its trek to the Pacific. With them as a guide was mountain man Jean Baptiste Charbonneau. The forty-two-year-old trapper had a peculiarly appropriate pedigree. He had been born in February 1805 at Fort Mandan, in what is today North Dakota, across the Missouri River from the villages of the Mandan Indians. His mother was a teenage Shoshone girl whom his father, a French trapper named Toussaint Charbonneau, had purchased from the Hidatsa, who had kidnapped her from her home. Her name was Sacagawea, and she was the only female member of the Lewis and Clark expedition. On her back the infant Jean Baptiste had accompanied the expedition to the

Pacific and back. Educated in St. Louis at Clark's expense, he had met a German prince and at his invitation had spent six years traveling around Europe, learning German, French, and Spanish. On his return to America, he had become a trapper, working with many of the great mountain men. Cooke and his Mormon Battalion could hardly have had a more ideal guide. With Charbonneau's assistance, the battalion made its way through the deserts and mountains of the Southwest, in one place getting through a seemingly impassable mountain range by hoisting their wagons up steep slopes at the end of long ropes and lowering them down the other side.

Their arrival in California on January 29, 1847, was timely for Kearny. With the Mormon Battalion on hand, Kearny finally had the manpower he needed to oppose Frémont's mutiny. More help came a few days later when Commodore William Branford Shubrick arrived in California with orders to supersede Stockton, much to the relief of army, navy, and Californios, as he lifted martial law and generally ran a much more reasonable regime than his predecessor. He also pledged his support to Kearny. About the same time, the navy's sloop-of-war USS *Lexington* arrived carrying a large company of regular artillery. Its arrival more than doubled the number of regular troops Kearny had in California. Finally, on February 13, Colonel Richard B. Mason arrived with further orders from Polk. Kearny was indeed to be governor and then was to turn the job over to Mason at such time as he deemed California to be "pacified."[64]

Thus strengthened, Kearny proceeded to assert his authority. Frémont was furious. At first, he appeared ready to obey orders, but within a few days he was back in old form, defying Kearny's orders, per instructions from Washington, to have the California Battalion mustered into United States service. When Kearny sent for the return of the howitzer belonging to his dragoons, lost at San Pasqual and surrendered by the Californios at Cahuenga, Frémont ordered his subordinates to refuse. After coming to Monterey for a direct confrontation with Kearny, Frémont backed down and agreed henceforth to obey orders.[65]

In early April Mason and Frémont were in Los Angeles while the former straightened out various administrative matters pending in the wake of the recent occupation of the province. After obeying several routine orders, Frémont became balky again, several times refusing a summons to report to Mason. When he did appear, the famous Pathfinder was surly and belligerent. Several days later Mason once more needed to see Frémont, and the same unpleasant process played out again. When requested to account for some of the public property used by the troops under his command, Frémont exploded in a torrent of angry words.

"None of your insolence," replied the exasperated Mason, "or I'll put you in irons."

Frémont stopped in mid-tirade, shocked that Mason would dare to speak to him in such a way. He demanded that Mason apologize. The colonel refused, whereupon Frémont left the room in a huff. Shortly thereafter, an officer of the California Battalion arrived at Mason's headquarters with a message from Frémont demanding that Mason apologize. Mason again refused, and the officer then presented him with a challenge from Frémont to fight a duel. By this time, Mason's frame of mind made him only too glad for the chance to take a shot at Frémont, so he accepted and, as the challenged party, chose as the weapons for the duel shotguns loaded with buckshot.

By the next day, Mason had calmed down enough to realize that it would not do to have the two senior U.S. officers in Los Angeles engaging in personal combat, however much it might have helped the American cause and made the world a better place generally for someone— anyone—to shoot John C. Frémont. So he sent Frémont a note informing him that they would have to postpone the duel until they got back to Monterey. Before that could happen, however, news of the planned contest reached Kearny, and he quickly nixed the whole thing.[66]

Thereafter, Frémont more or less obeyed Kearny's and Mason's orders, though slowly and not within the time frame Kearny gave him for such tasks as mustering out the California Battalion. The Pathfinder even occasionally continued to represent himself as governor of California, particularly when he found it necessary in order to interfere with the local collector of customs in such a way as to cover his tracks for previous financial irregularities.[67]

With his mission in California completed, in August 1847 Kearny set out for Washington. Frémont realized that he might as well go too. Upon reaching Fort Leavenworth, the first army post on their way, Kearny duly had Frémont arrested and charged with mutiny for his behavior in California. When they arrived in the national capital, Kearny received a hero's welcome and Frémont a court-martial, ending in a conviction and sentence of dishonorable discharge. Polk recognized Frémont's guilt, but in appreciation of his help in securing California, he commuted the sentence. Frémont was furious that the president had not instead overturned the conviction and demanded that Polk do so. When he did not, the offended Pathfinder resigned.[68]

CHAPTER THIRTEEN

Buena Vista

BACK IN WASHINGTON, Polk was disappointed at the failure to bring the Mexicans to the negotiating table. The year 1846 had seen impressive military victories, but the foe remained adamant. Polk was also disappointed that Santa Anna had not delivered on the promises that had led Polk to give orders allowing him to slip through the U.S. blockade and into Mexico a few months before. In August 1846, in another of Mexico's seemingly endless coups, General José Mariano Salas had deposed President Paredes and seized control of the country on behalf of Santa Anna, who was soon exercising power in Mexico City. When a message bearing a peace proposal from Secretary of State James Buchanan arrived shortly thereafter, Santa Anna indignantly rejected it, calling on his fellow Mexicans to rally to his standard and drive out the invaders. Stunned by Santa Anna's duplicity, Polk considered his next move.[1]

For several weeks Polk and his advisors had been contemplating a possible expedition, detached from Taylor's army, to capture the Mexican Gulf–coast port of Tampico. After news arrived of Santa Anna's decision to continue the war, Polk decided that a deeper strike was needed and began to consider instead a move to capture the more important and southerly port of Veracruz. To lead the expedition he had in mind Major General Robert Patterson. Born in Ireland, Patterson had migrated to Philadelphia with his family at the age of seven. In the War of 1812 he served first with the Pennsylvania volunteers and then with the regular U.S. Army, mustering out at the end of hostilities as a captain. Returning to Philadelphia, Patterson took up banking and politics, and his prominence won him a commission as major general of Pennsylvania volunteers when the Mexican War broke out. What made the fifty-four-year-old Patterson especially attractive to Polk was that he was a good Democrat, unlike Taylor and Scott, who were Whigs and, as Polk correctly surmised, who both entertained ideas about future residence in the White House.[2]

Taylor had recently been reinforced by the three thousand men under

Brigadier General John E. Wool. Wool's career as a professional soldier presented a contrast to that of the occasional amateur officer Patterson. Born in Newburgh, New York, in 1784, Wool had been practicing law at the outbreak of the War of 1812. Joining the regular army, he distinguished himself at the Battles of Queenston Heights and Plattsburg, rising to the rank of colonel. After the war he never looked back to his law career; he remained in the army and by 1841 had achieved promotion to brigadier general, a very senior rank in the small regular army. His first assignment in the Mexican War had been to lead the Center Division on a march from San Antonio to capture Chihuahua City. Finding the route impracticable, Wool had diverted to join Taylor.[3]

The midterm congressional elections that fall went as midterm elections usually do, with the party that controlled the presidency losing seats in Congress. That was enough to give the Whigs a slim 117–110 margin in the House of Representatives. Although not unexpected, the outcome was disquieting to Polk and his fellow Democrats. Senate Democratic stalwart Thomas Hart Benton believed he knew the reason for the voters' dissatisfaction. It lay in the passive way the United States was currently prosecuting its war with Mexico. The American people, he told Polk when he stopped by the White House in mid-November, wanted energetic action, with steady "going ahead" until the job was finished. "Ours were a go-ahead people," as Polk summarized Benton's conversation in his diary, and the "only policy either to obtain a peace or save ourselves was to press the war boldly." Merely sitting down and occupying the northern tier of Mexican provinces would not do. That policy would produce a long-drawn-out conflict that would play directly to one of the great weaknesses of the American people, their impatience, and at the same time to perhaps the great strength of the Mexican people, their ability to endure long-term low-grade conflict. Benton wanted instead a vigorous, aggressive prosecution of the war all the way to victory, and he had a plan for it, which he gave the president in writing.[4]

Thomas Hart Benton was born in 1782 in Harts Mill, North Carolina, the son of a wealthy lawyer and landowner. He studied law himself, at the University of North Carolina, but left before graduating in order to manage his family's extensive holdings, his father having died several years before. A few years later Benton moved his family to the Nashville Basin in Middle Tennessee, where he acquired a forty-thousand-acre plantation. In Tennessee he became a lawyer, a member of the state legislature—for one term—and, more important, a protégé of Andrew Jackson. When the War of 1812 began, Jackson made Benton his aide-de-camp with a commission as lieutenant colonel. All went well until Benton heard that Jackson had spoken disparagingly of his brother, Jesse. Enraged, the Bentons attacked Jackson in a Nashville hotel, leading to a free-for-all between their entourages. Before it was over, Jackson had one of the Bentons' bullets in his shoulder and another in his arm, while Jesse Benton had received one of Jackson's shots in return. The men survived, and so did their animosity.

After the war Benton had once again relocated his massive estate, this time to the Missouri Territory. He settled in St. Louis and there added to his law practice the duties—and influence—of editing the *Missouri Enquirer*. In 1817 he clashed with a fellow lawyer, Charles Lucas. Each man called the other a liar, and then Benton upped the ante by calling Lucas a "puppy." That led to a duel in which Benton shot Lucas dead.

This was frontier Missouri, and shooting another man in a duel was as likely to help as to hurt a man's reputation. It seemed to do Benton's little harm, as in 1821 he was selected as one of the two original U.S. senators of the brand-new state of Missouri. Reelected in 1826, 1832, 1838, and 1844, Benton had become the first member of the Senate to win election to that body five times over. His Senate career was marked by staunch opposition to special privileges for big banks, especially the biggest of them all, Henry Clay's cherished Second Bank of the United States. Benton's devotion to sound money won him the nickname Old Bullion, and though his policy positions made it a natural alliance, there was certainly irony in the fact that Benton became the staunchest congressional ally of President Andrew Jackson.

Perhaps the issue nearest Benton's heart was westward expansion. Like many another American, Benton had been an enthusiastic advocate of the concept of Manifest Destiny long before O'Sullivan had coined the term. Benton had consistently supported policies that promoted settlement of the West, from his opposition to the kind of credit expansion that encouraged land speculation to his advocacy of a generous land policy that would, four years after his death, eventually be realized in the Homestead Act.

It was therefore appropriate, in one sense, or perhaps ironic, that Benton's favorite daughter, the headstrong and willful Jessie, had in 1841, at the age of seventeen, eloped from her young ladies' finishing school with the dashing twenty-eight-year-old Lieutenant John C. Frémont of the Corps of Topographical Engineers. Old Bullion had at first strongly disapproved, but he soon came around and became an enthusiastic backer of his pathfinding son-in-law. He provided strong political sponsorship for Frémont's 1842 exploring expedition to South Pass and subsequent expeditions into the Sierra Nevada that won the young lieutenant the sobriquet of Pathfinder.

As one would expect coming from such a man, Senator Benton's plan for winning the war with Mexico was nothing if not aggressive. He called for an American army to land at Veracruz, capture the city, and then march inland to take Mexico City itself, duplicating the accomplishment of Hernán Cortés more than three centuries before. The idea was not entirely novel. Late in October Winfield Scott had, at Polk's behest, submitted a plan for the capture of Veracruz. Scott, the opposite of Benton in perhaps every respect except an outsized ego, had urged in his plan the necessity of the same course of action Benton was advocating a fortnight later. "To conquer a peace," Scott wrote, "I am now persuaded that we must take the city of Mexico, or place it in imminent danger of capture."[5]

As to the advisability of the campaign, then, there seemed to be no doubt, with the country's foremost general and one of its most astute politicians recommending it for reasons both military and political. The question for Polk to decide was who should command the campaign. Benton suggested that Polk persuade Congress to re-create the rank of lieutenant general, a rank not held since the retirement of George Washington, thus giving the commander of the great expedition instant seniority over all the army's current generals, including the odious Whigs Scott and Taylor. Furthermore, a peace commissioner should accompany the army to Mexico City, with full powers to negotiate with the Mexican government on all the issues that had brought on the war and to conclude a treaty of peace. Benton let Polk know that he personally was available to fill either or, preferably, both positions.[6]

Polk presented Benton's plan to the cabinet, which received it with some skepticism. Polk, and presumably also the members of the cabinet, would have been comfortable with Benton as a peace commissioner, but, as several members of the cabinet pointed out, brief service as a staff lieutenant colonel whose chief duty had been to represent Andrew Jackson's concerns in Washington, D.C., during the War of 1812 was hardly a sufficient qualification for appointment as supreme commander of the Republic's armies for the express purpose of leading the boldest military venture of its not-quite-seventy-one-year history. The president dryly informed Old Bullion that he did not believe Congress would see fit to authorize the new rank, and, as expected, Benton had no interest in accepting a lower one.[7]

Still, Scott's and Benton's arguments in favor of a campaign to take Mexico City had won the support of the president and the somewhat more grudging support of the cabinet as well. With Benton out of the running to command such an endeavor, the question remained as to who should. Polk was deeply displeased with Taylor, who he felt had been playing politics with his command, angling for the next presidential election, and who had recently written some ill-advised letters to the secretary of war denouncing the administration's policies. Winfield Scott's well-known pride, ill temper, and Whiggish politics made him an unattractive choice too. Polk suggested Patterson, but the cabinet once again balked at the idea of giving such a command to a rank amateur. Polk brought up the name of another volunteer, William O. Butler, but the same objection also applied to him. Though a veteran of the War of 1812, including the Battle of New Orleans, the Kentuckian had spent the intervening years as a lawyer and politician, and brief service as a junior officer three decades ago was not sufficient to win the cabinet's confidence nor to prompt Polk to proceed against that body's advice.[8]

Instead, much against his inclinations, the president saw no choice but to give the command to Winfield Scott, who at least had lately been behaving a bit more circumspectly. The cabinet felt much the same way. Its members were divided, and even those who supported Scott held serious misgivings. Still, it seemed the only thing to do. Polk called the general in for a conference and assured him he was "willing that by-gones should be by-gones." If Scott had confidence in the administration, Polk would have confidence enough to give him command of the Mexico City expedition. Scott was overjoyed with the assignment. Indeed, when Polk told him about it, the general was almost moved to tears. Assuring Polk of his confidence and gratitude, the exuberant general took his leave of the president, "the most delighted man," Polk noted in his diary, "I have seen for a long time." Scott quickly made his preparations and set off for the mouth of the Rio Grande, where he would acquire his army—borrowed, for this expedition, from Taylor.[9]

Relations between the president and his top-ranking general were not to remain so pleasant. About the time Scott arrived at the Rio Grande, Polk, who was still far from satisfied with Old Fuss and Feathers, had decided to go ahead and see if Congress would be willing to create the rank of lieutenant general, thus giving him the ability to appoint someone—Benton, of course—who would outrank Scott and could thus take the command of the expedition away from him. Congress refused, but Scott got word of the proceeding and remarked bitterly that Polk was "an enemy more to be feared than Santa Anna with all his hosts."[10]

Scott arrived in Camargo, in the Rio Grande Valley, on January 3, 1847. Seven hundred miles to the northwest, Alexander Doniphan and his men were enjoying their rest in El Paso after crossing the Jornada del Muerto and their victory at El Brazito and preparing for their continued march toward Chihuahua City. Another seven hundred miles west-northwest of El Paso, Kearny's troops in San Diego were also resting after the grueling journey through the Gila River valley and their brutal treatment at San Pasqual. They too were planning further operations— the reconquest, along with Stockton's sailors and marines, of the province of California. While those operations took their course, Scott eagerly prepared for his own much more ambitious campaign.

On the day of his arrival, Scott wrote to Taylor requesting that he come to Camargo to discuss preparations for the new expedition. This was a follow-up to a letter Scott had written Taylor in November from New York and another he had written from New Orleans in December; in both he had explained that he would be compelled to take most of Taylor's troops for another expedition and that Taylor in the meantime would have to be content to remain at Monterrey, on the defensive. But by the time Scott reached the Rio Grande, Taylor's army was no longer concentrated at Monterrey, where both Scott and the authorities in Washington had supposed it to be. Before learning of Scott's campaign, Taylor had made plans to advance to Saltillo, about fifty-five miles far-ther to the southwest, and despite a dispatch from the secretary of war ordering him to stay put in Monterrey, as well as the letters from Scott, Old Rough and Ready had chosen to advance to Saltillo anyway. Now, in the face of Scott's request—an order really—that he come to Camargo, Taylor again chose not to obey.[11]

Scott could not afford to dally on the Rio Grande. He had to get his campaign under way so that his army could take Veracruz and then move inland, getting clear of the coastal lowlands before the advent of the season of the dreaded *vómito*—yellow fever—which would be raging there by late spring. That meant Scott had no time to lose. He therefore sent a requisition for the necessary troops directly to Taylor's subordi-nate, Major General Butler. It called for nearly all of Taylor's regulars and some of his most experienced volunteers. To make sure Taylor knew what was happening, Scott sent a copy of the letter to him as well.[12]

Taylor was furious. He sent the troops as ordered, but he continued to defy Scott's command to fall back on Monterrey, keeping his army near Saltillo. Meanwhile, he wrote bitter, self-pitying letters, one of them to Scott, complaining that the government was out to ruin him. Privately he fumed that there must be a conspiracy between Polk and Scott to derail his future presidential prospects. Worse, he allowed a friend back in the States to publish another of his letters, this one denouncing the conduct of the war and especially the planned campaign against Veracruz. A number of newspapers picked it up, and now it was the president's turn to be furious. This was not only public criticism but a severe breach of security. He had the secretary of war send Taylor a stern warning that the penalty prescribed in regulations for the unauthorized publication of military reports was dismissal from the service.[13]

Taylor's security breach may not have mattered. There had actually been two copies of Scott's letter to Taylor, sent on separate routes to assure the fastest possible arrival. One of those copies had been entrusted to Lieutenant John Ritchey, who was near Linares on the evening of January 11, 1847, when Mexican vaqueros came on him, lassoed him and dragged him to his death, and took his dispatch case. Whether the captured missive actually found its way to Santa Anna is disputed, but by early February, Scott and Taylor had learned of the loss of Ritchey's copy of the dispatch and had to assume that Santa Anna was aware of U.S. plans and dispositions in Mexico. Both Scott and Taylor, however, miscalculated the Mexican generalissimo's response. The correct military move would have been for Santa Anna to take his army to Veracruz to oppose Scott's landing, and that is what the Americans expected. What they had left out of their calculations was the overwhelming thirst for glory of the man who liked to be called the Napoleon of the West. Santa Anna much preferred the prospect of a glorious victory over Taylor's diminished army to that of taking the course of action that would give him the best chance of saving his country's capital. Even as Scott and Taylor weighed the probabilities, Santa Anna was already driving his army on a brutal march across the deserts from his base at San Luis Potosí toward Saltillo.[14]

Santa Anna had assembled at San Luis Potosí every last *soldado* he could find or make, drawing in Ampudia's defeated army from Monterrey, new levies from Mexico's more distant states, and the hapless peasants his press gangs swept up in nearby regions. He even pulled the garrison out of Tampico. All told, he brought together twenty thousand troops, of widely varying degrees of training and experience. He was less successful in procuring supplies and equipment for his greatly expanded host. Poorly clothed and fed and sometimes unpaid, Santa Anna's troops did not always have the best morale. Still, the Napoleon of the West's accomplishment in drawing together—and holding together—an army of that size in northern Mexico was impressive.[15]

By far the most unusual unit in Santa Anna's army was the San Patricio Battalion, composed entirely of deserters from the U.S. Army. These were mostly recent immigrants to the United States, a demographic heavily represented in the ranks of the regular army. The San Patricios were Catholic, and the Mexican government had made a concerted effort to depict the war as a conflict between Catholic Mexico and the Protestant United States and to encourage Catholic soldiers in the U.S. Army to cross over to the Mexican side. Leaflets printed by order of General Ampudia offered generous land bounties to deserters from the United States who would enlist under the banner of Mexico. Ironically, Scott had always been at pains to cultivate the goodwill of local Catholics, while Santa Anna was much at odds with the Catholic Church in Mexico, having plundered its holdings extensively to finance his war effort. Some of the San Patricios came from Germany, but most hailed from Ireland. The battalion carried a green flag bearing images of a shamrock, a harp of Erin, and Saint Patrick, who would no doubt have been astonished if he could have seen the proceedings.

Their commander was thirty-year-old John Riley, a veteran sergeant of the British Army and its colonial wars who had come to America after his discharge in 1843 and enlisted in the Fifth U.S. Infantry Regiment in 1845. In April of the following year he had deserted from Taylor's army along the Rio Grande. He had sought and received from his captain a pass to attend Catholic services just outside camp and had taken advantage of the opportunity to clear the picket line and desert to the enemy. Ampudia had commissioned him a first lieutenant in the Mexican army and had him raise a company of his fellow deserters for service as artillerymen. Serving in that capacity with the Mexican batteries at Matamoros, they had helped bombard their erstwhile comrades in Fort Brown. At Monterrey, Riley and his men had fired again on the U.S. flag and U.S. soldiers. In preparing the army for the march north to battle, Santa Anna had given Riley and his company, now grown to some 150 men, charge of the Mexican army's heaviest field guns, big sixteen- and twenty-four-pounders.[16]

Santa Anna's army left San Luis Potosí on January 26, 1847, and the northward march across 275 miles of sparsely settled country was an ordeal. The troops suffered for lack of water, as the sources along the route were few and of small volume. Mid-winter temperatures were low in this high desert, and the inadequately clad troops shivered under cold wind and rain and even occasional snow. Some froze to death, others deserted. Perhaps sixteen thousand completed the march.[17]

Taylor did not have the luxury of even that large a force, and his men had, on the average, even less experience than Santa Anna's. After the heavy detachments of troops to Scott, Old Rough and Ready's army numbered fewer than 4,800 men, including 209 dragoons and three batteries of regular artillery. The rest were volunteers, and among those citizen-soldiers only the 368 men of Jefferson Davis's Mississippi Rifles, along with a handful of Texas Rangers, had previously seen action. The rest had no experience of battle at all.[18]

Taylor did not believe Santa Anna could bring any significant number of troops across the deserts from San Luis Potosí and so did not expect a major attack. He rather hoped for a minor one, however, since another victory would be useful in the future presidential campaign that was coming to be more and more on Taylor's mind. In hopes of making contact with the enemy, Taylor flouted his orders still further by advancing his army nineteen miles beyond Saltillo to Agua Nueva, a pleasant hacienda situated amid the desert scrub in a broad, level valley.[19]

On February 17 a patrol of Texas Rangers led by Ben McCulloch clashed with the advance cavalry of Santa Anna's army near La Encarnación, thirty-five miles from Agua Nueva. A small body of Mexican cavalry under General J. V. Minon had been hovering in front of Taylor's army for several weeks, but McCulloch was convinced that the troopers his men had fought and driven out of La Encarnación were not their familiar foes of Minon's cavalry but belonged to an entirely different Mexican formation. McCulloch reported the news to Taylor, who decided to find out more about the unusual enemy activity to the south. On February 20 he dispatched Captain Charles A. May with all of the army's dragoons and a section of light artillery to scout to the east of Agua Nueva while McCulloch and seven or eight of his rangers, dressed as Mexican vaqueros, rode back to La Encarnación for a closer reconnaissance of the Mexican force there.[20]

May's dragoons had ridden as far as Rancho Hediona, thirty miles from Agua Nueva, when they clashed with Mexican cavalry, Minon's troopers this time, and captured a vaquero who claimed to have ridden that day from La Encarnación, where he said Santa Anna had arrived with a large army. May turned back toward Agua Nueva and arrived early the following morning, Sunday, February 21, to report the news to

Taylor. At about the same time May was making his report, and thirty-five miles to the south, McCulloch and one of his comrades nonchalantly walked their horses through the Mexican encampment at La Encarnación, just as the *soldados* were emerging from their tents to kindle their morning cook fires. Once clear of the camp and reunited with the rest of his scouting group, McCulloch rode hard for Agua Nueva, arriving a little before noon to report to Taylor that Santa Anna was indeed present at La Encarnación and with an army that McCulloch estimated at twenty thousand men.[21]

Deep in enemy territory and far from the aid of friendly forces, the Americans had no way of avoiding the coming clash with a foe that outnumbered them more than three times over. They may have been few, but these Americans were not necessarily a happy few, nor were they any band of brothers—at least, not all of them. Two of Taylor's volunteer regiments were the Second and Third Indiana, commanded by Colonels William A. Bowles and James H. Lane. Together the two regiments formed a brigade under the command of Brigadier General Joseph Lane. The Lanes were unrelated and glad of it. In fact, the two men hated each other. Born in Buncombe County, North Carolina, the forty-one-year-old Joseph Lane had grown up in Kentucky and Indiana. Portly and dignified in appearance, Lane had been a fixture in the Indiana legislature for almost a quarter of a century until appointed at the outbreak of the Mexican War to command the Second Indiana Volunteers, which he had turned over to Bowles when promoted to brigadier. James H. Lane was a wiry, fiery thirty-two-year-old lawyer from Lawrenceburg, Indiana.

On Saturday, February 20, the day on which Taylor dispatched his two scouting parties and on which the last of Santa Anna's troops arrived at La Encarnación, Colonel Lane was drilling his regiment at Agua Nueva while General Lane stood looking on. The two exchanged pointed remarks, and then the general took a swing at the colonel, who blocked the punch and landed one of his own squarely in his commanding officer's chops. Other officers jumped in to separate the two. Shouting for the colonel to prepare himself for a duel, the general stalked off to his tent, retrieved a rifle, approached to a range of thirty yards, and shouted, "Ready!" Many soldiers in the Third Indiana hastily began loading their weapons with a view to shooting their general if he shot their colonel. Fortunately at this moment the provost guard arrived on the scene and somewhat gingerly escorted the general away. Taylor took no disciplinary action pursuant to the incident, but he did take steps to avoid any future intersection of the Lanes by keeping the Second and Third Indiana regiments strictly separated. Although Joseph Lane continued in nominal command of both, he accompanied the Second, which thus in effect had two commanders.[22]

The impending clash with Santa Anna's mighty host was considerably more than Taylor had bargained for when he had moved his army forward to Agua Nueva. The broad, flat valley around the hacienda was not a good place for the smaller American army to make a desperate stand against its vastly larger Mexican opponent. Both of Taylor's flanks were "in the air"—not anchored on any strong natural feature—and the ground was favorable for the operation of the large Mexican cavalry force, which would undoubtedly sweep around both sides of the small American army. Wool urged Taylor that the army should fall back a short distance to the Angostura—Spanish for "narrows"—a pass about forty feet wide through a range of hills. There, near the hacienda of Buena Vista, Wool argued, the army could find better ground for defense. Taylor, however, was more concerned with avoiding the appearance of retreating, and so he refused—heatedly, according to one account. Wool persisted, and at last Taylor gave the order for the army to redeploy.[23]

The army's baggage and the large stock of supplies at Agua Nueva were more than the available wagons could carry, so Taylor had them load up and haul what they could and left a regiment of Arkansas cavalry to cover the remainder until the wagons could come back for it—provided they could do so before Santa Anna arrived. They rolled out of Agua Nueva early on the afternoon of the twenty-first and were at Buena Vista before sundown.[24]

The position around Buena Vista was a strong one. A low plateau stood at the foot of a range of mountains. The road from the south approached across a plain and then climbed to the plateau through the Angostura, closely flanked on the east by the steep bluffs of the plateau and on the west by a small river. The plateau was cut by numerous ravines carrying streams down from the mountains.

Having acquiesced to Wool's suggestion to move the army to Buena Vista, Taylor allowed Wool to position the troops, and he did so skillfully. He placed three pieces of artillery along with elements of the First Illinois on the main Saltillo–San Luis Potosí Road, where it passed through the Angostura itself. Atop the bluffs east of the road—on the plateau—was an open area well suited to artillery and cavalry but accessible to those arms only via a gully about a mile and a half east of the Angostura. To cover this plain, Wool deployed, from west to east, elements of the

First Illinois and then all of the Second Kentucky, Second Illinois, and Second Indiana—with another eight pieces of artillery interspersed between regiments. The line on the plateau angled northwest to southeast and faced to the southwest, in the direction of the main road. The plateau stretched another half mile beyond the right flank of the Second Indiana—and thus the right flank of the army—and the base of the mountains, and that was a potential source of danger. Wool, however, had kept almost half his total force in reserve, most of it grouped around the hacienda of Buena Vista, about a mile north of the Angostura.[25]

After observing the posting of his army, Taylor proceeded up the road to spend the night at Saltillo, seven miles from Buena Vista. With him as escort went May's dragoons, the regular artillery batteries of Captains Braxton Bragg and Thomas W. Sherman, and Taylor's favorite volunteer infantry regiment, the Mississippi Rifles, natty in their red shirts and white duck pants.[26]

By the evening of February 21, when the U.S. wagon train, escorted by a regiment of Kentucky cavalry, turned back toward Agua Nueva for its second load of supplies, Santa Anna's lead elements were barely six miles from that place. The wagoners and Kentuckians had orders to load as much as they could before midnight, then set fire to the rest and get out of there. They were still loading supplies at about 11:00 p.m. when their pickets on the south side of Agua Nueva reported that the Mexicans were approaching. Hastily the wagoners whipped up their mules and headed north, while the cavalrymen hurried about with torches, setting fire to the remaining stockpiles. In the confusion of the nocturnal exodus, five wagons were wrecked and left behind.[27]

Santa Anna's army had marched from La Encarnación around noon on February 21 and had made a cold and cheerless bivouac along the road that night. They marched at dawn, and it was still early on the morning of February 22 when the main body reached the smoldering remains of Agua Nueva. Having made considerable efforts at operational secrecy, Santa Anna was bitterly disappointed at failing to catch the Americans in their vulnerable position. He took heart, however, from the reports of the local peasants that the Americans had left in quite a hurry. The sight of the five wrecked wagons further confirmed in Santa Anna's mind the idea that his enemy was in headlong flight. That prospect was particularly encouraging to the Napoleon of the West because he had made special preparations for it, giving orders to Minon's cavalry and to numerous irregular *rancheros* and vaqueros north of Saltillo to harass the retreating Americans in hopes of turning their withdrawal into a slaughter. If he now aggressively pursued Taylor's retiring force, his plans for its destruction might become reality.[28]

He therefore ordered his troops to proceed without halting for rest at Agua Nueva, pausing only to fill their canteens before pressing on up the road toward Saltillo as fast as they could march. Another ten miles or so of hard slogging brought them within sight of the American army at bay and offering battle at the Angostura and the adjoining plateau. Dismayed, Santa Anna halted and at last gave his tired soldiers a chance to rest. Studying the American position, he decided his situation was still favorable. With his massive advantage in numbers, he could pin the Americans down in the center, near the Angostura, and then sweep around their eastern flank and crush them. The rest of the morning he spent both resting his troops and getting them into position for the coming battle.[29]

The morning of February 22 held no such surprises for the Americans, who were expecting Santa Anna's arrival. Tents were struck and stowed in the baggage wagons within half an hour of sunrise, and each man drew forty rounds of ammunition. A regimental band near the hacienda played "Hail, Columbia," and General Wool, remembering that it was Washington's birthday, still a major patriotic holiday in mid-nineteenth-century America, set the day's password as "Remember Washington." About nine o'clock Taylor arrived from Saltillo, still accompanied by May's dragoons, Bragg's and Sherman's batteries, and Davis's Mississippi Rifles, drawing resounding cheers from the troops around Buena Vista and across the plateau.[30]

The commanding general cut a curious figure, evoking anything but the pomp of war, but his men loved him. One of them described him as "a plain-looking gentleman, mounted upon a brown horse, having upon his head a Mexican sombrero, dressed in a brown, olive-colored, loose-frock-coat, gray pants, wool socks, and shoes; beneath the frock appears the scabbard of a sword." With him in command, the troops were confident that they "can not be whipped by a Mexican army."[31]

Around midday, a note arrived from Santa Anna via flag of truce. "You are surrounded by twenty thousand men," the Mexican general wrote, "and cannot in any human probability avoid suffering a rout, and being cut to pieces with your troops, but as you deserve consideration and particular esteem, I wish to save you from a catastrophe and for that purpose give you this notice, in order that you may surrender at discretion." That was vintage Santa Anna. "Surrender at discretion" was the same deal he had offered the defenders of the Alamo just one day short of

The Battle of Buena Vista, February 23, 1847

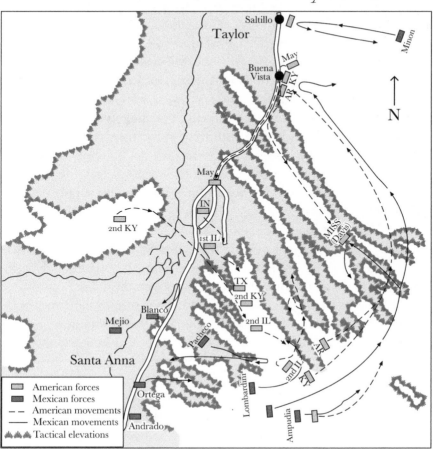

eleven years before. Of course, Santa Anna might not have massacred Taylor and his army, but there was no denying that the Napoleon of the West had a bad track record in such matters. Not that it made any difference to Taylor, who had no intention of surrendering on any terms whatsoever. Witnesses say the surrender demand prompted a profane outburst from Old Rough and Ready, though one of his soldiers heard the reply reported as merely, "If you want us, come and take us!" Taylor's note of reply to Santa Anna was polite, however: "I decline accepting your request." That almost certainly came as no surprise to Santa Anna. The flag of truce and exchange of messages were really little more than a ploy to distract the Americans and keep them from launching any possible spoiling attacks while the Mexican army took up its positions and prepared for the assault.[32]

Around 3:00 p.m. firing flared as Mexicans probed up the road toward the Angostura. Nothing much came of this. Of far greater import was a probe by two Mexican brigades along the high ridge to the east of the plateau, on the far left of the American position. This was serious since the ridge would lead the Mexicans to a position on the Saltillo Road near the hacienda of Buena Vista, directly in the rear of the American lines. Taylor countered the movement by sending the Arkansas and Kentucky cavalry regiments, but after several hours of skirmishing the Americans had to withdraw to the base of the mountain. Mexican casualties had been higher, but they held more advantageous ground for the morrow's contest.[33]

Taylor continued to worry about the security of his supply depot at Saltillo, and so he once again decided to spend the night there while his army remained at Buena Vista and the Angostura, and on the plateau. As he had done the night before, Taylor brought with him May's dragoons and Davis's Mississippi Rifles, but this time he brought only a single gun of Bragg's battery, leaving the others with the army.[34]

That night a chill wind drove a thin drizzle over the two armies encamped in front of the mountain pass. The soldiers spent a cold and mostly sleepless night, especially those of the Second Indiana, nervously contemplating their position on the vulnerable flank of Taylor's army and listening intently to nocturnal sounds amplified by nerves. Sergeant Benjamin Franklin Scribner especially remembered the sound of Mexican trumpets during the night: "I never shall forget the peculiar melody of those sounds as we lay upon our arms, hungry, and shivering with cold." A false alarm brought the Hoosiers to their feet sometime after midnight. Word had it that Mexican lancers were probing their position. Investigation showed this to be false, and that was just as well, since the inexperienced Colonel Bowles had gotten the regiment deployed backward. His confused responses for the duration of the scare did little to build his soldiers' confidence in him or his in himself.[35]

The morning of Tuesday, February 23, dawned crisp and bright, the rain and clouds having moved off in the hours before daylight. Reveille sounded in one Mexican regiment after another—no two at the same time by Santa Anna's order, so that the listening Americans might reflect on the overwhelming size of his army. Then, like a snake slowly uncoiling itself, the Mexican army spread into a single long line of battle, impressive with brightly colored uniforms, a brilliant spectacle in the clear morning air. Bands played religious music, and priests in resplendent vestments passed along the line with smoking incense pots, blessing each unit in turn. Across the broad expanse of ground between the lines, the Americans could hear massed shouts of *"Viva,"* first from one sector and then from another of the long Mexican line.[36]

Santa Anna's plan called for a diversionary assault along the road while his main effort aimed at flanking and rolling up the U.S. line on the plateau. With the priests' blessings complete, the Mexican army swung into motion, its various components marching this way and that to form columns of attack according to Santa Anna's orders. The two blows he had envisioned fell almost simultaneously on the Americans, opening the day's fighting. Taylor was not present, since at that hour he was just setting out from Saltillo along with his escort, having satisfied himself as to the safety of the supplies there and having left an ample detachment to guard them. He was still a good two hours from the battlefield, and Wool commanded in his absence. Unfortunately, Wool bought Santa Anna's feint, focusing his attention on the attack along the road and paying no attention to the movement of Mexican forces toward other parts of his line. The Angostura, at least, proved as strong a position as Wool had anticipated. American guns posted there easily broke up the Mexican column advancing up the San Luis Potosí–Saltillo Road.[37]

Meanwhile, a desperate fight broke out on the plateau, on the extreme left flank of the U.S. position, where another Mexican column, taking advantage of cover from the position seized the evening before, had succeeded in gaining the plateau almost unobserved by the defenders. Mexican troops poured out of a ravine giving access from below and swarmed the high ground. Their onslaught quickly routed the Kentucky and Arkansas cavalry that had been holding that sector.

The pressure next fell on the Second Indiana. In the vain hope of catching the Mexicans before they could emerge from the ravine, Brigadier General Joseph Lane had ordered the regiment to advance but had not told Colonel Bowles his reason for doing so. On the left wing of the Second Indiana, the extreme left of the army, Sergeant Scribner could not understand why they were so far forward, three-quarters of a mile from the support of the rest of the army, but he and his comrades tried their best to hold the advanced ground to which they had been assigned. Along with a small battery of the Fourth Artillery—one twelve-pounder howitzer, one six-pounder, and one four-pounder under the command of Lieutenant John Paul Jones O'Brien—they constituted the only defenders of the American left flank against what was clearly developing as Santa Anna's main thrust, about four hundred men fighting desperately to stave off the advance of ten times their number.[38]

Scribner was doing his job as a file closer, standing just behind the rear rank and striving to keep the men of his squad in an orderly line without gaps, when his captain shouted to him, "Never mind, Frank, fire away!" Scribner obeyed, ignored the niceties of the line, and began plying his rifle on the enemy as rapidly as he could. The air around him seemed to buzz with the whizzing of grapeshot from the Mexican cannon. He was in the act of reloading when a grapeshot, an iron ball about an inch in diameter, slammed into the head of Private Apollos Stephens, a friend of Scribner's from back in New Albany, Indiana. Stephens toppled backward, almost striking Scribner in his fall, and the twenty-one-year-old sergeant glanced for an unforgettable moment at the already glazing eyes of his friend. With effort, Scribner fought down his emotions, stepped around the body, and fired again. Moments later, his captain fell, and the thought crossed Scribner's mind that the ball must have passed very close to him before striking the captain, since that officer had been standing almost directly behind him. After that, there was no time for thought or reflection, just loading and firing as rapidly as one could: "All was hurry and excitement, each working hard and doing his best."[39]

At the other end of the Indiana line, Colonel Bowles was not handling the stress of battle quite as well as his men were. Perhaps he would have been better off if, like them, he could have occupied his hands and mind with the intricate, repetitive steps of loading and firing a muzzle-loading musket. Someone noticed him getting off his horse, turning the animal broadside to the enemy, and cowering behind its flank. The fight grew more desperate, and still the Hoosiers, along with O'Brien's artillerists, hung on grimly, their casualties climbing above 20 percent. Then Bowles cracked. "Cease firing and retreat!" he shrieked. At first his hard-pressed soldiers did not even notice him, but Bowles kept bawling his order to retreat. He was on the right of the regiment's line, and gradually, by ones and twos and small groups, the men there began breaking for the rear. Then the rest of the regimental line started to unravel from right to left.[40]

On the left, Scribner was compulsively counting his shots as he fired. He had reached twenty-one when someone shouted, "They are all retreating!" Looking to the right, he saw that wing of the regiment in headlong flight and the left beginning to follow. Nearby, several officers who had not heard Bowles were shouting, "Halt, men! For God's sake, stop!" Scribner's own company did stand its ground briefly. But as it became clear that the rest of the regiment was going and that the Mexican lancers were bearing down on them, the lieutenant who now commanded the company remarked, "It's no use, boys, to stay here alone; let *us* retreat!" They set off for the rear at a run, with the Mexicans on their heels.[41]

The situation on the American left was quickly becoming critical. O'Brien had been blasting double canister into the faces of the charging Mexican infantry. Now, abandoned by his supporting infantry, the lieutenant faced the desperate necessity of getting his guns out of the path of the Mexican infantry, which rushed toward his position cheering and flushed with success. Every horse of the four-pounder's team was dead, every man of its crew dead or wounded. Nothing could save that gun, but somehow O'Brien and his surviving men got away with the other two.[42]

The collapse of the Second Indiana allowed the two-sided pressure of front and flank attack to fall next on the Second Illinois, which now found itself in an equally desperate fight. Help soon arrived, however, in the form of the Second Kentucky Regiment, moving up to reinforce the Illinoisans. Even more valuable was the American flying artillery. Galloping across the battlefield to the critical point, a section of Bragg's battery, led by Lieutenant George H. Thomas, wheeled into position alongside the Second Illinois, unlimbered, and opened a deadly fire in time to help blunt the Mexican attack. More help came from Captain Thomas W. Sherman's battery, which moved up in support of the Kentuckians. The surge of advancing Mexican troops ground to a halt.[43]

The danger was by no means past, however. Though the American left-center had steadied and held—just barely—the open ground between the mountains and the left flank, now driven back on the center, had allowed Mexican troops to pour northward along the foot of the mountains, heading straight for Buena Vista and the American rear. Large numbers of Mexican cavalry swept through, and behind them toiled the San Patricios, bringing up Santa Anna's heaviest guns— indeed, the heaviest guns on the battlefield—a sixteen-pounder and two ponderous twenty-four pounders.[44]

At this point, about 9:00 a.m., Taylor rode onto the battlefield. He met Wool, who was distraught, believing the battle lost. Taylor assigned him to try to rally stragglers in the rear. Then he rode forward to survey the situation. Regrouping not far from the hacienda of Buena Vista were Colonel Humphrey Marshall's Kentucky and Colonel Archibald Yell's Arkansas cavalry regiments, which had both been driven from their positions on the far left at the first Mexican onslaught that morning. At the moment those two somewhat shaky formations were all that stood between the U.S. wagon park at the hacienda and the large force of Mexican cavalry massing at the foot of the mountain after having swept around the American left flank. Taylor dispatched Davis's Mississippi Rifles to help defend against the Mexican thrust that was sure to begin soon, and then he galloped to the center.[45]

American fortunes in that sector had improved. O'Brien had brought his two guns back into action alongside those of Bragg and Sherman, making a total of eight American cannon firing across the plateau. The San Patricios answered with their big guns, but within the relatively narrow confines of the plateau, the lighter American guns still had the range to reply effectively, firing grapeshot into the infantry adjacent to the Mexican guns until the foot soldiers fell back and left the guns unsupported. Santa Anna, who had ridden onto the plateau in order to be present to receive the cheers of his exultant troops as they swept forward to the final triumph, had his horse shot from under him and, upon acquiring a replacement, made a hasty personal retreat to safer ground for a general.[46]

Eager to regain at least some of the ground U.S. forces had lost on the left center, Colonel William Bissell of the Second Illinois and Colonel William R. McKee of the Second Kentucky led a counterattack. Colonel John J. Hardin brought four companies of the First Illinois over from the Angostura sector to join in the attack, launching a bold bayonet charge when some of the Mexicans stubbornly hung on in one of the many ravines that scored the plateau. Hardin's men, going into battle for the first time, plunged into the ravine and killed, wounded, or captured 150 of the enemy in hand-to-hand fighting.[47]

Seeing the encouraging state of affairs in the center, Taylor decided to take the risk of weakening his forces there in order to send help to the handful of defenders facing a desperate situation on the left rear of the U.S. position. He chose the units that combined maximum combat power with rapid movement on the battlefield, and those were the guns of his flying artillery batteries—Captain Thomas Sherman with one of his guns, Lieutenant John Reynolds with another, and Captain Braxton Bragg with a two-gun section of his battery. With them Taylor dispatched May's dragoons.[48]

The need was acute. About a thousand Mexican lancers were bearing down on Buena Vista from the southeast, and to their left more lancers backed by an even larger force of infantry were advancing on a parallel course that would, if unchecked, give them possession of the San Luis Potosí–Saltillo Road between the hacienda and the Angostura, cutting off the retreat of the American troops defending the center. In their path stood Jefferson Davis and fewer than four hundred men of the Mississippi Rifles. Nearby, Wool and various officers of the Second Indiana were rallying the fugitives of that regiment. Many of the men had only been looking for a place to rally and some leadership to show them where to form up. These men eagerly got into line; others kept running. At least one company had already regrouped and was ready to move into position immediately. Even a remorseful Colonel Bowles picked up a musket and cartridge box and took his place in the ranks as a private. In all, about two-thirds of the regiment's survivors came into line at this point.[49]

Seeing the odds against him, Davis asked Wool for reinforcements. The only unit Wool could send was Colonel James H. Lane's Third Indiana, which had been waiting in reserve on a knoll just behind the Angostura. On Wool's orders Lane led his regiment toward Davis's position, marching up one of the many ravines that slashed the plateau. As the regiment advanced, more of the fugitives from the Second Indiana attached themselves to it. Other members of that regiment rallied when some of Taylor's staff officers, farther to the rear, came upon a party of them bearing the regimental flag and persuaded them to turn back into the battle, providing an additional nucleus around which the regiment's shattered fragments could coalesce.[50]

Meanwhile, Davis had his regiment slowly advance toward the threatening Mexican cavalry and infantry. Ordering his men to "advance firing," he led them across a shallow ravine, driving the Mexicans back ahead of them. A bullet struck Davis's heel, but he stayed in the saddle. With no supporting U.S. troops yet in sight and the Mexicans threatening his flanks, Davis commanded his men to pull back across the gully, which they did in good order.[51]

It was about this time that the Third Indiana, also advancing along with part of the rallied Second, emerged from its own gully to find itself not alongside the Mississippians but rather two or three hundred yards to Davis's right, having inadvertently taken a diverging course across the broken terrain. To their shock, the Hoosiers had come face-to-face, at a range of only two hundred yards, with a large formation of Mexican infantry, who began to advance toward them. Farther away, the traitors of the San Patricio Battalion spotted them and eagerly opened up on their fellow Americans with their big guns. The Indiana troops fired volley after volley into the ranks of the advancing infantry, driving it back, while the San Patricios at first had difficulty getting the range. Forced back across a ravine, the Hoosiers rallied again and held their ground on the rim of the declivity. On sending a scouting party forward into the ravine they had just crossed, they found and drove off Mexicans who had been slitting the throats of the American wounded and stripping them of their clothes.[52]

With the initial threat turned back, Lane noticed that Mexican cavalry were swinging around the infantry to reach a position from which they could charge Davis. He ordered his regiment to march by the flank, cross an intervening ravine, and come up on the Mississippians' right. As they did, the remnants of the Second Indiana, now almost completely reconstituted, came together between the other two regiments, so that the Americans formed a line of some eight hundred men in all, spanning the ridge between two deep ravines that ran down toward Buena Vista. The Mississippians' line angled forward from that of the Indianans, forming a shallow V with its open side toward the advancing enemy.[53]

The Mexican cavalry began to trot forward, then accelerated gracefully to the lope and finally the gallop. "I shall never forget the imposing appearance of the Mexicans as they bore down upon us with their immense columns, glittering lances, and parti-colored banners," recalled Sergeant Scribner. "There was one company mounted upon white horses, and wearing brass mounted caps, with red plumes." It was a sight to sober more experienced soldiers than the Indiana and Mississippi volunteers who waited to receive the lancers' onslaught. Davis glanced along the line of his red-shirted Mississippians and noted with satisfaction that they were standing steadily "at shouldered arms waiting an attack."[54]

As the horsemen neared, their pace slowed again, first to a lope, then a trot. Perhaps their horses were exhausted, or they may have been hoping to draw an ineffective long-range volley from the inexperienced Americans. Then the lancers could have charged home against the Yankee infantry while they struggled to reload. "Hold your fire, men, until they get close," shouted Colonel Davis, "then give it to them." The Indiana officers were yelling the same orders to their men. For a few moments of tense expectation, the action seemed almost to stop. One witness claimed the Mexicans were singing a song of some sort as they approached. As the range continued to close, the Mexican horsemen reduced their pace to a walk and finally slowed almost to a stop about eighty yards from the American line. Young Benjamin Scribner thought it was more like twenty.

"Fire!" shouted several American officers, and the combined volley of the three regiments decimated the Mexican cavalry. "Whole platoons appeared to droop and fall," recalled one of the Americans, while he and his comrades continued loading and firing as fast as they could. The Mexican survivors were soon retreating in disorder, while the San Patricio Battalion, still banging away with its heavy guns from a distant position across several ravines, tried to cover the withdrawal of the defeated lancers.[55]

The powder-grimed Indiana and Mississippi volunteers threw their caps in the air and whooped and cheered in triumph as they saw their foes retreating. The feeling of euphoria at having both survived and triumphed conveyed a sense of invulnerability. "I almost thought that I could not be killed," recalled Scribner. General Lane had suffered a wound in his arm, but he seemed to have forgotten the injury as he rode along the line, hurrahing and shouting, "We'll whip them yet!"[56]

Meanwhile, to the left of the Hoosiers and Mississippians, across another deep ravine, another large body of Mexican cavalry charged down on the hacienda of Buena Vista. May's dragoons and the Arkansas and Kentucky volunteer cavalry regiments met them in a crashing mounted charge. The larger, heavier American horses gave their riders the initial advantage as they thundered through the Mexican formation, but the American steeds tended to get out of control, bolting along with the Mexican charge in one grand stampede and mounted mêlée that thundered past the buildings of the hacienda in a cloud of dust with a blur of flashing sabers and fluttering lance pennants. Wool had posted American riflemen at the hacienda, whose steady and accurate fire from behind the walls of the hacienda's enclosed yards finally drove off the Mexican horsemen.[57]

With the repulse of these Mexican attacks, the surviving troops of the Mexican flanking column were left in a vulnerable position, having fallen back against the foot of the mountains and needing time and space to turn southward, along the front of the victorious Americans, in order to make their escape. As the victorious Americans prepared to follow up their success and inflict much heavier casualties on the defeated Mexican attacking column, a small group of Mexican officers advanced under a flag of truce. Met by American officers, they presented their message, a question: What did the U.S. commander "want"? This nonsensical query so perplexed General Wool that he took a flag of truce himself and started to ride out to try to find Santa Anna. The San Patricios never slackened the fire of their big guns, however, and Wool soon made a hasty retreat to U.S. lines. The object of the strange flag-of-truce party now became apparent. It had been a dishonest but completely successful ploy to allow the safe withdrawal of the defeated attacking column.[58]

At this point Taylor, or perhaps Wool, decided to launch an attack by the units on the plateau. The First and Second Illinois regiments and the Second Kentucky advanced aggressively, but the Mexicans rallied and turned on the attackers in overwhelming numbers. The Americans had to fall back. Casualties were heavy among the U.S. officers. Colonel Hardin of the First Illinois died while fighting off the enemy with his saber. Colonel McKee of the Second Kentucky also fell, as did his subordinate officer Henry Clay Jr. Seeing the hopelessness of the situation, the wounded Clay ordered his men to retreat while he lay on the ground, unable to follow them. He then fought on with his pistols until killed.[59]

The Mexicans in turn tried to follow up their advantage by pursuing the retreating Americans, but heavy fire from the mobile U.S. artillery, backed by solid ranks of infantry diligently plying their muskets, soon put a stop to the chase as yet another Mexican assault broke in blood before the batteries of Bragg, Sherman, and Captain J. M. Washington.[60]

That night and early the next morning Taylor received two regiments of reinforcements, moving up from Saltillo, and forty wagons of supplies. Both arrivals were badly needed. The fresh troops would just about make good his losses of February 23—673 men killed or wounded and some fifteen hundred missing—and the supply wagons remedied what was becoming a critical ammunition shortage.[61]

Morning light on February 24 revealed that Santa Anna had retreated, leaving his campfires burning to mask the withdrawal. As the realization of what this meant spread through Taylor's army, cheer after cheer swept along the U.S. lines.[62]

CHAPTER FOURTEEN

Veracruz, Cerro Gordo, and the Politics of Expansion

BACK IN THE UNITED STATES, politics took no holiday while the armies fought in Mexico. As in nearly all the nation's wars, there were Americans who opposed the conflict. Some were politicians who would have attacked any policy of their electoral opponents, warlike or pacific. Others represented the cultural elites who would have opposed the common people of their own country—whatever might have been its cause or its enemies—out of pure intellectual refinement and social snobbery. But this war had another class of detractors, and those opponents had a more substantive issue in view. The question of whether the United States would or should be a predominantly slave or free society had now resolved itself for the moment into the more specific and immediate question of whether the present conflict was a necessary defense of the nation's honor and territory—which might also yield a dividend of more national territory—or whether it was in fact an effort to skew national politics in favor of slavery by adding to the nation's territory vast tracts of land presumed to be suitable for the spread of the South's peculiar institution.

Political developments during the war's first summer made that question an instant topic of heated debate in every national forum. From the outset, Polk was eager to conclude a negotiated peace with Mexico. Early in August 1846 he asked Congress to appropriate $2 million to be kept on hand ready for payment to any Mexican regime that would enter into a peace treaty with the United States. Knowing the turbulent state of Mexican politics, Polk thought the funds might be necessary to prop up such a government from the time the treaty was first signed until it was ratified by the Senate, and he considered it a down payment on the purchase of lands that he hoped the United States would acquire as part of any treaty settlement. It was a curious assumption in one way, since European wars of that era generally concluded with the winner simply taking a piece of the loser's land and sometimes demanding a large cash payment to boot, but somehow in this war everyone seemed to assume that any U.S. acquisition of territory would be by purchase, no matter how overwhelming the U.S. military victory might be.[1]

It was the assumption of an impending land purchase that drew unusual congressional attention to Polk's requested $2 million appropriation.[2] That prospect gave concrete reality to the question of the war's purpose and its ultimate effect on the American polity. If new land was to be acquired from Mexico, would it become slave territory or free? Was this war a contest to spread America's free institutions or a plot to extend the realm of what many were already calling the "slave power conspiracy"? The question was made all the more awkward by the fact that Polk had succeeded in achieving a compromise solution with Britain regarding Oregon—without either gaining the 54°40' boundary or fighting—but had accepted war with Mexico over the question of the United States' southern boundary.

Eager to show his constituents and the world that the present contest was not a war to spread slavery, freshman Pennsylvania Democratic congressman David Wilmot, formerly a loyal supporter of the administration, introduced an amendment to the $2 million appropriation bill, stipulating that "as an express and fundamental condition to the acquisition of any territory from the Republic of Mexico by the United States . . . neither slavery nor involuntary servitude shall ever exist in any part of said territory."[3]

The Wilmot Proviso was immediately the subject of intense controversy. Southerners denounced it in intemperate terms, partially because it implied a sort of ethical taint to slavery, as though their vaunted peculiar institution were a kind of moral plague that had infected them all and must be quarantined from the as-yet-uncontaminated new lands. In part, their opposition sprang from the fact that they had indeed hoped the war would accomplish exactly what antislavery Americans feared it would: introduce vast new lands for the spread of slavery and creation of new slave states, increasing the power of the slave state bloc in Congress and the electoral college.

For the moment, the legislative result of the introduction of the proviso and its successful attachment to the bill was that although the House passed the measure by a narrow margin, the Senate failed to do so because of a southern filibuster. Polk was more of a national expansionist than a slave expansionist, though he supported slavery. He was disgusted with the Wilmot Proviso primarily because he considered it an unnecessary distraction from the business at hand, that of concluding a successful peace with Mexico. Why obstruct that purpose by serving a cause as worthless—in Polk's eyes—as opposition to slavery? The proviso, Polk said, was "mischievous."[4]

By the time Taylor won his victory at Buena Vista, Winfield Scott was already in the process of moving his army to a position from which to seize the Mexican Gulf port of Veracruz. Preparations had been extensive for what would be the largest amphibious operation to that point in military history. Scott had the War Department lease merchant ships for transports and purchase a large number of specially designed shallow-draft surfboats for use as landing craft. With troops coming directly from the United States embarking at Brazos Santiago, near the mouth of the Rio Grande—usually after a voyage from New Orleans—and those transferring from Taylor's command taking ship at Tampico, which the Mexicans had recently abandoned, Scott needed a unified staging area. He chose the sandy coral harbor of little hundred-acre Lobos Island, eight miles from the Mexican coast and about sixty miles south of Tampico, where his troops began arriving in February 1847. Scott himself arrived there on the twenty-first of the month.[5]

Lush, green, and tropical, Lobos was beautiful when viewed from the sea—"this little gem of the ocean," an American officer described it, with the aroma of wild citrus blossoms wafting across the waters and "filling the evening air with delicious fragrance." Ashore the soldiers found they were sharing their paradise with numerous lizards, sand crabs, and rats. During the last week of February both volunteer and regular regiments continued to arrive on Lobos until Scott's army numbered some ten thousand men. Supplies and equipment did not come in as fast as Scott had hoped. Food was scarce at times. And Scott had only about two-thirds the ordnance and half the supply wagons he felt he ought to have. Worse, of the 141 surfboats he had ordered for carrying his troops to the landing beach on the Mexican mainland, only 67 were on hand. The shortage of boats would slow the rate at which the army could be put ashore, making the highly vulnerable process of landing that much more so. Nevertheless, Scott believed further delay would be more dangerous still.[6]

On March 2, Scott gave the order to sail. Three days later, the snow-capped summit of Pico de Orizaba, Mexico's highest mountain, hove into view, and only later the spires of Veracruz on the coast below it. Much history had already played out in Mexico's chief port city. In 1519 Hernán Cortés had landed there on his quest to conquer the Aztec empire and had given the harbor its present name. In the years that followed, the wealth of the Aztecs and later the spices of the distant Philippines, the latter having reached Acapulco on the Manila galleons and come overland across Mexico, had passed through the port of Veracruz and into other galleons that would carry them to Spain. In the harbor of Veracruz a Spanish fleet in 1569 had broken a truce to attack and largely destroy the English fleet of Sir John Hawkins, rendering the escaped Hawkins and his protégé, Sir Francis Drake, the implacable scourges of the Spanish Main. Here in more recent times, Santa Anna in 1838 had led Mexican troops against French invaders, come to collect outstanding Mexican debts. He had lost a leg in the fighting but had won enough public sympathy to regain power in Mexico, which he had lost two years earlier when he lost the province of Tejas.[7]

The city was powerfully fortified, surrounded by a stout stone wall fifteen feet high and studded with three forts. Dominating the harbor was the even more formidable fortress of San Juan de Ulúa, located on a reef about half a mile from the port itself. Begun in 1565, the fortress boasted sixty-foot-high stone walls, 150 cannon, and more than one thousand defenders. Despite such daunting defenses, many of Scott's officers recommended that the army should attempt to take the city by storm. The reason for this was the most deadly of all the dangers that awaited the Americans at Veracruz: the dreaded *vómito*—yellow fever—would come in late spring and summer and could easily inflict more casualties than a desperate battle. Nevertheless, Scott determined to spare his troops the slaughter of an assault and take the city by siege, betting that he could do so before the *vómito* arrived.[8]

During the first days of March, Scott, together with Commodore David E. Conner, the cooperating naval commander, reconnoitered the coastline around Veracruz, sometimes drawing fire from the big guns of the city's defenses, and selected Collado Beach, about two miles south of the city and safely out of reach of its guns, as the landing site. There the fleet assembled over the next few days. Some Americans expected the landing to be a hard fight. An officer wrote to his wife, "If they do not oppose our landing, they will lose their best opportunity. Many think they will not oppose us, but I think they cannot be so blind as to permit so favorable a chance to pass." If the Mexicans did make such a blunder, he thought, they would have no chance of saving Veracruz from the inexorable progress of American siegecraft.[9]

On the afternoon of March 9, the army and navy, working together, made final preparations for the landing. The troops were carried in surfboats from their transports to the warships that would actually move into the sheltered waters immediately off Collado Beach. A controlled excite-

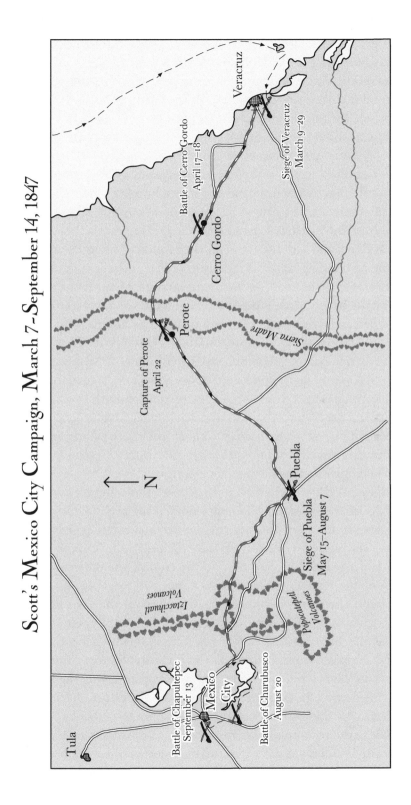

Scott's Mexico City Campaign, March 7–September 14, 1847

Tula

Battle of Chapultepec
September 13

Mexico City

Battle of Churubusco
August 20

Iztaccihuatl
Volcanoes

Popocatepetl
Volcanoes

N

Puebla

Siege of Puebla
May 15–August 7

Capture of Perote
April 22

Perote

Sierra Madre

Cerro Gordo

Battle of Cerro Gordo
April 17–18

Veracruz

Siege of Veracruz
March 9–29

ment prevailed among the men, who were aware that they were part of something very big. A Pennsylvania volunteer wrote in his diary of "soldiers mingling with the sailors in singing their favorite songs." The warships bearing the troops then sailed past the Isla de Sacrificios and moved into position for the debarkation.[10]

About an hour before sunset, the twenty-five hundred regulars of Worth's division, about one-fourth of Scott's army, piled into the surfboats for landing in the first wave of the assault. Once the boats had loaded and pulled away from the ships, they formed a rough line abreast facing the shore and the rowers lay on their oars. At the sound of the signal gun from the flagship *Massachusetts*, they set out for the beach, the soldiers cheering and the sailors at the oars pulling mightily in order to cover the intervening water as rapidly as possible. Shallow-draft steamers moved in close to shore, firing their cannon over the surfboats toward the dunes on the beach, where the Americans could see a few scattered Mexican soldiers and where other defenders might be lurking.[11]

On the ships waiting offshore, bands ran through their repertoire of patriotic airs, including "The Star-Spangled Banner," "Yankee Doodle," and "Hail, Columbia." The rest of the army, waiting its turn to board the surfboats, raised cheer after cheer. One of the volunteers watching from a ship looked around at the masts and rigging filled with eager spectators and thought the scene reminded him of robins crowding into a wild cherry tree or, perhaps more ominously, of a flock of crows perching in trees "watching the dead carcass lying beneath."[12]

General Worth was the first man ashore, and a huge cheer went up from the surfboats and the watching ships. As the keels of the other surfboats grated one after another on the sandy beach, Worth's division splashed through the waist-deep surf behind him, deployed on the beach, and advanced rapidly beyond the crest of the dunes to cover the landing of the rest of the army. Not a shot was fired onshore. Another great cheer rose from the thousands watching on the fleet as they saw Worth's men surge over the dunes and move inland. By ten o'clock that night, as the hardworking sailors plied their surfboats back and forth between ship and shore, Patterson's division of volunteers and David E. Twiggs's division of regulars were also ashore, completing the landing of Scott's small army. In all, some nine thousand Americans had landed on Collado Beach that day, and to the surprise and relief of Scott and his men, Mexican resistance was negligible. The Americans would have been highly vulnerable during the early stages of their landing, but the Mexican commander decided to place his trust in the powerful defenses of Veracruz. He kept most of his men behind the walls, trusting that Scott would either send his troops to their deaths in a frontal assault or else wait and have them laid low in their thousands by the *vómito*.[13]

During the days that followed, Scott pushed his lines behind the city, cutting it off from the interior of Mexico and preparing to besiege it. The American troops struggled through soft sand and dense chaparral, which was especially galling to the volunteers making their first hard marches. Gradually the army worked northward along the west side of the city, sometimes skirmishing with small bodies of Mexican cavalry. The bulk of Scott's troops remained encamped just behind Collado Beach, suffering, particularly during the first few days, from a lack of supplies and equipment while ordnance and quartermaster personnel labored to move such articles via surfboat and across the beach. Small Mexican detachments occasionally lobbed a cannonball onto the beach from maximum range somewhere off in the interior.[14]

During this period of the operation, General Patterson visited some of the volunteer troops of his division and in a brief speech thanked them for their good performance so far. While he was speaking, Mexican shot and shell were whistling over the position, and Patterson ordered the men to lie down. "Lay down yourself, General," shouted a Tennessee volunteer, "or the Mexicans will presently knock you over." "No, sir," answered Patterson. "My duty requires me to be where I am. The President of the United States can make generals every day, but he cannot make soldiers." The men laughed and cheered.[15]

On March 12 a cold northerly windstorm, or norther, came up, blowing sand and dust into the soldiers' eyes—as well as their mouths, noses, ears, bedding, and food. The wind also doused cook fires, knocked down tents, and temporarily cut off communication with the fleet. Several supply schooners were driven ashore with the loss of their cargoes in the wildly breaking surf. Ashore, some of the troops had to move their camps from the drifting dunes to the prickly chaparral a little farther inland.[16]

The winds howled through the next several days, but the process of encircling Veracruz continued, even if the landing of additional guns and stores from the fleet was temporarily impossible. With Worth's division holding the southern end of the American line, Patterson's volunteers extended their positions farther north, their line meandering a mile to a mile and a half from the walls of the city, as dictated by terrain. At the far end of the line, Twiggs's division of regulars finally reached the coast north of Veracruz on March 13, completing the investment of the city.[17]

For the next week the American army labored steadily, digging zigzag trenches forward from its lines so as to emplace batteries of heavy guns close enough to do major damage to the city walls. Morale was high, and the men felt confident of success. "Great enthusiasm prevails throughout the Army," wrote Captain Robert Anderson of the Third Artillery, "and all cheerfully perform the duties required of them."[18]

To choose the locations for his batteries, Scott relied on the services of a group of highly skilled engineer officers, each of whom had graduated near the top of his class in America's foremost engineering school of that era, West Point. Senior among these was Colonel Joseph G. Totten. A native of New Haven, Connecticut, the fifty-eight-year-old Totten had graduated from West Point in 1805—at the age of sixteen—and had served as a military engineer in the War of 1812. Like most army engineers, he had supervised the construction of forts during the postwar years, and since 1838 he had been chief engineer of the United States Army. Assisting him were a number of younger officers. Almost twenty years Totten's junior, Captain Robert E. Lee had graduated second in the forty-six-man West Point class of 1829. The other members of the group were younger still: First Lieutenant Pierre Gustave Toutant Beauregard was a Louisiana Creole, second in the class of 1838; Second Lieutenant Gustavus Smith, a Kentuckian, was eighth in the class of 1842; and twenty-year-old Second Lieutenant George McClellan was less than a year out of West Point, where he had finished second in the class of 1846.[19]

These young engineers, supervised by their seniors Totten and Lee, used their skills to select positions, some as close as half a mile from the city walls, from which the American guns could do the most damage without being exposed to dangerous Mexican counterfire. On one occasion, Totten assigned Beauregard to supervise a party of sappers in digging certain gun emplacements in a specific location. On arriving at the site, Beauregard had doubts, and after careful examination he decided, with some trepidation, to halt the work and go back and tell the chief engineer of the army that his selected position could be easily enfiladed by Mexican artillery. It was an indication of the degree of professionalism prevailing among the small group of engineer officers that Totten readily agreed to come and reexamine the ground and on doing so admitted that Beauregard was right and ordered the guns emplaced elsewhere.[20]

To Scott's dismay, a large proportion of the siege artillery he had planned to use against Veracruz had not yet arrived. It was the usual story of delays in transportation at various stages of the journey from the arsenals back home, but Scott's situation did not permit delay since he believed he needed to capture the city and move his army inland by April 1 in order to escape the *vómito*. Thus on March 21 he held a conference with Commodore Conner and with Commodore Matthew Perry, recently arrived on station as Conner's replacement. Perry readily agreed to provide a battery of six heavy guns, taken from his warships and manned by sailors. About fifteen hundred men were involved in the process of moving the guns, some of which weighed as much as three and a half tons, from the ships to their positions in emplacements Captain Lee had sited and the men of Patterson's division had dug for them only seven hundred yards from the walls, making the naval battery, as it was called, the closest of all the American batteries. Expectations were high for the effectiveness of the three thirty-two-pounders and three sixty-eight-pounder shell guns once they finally got into action.[21]

By March 22 most of the gun emplacements were complete, their artillery in place and ready to fire. Though work continued on the naval battery and several others, Scott sent a note under flag of truce to General Juan Morales, commander of the Mexican garrison of Veracruz, courteously inviting him to surrender the city before the siege batteries opened fire. Morales replied just as courteously that he felt it his duty to resist. With the niceties out of the way, the heavy guns roared into action at four o'clock that afternoon.[22]

Offshore, several naval vessels added their fire to the bombardment. The little gunboat *Spitfire*, commanded by thirty-three-year-old Lieutenant David Dixon Porter, pressed close in to shore to ply its cannon against the Mexican fortifications. The warships drew off at nightfall and suspended their fire, but the land batteries thundered on, though at a slower rate. The Mexicans, for their part, kept up a steady return fire from a larger number of guns. That evening another fierce storm rolled in, forcing details of soldiers to shovel sand out of the trenches constantly in order to keep them from filling in. Yet the bombardment continued, with the second day being much like the first. Great clouds of powder smoke overshadowed the city, beneath which the muzzle blasts of the cannon and the bursting of shells flashed like lightning. "The earth shook," an American officer wrote. "The steeples and domes seemed to quiver. The bells tolled without human aid. The air was rent with a thousand confused sounds."[23]

On the twenty-fourth several new batteries went into action, including the powerful naval battery, which drew the heaviest Mexican return fire, pounding the sandbag revetments and killing several sailors and a midshipman. The bluejackets stood to their guns manfully, at one point keeping up such a rapid fire that they were forced to pause to prevent the guns from overheating. The quartermaster department kept its wagons shuttling constantly to maintain adequate supplies of ammunition for all of the batteries.[24]

By the early morning of March 25, the Mexicans had had enough and requested surrender negotiations. The bombardment ceased by Scott's order at 8:00 a.m., after eighty-eight hours and sixty-seven hundred rounds of shot and shell. As at Monterrey, the Mexicans initially proposed ridiculously favorable terms—their garrison to be allowed to leave intact, armed, and free to continue the war. Scott, who could profit by the example of Taylor's unpopular agreement after the previous battle, insisted on a capitulation. Nevertheless, the terms to which he finally agreed were nearly as generous as those the Mexicans had first requested. The Mexican enlisted men were to surrender their arms, but the soldiers themselves were to be paroled—released on their word of honor not to take any further part in the war until properly exchanged. Mexico in general and Santa Anna in particular had a bad track record in such matters, and the present case proved no exception, as the paroled troops from Veracruz were soon back in the ranks of Santa Anna's army without any pretense of exchange.[25]

But the victory had given Scott what he needed—control of the port of Veracruz, including the fortress of San Juan de Ulúa—and it had done so in time to allow Scott's army to get into the interior highlands before the arrival of the *vómito*. The 350 surrendered Mexican cannon were a bonus. The cost to the Americans had been thirteen killed and fifty-five wounded. Perhaps one hundred Mexican civilians had died in the bombardment. The surrender ceremony took place on the open plain outside the walls on March 29, as five thousand Mexican troops marched out, grounded arms, and marched away.[26]

Scott's army took possession of Veracruz, gave it and the fortress of San Juan de Ulúa a thorough cleaning, distributed ten thousand rations to hungry citizens, and imposed martial law, chiefly in order to prevent crimes by American soldiers against Mexican civilians. In that effort it did not succeed perfectly, but it nevertheless kept such breaches to a minimum. Scott was concerned to maintain the efficiency and honor of his army but also to prevent behavior that would drive the Mexican people into desperate guerrilla resistance. If possible, he hoped, not only in Veracruz but throughout his campaign into the interior of Mexico, to keep the civilian population friendly or at least neutral. In that endeavor, he clearly got off to a good start in the port city.[27]

While Scott had been preparing his campaign and taking Veracruz, Santa Anna and his army had been making their weary way back from the defeat at Buena Vista. The Mexican strongman returned to San Luis Potosí with less than half the men he had taken north in his grand army scarcely a month before. The rest had fallen to American rifles and muskets, canister and shells, bayonets and sabers—and even more to the rigors of the march. Santa Anna's next concern was to deal with yet another attempted coup d'état in Mexico City. The generalissimo's presence in the capital—combined with Scott's presence in Veracruz—sufficed to quiet the factions warring for control of the government and refocus attention on warring against the Americans.[28]

Always the consummate politician, Santa Anna claimed he had won a victory at Buena Vista and promised the populace of the capital that he would now march against the gringos on the coast and win another. He reinforced his depleted army back up to a strength of more than twelve thousand men and marched east to confront Scott. He guessed that Scott would probably seek to proceed toward the capital along the National Road, and he took up a strong position to block that route where it climbed a steep and narrow defile to reach a higher plateau about fifty miles inland from Veracruz. With his army deployed around the head of this steep gorge, he could slaughter the Americans as they tried to fight their way up the road. At the summit of the pass, and thus the center of Santa Anna's position, was the village of Cerro Gordo.[29]

Scott did indeed plan to use the National Road, and after a brief delay to attend to matters of logistics, his army, led by Twiggs's division of regulars, began its march from Veracruz on the morning of April 8. The first day's march covered only about eleven miles. The road underfoot was soft sand and the sun overhead blazed down mercilessly. A lieutenant in the Seventh Infantry thought it the hardest march they had yet made. Many soldiers threw away their overcoats, blankets, knapsacks, and sometimes even extra rations, "so that the road was strewn for miles with clothing." Indeed, as another American officer observed, many soldiers still could not keep up the pace. "We strewed the road with men," he wrote, "and when we arrived at our halting place for the night, not two-thirds of the men are up." Earlier starts and gradually increasing altitude rendered the succeeding days' marches more bearable. On April 11, Twiggs and his division arrived at Plan del Rio, about three miles from Cerro Gordo, where reports had it that the Mexicans were fortifying. On encountering a patrol of Mexican lancers, the general halted to reconnoiter.[30]

The fifty-seven-year-old son of a Georgia planter, Twiggs had volunteered for service in the War of 1812 and stayed in the army afterward, rising to fairly senior rank. Seniority and pugnacity counted far more than brains in the peacetime army of that day, and that was as well for Twiggs, who was a man of very little brain. Encamped at Plan del Rio on the evening of April 11, he was able to grasp the twin facts that Mexicans were in front of him and that behind him was the rest of his own army, including Brigadier General William J. Worth, with whom Twiggs was involved in a bitter dispute over rank. The thing to do, clearly, was to win glory before Worth could arrive. Twiggs's idea of a reconnaissance, therefore, was to put his division into column on the morning of April 12 and hurl it headlong into the gorge in front of Cerro Gordo.[31]

As the lead unit of the division, a regiment of *voltigeurs*, or light infantry, under Lieutenant Colonel Joseph E. Johnston, began to enter the gorge, Mexican troops opened fire. Johnston went down wounded, and his men carried him to the rear. A West Point classmate of Captain Lee, as well as a fellow Virginian, Johnston had vaulted to the temporary rank of lieutenant colonel to command the wartime-only regiment of *voltigeurs*. Already in his participation in the Indian wars Johnston had shown a propensity to collect enemy projectiles, and in this brief encounter he added two Mexican grapeshot to his tally. Surgeons removed one from his arm and the other from his side just above his hip. He would soon recover, and his April 12 wounds, the result of overeager Mexican troops opening fire prematurely, were sufficient to warn even a man of Twiggs's pedestrian intellect that the division was about to march into a trap. Reluctantly he halted the advance and pulled the troops back to their previous camp.[32]

During the next two days, Twiggs's engineer officers surveyed the terrain and the enemy position, and Patterson's division came up to join Twiggs's. Scott was not on hand yet, and Patterson should have taken over command of the force confronting Cerro Gordo, since as a major general he outranked Twiggs, a brigadier. Patterson, however, was unfit for duty because of sickness. Impatient and still eager to seize some glory before the hated Worth arrived on the scene, Twiggs listened with interest to Lieutenant Beauregard's report that the left, or northern, flank of the Mexican position, anchored on a hill called El Telégrafo, was weak and vulnerable to attack. Twiggs decided to take his own division by a roundabout route past the Mexican left and strike that flank while Patterson's division, spearheaded by Gideon J. Pillow's brigade, attacked directly up the National Road, straight into the teeth of Santa Anna's artillery batteries. He set the morning of April 14 as the time for the attack.[33]

Gideon Pillow was an interesting character. A forty-year-old Tennessee lawyer and politician, he was a friend and political ally of James Polk, for whom he had helped to secure the 1844 Democratic nomination. Though devoid of military qualification of any sort, Pillow entered the army as a brigadier general, courtesy of his friend in the White House; after all, a number of volunteer generals received similar appointments during the war on the strength of little more qualification than Pillow's. The Tennessean's assignment to Scott's army served two purposes. First, it provided for a prominent Democratic general to gain a share of the military glory and political dividends in an army whose higher ranks were dominated by Whigs, and second, it gave Polk eyes and ears within the army, so as to keep track of what Scott was up to. Unfortunately, Pillow was not only militarily incompetent but also headstrong. Well aware that his friend Polk would sustain him in any controversy and that the rest of the army was also aware of that fact, Pillow had already shown a propensity to obey orders only when he found them to his liking. In this case, the order for the attack seemed to carry the prospect of military glory and future political advancement, which was exactly to Pillow's liking.[34]

It was not at all to the liking of many of the other officers of both divisions, especially those that possessed a modicum of military knowledge or of good sense. On the evening of the thirteenth, Patterson summoned Beauregard to his tent and asked him what he thought of the situation. The Creole said he thought they should wait until the army's Third Division arrived and then should flank the Mexican left via a route that his fellow engineer Lieutenant W. H. T. Brooks had shown him. Patterson sent Beauregard to present his case to Twiggs.[35]

The old dragoon listened to what Beauregard had to say but insisted that it was too late to change his plans. "Don't you think we will succeed any how?" he pointedly asked the young lieutenant. "Certainly, Sir," Beauregard replied, perhaps without much conviction.[36]

It thus appeared that nothing could avert an American bloodbath the following day, and the troops of Twiggs's and Patterson's divisions spent the evening glumly contemplating their slim chances of personal survival for the next twenty-four hours. About 11:00 p.m., however, Patterson became sufficiently concerned to report himself fit for duty, assume the command, and order the postponement of the attack.[37]

Scott arrived about noon the next day, and his troops welcomed him joyfully but respectfully, lining the road as he rode into camp and raising their hats or, if they had no hats, tapping their heads with their right hands in salute. Everyone seemed confident of success with Old Fuss and Feathers on hand. Scott was immediately taken by the idea of turning the Mexican left in the manner Beauregard had suggested. Beauregard himself was on the sick list by this time, but Scott assigned Captain Lee to reconnoiter the roundabout route through the hills north of the National Road.[38]

In a daring personal reconnaissance on April 15, Lee scouted much farther than Beauregard had gone, continuing until he was behind the Mexican army. While there, Lee had a harrowing experience. He was near a small stream when he heard the sounds of men approaching and hastily hid behind a large log. To his dismay, he realized that the stream was a watering source for the Mexican army, and soldiers came and went from it in a constant succession throughout the rest of the day, some of them even sitting on the log behind which Lee was concealed. Somehow they failed to notice him, and after nightfall he was able to leave his unpleasant hiding place and make his way back to American lines. With him he brought the news that the flanking maneuver would be difficult but feasible.[39]

Based on the information provided by Lee and, indirectly, by Beauregard, Scott devised a plan. Twiggs was to advance around Santa Anna's left flank to reach the rear of his army, taking possession of the National Road behind the Mexicans. As a diversion, Pillow was to launch a small assault toward three ridges that paralleled the highway on the south. His plan would allow Twiggs—with adult supervision provided by the engineer officers—to perform the flanking maneuver he had set his heart on, but to do so in a more sensible way than he had originally planned. The diversionary attack would spare the army the casualties of a full-scale assault into the gorge of Cerro Gordo, but would give Pillow the illusion of accomplishing something important while actually keeping him as far as possible from the scene of decisive action. Worth's division, just arriving at Plan del Rio, would be held in reserve, ready to exploit success.[40]

With his full army now on hand, Scott had about eighty-five hundred men against Santa Anna's force estimated at between twelve thousand and eighteen thousand. Still, he was confident. Once his troops breached the Mexican lines and threw Santa Anna's army into flight, Scott's orders called for a vigorous pursuit until nightfall.[41]

Over the next two days Scott's pioneer troops laboriously cut a track through the woods and chaparral so as to allow infantry and artillery to traverse the rough ground and dense foliage around the Mexican left. By April 17 the road was complete, and Scott dispatched Twiggs's division on an approach march along the new path to take up a position in readiness for an all-out attack on the following day. Twiggs was to occupy a hill known as La Atalaya, east of Cerro Gordo and only a few hundred yards from El Telégrafo. Much depended on maintaining the element of surprise. If all went well, the approach march should encounter no opposition.[42]

Unfortunately Twiggs disregarded Lee's advice as to how to conceal his division's march from observers on the hills ahead. The Mexicans spotted the movement and advanced a detachment to contest control of an outlying hill in the Americans' path. Twiggs pitched into them directly, and an extended skirmish raged on the hilltop. Twiggs upped the ante with the brigade of Colonel William S. Harney, whose regulars finally cleared this minor eminence and then pushed on to the foot of La Atalaya. Harney ordered them up the hill, where they found the Mexicans entrenched and ready for a fight. After a short, sharp conflict, Harney's men cleared this hilltop as well and paused. By this time, old Twiggs himself had reached the crest. What were the general's orders, a captain wanted to know. "Charge 'em to hell!" Twiggs bawled, and the troops rushed down the southwest side of La Atalaya in pursuit of the fleeing Mexicans, who were making for El Telégrafo.[43]

On this side of La Atalaya, however, the advantage lay with the Mexicans, as the badly outnumbered Americans were exposed to heavy fire from El Telégrafo. A number were hit, and the others went to ground, seeking such cover as they could find behind mesquite trees and uneven terrain. A few made a break for the shelter of the northeast side of the hill but were cut down by Mexican bullets. The rest of the command remained pinned down on the south slope.[44]

Seeing that U.S. troops were trapped on the exposed hillside, Captain Edwin V. Sumner acted quickly to bring additional troops to the crest of La Atalaya to provide the covering fire necessary for most of the troops to get off the slope. A few had to hold on until nightfall and then made their retreat back across the crest. Sumner was another prime specimen of the regular U.S. Army of those years. Born in Boston, Massachusetts, fifty

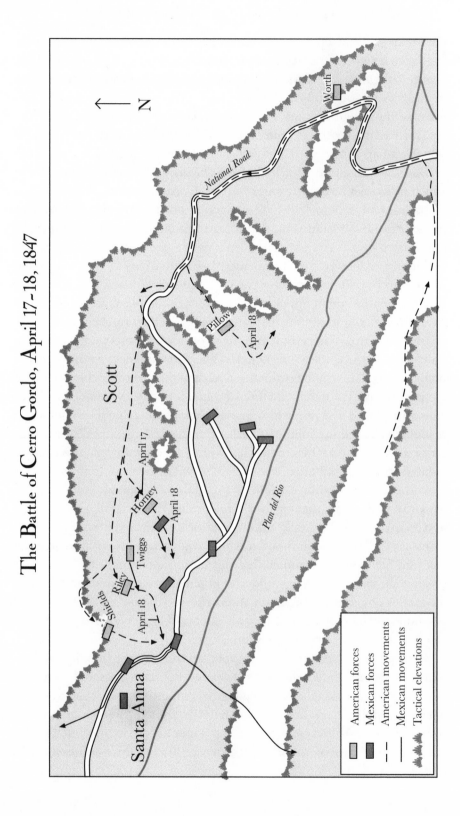

The Battle of Cerro Gordo, April 17–18, 1847

N

Worth

National Road

Pillow

April 18

Scott

April 17

Harney

April 18

Twiggs

Riley

Shields

April 18

Santa Anna

Plan del Rio

American forces
Mexican forces
American movements
Mexican movements
Tactical elevations

years earlier, Sumner had gained a second lieutenant's commission in 1825 direct from civilian life. Through his more than twenty years of service he had won a reputation for sober, austere, hardheaded devotion to duty that led one junior officer to liken him to Oliver Cromwell's formidable Puritan soldiers.[45]

While directing his troops this day on top of La Atalaya, Sumner took a musket ball in the forehead. The round partially deflected from the metal star emblem on the front of Sumner's cap, leaving a wound from which he soon recovered, though the report circulated in the camps that night that he had been killed. The narrow escape only enhanced his reputation, as the story was soon making the rounds in the regular army that Sumner was so bullheaded that a bullet had bounced harmlessly off his forehead, winning him the admiring nickname Old Bull.[46]

Twiggs's "charge 'em to hell" excursion to the southwest slope of La Atalaya cost the army about ninety casualties, all told. The entire episode, from the Mexicans' sighting of Twiggs's column through the fight on the hill, had served to alert Santa Anna that an American force was bearing down on his vulnerable left flank. In fact, the Mexican general's chief engineer had already warned him of the flawed position at Cerro Gordo—strong against an assault directly up the National Road, vulnerable on the left flank—but Santa Anna had not believed him. The Americans, he maintained, would not be able to get through the rough country to the north of the road. Now Twiggs had done him the favor of announcing that they had.[47]

Thus warned, Santa Anna had his troops work through the night to strengthen the defenses of his left flank, dragging up additional cannon and digging emplacements for them. He also shifted more troops into the sector. Still, he considered this a mere precaution, partially because he believed he had repulsed a major American thrust that day, thus proving that his flank was strong enough, and partially because his wishful thinking still led him to imagine that the main American effort was going to come along the National Road and be aimed at the three ridges to the south of it.[48]

While Santa Anna and his men made their preparations, Scott dispatched one of Patterson's two brigades to reinforce Twiggs and sent written orders to all of his subordinate commanders spelling out exactly what he wanted them to do the following day and how he expected the battle to develop. Colonels read out the orders to their regiments, and the men received the news soberly but with a fair amount of confidence. Soldiers in the First Pennsylvania spent the evening swimming and washing in the river, making final checks of their weapons and accoutrements, and writing letters home. The men in Harney's Second Brigade had no leisure for such activities. They spent the night dragging one twenty-four-pounder and three twelve-pounder howitzers to a hilltop position on La Atalaya from which they could enfilade the Mexican flank on El Telégrafo.[49]

The next morning, April 18, one soldier noted that his comrades preparing to go into battle "looked more like preparing to go on a Fourth of July spree." While some finished up their letters home, others were "eating and drinking, and some whistling, and some boast and talking loud of what they intended to do." Beneath the good spirit, of course, was an undercurrent of nervousness, betrayed by the too-loud talking and boasting. Nonetheless, they were ready and eager for battle.[50]

Harney's regulars led off the attack, advancing from their position atop La Atalaya against El Telégrafo. With Captain Lee directing, Twiggs took his other brigade around the Mexican flank. Then the two brigades of Twiggs's division struck El Telégrafo from two sides. The slopes were steep, overgrown with tangled chaparral, and thickly strewn with loose, jagged rocks. After their hard climb under heavy fire, the Americans paused under the shelter of the upper slope before charging into the Mexican defenses. The fight became hand to hand, with soldiers plying their bayonets and officers their swords with deadly effect. The Mexican general commanding the position fell dead, shot in the face, and his troops were soon streaming down the reverse slope of the hill in retreat. Captain Gabriel Paul, Lieutenant John Henshaw, and Sergeant Major Thomas Henry, all of the Seventh Infantry, raced one another to the Mexican signal tower atop El Telégrafo. The sergeant major won the race, hauled down the Mexican colors, and raised the Seventh's own United States flag in their place. Meanwhile, other American troops turned a captured Mexican cannon around to fire on its former owners.[51]

Lee led James Shields's brigade around the flank of the Mexican position on El Telégrafo and brought it out into a position from which it could charge directly into the village of Cerro Gordo and the main Mexican camp. This was the opportunity Shields and his men had been hoping for. Born in County Tyrone, Ireland, almost thirty-seven years before, Shields had immigrated to Illinois, become a lawyer, entered the legislature as a Democrat, and in 1842 nearly fought a duel with a Whig legislator named Abraham Lincoln. Ten years prior to that, Shields, like Lincoln, had served in the Illinois militia during the Black Hawk War. Like Pillow, Shields had used politics as a springboard for the leap to general's rank, with potential for further political benefits to come. Unlike Pillow, Shields showed a fair degree of competence.

As his brigade charged into the village of Cerro Gordo and the Mexican camp, Shields went down, shot through the lungs, but nothing could stop the American onslaught now. The Mexican lines on El Telégrafo finally collapsed completely, and Twiggs's division dashed after the fleeing Mexicans, many of whom now found Shields's troops blocking their escape route. With the situation on his left rapidly deteriorating, Santa Anna rushed to that part of the field to try to rally his troops, but things there were quickly becoming hopeless.[52]

Despite Mexican preoccupation with the growing disaster on their left, Pillow's diversionary assault had begun as a fiasco, for which Pillow blamed Scott's orders. The fact was, however, that Pillow had bungled the assault in every possible way. He quarreled with his attached engineer officer, Lieutenant Zealous B. Tower, rejecting that highly trained professional's recommended route and choosing instead one that would expose his troops to more enemy fire and greatly delay their attack. As his force approached the Mexican position, Pillow plunged the regiments into disarray, causing further delay. They were nearing the Mexican positions and could clearly hear the voices of the defenders in the fortifications just above and ahead, obscured by dense thickets, when Pillow noticed that Colonel Francis M. Wynkoop's First Pennsylvania Regiment, thanks to Pillow's mismanagement of the brigade, was still not in position.[53]

"Why the hell don't Colonel Wynkoop file to the right?" bellowed the irate Pillow. In response, a bugle sounded from the fortifications in front, and the Mexican cannon, their owners now thoroughly alerted, opened fire. Pillow ordered the nearest regiment to charge, even though it was still not in position to do so. Bravely the troops of the Second Tennessee floundered forward through the thorny chaparral, taking heavy casualties and scarcely getting within sixty yards of the Mexican redoubt before streaming back in retreat. Pillow's other three regiments were so poorly positioned that they could not get into the fight at all, much to the disgust of their soldiers. Having received a minor wound in the arm, Pillow promptly betook himself to a place of safety in the rear and, as one of his soldiers dryly noted, "was no more seen or heard from until the engagement was all over."[54]

It was a difficult situation for the inexperienced volunteers of his brigade. The two regiments of Pennsylvanians and two of Tennesseans had cheered the prebattle speeches of General Patterson and their regimental commanders, but then they had been sobered by the sight of some of Twiggs's wounded men making their way painfully to the rear. "I assure you," wrote one of the volunteers, "it was not very encouraging to those soldiers who were just going into the field of battle." Now their commander had gotten them into a tight spot and then fled the field, leaving them under a heavy fire and without orders.[55]

Round shot, grape, and canister shrieked and whistled around them, shells exploded, and severed tree branches, twigs, and leaves rained down on their heads. In scattered gaps in the cacophony of sound from the munitions passing over and around them they could hear from the Mexican fortifications in front of them shouts of *"Bravo! De la Mexicano!"* as the defenders celebrated the repulse of the American attack in this sector. Three times Wynkoop sent to the rear for orders, but his couriers could find neither Pillow nor Patterson, their division commander. The only consolation in the whole sorry affair was that the Mexicans' aim tended to be high. If they had been better shots, Pillow's brigade could hardly have escaped annihilation.[56]

When Scott received word of the situation on Pillow's front, he seemed neither surprised nor disturbed. Sending orders for Pillow to renew the assault or not, as he might please, Scott directed Worth's division of regulars to follow in the track of Twiggs's victorious division, wisely choosing to reinforce success rather than failure. With the Mexican left wing destroyed, it mattered little what Pillow might do. Let the president's friend amuse himself as he might. Scott would win the battle elsewhere, and no matter what sort of fiasco Pillow's attack might have been, it at least drew the attention of the Mexicans exactly where Scott wanted it.[57]

Thanks to the success of Twiggs's division, Mexican resistance collapsed all along the line by about 10:00 a.m. Pillow's long-suffering volunteers were surprised to notice the Mexican fire slacken and then stop. White flags went up along the Mexican breastworks as the defenders found themselves taken in the rear and trapped by Twiggs's troops. Caught up in the disintegration of his army, Santa Anna lost his carriage and his baggage, including a massive and ornate silver service and what was apparently a spare cork leg. Cutting loose one of the fine black mules in his matched team of four, the general made his escape, one of thousands of Mexican fugitives of all ranks struggling through the woods and chaparral to evade Scott's victorious legions. Santa Anna succeeded in getting away, but three thousand of his men did not and became prisoners of war. The Americans also bagged thirty-nine cannon and more than four thousand muskets left on the battlefield. By any measure, the Battle of Cerro Gordo had been a resounding American victory.[58]

Two thousand four hundred miles away, in Washington, D.C., Polk had been contemplating the best and quickest way to parlay Scott's capture of Veracruz and subsequent, presumably successful, advance into the interior of Mexico into a satisfactory peace treaty. Toward that end, and even before the Battle of Cerro Gordo, Polk had determined to send an emissary to accompany Scott's army and be on hand to open negotiations the moment Mexican authorities showed a willingness to talk. After receiving word of Scott's capture of Veracruz, Polk turned to serious consideration of who best should fill that role. Various political objections weighed against many of the senior politicians of his party. Secretary of State James Buchanan would have been acceptable but could hardly remain away from the capital for the amount of time involved. The choice finally fell on the chief clerk of the State Department, Nicholas P. Trist. A lawyer, former West Point cadet, and onetime private secretary to Andrew Jackson, Trist spoke Spanish fluently and was the senior professional officer of the State Department. Polk made the selection on April 10, 1847, and Trist set out shortly thereafter for Mexico. Perhaps with Scott's impressive victories and Trist's negotiating skill, peace might not be far off, but whether it came sooner or later, the peace would only make the question of the Wilmot Proviso that much more insistent.[59]

CHAPTER FIFTEEN

To the Gates of Mexico City

U.S. TROOPS PURSUED the Mexicans aggressively after the victory at Cerro Gordo, not stopping until darkness overtook them near Santa Anna's hacienda, Encerro, eight miles from the battlefield. During the pursuit they captured many additional prisoners and one of the cork legs Santa Anna used in place of his original equipment, shot away by a French cannonball nine years before. Soldiers of the Fourth Illinois found the prosthesis in the general's abandoned baggage, and the state of Illinois proudly displayed the artificial limb in its capitol for many years after. The American soldiers quickly invented an appropriate parody of one of their favorite marching songs, adapting "The Girl I Left Behind Me" into "The Leg I Left Behind Me." When the results of the battle were totaled up, U.S. losses came to fewer than five hundred men, while the Mexicans had perhaps one thousand men killed or wounded and another three thousand captured. Scott's troops were exuberant at the victory, although the Pennsylvania and Tennessee volunteers were "cursing and condemning every bone in Brig.-Gen. Pillow's body" for leading them into a hopeless position and leaving them there.[1]

Unwilling to grapple with the logistical problems inherent in keeping so many prisoners, Scott paroled those he had taken at Cerro Gordo. Within weeks most of them had violated their paroles by joining the new army that Santa Anna was once again cobbling together in the interior of the country. Scott was not so naïve as to doubt that this would be the case, but, as one observer noted, "Gen. Scott considers it easier to take them prisoners again than to lead and guard them." Despite forcing paroled prisoners of war back into the ranks without exchange, Santa Anna would pose little threat for some time to come. The completeness of his army's disintegration at Cerro Gordo meant that it would be months before he would have anything like a respectable force at his command.[2]

At the moment, though, Scott was far more inclined to worry about suspected enemies in his own camp than real ones outside it. Nicholas

Trist arrived with the army in May 1847. For all Scott's military brilliance, he could be a pompous buffoon when he imagined—as he often did—that his superiors were slighting his prerogatives or his public acclaim. That is exactly what he saw in Trist's mission—a foul plot to take from his hands the control of the army and the war. Trist could be charming when he chose to be. On this occasion he chose not to be, and in any case he was almost as proud as Scott himself. The two men's relationship went sour on an initial exchange of notes before they had even had a chance to meet face-to-face, which they subsequently refused to do, instead communicating by means of puerile and abusive letters sent across the camp. Thus matters were to remain for some time.[3]

Scott's army stopped for several weeks in the pleasant up-country town of Jalapa, about sixty-five miles from Veracruz. At an altitude of forty-seven hundred feet, Jalapa enjoyed a refreshing climate, with cool nights and warm days, while the rich soil of the surrounding region provided an abundance of many fruits as well as grain and coffee. The commissary department of Scott's army regularly made large purchases from local farmers and merchants, enhancing the already favorable attitude of most of the inhabitants toward their guests. The middle class was particularly well disposed toward the Americans, and they in turn found the residents smart, thrifty, and industrious, overturning previously held stereotypes among the conquerors, one of whom wrote, "We imagine ourselves in some thriving Yankee town." The town itself was neat, clean, and well built, with red tile roofs giving it a picturesque appearance, set as it was against the backdrop of mountains highlighted by the snowcapped volcanic cone of 18,490-foot Pico de Orizaba. The scenery, explained Lieutenant Henshaw in a letter home, "is grand, sublime and delicious."[4] Another American officer called Jalapa "one of the most delightful spots that I have ever seen in all my life."

The army greatly enjoyed its sojourn in this garden spot of Mexico, though the men of Patterson's volunteer division were disgusted that they had to camp outside Jalapa and were not allowed to enter the town except in small groups, carefully selected, on special passes. Scott knew enough about the volunteers' lack of discipline to realize the importance of guarding them from temptation, and he posted sentries to see to it that the citizen-soldiers had no opportunity for looting or other offenses.[5]

While the army was at Jalapa, seven volunteer regiments came to the end of their one-year enlistments. Almost to a man, they decided they had seen enough of war and opted to go home. Patterson had urged Scott to press farther into Mexico so that when the men's enlistments expired they would choose reenlistment instead of the dangerous journey back to Veracruz. Scott saw things differently, however. He let them go early. Partially this was an act of humanity, since it would allow them to pass through Veracruz before the yellow fever season was at its height. Partially it was a practical move. As short-timers, the volunteers probably would not fight very well, and in any case Scott planned no fighting in the near future, so keeping them meant feeding that many more mouths to no purpose.[6]

Their departure left Scott with scarcely more than seventy-one hundred men. That was not enough to provide the powerful escorts that were needed to secure the safety of supply trains against the threat of Mexican guerrillas ranging the roads between the army and the coast. Despite the friendly, or at least accommodating, attitude of many Mexican civilians, others were hostile, and some, either individually or in guerrilla bands, had taken to attacking American supply convoys and murdering individual American soldiers they found alone and at a distance from their comrades. So Scott took the bold step of shutting down his supply line. Henceforth, he would advance deeper into the heart of Mexico cut off from his base on the coast and dependent on the countryside to feed his troops. It was an extremely daring move, as Scott's officers at once recognized. When Captain Ephraim Kirby Smith of the Fifth Infantry heard the report, he at first could not believe it. "It must be all gammon!" he wrote to his wife. On the opposite side of the Atlantic Ocean, the Duke of Wellington, the British general who thirty-two years before had defeated Napoleon at Waterloo, had been following the newspaper reports of Scott's campaign with great interest. On learning of this latest daring move, the old general shook his head. "Scott is lost!" he exclaimed. "He has been carried away by successes! He can't take the city, and he can't fall back on his bases."[7]

But Scott seemed unconcerned. From Jalapa, he advanced his army during May about sixty miles to Puebla, shuffling his units so as to keep his forces spread out along the route and able to gather the largest possible amount of supplies. Before the last American troops marched out of Jalapa, the leading elements of the army had already been in Puebla for ten days. Scott kept his army in and around Puebla for the next three months, awaiting heavy reinforcements known to be on the way from the United States. The men found Puebla almost as pleasing as Jalapa. The town was clean, and the houses well built. The region yielded abundant fruit, "and dirt cheap," including "the cocoa Nut and Pine apple." The men were even delighted to find that among the many items they could buy on the plaza was "the finest Ice Cream in the world," made with ice hauled from the nearby mountains. Puebla also offered the exotic. The grandeur of the city's cathedral moved one officer to write that it "baffles my powers of description." A circus came through town, and some of the soldiers also went to see bullfights, which one of them called "the most cruel amusement that I ever witnessed."[8]

Scott spent the time in Puebla developing supply and intelligence networks in the region, drilling his army, and, astonishingly, making friends with Nicholas Trist. Such an event had hardly seemed likely on the army's first arriving in Puebla, when Scott and Trist were still writing each other lengthy letters of insults and sarcasm. The first step toward a détente between general and diplomat came in the form of a letter from Secretary of War William L. Marcy in Washington. Having read the previous venomous correspondence between Scott and Trist, Marcy hastened to try to smooth over the difference, assuring Scott that the falling out had been the result of a misunderstanding. A few weeks later Trist had the courtesy to inform Scott of some diplomatic developments, and Scott responded in like manner. Then Trist took ill and was confined to bed for a fortnight. Scott sent him a box of guava marmalade to help speed his recovery, and the two became warm friends.[9]

Their rapprochement came just in time to deal with another behind-the-scenes overture from Santa Anna. Indeed, the arrival of the Mexican general's communication had helped to further the thaw in relations between the two high-ranking Americans. This time, using the British minister as his conduit, Santa Anna informed Scott and Trist that he was willing to negotiate a treaty with the United States in exchange for a handsome personal bribe, to be paid in advance. The idea appealed to the devious natures of Scott and Trist, but Scott's generals, both regulars and volunteers, were distinctly queasy about it. Undeterred, Scott and Trist decided to give Santa Anna a $10,000 down payment on $1 million, with the rest to follow when negotiations got under way.[10]

By this time, however, late July 1847, Santa Anna had succeeded in assembling a new army of some thirty thousand men with which to resist any further advance by Scott. Liking his chances in battle much better than he had three months before, the wily Mexican general pocketed the $10,000 payment and then blandly informed the Americans that an April 20, 1847, Mexican law made it treason for any Mexican official to negotiate with the United States. Once again he proclaimed to the Mexican people that he was prepared to fight to the death in leading them against the hated gringo invaders. Even such occasionally slippery Americans as Scott and Trist had simply been unable to imagine someone so completely unhindered by any vestige of a moral scruple as Santa Anna repeatedly proved himself to be.[11]

Nothing remained for Scott and his army but to march on and attempt to take the capital of Mexico, and that, as the Duke of Wellington had noted, was a most daunting, seemingly impossible task. Though at an elevation of seven thousand feet, Mexico City lay on the bottom of a flat valley floor, surrounded by lakes as well as by marshes that were impassable to cannon, wagons, and large groups of men or horses. An army could approach the city only by way of several narrow causeways, seemingly tailor-made for defense.

Reinforcements had brought Scott's army up to a fighting strength of 10,700 men, not counting another 2,500 who were debilitated by sickness, and Scott now organized it into four divisions. Twiggs and Worth each still commanded a division. Patterson had returned to the United States along with the units whose enlistments had expired, and the reconstituted volunteer contingent now comprised two undersized divisions. One of these was commanded by Gideon Pillow, who had returned to duty after recovering from his Cerro Gordo wound. Fortunately for the army, and especially for the men in his division, Pillow generally followed the advice of his new adjutant general, regular army captain Joseph Hooker, and even allowed Hooker to give orders for him in his absence. It was a vast improvement.[12]

The other volunteer division was under the command of the Mississippian John A. Quitman. Born in 1798 in Rhinebeck, New York, Quitman opened a law practice in Chillicothe, Ohio, in 1820, then moved to Natchez, Mississippi, the following year. By 1826 he had been successful enough to fulfill almost every southern lawyer's dream and buy himself a plantation near Natchez. That same year he went into politics, winning election to the state legislature. He continued thereafter in various political positions, including governor and state supreme court judge. A Whig in the 1830s, Quitman became a Democrat in the following decade. Like Pillow, he was a purely political general, devoid of military qualifications for his job. Still, he complained that it was he who ought to be commanding a division of regulars rather than Twiggs or Worth, since they were brigadier generals and Polk had given him the rank of major general. Scott told the ambitious Mississippian that he would have to be content with his division of volunteers, unless he wanted to transfer to the Rio Grande theater of the war. That shut him up.[13]

The vanguard of Scott's army marched out of Puebla on August 7.

"We are, at last, off for the far famed City of Mexico," wrote an American officer. Their march took them along dusty roads between fields of corn and beans and then, steadily rising, through forests of oak, cedar, and pine. On the tenth they finally topped the ten-thousand-foot-high ridge forming the eastern wall of the Valley of Mexico and viewed for the first time the vast basin spread out three thousand feet below, flat and green and dotted with lakes and villages, stretching thirty miles wide and forty-five long and rimmed by still more towering mountains fading into the distant haze—"a most glorious spectacle," thought Captain Smith. Ahead and to their right, twenty-five miles away and barely visible across the flat valley floor, the soldiers could just make out the spires of the city that had once been Montezuma's, and Smith reflected that the Americans were now gazing on it from the same vantage point from which Cortés had first seen it more than three centuries before.[14]

The army's march along the National Road took it down into the valley, where many of the soldiers found the close-up view less enchanting than the distant vista. "As we come closer its beauty vanishes," wrote one American. "The lakes turn to marshes, the fields are not cultivated, the villages are mud, and the residents are wretched-looking Indian peons in rags and squalid misery."[15]

By August 12, Scott's vanguard was approaching the capital. Lakes and marshes clustered around the city of Montezuma, allowing access only via narrow belts of natural dry land or even narrower man-made causeways. The National Road entered Mexico City by a combination of both; threading its way between the south shore of Lake Texcoco and the north shore of Lake Chalco, it then passed over a broad marshland via a long, narrow causeway before finally reaching the city.

At the very southern tip of Lake Texcoco, a shorter causeway carried the road across a narrow arm of the lake. From the far shore of the lake a high hill rose incongruously from the level plain, its crown towering some four hundred feet above the waters of the lake. Its name was El Peñon, and it extended one thousand yards along the west shore of the lake, looking down onto Texcoco on the east and the broad marsh on the west and completely dominating the National Road on both sides. Santa Anna had fortified El Peñon with three tiers of entrenchments and artillery positions housing thirty cannon and seven thousand soldiers. Covered on the left by the waters of Texcoco and on the right by the marsh, the position on El Peñon could not be flanked, and Santa Anna was longing to see Scott hurl his troops down the National Road right into the teeth of the bristling fortress hill.[16]

Scott did not wish to oblige. Scouts had informed him of the lay of the land and the existence of the position at El Peñon before he left Puebla, and reports had claimed as many as two thousand Mexicans at work fortifying the position since June. Scott had been planning to circumvent the hill fortress by taking his army off the National Road and marching south via byways skirting Lake Chalco and neighboring Lake Xochimilco to reach the village of San Agustín, whence the main Acapulco Road led into Mexico City from the south. The road was bad. Santa Anna considered it impassable for an army and therefore had not guarded it, but, just to be certain, he had ordered boulders rolled onto it and trees felled across it. Scouting reports of the obstructions in the road gave Scott pause, and the army remained encamped in front of El Peñon while Lee and the other engineer officers reconnoitered every available avenue of advance. Their verdict was that the Chalco route would be difficult but possible, while all other paths to the city led directly into heavy Mexican defenses.[17]

On August 15 Scott made his decision, issuing orders for the army to take the Chalco route and march for San Agustín. It was a daring move, leaving as it would the Mexicans at El Peñon effectively between his army and the coast, but since he had already cut himself off from the coast, it mattered less than it would have had he still been trying to maintain a supply line. Having already chosen an audacious course, Scott showed a readiness to play it out to its logical conclusion.[18]

The army took up the march that afternoon under a light drizzle with Worth's division in the lead, accompanied by an engineer company and a five-hundred-man fatigue party to help clear the way. Pillow's and Quitman's divisions followed. Their road led past cornfields and olive orchards, with an occasional small village and distant glimpses of a spire of the capital. "We go to victory or death," wrote Captain Smith that evening in a letter he hoped would someday reach his wife. "Our spirits and courage are good, we have confidence in ourselves, and confidence in our generals." For the next several days the troops toiled over the difficult, often muddy road, with occasional Mexican obstructions and light resistance, and covered the twenty-five miles to San Agustín by August 18.[19]

On that day the U.S. advance guard began moving northward up the Acapulco Road toward the capital. They had gone only three miles when they drew the fire of large numbers of Mexican cannon emplaced near the village of San Antonio, bringing the advance to a halt. The first shot scored a direct hit on Captain Seth Thornton of the dragoons, captured in the war's first skirmish and since exchanged, only to find death almost within sight of Mexico City.[20]

A quick reconnaissance revealed that the position was a strong one, with numerous guns and heavy infantry support. Worse, it could not be flanked on the east, where the waters of Lake Xochimilco blocked passage, nor on the west, where a weird landscape called the Pedregal seemed equally forbidding. A lava flow that had crystallized long ago, the Pedregal seemed like a choppy sea that had suddenly congealed, its waves preserved as billows of hard black rock. It extended about five miles east and west and about three north and south. Between the Pedregal and Lake Xochimilco, the Americans were confined within a narrow causeway and their further advance was blocked by another powerful defensive position. As soon as Santa Anna had realized that the Americans were not going to assault El Peñon, he had shifted his forces to meet Scott's army at San Antonio, and now his position seemed almost as forbidding as the one he had held on the east side of the capital city.[21]

That evening Scott met with his officers to discuss the situation and to listen to their proposed solutions. James Mason, chief engineer of Worth's division, recommended that the army should assault San Antonio, battering its way straight up the Acapulco Road into the capital and hoping to work some of its infantry through the eastern edge of the Pedregal to take the defenders in flank. Lee was of a different opinion. Together with Beauregard, he had scouted a road—really scarcely more than a mule track—that skirted the southern edge of the Pedregal. The route was passable for infantry and with a bit of labor could be made passable for artillery. Near the southwest corner of the Pedregal this rough track connected with a much better road—the San Angel Road— which led northeastward toward Mexico City, passing through the villages of Churubusco, Padierna, and San Angel before it joined the Acapulco Road north of San Antonio. Lee urged that the army use this route, bypassing the powerful Mexican fortifications.[22]

Lee was not only highly intelligent but also tactful and persuasive. After the conference, Scott weighed the decision overnight, and on the morning of August 19 he gave orders for Worth's division to continue to threaten a frontal assault at San Antonio, Quitman's to guard the army's wagon train and supplies at San Agustín, and Pillow's and Twiggs's to follow Lee's route around the Pedregal. Lee himself was to lead the way with a pioneer battalion of five hundred men, drawn from the leading division, Pillow's, to make the road passable for the artillery to follow.[23]

The roadwork proceeded well, and by early afternoon they had nearly reached the far side of the Pedregal. From a hill called Zacatepec, Pillow and his staff could see the junction with the San Angel Road, somewhat more than half a mile away. Around the junction lay the village of Padierna, which all of the Americans consistently misidentified as Contreras, the next village to the southwest. Mexican troops were in evidence in the vicinity of Padierna, and a large number of them were strongly entrenched on high ground several hundred yards beyond the village, about a mile from Pillow's vantage point on Zacatepec. Of more immediate concern, Mexican skirmishers were sheltering among the numerous boulders and rock outcrops on the slope that led down from Zacatepec to Padierna, posing a direct threat to the safety of the road-building detachment.[24]

The Mexican force opposing Pillow's advance was under the command of General Gabriel Valencia, and its presence on the San Angel Road was an illustration of the poor state of discipline among the ranking officers of the Mexican army. Valencia was five miles in advance of the point Santa Anna had told him to defend, but he had no intention of obeying his nominal commander's orders. He was a headstrong and ambitious man who harbored serious hopes of unseating Santa Anna and making himself ruler of Mexico sometime in the near future. He had the best division in the Mexican army, and at a strength of seven thousand men it was almost as large as Scott's entire army. Valencia also possessed twenty-two cannon, including heavy sixteen- and twenty-four-pounders that could dominate the San Angel Road. He planned to fight an independent battle, separate from the rest of Santa Anna's army, so that all the glory—and the political credit—would be his. His troops occupied heights that lay several hundred yards to the west of the San Angel Road and stretched from the village of Contreras, southwest of Padierna, to San Geronimo, to the northeast of the crossroads hamlet. As for the yawning gap between his force and the rest of Santa Anna's army, Valencia was confident that the Pedregal would effectively seal it from American access.[25]

Pillow had strict orders from Scott not to bring on a general engagement that day, but such orders did not preclude driving back a few hundred skirmishers sheltering among the rocks between Zacatepec and Padierna so as to allow the road builders to complete their task. Accordingly, Pillow ordered his own skirmishers forward to rout the Mexicans out of their coverts and push them back beyond the village. The American skirmishers, dismounted troopers of Major William W. Loring's Mounted Rifle Regiment, readily carried out their task, reaching Padierna but immediately coming under intense artillery fire from Valencia's massive conglomeration of heavy guns on the heights to the west. Pillow, drawing on his own resources and those of Twiggs's division, which was just coming up, responded at once by ordering forward two U.S. batteries, with supporting infantry, to answer the Mexican guns. With that, the full-scale battle that Scott had been trying to postpone was fairly joined.[26]

It started badly for the Americans. Only a rank amateur like Pillow would have thought to try to neutralize Valencia's massive array of heavy guns with the eight relatively tiny six-pounders and even smaller mountain howitzers of the two American batteries. The fast-moving U.S. guns could dominate battlefields where mobile firepower was at a premium, but they were at a hopeless disadvantage in the face of the more numerous and much heavier Mexican guns dug in on the high ground overlooking the San Angel Road. Mexican shot were soon crashing into limbers, caissons, guns, and gunners, but the artillerymen, who had performed prodigies in merely moving their guns into position across the rough ground, stood grimly to their tasks until nearly all their guns were disabled. Lieutenant Thomas J. Jackson, just fifteen months out of West Point, commanded a two-gun section of one of the batteries and was especially noticeable for his courage and extreme determination, keeping his last remaining gun in action with his few surviving men until ordered to withdraw.[27]

Meanwhile, Pillow, who as a major general outranked Brigadier General Twiggs, much to the latter's annoyance, was exercising command over both divisions. Pillow's solution to the problem at Padierna was to dispatch thirty-five hundred of his troops to advance across the southwest corner of the Pedregal to take the village of San Geronimo, on the San Angel Road near Valencia's left flank and in a position, theoretically, to turn the Mexican position and cut off Valencia's division from Santa Anna's main body several miles to the northeast.[28]

As Pillow apparently did not pause to reflect, this would also cut off the thirty-five hundred Americans, who would potentially be caught between the upper and nether millstones of Santa Anna and Valencia. Fortunately for the Americans, Valencia paid little attention to the movement, being almost entranced with the ongoing artillery duel. The American advance force, a brigade of Pillow's division led by Colonel Bennett C. Riley, successfully occupied San Geronimo after only a couple of minor brushes with Mexican cavalry. That evening the unequal artillery contest ended, but Valencia still gave no heed to the Americans on his flank. Imagining himself to have won a great victory, he spent the evening getting drunk and giving promotions to all of his officers.[29]

Pillow was apparently sober, but remained equally oblivious to his own potential tactical danger. His subordinate Persifor F. Smith was more alert. A native of Philadelphia and graduate of Princeton, Smith had been a lawyer before turning soldier. Brevetted for his service at Monterrey almost a year earlier, Smith was highly respected and popular within the army. He commanded the brigade of Pillow's division assigned to support the artillery, but he had decided that his troops were needed with the advance force at San Geronimo. On his own initiative he led his brigade there and as senior officer present took over command of the advance force that evening. During the night James Shields led his brigade into San Geronimo as well. Shields was acting on orders from Scott. From his vantage point at San Agustín, the commanding general had observed the outbreak of the battle he had ordered Pillow to avoid. Hurrying to the scene, Scott took steps to remedy the situation. By strengthening the force at San Geronimo to 40 percent of his total manpower, Scott hoped to secure it against Mexican attack and enable Smith to exploit his position between the two severed portions of the Mexican army.[30]

Smith determined that the best course of action was to seize the initiative by attacking Valencia's force at dawn. Riley and several engineer officers had done some scouting, and it was clear that the Americans could exploit a ravine just south of San Geronimo to hit Valencia in both flank and rear. To complete his plan, Smith needed the other U.S. forces—those still facing Padierna—to add their weight by attacking the front of the Mexican position. Captain Lee volunteered to carry a message to Scott to report the situation and request the cooperative attack at dawn. After a difficult journey across the Pedregal in darkness made deeper by solid cloud cover and a steady rain, Lee found Scott at San Agustín and quickly gained his approval.[31]

Scott was relieved to receive Lee's report, as he had already dispatched several staff officers to make their way across the Pedregal and check on the status of Smith's command, but none of them had been able to get through the weird and rugged terrain in the rain-sodden darkness. In preparation for the next morning's assault, Scott dispatched Twiggs and the weary Lee to round up the additional troops needed for the attack. The fifty-seven-year-old general quickly gave out and sat down to rest, but Lee persevered. By dawn he had Franklin Pierce's brigade ready to join the assault on the Padierna front, along with a detachment of the Mounted Rifles and what was left of Captain John B. Magruder's badly shot-up battery, including young Lieutenant Jackson.[32]

The American soldiers, both at Padierna and around San Geronimo, spent an unpleasant night huddling under the downpour and listening to cheers and sounds of raucous celebration across the way, where the Mexicans were making merry over the great victory they believed they had won on August 19. Those of Smith's men who got some sleep found their slumbers cut short when their officers and noncommissioned officers shook them awake at 2:00 a.m. and directed them to prepare to march. Ignorant of the plan for the coming day's attack, the men stumbled into their ranks and prepared to set off with such fortitude as they could muster. The march, which began about 3:00 a.m., was a nightmare of stumbling and slipping through water sometimes ankle-deep and heavy clay mud that one American described as being both as soft and as slippery as "soft soap." On orders from their officers, the men tried to stay close enough together for each soldier to maintain physical contact with the man in front of him, but this sometimes proved impossible, and whole units went astray, only to be herded back into the column by the tireless engineer officers who had reconnoitered the route.[33]

By six o'clock on August 20, the early-morning light was struggling to illumine the landscape through a mist that had replaced the night's rain. Despite the foul weather, Valencia's cavalry had detected the American march. In his complacent and perhaps somewhat bleary-eyed state, the Mexican general had responded by posting a detachment on his flank, facing north. As the light rose, the Americans surged up out of their ravine. As the Mexican flank guards prepared to fire on the charging Yankees to the north, they were astonished to find still more Americans storming toward them from the west, the rear of the Mexican position. Valencia had grossly underestimated the extent of the U.S. flanking movement, which had placed attackers both on his flank and in his rear.

At first Valencia's troops held their ground as the Americans charged directly into their positions and the battle became a massive hand-to-hand mêlée. The detachment guarding the flank broke first, fleeing toward the main body with the Americans on their heels. Hearing the din of battle rising from the north, Pierce's men and the other American troops around Padierna charged toward the front of Valencia's division just as it wavered and began to give way. Approximately seventeen minutes after Smith's troops had emerged from their ravine, the battle, as such, was over, as Mexican resistance collapsed into panicked flight.[34]

The Americans chased fugitive Mexicans all the way to San Angel, five miles northeast of the battlefield. Valencia himself escaped but became a fugitive from his own army as well when he learned that Santa Anna had given orders that he be shot on sight. Santa Anna himself was almost equally to blame for the debacle, however. Whether because of his by now well-established deficiencies as a battlefield commander or out of a desire to see his dangerous political rival destroyed, he had failed to advance at a time when he had a good opportunity to relieve Valencia and trap the Americans at San Geronimo the afternoon before.[35]

Although the battle had been fought around the villages of Padierna and San Geronimo, the Americans, thanks to a mistake about local geography, would refer to it as the Battle of Contreras. The contest had pitted 4,500 U.S. troops against 7,000 Mexicans and had ended in a rout, with 700 Mexicans dead, according to Scott's report, and 813 captured, including 4 generals. Among the twenty-two cannon the Americans captured were two six-pounders that the Mexicans had captured from a battery of the Fourth U.S. Artillery at Buena Vista. Appropriately, the troops who retook the guns were also part of the Fourth Artillery, serving now as infantry. Throughout the entire battle, Santa Anna's 12,000 additional Mexican troops at San Angel had stood idly by. Scott had neither planned nor expected the battle, not knowing of Valencia's presence south of San Geronimo until his troops had made contact with that Mexican force on the nineteenth. For Scott's army, the fight they would call the Battle of Contreras was an incident along the road to Churubusco.[36]

Churubusco was the name of a river that flowed northeast and then east to enter Lake Xochimilco northeast of San Antonio. It was also the name of the town on the Acapulco Road where that thoroughfare spanned the river. The bridge at Churubusco would be Santa Anna's primary route for getting his badly shaken army back to Mexico City, where it could regroup within the capital's fortifications. The town and its bridge were therefore key points for both armies and the obvious next objective. With almost the whole of August 20 still available after the early-morning triumph at Contreras, Scott ordered an aggressive pursuit of the defeated Mexicans, sending Twiggs's victorious troops marching up the road from Padierna to Churubusco.[37]

Covering the Churubusco crossing were two Mexican strongpoints. One was a powerfully built fort immediately covering the bridge and known in the military parlance of the time as a *tête de pont*. The other was the Convent of San Mateo, taken over by the Mexican military and converted into a fort. The convent's four-foot-thick walls made it well suited to the purpose. To hold these works and the line of entrenchments link-ing them and covering Churubusco, Santa Anna shifted seven thousand men from the defenses of San Antonio, which was in any case now threatened with being turned by the American advance.[38]

Flying over the walls of San Mateo was a green flag with images of the harp and Saint Patrick that was by now familiar to the U.S. troops. Among the defenders was the San Patricio Battalion, the unit of deserters from the regular U.S. Army. Enough had deserted by August 1847 to form a battalion of more than two hundred men.

With smaller numbers the San Patricios had served with distinction as an artillery battery at the Battles of Monterrey and Buena Vista. They had fought tenaciously at Cerro Gordo, where they had nevertheless lost their prized heavy cannon. According to one story of that battle, they had held neighboring Mexican units to their work with threats to fire on them if they broke for the rear. Only when the San Patricios were completely occupied killing their fellow Americans in front of them did the Mexican line around them give way. One reason for the tenacious fighting of the battalion was the awareness of every one of its members that the U.S. Articles of War knew only one fate for the soldier who deserted to the enemy in time of war.[39]

The American army reached Churubusco around noon on August 20, and skirmishing broke out immediately as Twiggs ordered his skirmishers forward to learn the strength of the Mexican position, which was difficult to discern from a distance because of the intervening fields of dense, tall corn. The defenses proved to be much stronger and more heavily guarded than the Americans had anticipated, and the Third U.S. Infantry Regiment was soon pinned down in cornfields and ditches in front of San Mateo. There the deserters of the San Patricio Battalion manned four eight-pounder guns, while other members of the battalion fired muskets, and hundreds of additional Mexican defenders in the convent fired more muskets and three additional cannon. In the ranks of the Seventh Infantry, Lieutenant Henshaw thought the musketry was the heaviest he had heard so far in the war. He could think of nothing to liken it to but the sound of a very heavy hailstorm beating against a window.[40]

Engineer lieutenants Gustavus Smith and George McClellan ordered an artillery battery to support the foot soldiers. Its commander brought his guns up to 150 yards from the convent walls and opened an unequal duel with the seven guns, and hundreds of muskets, of the defenders. Despite the disadvantage of numbers, the American gunners kept up their short-range slugging match for an hour and a half.[41]

Meanwhile, Worth's division had advanced through San Antonio. Hearing of Twiggs's success at Padierna and San Geronimo, he determined to attack the force in front of him, now much weakened by Santa Anna's ordering most of its defenders back up the road to Churubusco. Worth sent one of his brigades working through the eastern edge of the Pedregal, almost within gunshot of the Mexicans, to turn the defensive position at San Antonio. After a two-hour scramble over and around the jagged boulders and crags, the flanking columns charged out of the Pedregal at the double-quick. Hit in front and flank, the defenders fled after only brief resistance. The rout that followed was as great a debacle for the Mexicans as that which had taken place along the opposite side of the Pedregal a few hours before. Up the road from San Antonio toward Churubusco the whooping Americans pursued their fleeing quarry. Mexican supply wagons ran off the road, bogged down in ditches, and had to be abandoned, and hundreds of winded *soldados* gave themselves up.[42]

By the time Worth's division arrived on the southeastern outskirts of Churubusco, Twiggs's division had been in action for an hour on the southwestern side of town. Worth probably was unaware that Twiggs had gotten himself into trouble by an overaggressive reconnaissance, but he avoided that particular blunder by omitting any reconnaissance at all. Elated by his success at San Antonio and eager to outdo his hated rival Twiggs, Worth simply ordered his division to deploy and charge. Advancing rapidly toward the *tête de pont*, Worth's men received their first indication of the strength of the enemy's position in the form of short-range blasts of grapeshot from the Mexican guns. They were soon, like much of Twiggs's division, pinned down in cornfields and along irrigation ditches. "The roar of the cannon and musketry, the screams of the wounded, the awful cry of terrified horses and mules, and the yells of the fierce combatants all combined in a sound as hellish as can be conceived," recalled an American officer. Casualties mounted alarmingly during the early-afternoon hours. After the exhilaration of the morning's easy victories and headlong pursuit, the Americans hung on grimly and marveled at the tenacity of the Mexican defense.[43]

At his headquarters at Coyoacán, a village about half a mile behind Twiggs's division on the road that led back to Padierna, Scott was worried about the situation of his outnumbered army and tried to think of a solution for the increasingly dangerous deadlock at Churubusco. The answer came from an American who had lived in the area for several years. Noah Smith suggested that Scott could flank the Mexicans by sending troops across the bridge over the Churubusco River at

The Battle of Churubusco, August 20, 1847

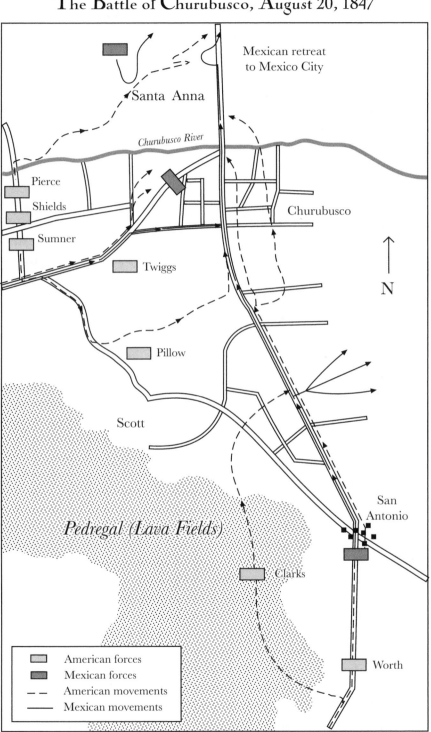

Mexican retreat
to Mexico City

Santa Anna

Churubusco River

Pierce

Shields

Sumner

Churubusco

N

Twiggs

Pillow

Scott

San
Antonio

Pedregal (Lava Fields)

Clarks

Worth

American forces
Mexican forces
American movements
Mexican movements

Coyoacán. These troops could then march east along the north bank of the river to come in behind the Mexicans holding the town of Churubusco on the south bank. It was a risky move that would require Scott to commit his last available reserve, other than the troops guarding the supply wagons, but he did not hesitate. Orders went out immediately for Franklin Pierce's volunteer brigade to cross the bridge, followed by Shields's brigade. Pierce had badly injured his foot the night before when his horse had slipped on the wet basalt of the Pedregal and fallen on him. It was so sore now that he could not put it in the stirrup. Still, he begged Scott not to order him to the rear. This might be the last big fight, and Pierce wanted to be with his men. Scott relented and let him go.[44]

The two brigades advanced through cornfields and across irrigation ditches similar to those their comrades in Twiggs's and Worth's divisions had encountered south of the river. Then they ran into determined Mexican defenders, who brought their advance to an abrupt halt. Intense fighting raged now on the north as well as the south side of the river, but here too the Mexican defenders stood firm. Along the line of the New York volunteers, Episcopal chaplain John McCarty ignored the heavy fire and busied himself consoling the wounded and encouraging the other men to go on fighting.[45]

Shields tried to extend his line to the north so as to flank the defenders, but they matched his move and again stymied the attackers. In response to the north bank commanders' pleas for reinforcements, all Scott could do was pull the Second Dragoons and Mounted Rifles off the southern front and send them around to join Pierce and Shields, but the added force still brought no breakthrough. Three o'clock was approaching, and it appeared that Santa Anna had won his first victory over Scott and the first Mexican victory of the war.[46]

In order to protect his line of retreat and communication from the threat posed by Pierce and Shields, Santa Anna had pulled some of the defenders out of the *tête de pont*, almost imperceptibly shifting the delicate balance of forces that had held the Americans at bay on that front for more than two hours. It was junior officers in the U.S. ranks, pinned down with their men out on the front lines, who first seemed to sense the subtle change, perhaps by noticing a slightly diminished volume of fire coming out of the Mexican fortifications.

On the line of the Eighth Infantry, Captain James V. Bomford believed he saw an opportunity. Climbing to his feet and calling on his men to follow him, he charged toward the Mexican fortifications. A few yards away Lieutenant James Longstreet sprang forward with the regimental colors. Soon the Eighth's entire line was advancing. The Fifth Infantry joined the charge, its commander, Colonel Charles F. Smith, leading his men and shouting, "Forward!" Then the rest of Worth's division surged forward. This time the Mexican fire was not enough to stop them. Wading the shallow waters of the ditch in front of the fort, they boosted one another up the glacis and onto the parapet, where they fought hand to hand with the defenders. Within minutes the Americans had overrun the *tête de pont*, and Longstreet had planted his flag on the ramparts.[47]

The situation for the defenders of San Mateo was now desperate. The fall of the *tête de pont* had cut off their retreat, and soon American fire was pouring into the convent from several directions, including that of the *tête de pont* itself, where the victors had turned a captured four-pounder cannon so as to enfilade San Mateo. In front, another American battery galloped up and unlimbered in place of the one the Mexican gunners had beaten off in a long artillery duel that had ended an hour ago. Now shot and shell slammed into the convent more frequently than before. Under the cover of the bombardment, American troops, led by the Third Infantry, charged again and this time succeeded in climbing and battering their way into the walled courtyard. Fighting with bayonets, they cleared the courtyard in short order as what was left of the garrison pulled back into the church building itself.

Braving their way through intense blasts of musketry from the interior, the Americans battered their way into the building and then began the task of clearing its first floor in vicious hand-to-hand fighting. As the defenders finally retreated to the second floor, one of the Mexicans attempted to display a white flag, but a San Patricio snatched it away from him. Twice more Mexicans tried to signal a general surrender as the fighting raged in the stifling, smoke-filled upstairs corridor, and both times the desperate San Patricios thwarted the attempt. Finally, cornered and hopeless, the surviving members of the battalion surrendered and resistance in the convent ceased. Among the captured were eighty-five members of the San Patricio Battalion, including their commander, John Riley, a deserter from Company K, Fifth U.S. Infantry, who by this time had risen to the rank of lieutenant colonel in the Mexican army. Meanwhile, the Mexican troops who had escaped the fall of the *tête de pont*, along with those who had been fighting north of the river, fled in disorder up the causeway toward the inner defenses of Mexico City.[48]

The city walls were five miles away from Churubusco, and the American infantry covered two of those miles in pursuit before Scott's orders brought them to a halt. Racing past the foot soldiers, Scott's own personal escort, Company F, First Dragoons, kept up the chase. In the lead were Lieutenant Richard S. Ewell and the company's commander, Captain Philip Kearny. A nephew of First Dragoons commanding officer Brigadier General Stephen W. Kearny, the thirty-two-year-old Captain Kearny was the scion of a wealthy New York family who had sought adventure in a military career. After earning, at the insistence of his family, a law degree at Columbia College, Kearny had in 1836 obtained a second lieutenant's commission in his uncle's regiment. Three years later the army sent him to France to study cavalry tactics at the famous French military school at Saumur, but Kearny had done more than study, participating in combat on several occasions in Algeria, where his boldness in battle won him the nickname Kearny le Magnifique. Back in the States and bored with the routine of the peacetime army, Kearny had been at the point of resignation when the Mexican War broke out, rescuing him from the torments of ennui. Assigned to raise a new company of the First Dragoons, he recruited his men in Terre Haute, Indiana, and mounted them on 120 beautiful dapple-gray horses at his own expense.

Now, on the late afternoon of August 20, the young captain was once again, in the eyes of many who saw him, Kearny the Magnificent as he led his splendidly mounted company at a gallop up the road from Churubusco to the San Antonio Garita, the fortified gate that formed the southern entrance to the walls of Mexico City. Spotting a battery of Mexican guns in action near the gate, Kearny made for them with single-minded fixation, leading his horsemen racing through the swarms of fleeing Mexican soldiers desperate to reach the safety of the gate. Frantic to stop Kearny and his dragoons, the gunners cut loose while their own comrades were still in the line of fire. Mexican soldiers and American dragoons toppled like tenpins under blast after blast of grapeshot. Ewell's horse went down, pitching him to the ground to make his escape on foot. One of the grapeshot shattered Kearny's left arm, which would require amputation, and the battered dragoons had to fall back.[49]

The day's two battles, Contreras and Churubusco, added up to a resounding victory for Winfield Scott and his army. Of 25,000 Mexican troops who had taken part in the day's fighting, 4,000 were killed or wounded and another 2,700 were captured, including 8 generals, 200 other officers, and the deserters of the San Patricio Battalion. Scott's troops had taken thirty-seven Mexican cannon, hundreds of wagons, uncounted numbers of muskets, and vast supplies of ammunition. The triumph had not come without cost. Of the 8,500 Americans engaged in the battles, 137 were killed and 877 wounded. Nevertheless, it had been exactly the victory the Americans had needed, bringing them past the outlying obstructions of Mexico City—lakes, marshes, the Pedregal—and to within striking distance of the very walls of the city itself.[50]

CHAPTER SIXTEEN

A Conquered Capital and a Negotiated Peace

ON AUGUST 21, 1847, the day after the victories at Contreras and Churubusco, Scott and his headquarters entourage moved toward Tacubaya to begin preparations for the climactic assault on the capital city. It was an assault he very much did not wish to make. As he had after every battle in his virtual hesitation waltz across Mexico, Scott hoped that the Mexicans would respond to the American victory by suing for peace. He would rather have had a negotiated peace than one dictated from the enemy's capital over the bodies of vast numbers of his own and the enemy's slain, and his several previous failed attempts at negotiations had not convinced him of the hopelessness of further talks.[1]

His attempts had, however, excited the disgust of his men. Avoiding unnecessary bloodshed was all very well, especially to those who might be called upon to shed it, but many felt that long before this it should have been clear to Scott that such pauses for negotiations only gave the Mexicans opportunity to recover from their defeats and thus shed even more American blood when the next advance became necessary, as constant Mexican intransigence assured that it would. Indeed, some believed Scott's actions may even have served to convince the Mexicans that the American position was weaker than it seemed and that the Yankees were desperate for peace. "After every victory we are down upon our knees suing for peace," grumbled a disgruntled infantry officer after one of Scott's previous pauses. Scott's renewed hesitation at the very gates of the enemy capital occasioned "much muttering and grumbling throughout the army" as the soldiers expressed their opinion that their general was wasting the fruits of their recent victories. Noting the large number of flag-of-truce parties coming and going between Mexico City during the days after Churubusco, an American news correspondent wrote wryly, "At this game the Mexicans can beat us."[2]

Accompanied by his staff and newfound friend Nicholas Trist, Scott arranged a meeting with General Ignacio Mora y Villamil outside Mexico City on the road to Tacubaya. The general, who was the chief engineer of the Mexican army, produced two letters. One was from the British minister to Mexico, expressing the rather superfluous hope that the hostilities would soon end and that the Americans would not sack the city when they took it. Of course, if the Americans had wanted to go into the sacking business, they could have started with Veracruz and honed their technique on Jalapa and Puebla. The other letter was somewhat more interesting. It was from José Ramón Pacheco, Mexico's foreign minister, stating that he was now prepared to receive Trist as an American emissary and that he would consider whether previous U.S. peace proposals were consistent with his country's "honor." In the meantime, he suggested a one-year truce.[3]

The prospect was laughable, and there the matter might have ended. Seeing the Americans disinclined to fall for such an obvious ploy, however, General Mora y Villamil tried a more subtle one. Santa Anna, he told Scott informally, would probably be willing to settle instead for an immediate short truce to allow negotiations. The concept appealed to both Trist and Scott. It was in keeping with Scott's long-held plan of stopping short of actually entering the Mexican capital, once he had it at his mercy, so as not to humiliate the nation completely. Now that a negotiated peace finally seemed possible, both American leaders, military and diplomatic, were eager to try. The truce was soon concluded. Its terms provided that neither side should make military preparations during its continuance, neither army receiving reinforcements or improving its position. The Americans were to allow free traffic into and out of Mexico City, so that Santa Anna's forces could bring in supplies, and in exchange should be allowed to purchase supplies from the city. Either side could terminate the agreement on forty-eight hours' notice.[4]

Of course Santa Anna never had any thought of abiding by these terms. The truce and the recent talk of negotiations had been nothing more than a ploy to gain time while he prepared for further military operations, a large-scale version of the trick he had used on Taylor at Buena Vista in displaying a flag of truce for no other purpose than to cover the retreat of some of his troops. From the outset, while Scott carefully observed the terms, making sure that his troops behaved with scrupulous respect toward Mexican citizens, Santa Anna flouted the agreement. His military preparations went on apace, and when columns of U.S. supply wagons sought to enter the city for provisions, they were either refused admittance or threatened with mob violence. The first train of American supply wagons to enter the city was met with a riot that left two American teamsters dead, infuriating Scott's soldiers. If U.S.

forces had not succeeded in gathering supplies from the surrounding countryside, the food situation in Scott's army would have become critical. Even then the Americans had to make their purchases at gunpoint from terrified civilians whom Santa Anna, in another blatant violation of the truce, had ordered not to sell to the Yankees.[5]

To the disgust of his officers, many of whom had recognized the truce for what it was from the beginning, Scott at first refused to believe the abundant evidence of Santa Anna's perfidy. What finally opened his eyes was the complete intransigence of the Mexican "negotiators." When Trist insisted that the talks had to deal with serious proposals for settling the issues that had brought the two countries to war, the Mexicans countered with a demand that the United States accept the Nueces River boundary for Texas, as if the negotiations were being carried on by a victorious Mexican army on the banks of the Potomac. Meanwhile, Santa Anna carried on his military preparations so openly, constructing fortifications and bringing in reinforcements, that at last even Scott could not deny them. By September 6 Scott had finally had enough and gave the Mexicans notice that he would no longer consider the truce to be in force. The strange one-sided arrangement officially came to an end forty-eight hours later. The Americans would have to storm Mexico City, and it would be a good deal harder, riskier, and more costly now than it would have been two and a half weeks earlier, when the Mexican army was weakened and in disarray after the defeats at Contreras and Churubusco.[6]

Scott cast about for a direction from which to launch his new effort against the city and, on the advice of several of his officers, began seriously considering a southern approach, keeping well clear of the formidable Castle of Chapultepec, on the city's west side. That plan quickly suffered a setback, however, when a battalion-sized patrol covering Lieutenant Beauregard on a reconnaissance in front of the southern gates clashed with a Mexican patrol on the night of September 7, drawing Santa Anna's attention to that quarter. The Mexican leader immediately began shifting forces to the southern walls, and intelligence reports of the Mexican movements reached Scott that same night, making the southern approach seem less appealing.[7]

Several Mexican outworks commanded the outer ends of the western causeways. Among the outermost of these was a three-hundred-yard-long complex of stone buildings that had been at various times a flour mill and cannon foundry. It was called Molino del Rey. Six hundred yards west of the Molino was a smaller dependent work known as Casa de la Mata, and about one thousand yards east stood the Castle of Chapultepec on its hill. Reports indicated that the Mexicans in the Molino were casting church bells into new cannon and also had a large stockpile of powder. Scott therefore decided to take and destroy it and its satellite work in what he assumed would be a minor engagement, to be executed by Worth's division on September 8, thus both denying Santa Anna some additional cannon and taking a first step toward weakening the city's western defenses.[8]

Molino del Rey and Casa de la Mata (also called Casa Mata) were in fact very strongly held by the Mexicans. At least eight or nine thousand troops occupied the two mutually supporting positions and their associated entrenchments, with additional Mexican cavalry hovering to the west ready to swoop down on the flank of the attackers. The positions were strong for defense, with open fields of fire. Some of Scott's officers urged him to leave the Molino alone, but Scott was determined to attack. Upon receiving orders for an attack on the Molino the next day, Captain Ephraim Kirby Smith of the Fifth Infantry wrote to his wife, "Tomorrow will be a day of slaughter," adding, "I am thankful that you do not know the peril we are in."[9]

In the predawn hours of September 8, Worth deployed his 3,450-man division for the attack. In their positions and ready to go, his men waited apprehensively for orders to advance. The position in front of them looked forbidding in the gray light of dawn, and its aspect grew more so as the light rose. Finally, at about six o'clock, Worth gave the order, and the American artillery opened its preparatory barrage. Mainstays of the American guns firing on the Molino were two big twenty-four-pounder siege pieces under the command of Captain Benjamin Huger. No Mexican guns answered the bombardment, and two American engineer officers observing the defenses from an advanced position detected no activity and sent word back that the Molino appeared to have been abandoned and that the infantry should advance at once.[10]

In fact, the Mexicans had gone nowhere and were merely biding their time. As the assaulting column charged toward the Molino, they opened up with both artillery and musketry. The attackers were a special storming party of five hundred men handpicked from all the units of Worth's division and commanded by Brevet Major George Wright. The Mexican fire mowed them down, toppling three-quarters of the storming party's officers, including Wright himself. The attackers pressed home their assault grimly, and they briefly got in among the Mexican guns but could not stay there against a powerful counterattack bolstered by reinforcements from Chapultepec.[11]

Several hundred yards farther west, Colonel James S. McIntosh's brigade charged toward Casa de la Mata and met a similar reception, coming under heavy musketry fire at a range of seventy yards as the Mexicans poured volley after volley into the American ranks. Advancing with the Sixth Infantry, Lieutenant Ralph W. Kirkham saw his friend Lieutenant William T. Burwell go down, shot in the leg just above the knee. Since his friend's wound did not appear life-threatening, Kirkham pressed on with the regiment. Amid heavy casualties, including McIntosh himself, the brigade pushed to within thirty yards of the fortified building before the fire became unbearable and the troops had to fall back. Then the Americans could only watch in horror from a position several hundred yards away as Mexicans dashed out of Casa de la Mata to kill and mutilate the American wounded who had been left on the ground outside when the attack fell back. As Burwell lay helpless, a Mexican lancer laid his head open and an infantryman repeatedly bayoneted him and began to plunder his corpse. Another wounded American officer, Captain William H. T. Walker of the Sixth Infantry, escaped death by feigning it. Captain Smith, who had written his wife with such foreboding the night before, was also badly wounded and succumbed a few days later.[12]

Colonel John Garland's brigade renewed the assault on Molino del Rey, joined by what was left of the original storming party. Again the Mexican fire tore into them, and the attack stalled. This time, however, the Americans simply refused to accept repulse. Daring artillery officers raced their six-pounders up to point-blank range, then unlimbered and began to blast shot and shell into the structures. Infantrymen doggedly worked their way forward, driving the Mexicans back from their outer defensive positions and battering in the gates of walled courtyards. Lieutenant Ulysses Grant found a wagon, got some of his men to prop it against the wall of one of the buildings, and used it as an impromptu scaling ladder to reach the roof. A squad of his men followed him, securing several Mexican prisoners. Once the Americans got into the complex, the fight became a bitter building-by-building and room-by-room contest in which defenders sometimes held a chamber or corridor to the last man. Other Mexicans surrendered, especially as it became increasingly apparent that the Americans would carry the position.[13]

Casa de la Mata remained defiant, but Worth did not immediately renew the assault. Instead, his men allowed their excellent artillery to proceed with the methodical destruction of the fort. The Mexicans brought their cavalry charging in from the left to flank the Americans, but Sumner's dragoons twice headed them off and drove them back. Finally, about two hours after the first shots of the battle had been fired, the defenders of Casa de la Mata fled, leaving what remained of the building in U.S. hands.[14]

U.S. losses totaled 116 dead and 673 wounded, including half the officers in McIntosh's brigade and similar losses in the others. The Mexicans left 269 dead on the battlefield and suffered about another 500 wounded. The Americans captured 852 Mexican soldiers, four cannon, and a collection of battered stone buildings. As U.S. troops moved about the site, securing the dead and wounded, Mexican artillery in Chapultepec took them under fire, stoking the American anger that had been kindled by the sight of their wounded comrades being murdered in front of Casa de la Mata. The crowning discovery of the day, however, as the Americans took stock of their conquest, was that the prebattle reports had been wrong about Molino del Rey. No one had been making any cannon there in recent weeks.[15]

The mood of the army that night was surly and dissatisfied. The troops, and especially their officers, seethed with even more discontentment at Scott's almost three-week pause, which had allowed Santa Anna to marshal his troops and strengthen his defenses. That blunder looked all the worse now that it had cost a large number of American lives— "brave men who deserved a better fate," as one of their comrades wrote. The troops were also angry at the ill-informed decision to attack Molino del Rey. A Pennsylvania soldier wrote that the decision "is condemned by the entire army and reflects anything but credit upon General Scott."[16]

Lieutenant Ulysses S. "Sam" Grant, of the Eighth Infantry, felt frustration that Scott and Worth had not followed up the costly victory by pursuing the fleeing defenders of Molino del Rey and Casa de la Mata right into the Castle of Chapultepec, which he believed could then have been taken with minimal additional cost. Another American officer summed up the mood of dissatisfaction with Scott when he wrote, "How much bloodshed would have been spared had General Scott only had a little more of the go-ahead Napoleon spirit about him." Along with the bitterness toward Scott, however, the soldiers felt a deep anger at the Mexicans and a desire to settle scores.[17]

Even as the army had been preparing for the final phase of the campaign against Mexico City, a number of its officers had during recent days been attending to another duty. The army had to deal somehow with the captured members of the San Patricio Battalion. Two separate group trials were held for different contingents of prisoners. Colonel

Bennett Riley, an Irish-American Catholic, presided over one of these courts-martial. Colonel John Garland convened the other. The results were much the same. One soldier escaped the death sentence because he had never been properly enrolled in the U.S. Army, and another because he was judged to be of weak mind, "a perfect simpleton." The courts duly sentenced the rest as the Articles of War prescribed.

When news of the death sentences got out during the early days of September, while the truce was breaking down, various Mexicans and foreign residents of Mexico City had appealed for leniency, including the archbishop of Mexico City and the British minister. Scott had carefully reviewed the findings of both courts-martial and weighed them against the Articles of War. He pardoned eight more men because of their excessive youth, and another because he asserted that he had not voluntarily deserted but had in fact been kidnapped by Mexicans while drunk.

Scott also commuted the death sentence of San Patricio Battalion commander John Riley, who by the time of his capture had held a major's commission in the Mexican army. What saved Riley's life was the fact that he had deserted a few days before the technical outbreak of war between the United States and Mexico. Therefore, in precise adherence to what the Articles of War dictated for such cases, Riley received the standard punishment meted out to all peacetime deserters from the regular army—fifty lashes and branding with the letter D for "deserter." Thus, ironically, the man who had led the battalion escaped with his life, while his men, many of whom he had personally persuaded to enlist and fight for Mexico, awaited hanging.

Although the Articles of War were very clear about such cases, Scott would nevertheless have liked to have pardoned the rest, but with the truce breaking down and the prospect of bloody fighting ahead, he could not let their bad example go unpunished and thus risk the collapse of military discipline. Scott's army itself, from generals to enlisted men, was overwhelmingly and ferociously in favor of administering the full weight of justice, and the Irish-Americans who had remained faithful to the United States flag were some of the most vocal in that regard. Reluctantly Scott gave his approval, and the rest of the death sentences were confirmed. Twenty were hanged at San Angel on September 10, two days after the Battle of Molino del Rey.[18]

Twiggs had charge of the affair, which also included the whipping and branding of Riley. Like most other soldiers in Scott's army, Twiggs had not been among those who wanted clemency for Riley or any of the other deserters. The crusty old general believed there was only one proper fate for a man who had deserted and then killed his former comrades, and he desperately wanted to kill Riley. He hired a sturdy Mexican muleteer to wield the cat-o'-nine-tails, explaining that being struck by a member of the United States Army would confer too much honor on the former commander of the San Patricio Battalion, and he offered the muleteer a bonus if Riley should die under the lash. With that punishment concluded and the deserter still alive, Twiggs had him branded on the cheek with a *D*—and branded a second time because the general said the first *D* was upside down—and finally had the deserter's head shaved.[19]

The remaining thirty survivors of the San Patricio Battalion were under the charge of Colonel William S. Harney of the First Dragoons. The epitome of a hard-bitten regular, Harney had devotion to duty and country bred in his bones through seemingly countless years of frontier service. The San Patricios had offended the most sacred tenets of his value system. They had killed their fellow Americans. They had fired on the Stars and Stripes. Harney had orders to hang them, and hang them he would, but he determined to do so in a way that would symbolize the nature of their offense and the vindication of the nation and its flag in their punishment. His opportunity would come three days after the first hangings, on September 13.[20]

Meanwhile, Scott devoted September 9 and 10 to reconnaissance aimed at determining the best route of advance to breach the defenses of Mexico City. Lee, Beauregard, and the other engineer officers of Scott's staff carefully scouted the fortifications, and Scott's interests turned back to the southern front, where he joined Lee for a close reconnaissance of the *garitas* [gates] on that side of the city, but Scott was not pleased with the "net work of obstacles" he saw there.[21]

On Saturday morning, September 11, he summoned all his generals to meet with him and his staff at the church in the outlying village of Piedad. Scott opened the meeting by expressing his preference for an assault on the western gates. A southern approach would face serious problems, he explained, and the ground on the city's western side was more suitable for operations. True, a western approach would require the taking of Chapultepec, but Scott opined that the castle might surrender after a bombardment, without the necessity of assault, and after Chapultepec's surrender, the city itself might capitulate.[22]

This last was more of Scott's by now discredited optimism in the willingness of Mexican leaders to be reasonable, and it probably swayed few within the council of war. Gideon Pillow, who had counseled strongly against the attack on Molino del Rey, now urged adoption of a southern approach, and several of the engineer officers, including Lee, agreed with him, as did four other generals, lending the weight of vastly greater military expertise to Pillow's not very substantial credentials. Only Twiggs sided with Scott, and then Bennett Riley asked the engineers which approach would require less work digging battery emplacements. When told it was the western, he replied, "Well, I go in for less work and more fighting." Beauregard had not yet spoken up, and so Scott called on him. "You, young man, in that corner, what have you to say on the subject?"

The young Creole launched into an intense argument against the southern and in favor of the western attack. The difficulties attending the southern approach were too great, and besides, a southern attack was exactly what Santa Anna was expecting and, as Beauregard argued, hoping for. So powerful was the young engineer's presentation that Franklin Pierce announced that he was changing his vote from the southern to the western side, but it soon became apparent that there was only one vote in this meeting that would count. With finality Scott announced, "Gentlemen, we will attack by the western gates. The general officers present here will remain for further orders—the meeting is dissolved."[23]

Attacking from the west meant, first of all, reducing the forbidding Castle of Chapultepec, which stood high atop a rocky two-hundred-foot hill, frowning down on the outer ends of the western causeways. Built more than half a century before as the curiously fortresslike country residence of a Spanish viceroy, it had in 1841 become the seat of the Mexican military academy. The entire enclosure around the castle was about three-quarters of a mile east and west by about a quarter mile north and south and was defended by about six thousand Mexican troops, many of them in elaborate earthwork defenses constructed to strengthen the fortress still further. The castle itself held 260 additional defenders, including several dozen young cadets of the Mexican military academy who had refused to leave. The southern and western slopes of the hill were steep, those on the north and east precipitous.[24]

As always, Scott made careful plans for the assault. A heavy artillery bombardment on September 12, coupled with an infantry feint toward the southern gates, would precede the infantry assault against the castle on the morning of the thirteenth. Throughout the night of September 11, Captain Lee of the engineers and Captain Huger of the ordnance department directed American fatigue parties digging emplacements for the army's cannon within range of Chapultepec. By the morning of

Sunday, September 12, the guns were in place and opened fire on the castle. The American siege train had been enhanced by recently captured guns, including the sixteen- and twenty-four-pounders taken at Contreras, and so the fire of the American artillerists was more deadly than ever. They slammed solid shot into the castle walls and occasionally sent blasts of canister across the causeways leading from the castle to the city, preventing the Mexican troops there from reinforcing Chapultepec. Yet the effect of the American fire on the castle walls was disappointing. Mexican engineers were quick to repair the few minor holes knocked in the walls. Clearly a difficult task awaited the infantry the next day.[25]

After contemplating a night attack, largely out of fear that the Mexicans might reinforce Chapultepec from the city during the hours of darkness, Scott accepted Captain Lee's advice that the assault take place the following morning. At a meeting with his generals that evening, Scott listened patiently as Pillow foolishly expounded an amateurish plan of his own. Then the commanding general launched into a detailed briefing on what the army was going to do the next day. Pillow's division of volunteers would assault up the west face of Chapultepec Hill, advancing from Molino del Rey with Worth's division of regulars following behind in support. Spearheading the attack in this sector would be a special storming party of 250 regulars, who would be selected from among volunteers drawn from all of the regular regiments.[26]

That night in the army's camps, so many regulars stepped forward for this highly dangerous assignment that their officers had them draw lots to see who should have the privilege of being part of the storming party. Among themselves, the officers settled the matter by date of rank, with the seniors within each grade claiming the limited number of slots. In the Seventh Infantry, John Henshaw was disappointed when Captain Gabriel Paul and First Lieutenant Levi Gantt both claimed the honor of membership in the storming party, leaving Henshaw to remain with his regiment, earmarked for a reserve assignment the following day.[27]

Simultaneous with the attack of Pillow's and Worth's divisions and the storming party, Quitman's division of volunteers would advance from the south-southwest up the Tacubaya Road to strike the southeast quadrant of the castle compound, where Chapultepec's entrenchments reached the outer ends of the causeways leading to the capital itself. As with Pillow's and Worth's divisions, Twiggs's division of regulars would follow Quitman's in support but would provide a special 250-man storming party to spearhead the attack.[28]

The men regarded their coming ordeal with foreboding. Recent battles had been bloody, and this one threatened to be worse. Their officers were equally pessimistic, judging the chances for success uncertain at best. A young lieutenant in one of the storming parties recalled that the prospects "now looked dark and gloomy in the extreme." The doubts extended right up the chain of command. General Worth commented privately, "We shall be defeated," and Scott himself confided to a friend on his staff, "I have my misgivings."[29]

First light brought a renewal of the bombardment. The infantry formed up nervously for the advance, scheduled to begin at 8:00 a.m. On a knoll just behind U.S. lines and within plain sight of the castle ramparts, Colonel Harney and his dragoons had arranged a long row of mule carts beneath an equally long gallows, from which dangled thirty nooses. In the carts stood the remaining condemned San Patricios. Harney had come up with a setting for their execution that he felt would properly dramatize the gravity of their offense and vindicate the authority of the United States and its military law. He announced that as soon as he saw the Stars and Stripes rise above the ramparts of Chapultepec he would give the order and his men would drive the carts forward, hanging the thirty deserters. From this hilltop and elsewhere around the American lines, as well as from the walls and buildings of Mexico City, many eyes gazed intently at the castle as the first rays of the rising sun lit its walls.[30]

The attack stepped off as scheduled. Pillow's column advanced across a marsh and a grove of trees and fought its way into the compound from the west. Pillow went down with a wound in the ankle, but his troops pressed on. Particularly successful was Lieutenant Colonel Joseph E. Johnston, advancing at the head of his regiment of gray-uniformed *voltigeurs*, a regular army regiment that had been enlisted only for the duration of the war. Johnston's men, along with the storming party, broke through the outer defenses and started fighting their way up the hill.[31]

Lieutenant Thomas J. Jackson, commanding a section of two six-pounders advancing on Chapultepec from the west, found his progress halted when every one of his horses was shot down and one of his cannon disabled. His cannoneers took shelter in the ditches on either side of the road while Jackson strode up and down among the humming bullets exhorting his men to come back and help him fight with the remaining gun. Finally a single sergeant did so, and together they got the gun into action.[32]

On the southeast side of the compound, Quitman's attack stalled under heavy fire from the outer defenses of Chapultepec and a crack

Mexican battalion blocking the road ahead. After a period of deadlock, Quitman sent one of his brigades to the left to attack the center of the compound's southern wall. These troops were able to take advantage of the breakthrough Johnston's men had scored on the right flank of Pillow's column. Volunteer regiments from New York, Pennsylvania, and South Carolina fought their way into the compound and started up the hill. On both Pillow's and Quitman's fronts, the regulars and the marines soon moved up to reinforce the volunteers. Charging up the hill at the head of the Eighth Infantry, Lieutenant James Longstreet carried the regimental colors. When he fell with a musket ball in the thigh, he handed the colors to his friend Lieutenant George Pickett, who took the flag and continued up the slope.[33]

The troops reached the base of the castle wall, regulars and volunteers now thoroughly intermixed, and there they spent an unpleasant fifteen minutes waiting for the scaling ladders to come up. The Mexican fire was intense, and officers became concerned that their men might falter. Eager to boost morale, Beauregard called out to Johnston, who was nearby, "Colonel, what will you bet on this shot?"

"Drinks in the City of Mexico," Johnston shouted back. Beauregard drew a bead, fired, and claimed a hit. "You have lost," he shouted gleefully to Johnston. "You will have to pay it."[34]

At last the ladders arrived and the final stage of the assault began. The Mexicans resisted desperately, shoving back the first few ladders. American sharpshooters made this dangerous for them, and soon there were too many ladders anyway. Johnston believed that one of his *voltigeurs* was the first American atop the wall. Before long Americans were swarming over the parapet. Fierce hand-to-hand combat raged throughout the castle. Many of the attackers had seen their wounded comrades murdered on the ground outside Casa de la Mata five days before, and they were eager to avenge those deeds. The fighting was merciless. As the Americans began to gain the upper hand, the color guard of Johnston's *voltigeur* regiment rushed up to the tower where the castle's colors flew. Reaching the top, they hauled down the flag of Mexico and raised their own United States flag in its place.[35]

Watching from his knoll some distance from the base of the hill of Chapultepec, Colonel Harney gave the signal. His men whipped the mules. The carts rumbled forward, and the thirty convicted deserters who had fought in the San Patricio Battalion dropped on their ropes.[36]

Fighting continued inside the castle and the surrounding compound as the final knots of Mexican resisters were routed out. Many were killed.

The Battle of Chapultepec, September 13, 1847

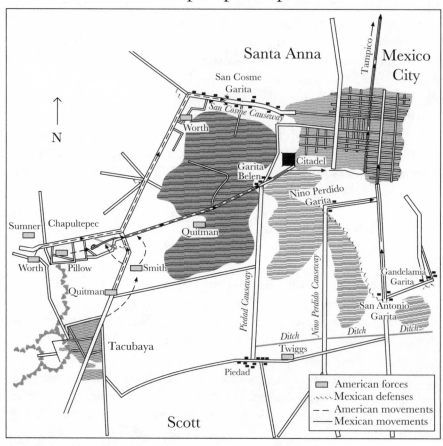

A few individual surrenders were accepted, and the rest of the Mexicans fled down the eastern slope of the hill for the causeways leading to the city. By 9:30 a.m. Chapultepec was in U.S. hands. Mexican casualties for the fight totaled around eighteen hundred, U.S. about one-fourth that.[37]

With the castle taken, Quitman lost no time in getting his own troops onto the causeways leading toward the city. He thought this might be his last chance of the war to win military glory, and he may have feared as well that Scott would repeat his performances after past victories by halting the army and allowing the enemy to regroup and prepare to kill more Americans in the next advance. So he and his staff quickly began massing his division at the eastern foot of Chapultepec Hill preparatory for an advance on the Belén Gate. It was as well that he did so, for Scott was indeed about to resume his preferred halting mode of warfare. Upon arriving atop Chapultepec, Scott was angered to learn of Quitman's preparations to advance and sent messengers galloping after him with orders to stop the movement. Fortunately for the American cause, he was too late. Realizing he could not stop Quitman, Scott directed Worth to march his division toward the San Cosme Gate. Several times during the hours that followed, however, Scott tried to get Quitman to stop and transform his advance into a feint so that Scott's old friend Worth could have the honor of taking the city. Quitman ignored the orders.[38]

The Mexicans stubbornly resisted Quitman's advance. An aqueduct ran along the center of the causeway, and the advancing Americans used it for cover, dashing from one archway to the next. Captain Simon H. Drum led his battery of light artillery up the causeway, firing his guns from both sides of the aqueduct until his six-pounder ammunition was expended, then taking a Mexican eight-pounder and firing captured ammunition until he was mortally wounded, whereupon the command of the battery devolved on a sergeant. Beauregard was with Quitman at the head of the column and suffered several minor wounds.[39]

Shortly after 1:00 p.m. Quitman's men, sensing weakening Mexican resistance, rushed the gate, clambered over the parapets, and cleared the fortified post with their bayonets, but the great bulk of the defenders merely fell back a few score yards to the Ciudadela, an old tobacco factory converted to a fort, and there continued the fight. When Quitman sent a staff officer to Scott requesting more ammunition and artillery, the commanding general replied peevishly that he had none to send. He raged that Quitman was in the wrong place, that the Belén Gate was the stronger sector of the Mexican defenses, and that the true American effort should be made at the San Cosme Gate, where Scott was even then following behind the advance of Worth's division. That might be, but the probability is that if Quitman had not forced the issue, Scott would not have made any advance on either gate that day.[40]

Meanwhile, Worth's division had been advancing on the San Cosme Gate. Even before Worth could get the division regrouped and formed up after the storming of Chapultepec that morning, two young lieutenants, Daniel Harvey Hill and Barnard Bee, had led a portion of the storming party of Twiggs's division, which had been assigned to Quitman, up the causeway toward the San Cosme Gate. They were joined by Thomas Jackson, who had made temporary repairs to his damaged cannon. With this small force they crowded the Mexican retreat along the causeway until General Anastacio Torrejón—who had led the Mexican horse against the hapless Captain Seth Thornton back at the beginning of the war—led fifteen hundred lancers in a charge along the causeway.

The narrow confines saved the Americans, as the Mexican horsemen could do nothing but charge straight toward them on a front the American guns could easily cover. Jackson blasted load after load of canister into the attackers, toppling many and driving the rest back.[41]

That afternoon Worth's division overtook Hill's, Bee's, and Jackson's scratch force and assumed the lead in the advance, continuing to fight its way toward the San Cosme Gate. Fairly dense suburbs lay outside the gate, and Mexican infantry and artillery had taken position in them. The Americans' fire soon drove the Mexican foot soldiers away from their rooftop positions, but Mexican artillery continued to sweep the streets with grapeshot. The leading American troops took shelter in the houses and then sent to the rear for picks. Thus equipped, they began to hack their way through the sidewalls of the houses, moving through the holes from one house to the next and thus gaining access to houses closer and closer to the gate without venturing into the deadly streets.[42]

After a bitter house-by-house fight through a suburb, Worth's men reached the gate late in the afternoon and found it heavily defended. Lieutenant Ulysses Grant took a detail of men and a mountain howitzer to a nearby church he had spotted. Disassembling the gun, they carried it to the bell tower, reassembled it, and began to lob shells into the gate fortifications so effectively as to attract the favorable attention of General Worth, who sent Lieutenant John C. Pemberton to summon Grant to the general for special commendation. On the other side of the road, Lieutenant Raphael Semmes got another howitzer into a good position and added its fire to the attack on the gate. Under the cover of Grant's and Semmes's fire, Lieutenant Henry J. Hunt, of the Second U.S. Artillery, brought a cannon up the road to blast round shot directly into the gate itself.[43]

Shortly before nightfall a detachment of U.S. marines attached to Worth's division and fighting house to house reached the roof of a three-story building adjacent to the gate from which they could fire down on the defenders. The advantage gained allowed the marines and army troops to rush the gate successfully. Taking possession of the cannon there, the Americans turned the guns and gave the retreating Mexicans several blasts as night was falling. With the day's fighting ended, Worth's men moved into the city and occupied a number of buildings near the gate.[44]

That night, at the urging of municipal leaders who wanted to avoid the destruction of their city, Santa Anna marched his remaining troops out of the capital. The Americans were surprised the next morning when municipal authorities advanced under flags of truce on both Worth's and

Quitman's fronts to inform them that the Mexican army was gone and the city was theirs. Quitman's battle-stained and bedraggled column marched into the city, and at 7:00 a.m. a marine lieutenant attached to Quitman's division raised the flag over the National Palace. Meanwhile, Scott had learned of Santa Anna's departure and had prepared to make a grand entrance at the head of Colonel Harney's dragoons. A short time later he rode into the central plaza resplendent in full dress uniform while the field music of Harney's regiment played "Yankee Doodle." Quitman's division was drawn up in review, and Worth's division marched in behind Scott. It was an impressive sight and marked the culmination of the campaign and of Scott's brilliant military career. Across the ocean, when the Duke of Wellington heard of the fall of Mexico City, he wrote that Scott's "campaign is unsurpassed in military annals. He is the greatest living soldier."[45]

The war was not over. Scott's triumphal entry into the plaza was the occasion of a mob uprising. A Mexican sniper wounded Colonel Garland, and a number of other shots were fired at the Americans. Rioters who had no firearms threw stones. The U.S. troops responded aggressively with volleys of musketry and blasts of canister from their cannon, sometimes clearing snipers' nests with bayonets and musket butts. House-to-house fighting raged in neighborhoods that had remained untouched in the previous day's battle and with even more destruction of property and considerable loss of life. An American officer wrote of seeing "furniture of every kind [and] ladies' and gentlemen's apparel . . . scattered in perfect confusion." The rabble, including jail inmates whom Santa Anna had released on his departure, proved no match for combat-hardened troops, and the riot was soon quelled. Sporadic violence continued for some days. Scott took a stern line, threatening to sack and raze the entire block of buildings from which any act of hostility was committed, and since the population had reason to believe he would do it, the acts of hostility generally ceased. Mexico City settled down to a more peaceful occupation.[46]

Outside the walls of the capital the war continued in desultory fashion. When a contingent of eleven hundred U.S. reinforcements marched from Veracruz to join Scott, a local Mexican governor marshaled his forces and tried to stop them at the old Cerro Gordo battlefield. The Americans used the same route Scott had taken to flank Santa Anna and served this Mexican force in the same way. Meanwhile, Santa Anna hoped to capture the American base at Puebla, where a small garrison guarded the sick and wounded personnel Scott had left behind there. The U.S. commander rebuffed Santa Anna's summons to surrender, and when the Mexican general arrayed his forces to storm the town, his men flatly refused to advance. Not long after, Santa Anna lost his command. Having turned over the presidency to José Manuel de la Peña y Peña several weeks before, he now found himself relieved of command and awaiting court-martial for his disastrous conduct of the war. Guerrilla warfare continued to sputter in the countryside, but with less and less prospect of affecting any aspect of the outcome of the war.[47]

Back in the United States, criticism of the war continued in some quarters, though the majority of Americans still supported it. Typically of a war that goes on for some time without further dramatic results, the conflict with Mexico began to be a target not only for quixotic idealist visionaries but also for the hard-eyed politicians of the opposition party, who hoped to score political points by denouncing a war that they devoutly hoped had grown boring and burdensome to the American people. During the course of 1847, the Whigs began taking potshots at Polk's decisions leading up to and during the war.

One eager young Whig freshman congressman, Abraham Lincoln of Illinois, presented on December 22, 1847, a series of resolutions in the House, calling on Polk to designate the "exact spot" where, as he had previously reported to Congress, "American blood [had] been shed on American soil." Lincoln's point was that the spot had been in disputed territory and therefore was not "American soil." Of course, to take that position was implicitly to side with Mexico in the dispute about the true borders of Texas and thus the United States, since the Texian and, subsequently, U.S. position had always been that American soil extended all the way to the north bank of the Rio Grande. The House was unimpressed and completely ignored the resolutions. Lincoln's constituents back in Illinois did not, and the move cost him a good deal of support. That it had been politically motivated became apparent the following year, when Lincoln enthusiastically supported a Whig presidential candidate who had been one of the war's chief generals. Older and politically wiser Whigs were inclined to be more circumspect in criticizing—if they did at all—a war that was still very popular with the vast majority of the American people.

While the U.S. Army waited in Mexico City, an unbecoming squabble arose among some of its generals. The instigator of the trouble was

Gideon Pillow. Those who had to deal with him in the army described him as a genial, ambitious fellow who wanted to get ahead in politics and did not care at all how he did it. Foul means would serve as well as fair, maybe better. His current tactic was to plant in various U.S. newspapers anonymous letters disparaging Scott and praising himself as a superlative warrior and the true architect of American victory. Scott got wind of the matter and had Pillow court-martialed for violating army regulations. Other officers became involved in the squabble, which became notorious within the army and affected officer relations for years after but could no longer influence the outcome of the current war.[48]

Peace negotiations proceeded slowly. Some Mexican politicians found hope in the fulminations of the antiwar movement in the United States, which encouraged them to think that the United States would eventually give up—or give much more favorable terms—if only Mexico remained sufficiently intransigent. In mid-November 1847 the whole process took a strange turn when orders arrived in Mexico City revoking Trist's authority to negotiate and recalling him to Washington. Polk had begun to fear that by keeping Trist in Mexico City month after month while the Mexicans stubbornly refused to negotiate seriously, he might be creating the impression that the United States was desperate for peace. When the order arrived, several of Trist's associates in Mexico City—Scott, British diplomat Edward Thornton, and newsman James Freaner—urged him to ignore it. Polk did not know the situation there, they argued, and would not send such an order if he did. Trist agreed to stay.[49]

Yet Polk's order did indeed produce somewhat the effect he had desired. On hearing of the order, José Manuel de la Peña y Peña, now serving as Mexican foreign minister, became alarmed. With Trist gone, the only way for Mexico to reopen negotiations would be to send a formal request to Washington, and that would be too humiliating for any Mexican politician to undertake. The U.S. occupation, and its attendant expense to Mexico, would then continue indefinitely. Eager to forestall this, Peña y Peña informed Trist that he was ready to begin negotiations in earnest. Even once serious talks got under way, progress was slow, partially because that was the way the Mexican government functioned and partially because the Mexicans were still occasionally encouraged by reports from the United States to the effect that the Whig opposition to the war would force Polk to grant more generous terms. The talks continued to drag on well into the new year of 1848.[50]

Finally, on February 2, 1848, Trist and the Mexican negotiators met at the traditional Mexican shrine of Guadalupe Hidalgo, a few miles outside Mexico City, and signed a peace treaty. It provided that the boundary between the two countries would follow the Rio Grande from its mouth to southern New Mexico, then west to the Gila River, down that stream to the Gulf of California, and then due west to the Pacific, passing south of the excellent natural harbor of San Diego. In exchange for the territory Mexico thus ceded, the victorious United States would pay $15 million and would assume Mexico's debts to U.S. citizens, variously estimated at from $2 million to $10 million.[51]

Polk was not particularly pleased with the treaty or with Trist. The former seemed far too generous to Mexico, and the latter had acted contrary to orders, which had revoked his authority and had recalled him to Washington, and had become snidely critical of Polk's administration. Still, the treaty secured all that Polk had hoped for at the beginning of the war, if at a hefty price, and the odious Trist could be ignored. The president therefore on February 22 submitted the treaty to the Senate for ratification.[52]

Such an outcome seemed far from certain. The Whigs opposed the treaty, denouncing any territorial acquisition. The Democrats were divided. Many believed the treaty was too favorable to Mexico, considering the magnitude of U.S. victory in the war. They also resented the fact that Trist had negotiated it after knowing that the president had revoked his authority and that he was even now heaping abuse on the administration. On the other hand, the influential Thomas Hart Benton had personal reasons for opposing the treaty. He was furious with Polk for refusing to intervene on behalf of the senator's son-in-law John C. Frémont, who had earned and received a court-martial and dismissal from the army for his insubordination in California. In retaliation, Benton was determined to oppose anything Polk favored. Then of course there were the antislavery senators, who as a matter of principle opposed any acquisition without a guarantee that slavery would be prohibited in the new lands.[53]

For some days the fate of the treaty seemed to be in serious doubt, but gradually most of the senators came around to a more pragmatic view. They began making various modifications to the treaty's fine print, and finally, on March 10, 1848, the Senate voted 38–14, with 4 abstentions, to ratify the revised version of the Treaty of Guadalupe Hidalgo. The Mexican government followed suit on May 25, and with that the war was formally at an end.[54]

PART FIVE

The Political System
and the Controversies
of Expansion

CHAPTER SEVENTEEN

The Election of 1848

BY THE TIME Nicholas Trist and the Mexican negotiators at Guadalupe Hidalgo signed the treaty of peace between their two nations, the election campaign of 1848 was already gearing up back in the States. Indeed, that year's campaign was in many ways a continuation of political controversies that had been building throughout the Polk years and especially during the war with Mexico. The concept of the Wilmot Proviso had not gone away after the first unsuccessful attempt to attach it to the $2 million appropriation to fund a negotiated settlement with Mexico. In December 1846, New York Democratic representative Preston King had introduced it again, reigniting the controversy in Congress, though with the same ultimate outcome: success in the House and failure in the Senate.[1]

Unlike Wilmot, King had not previously been a strong backer of Polk. Instead, he belonged to the Van Buren wing of the party. The Van Buren Democrats, always strongest in New York State, had been alienated from the Democratic Party's mainstream ever since Van Buren's shocking defeat for the 1844 nomination. Only Van Buren's own staunch commitment to unconditional party loyalty had kept them in line during the general election that year, and even the Little Magician's commitment to that cause had waned over the intervening four years. Polk had not favored Van Buren's faction of the party sufficiently with his appointments, and the Van Burenites felt that the administration had not done enough to aid one of their number, Silas Wright, in his unsuccessful 1846 bid for reelection as governor of New York.[2]

While northern Democrats struggled to bring the party around to their view, southern Democrats were just as determined to keep it hewing firmly to the proslavery line. Predictably, John C. Calhoun rose to the issue by introducing several resolutions in the Senate staking out the extreme proslavery view. According to Calhoun, the territories were not the property of the United States but rather the "joint and common property" of all the states together. Therefore, he argued, anything that was legal in any state had to be legal in all the territories, otherwise Congress would be guilty of denying some of the states their "full and equal rights" in the national domain. Nor had Congress the right to tell a nascent state what sort of constitution it could adopt, for that too would be denying somebody—the slaveholders, of course—their "full and equal rights." In short, as far as Calhoun was concerned, every territory should be a slave territory and every new state at least potentially a slave state. Of course, the resolutions had no chance of passage, but Calhoun intended them to rally all southerners into a unified bloc around a set of coherent demands.[3]

Southerners liked Calhoun's demands, but their enthusiasm for the resolutions was tempered by the fact that they quite accurately perceived that Calhoun was acting not merely on his fervent proslavery ideology but also on his even more fervent desire to be president. Clearly the gaunt South Carolinian intended that when a solid South rallied around his resolutions, it would also rally around him, and emphatically enough to win him the Democratic nomination and, perhaps, the presidency. Meanwhile, Democrats from the center of the party hoped Calhoun's efforts would fail, since they almost certainly would have split the party. As an alternative, Vice President George M. Dallas, a Pennsylvanian, floated a milder and vaguer version of Calhoun's demands by suggesting that the people of each territory be allowed to decide for themselves whether slavery would be legal there. The idea created little buzz at first, but it turned out to have legs.[4]

The fact was that the Democratic Party was already painfully close to a split of some kind. The fight over the Wilmot Proviso, and in particular its rejection by Polk's wing of the party, had added to the dissatisfaction of many northern Democrats. Van Buren's wing of the party came to be increasingly dominated by younger men who cared more about stopping the spread of slavery and defeating their intraparty enemies than they did about maintaining the unity and ascendancy of the Democratic Party as a whole. They staunchly backed Wilmot and every attempt to tack his incendiary proviso to bills passing through Congress, and they opposed the acquisition of southwestern lands from Mexico. To them such moves had become questions about slavery and not about the expansion of the United States. Within New York State Democratic politics, these antislavery Democrats came to be called Barnburners because they were, as their enemies said, willing to burn down the Democratic barn in order to rid it of the proslavery rats. Their opponents gained the nickname Hunkers.[5]

Van Buren might not have been in the front ranks of the Barnburners, but he definitely supported them. That support represented a curious transformation for the man who had once backed the Gag Rule and tried to keep slavery out of public discourse. Perhaps he was moved in part by the desire for revenge against the Hunkers. Perhaps he had come to recognize that the issue of slavery would neither go away nor remain submerged and that the way to save the Union was not to try to suppress the discussion of slavery but rather to halt the spread of the peculiar institution. At any rate, by the beginning of the 1848 presidential campaign, Van Buren had come almost to the point of opposition to the spread of slavery in the territories, and though he discouraged his Barnburner friends from attempting to win him the nomination, he took a definite interest in the campaign, giving plenty of advice to his younger colleagues.[6]

Barnburners and Hunkers came to a showdown at the September 1847 New York State Democratic Convention, held in Syracuse. The result was a resounding victory for the Hunkers, who showed themselves more adept at convention maneuvers. So complete was the Hunker triumph, so profound the frustration of the Barnburners, that the latter bolted, held their own convention a month later in Herkimer, New York, and passed resolutions demanding adoption of the Wilmot Proviso into the Democratic Party's platform. At yet another convention in Utica in February 1848, the Barnburners elected a rival slate of delegates from the state to that year's national convention. The bitter division of the party in the nation's most populous state did not bode well for Democratic prospects in the campaign then just getting under way.[7]

Meanwhile, the Whigs had their own problems. Strong antislavery Whigs in Massachusetts and Ohio, the so-called Conscience Whigs, made attempts similar to those of the Barnburners to gain the support of their party for at least the limitation of the spread of slavery. Yet mainline Whigs succeeded in state conventions in 1846 and 1847 in dominating their antislavery opponents as firmly as the Hunkers had overwhelmed the Barnburners. Conscience Whigs could not even get their state parties to adopt an endorsement of the Wilmot Proviso in their platforms. Clearly, on the issue of slavery there was no difference at all between the dominant factions of either the Whigs or the Democrats. Both party establishments were solidly entrenched and committed to allowing no rocking of the boat on the issue of slavery.[8]

Indeed, southern members of both parties constantly trumpeted that fact in their appeals for votes south of the Mason-Dixon Line. When

John C. Calhoun, the former Democrat turned quasi Whig turned semi-Democrat again, began agitating for southern political unity in demanding congressional protection of slavery in all of the nation's territories, the established southern wings of both parties soundly rebuffed the fierce South Carolinian and his followers throughout the South. Both Whigs and Democrats in the South boasted that the northern wings of their parties were staunchly beating back the attacks of abolitionists and "provisoists" against southern domestic institutions and the southern way of life. While the two parties competed with each other in assuring southern voters that their party was the staunchest bulwark of slavery, they tacitly agreed that slavery's security was to be found not in the kind of all-South political alliance that Calhoun advocated but rather in the support of nationwide parties that would suppress all agitation on the slavery issue, whether from proslavery zealots like Calhoun or from conscience-driven northern opponents of the institution.[9]

The 1848 Democratic National Convention came to order on May 22 in the Universalist Church in Baltimore. Its first serious problem was deciding between the rival Hunker and Barnburner delegations from New York. As a prerequisite to any compromise, the credentials committee demanded of each group a promise of unconditional support for the decisions of the convention and its nominee. With well-founded confidence, the Hunkers readily agreed. With equally well-founded distrust, the Barnburners declined, and the committee thereupon recommended seating the Hunkers only. The convention balked at this recommendation and, after several days of noisy and acrimonious debate, decided by a razor-thin vote to seat half of each delegation.[10]

With that matter settled to the satisfaction of neither faction, the convention could next turn its attention to the nomination of a presidential candidate. Polk had promised to be a one-term president, and though many of his supporters urged him to renege on that promise, he remained faithful to his word, leaving the race wide open. Various prominent Democrats had been maneuvering for the nomination during the past few months. On the first ballot Michigan senator Lewis Cass received 125 of the 251 votes cast, but though he was only one vote shy of a majority, he was still well short of the two-thirds vote that Democratic conventions traditionally required. His next closest competitor was Polk's secretary of state, James Buchanan of Pennsylvania, with 55 votes, closely followed by New Hampshire's Levi Woodbury. Calhoun and a couple of others trailed with single-digit vote totals. Through the next two ballots Cass's total crept up toward the needed 168 while Buchanan and Woodbury traded places but gained no ground. On the fourth ballot Cass went over the top with 179 votes and became the party's candidate.[11]

Born in Exeter, New Hampshire, in 1782, Cass had attended Phillips Exeter Academy before moving with his family to Marietta, Ohio, in 1800, where in 1806 he married Miss Elizabeth Spencer. During the War of 1812, Cass served as a brigadier general, seeing action at the Battle of the Thames along with such other future political figures as William Henry Harrison and Richard M. Johnson. In October 1813 President James Madison appointed Cass governor of the Michigan Territory, and he continued in that post until 1831. Leading an 1820 expedition into what was then the northwestern part of the territory, Cass discovered the lake in northern Minnesota that still bears his name and identified it, incorrectly as it turned out, as the source of the Mississippi River, the true headwaters of which are located thirty-five miles away at Lake Itasca. Cass then resigned as governor to take the position of secretary of war in the Jackson administration. In 1836 Jackson appointed him ambassador to France, where he continued to serve until 1842. In 1845 he won election to the Senate representing the state of Michigan; three years later he resigned to pursue his presidential campaign.[12]

Cass's position on slavery was popular sovereignty, a term he had coined in 1847 for what was in fact Vice President George Dallas's compromise suggestion earlier that same year, subsequently boosted by Senator Daniel Dickinson of New York. The idea aimed at removing the explosive issue of slavery's status in the territories from national politics by asserting that the people of each territory had the right to decide for themselves whether slavery would be legal in their territory. The name and the concept, at least when considered superficially, appealed to Americans, who tended to believe they favored the rule of the people, but popular sovereignty had its problems, both moral and practical. In a moral sense, as antislavery advocates would point out, the territorial residents who would be voting on the issue would not include the enslaved blacks, nor did American traditions of liberty, as notably expressed in the Declaration of Independence, allow that even a clear and legitimate majority had the right to take the rights of a single human being, much less to enslave him. Popular sovereignty's practical problems would become apparent in due time.[13]

What followed Cass's nomination was somewhat anticlimactic. The new candidate's doctrine left the door open for further expansion of slavery, and that was enough to alienate the opponents of the peculiar institution, including the Barnburners. Upon the announcement of Cass's nomination, the New York Barnburner delegation, acting on previous instructions from Van Buren, got up and walked out of the convention hall. In their absence the convention proceeded to nominate General William O. Butler of Kentucky for vice president. A volunteer officer in both the War of 1812 and the Mexican War, Butler had recently run for governor of Kentucky. Finally, the convention adopted a platform championing the traditional Democratic values of limited government and adherence to the Constitution and also, as a sort of afterthought, disavowing any congressional meddling with slavery. When the convention rejected a southern demand for stronger wording, asserting the federal government's duty to protect slavery throughout the national territories, the author of the measure, the fiery Alabama delegate William Lowndes Yancey, stalked out of the hall, followed by several other southerners.[14]

Sixteen days after the Democrats had convened in Baltimore, the Whigs held their own national convention, meeting in the salon of the Chinese Museum on Ninth Street in Philadelphia on June 7. As in the rival major party, several eager candidates hoped for the presidential nomination, chief among them Henry Clay and Daniel Webster. The two had been the foremost faces of congressional Whiggery since the party's inception. Both had served as secretary of state, and Clay was a three-time loser in presidential contests. The latter fact gave pause to some Whigs as they considered nominating the man who more than any other embodied Whig ideas. Being the intellectual fountainhead of Whiggery might not be a recommendation for the nomination if the voters had persistently shown a propensity to reject those very Whig ideas Clay had hatched, as they had done most emphatically when Clay served as standard-bearer.[15]

And Clay was getting old. He would celebrate his seventy-first birthday in April 1848, and he was beginning to show his age. Recent years especially had not been kind to Clay. His son John had suffered bouts of insanity, and his favorite son, Henry Jr., had died leading the Second Kentucky Volunteers at Buena Vista in February 1847. Perhaps in response to Frelinghuysen's exhortation after the 1844 electoral defeat, Clay had actually read several books on theology. In the wake of the devastating loss of his son, Clay took the step of joining the Episcopal Church and proceeding from baptism to confirmation and first communion in June and July 1847. In view of Clay's past life and continued political ambitions, some looked askance at his conversion as a cynical political ploy. His denominational choice was characterized more by gentility than by fervor, but in becoming an Episcopalian Clay was following the pattern of a large proportion of the southern plantation gentry. Nineteenth-century Episcopalianism contained a broad strain of evangelicalism, and Clay may have been sincere.[16]

One thing, at least, that had not changed about Clay during 1847 was his political ambition. The approach of another presidential election year was to Clay like the sound of a bugle call to an old cavalry horse, and once again he galloped into the fray. He had contacted political friends, criticizing other potential candidates. To test public reaction to another Clay presidential candidacy, he made a speaking tour of the East Coast during the summer of 1847. Enthusiastic crowds had greeted him in Philadelphia and elsewhere as his faithful supporters turned out once again to cheer their old political favorite. In his speeches during the tour and afterward, Clay had denounced the war more bitterly than ever as another blunder of the wicked and foolish Democrats. With every augury apparently favorable for his election, Clay on April 10, 1848, had placed a statement in his local newspaper, the *Lexington Observer and Kentucky Reporter,* announcing his candidacy for the Whig nomination.[17]

Yet not all Whigs thought Clay was the right candidate, and some of them had already begun casting about for another possibility. The Whigs had scored their only electoral success at the presidential level by entirely submerging their principles, nominating an old general, and focusing the campaign on hype and hoopla. Why not repeat the formula? Fortunately, two suitable generals were readily available, complete with glorious war records. Zachary Taylor and Winfield Scott both leaned toward the Whig Party, and their wartime squabbles with Polk ought to have made them more reliably Whiggish and more attractive to the party.

Scott had a habit of verbal indiscretions that could be a problem if he were the nominee. Taylor, on the other hand, had no known political views—the ideal candidate for the Whigs. Indeed, he had never even voted and did not seem to be entirely sure that he actually was a Whig. As an added bonus, Taylor owned a plantation and many slaves in Louisiana, so his candidacy would reassure the South. Taylor's Whig backers were ready to bet that northern voters would get over it. Of course, riding into power on the coattails of a victorious general of the war they had denounced nonstop since its inception would require a greater than usual degree of cynicism, even for politicians, but a number of young congressional Whigs, known as the Young Indians, thought their party was up to it and vigorously backed Old Rough and Ready for the nomination. Among them was first-term Illinois congressman Abraham Lincoln, who wrote to a political ally, "We cannot elect any other whig . . . [but with Taylor] we can . . . make great inroads among the rank and file of the Democrats."[18]

Worst of all for Clay, Taylor's backers included even Clay's previously staunch friend and political ally John J. Crittenden, who simply did not believe Clay could win the general election. A gambling, hard-drinking Kentucky lawyer and, since 1835, U.S. senator, the sixty-one-year-old Crittenden was the shrewdest of hardheaded politicians and an intense Whig partisan. He liked winning, and if winning required dumping his old friend Clay, Crittenden was ready to do it. He had had his eye on Taylor and Scott as possible war-hero presidential candidates, and for some months he had been in correspondence with both. Over time, Scott had demonstrated a tendency to write highly impolitic things to various correspondents, and Crittenden quickly made his judgment as to which man offered the better prospects for Whig victory in 1848. He soon became Taylor's chief advisor and manager. The general in his public statements steadfastly denied any interest in the presidency. "I am not and shall never be an aspirant for that honor," he wrote in a letter from Mexico in 1846. "My opinion has always been against the elevating of a military chief to that position." Crittenden took this with a grain of salt and continued his machinations to gain the Whig nomination for Old Rough and Ready.[19]

As Taylor's backers had plugged his candidacy in the months leading up to the convention, abolitionists within the Whig Party gnashed their teeth. The idea of nominating "one of the greatest slaveholders in the United States," as one Whig paper called him, and on top of that a man who had, in the view of many abolitionists, helped conquer a vast new expanse of territory for the spread of slavery in a war that the most radical abolitionists had from the first denounced as a vile scheme of the slave power conspiracy, was simply too much. Abolitionist Whigs spoke of Taylor with profound contempt. One disgruntled northern Whig snorted that Taylor's chief qualifications for the presidency were "sleeping forty years in the woods and cultivating moss on the calves of his legs."[20]

So it was that less than two months after Clay's formal announcement of his candidacy, a sharply divided Whig Party convened in Philadelphia's Chinese Museum to determine if the Old Coon would yet again carry his party's standard in the coming campaign. As the convention began to organize itself, many of its officers were nominal Clay supporters who seemed to act more the role of Taylor backers. They helped smooth the way for the old general, sidelining a resolution that only those committed to "Whig principles" were eligible for nomination and otherwise making sure the convention's rules favored Old Rough and Ready. On the first presidential ballot, Taylor led, with Clay close behind, while Webster, Scott, and a couple of others trailed in the distance. Opponents of Taylor complained loudly that he was "anything but a Whig," and a few lonely voices objected to his slave ownership, but to no avail. Old Rough and Ready gained votes at Clay's expense in the second ballot, leaped ahead in the third, and won the nomination on the fourth ballot, not with two-thirds support but with the simple majority that was all the Whigs required. While the supporters of the victor celebrated exuberantly, his opponents sat and looked on sullenly. Turning to the vice presidency, the convention chose New Yorker Millard Fillmore, a longtime party loyalist, holder of state offices, and more recently a U.S. representative. Fillmore was not, however, as many thought, a supporter of Henry Clay, nor was he an ally of the dominant Whig faction in New York, which was controlled by Senator William H. Seward and his political manager Thurlow Weed. Following the successful pattern of 1840, the Whigs declined adopting any platform at all.[21]

The majorities had prevailed within both the Whig and the Democratic parties, and the verdicts of both had been to steer clear of any possible divisiveness on the issue of slavery. The Democrats tried to have it both ways by means of popular sovereignty, while the Whigs preferred to have it no way at all, completely ignoring the issue and thus leaving the way open for Whigs throughout the country to present the party in whatever light seemed most likely to appeal to local voters. Yet discontentment seethed in the two major parties. Significant minorities within both had seen their intense concerns trampled in the stampede to maintain national party unity. The Democrats had the Barnburners to worry about, and the Whigs had their Conscience wing as well as the disgruntled supporters of Henry Clay to deal with. Some of the latter even urged their idol to run on a third-party ticket, but Clay would have none of it.[22]

The other two disgruntled minorities were driven by principle rather than devotion to a man, and they would not be so easily put off. In June 1848, a few weeks after the Whig convention, the Barnburner Democrats held a convention of their own, once again in Utica, New York. Van Buren's son John, a delegate at the convention, read a letter from his father stating that the founders had seen slavery as inconsistent with the "principles of the Revolution" and had not wanted it to grow. Now the Democratic Party platform, consistent with Cass, said Congress should leave the question of slavery up to the settlers in the territories, and Van Buren believed that this was wrong. He urged that "the evils of slavery" should be kept out of the territories. The enthusiastic Barnburner delegates responded by unanimously choosing the elder Van Buren as their presidential candidate. At first somewhat reluctant, Van Buren finally agreed to accept the nomination. Not so the Barnburners' vice-presidential candidate. Wisconsin senator Henry Dodge chose to remain loyal to the Democratic Party establishment and declined the Barnburner nomination.[23]

The emergence of the Barnburners opened new possibilities for the political cause of opposition to slavery. Some antislavery leaders at first eyed Van Buren suspiciously, in part because they were mostly former Whigs and he a former Democrat, but also because Van Buren had once stated that he would veto any bill for the abolition of slavery in the District of Columbia. Despite such concerns, the opportunity to broaden the movement seemed irresistible.[24]

The election cycle had already seen efforts at forming a grand coalition against slavery expansion. Salmon P. Chase, a Liberty Party leader in Ohio, had led a push the previous year to broaden the party's appeal by taking a stand on the Wilmot Proviso, with its ban on all future expansion of slavery, rather than the party's previous position for the immediate abolition of slavery. The purists within the party could not stomach such compromise, and the result was a split within the tiny Liberty Party. The hard-core abolitionists constituted themselves as the Liberty League and nominated Gerrit Smith for president, while the Liberty Party itself nominated New Hampshire senator John Parker Hale. Van Buren's nomination on the Barnburner ticket opened the way for exactly the kind of broader coalition Chase and others had been seeking, and Hale let it be known that he would be willing to stand aside in favor of Van Buren if a unified antislavery party could come together.[25]

Come together it did when, on August 9, 1848, thousands of political leaders of various stripes and degrees of antislavery zeal assembled in Buffalo, New York. Estimates ranged from ten thousand to twenty thousand nonresidents in the town. The official sessions of the convention took place in a large church building, while abolitionist speakers addressed overflow crowds of as many as ten thousand in the city park in an enormous tent belonging to Oberlin College and used for revival meetings. The 450 delegates hoped to put together a new antislavery political coalition. They came from every one of the free states as well as from three of the border slave states and the District of Columbia. Positions ranged from sincere support for universal freedom to a mere desire to keep the territories free from blacks, either slave or free, and thus reserved for white men. Some of the former Whigs and former Democrats brought with them the old party issues about banks and tariffs and federally financed internal improvements as well as lingering vestiges of the animosities of twenty years of intense partisan conflict, whether they personally had taken part in the full twenty years of wrangling or not.[26]

Despite these differences, the men in attendance at Buffalo managed to hammer together a new political party. Its platform was all that abolitionists and old Liberty Party men could have hoped for. Written largely under the direction of Ohioan Salmon P. Chase, the platform called for a thorough separation of the federal government from the institution of slavery. While admitting a lack of constitutional authority to end slavery in the states where it already existed, the platform stipulated that the federal government should ban slavery in every place where federal authority did prevail, including most especially all of the western territories. Joshua Leavitt, a Congregationalist minister and staunch abolitionist of the purest stripe, called the document "a thorough Liberty platform." Chase concluded the platform with the ringing slogan "Free Soil, Free Speech, Free Labor, and Free Men!" The delegates in the church building came to their feet and cheered when they heard it, and when a speaker read it in the tent outside a few minutes later, the crowd went wild. The slogan gave the new party its name, the Free-Soil Party.[27]

The delegates overwhelmingly selected Van Buren as the party's first presidential nominee and Charles Francis Adams, son of Van Buren's old political nemesis John Quincy Adams, as its vice-presidential nominee. Van Buren at once accepted the nomination and in his acceptance speech stressed that slaveholders had no right to take their slaves to the territories. In a further departure from his previous position, Van Buren even vowed to support the abolition of slavery in the District of Columbia. Some former Whigs and outright abolitionists were still not quite satisfied with the Little Magician as their candidate, but Massachusetts abolitionist politician Charles Sumner expressed their feelings when he said, "I am willing to take him. With him we can break the slave-power; that is our first aim." When the nominations were announced to the mass meeting out under the tent, pandemonium broke out again, with deafening cheers and shouts of "Van Buren and Free Soil."[28]

All in all, Van Buren and Adams formed the best ticket the new polyglot party could have found. It was customary in those days for conventions to conclude by formally declaring their nominations to be unanimous, even if they had to do so over noisy shouts of dissent from the supporters of defeated candidates. The Democratic and Whig conventions had done so earlier that year, though with an even more hollow ring than usual in both cases. As the Buffalo convention completed its nominations, Joshua Leavitt rose and with deep emotion appealed that the convention make the nominations unanimous. The roar of approval that filled the hall in response was evidence of a far stronger sense of unity than existed in either of the established parties.[29]

Both of those parties desperately feared the massive defection of their northern wings to the Free-Soil Party and at least the nonparticipation of many in their southern wings in response to the exhortations of proslavery fire-eaters like John C. Calhoun and William Lowndes Yancey. Calhoun openly advised southerners not to vote for either party's candidate. The Whigs had the added worry of Clay and his disconsolate supporters. The author of the American System and virtual founder of the Whig Party sat this one out, refusing to campaign for Taylor or the Whig ticket and opining that the convention had "placed the Whig Party"—with which he perhaps tended to confuse himself—"in a humiliating condition." In a similar vein, prominent Whig editor Horace Greeley of the widely read *New York Tribune* referred to "the putrid corpse of the party butchered at Philadelphia."[30]

Yet the reports of either party's demise turned out to be greatly exaggerated. Old loyalties died hard, and each party's establishment strove to see to it that when those loyalties failed, old hatreds and fears would serve in their place. Wavering Whigs were reminded that their staunch support for Taylor, while holding their noses if necessary, was all that stood between the Republic and the despised policies of the Democrats. At the same time, doubting Democrats were admonished that their defection to the ranks of the quixotic Free-Soilers would deliver their suffering country into the hands of the dreaded Whigs. A vote for the Free-Soilers was a wasted vote that would do nothing but give the government over to whichever party one had been fighting bitterly for the past generation. The Whigs (or the Democrats) were the true, practical antislavery (or proslavery) party—depending on the speaker and the local audience in need of being persuaded to stand by the old party. The tactic worked for both sides. Even a reluctant Greeley finally placed Taylor's and Fillmore's names on the *Tribune*'s masthead.[31]

Good old-fashioned partisan vituperation played its part as well. The Democratic Party establishment especially seethed with rage at Van Buren and the Free-Soilers—not surprisingly, since the Barnburners would represent a clear loss of votes for the party, particularly in the crucial swing state of New York. In private Polk called Van Buren "the most fallen man" he had ever known, while another southern Democrat referred to him as an "unprincipled intriguer." Mainstream Democrats circulated rumors that Van Buren owned a large southern plantation, complete with slaves, and that he was an infidel, both untrue.[32]

Party loyalties proved as solid in the South as in the North. Even with some voters staying home and a number of Democrats defecting to the Louisiana slaveholder Taylor, both parties retained most of their strength in the southern states. A prime example of southern party loyalty was Mississippi planter, politician, war hero, and, since shortly after his return from Mexico, U.S. senator Jefferson Davis. Taylor was the father of Davis's beloved first wife, Sarah Knox Taylor, who had died of malaria one month into their marriage thirteen years before. Davis had also been a protégé of Old Rough and Ready's during their campaigns in Mexico and had shared with him the glory of their victory at Buena Vista just the year before. As a committed proponent of the expansion of slavery, Davis had serious reservations about Cass's popular sovereignty, but he was a Democrat, and though his speeches included effusive praise of Taylor, he maintained that he "would be obliged to vote for Cass and Butler."[33]

The campaign included all of the by now standard features of American politics. There were barbecues, rallies, and parades with banners and bands. Each party had its campaign publications, and the nation's newspapers took sides openly rather than covertly, as they do today. Especially enthusiastic supporters organized themselves into clubs. There were Rough and Ready clubs and even Fillmore Ranger clubs. And there were hundreds of speeches. Van Buren's son John was one of the most sought-after Free-Soil stump speakers, as were Salmon Chase, David Wilmot, and Charles Sumner. The Democrats and Whigs had scores of speakers. The Democrats boasted Vice President George Dallas and Senator Thomas Hart Benton, as well as young up-and-coming politicians like Illinois's Stephen A. Douglas. The Whigs touted renowned orator Daniel Webster but also counted such lesser lights as Abraham Lincoln. Much to the relief of top Whigs, their candidate himself promised to make no speeches. Old Rough and Ready's propensity for verbal faux pas was the stuff of Whig managers' nightmares. They breathed easier when the old general stayed at his plantation near Baton Rouge, Cypress Grove, quietly awaiting the decision of the people as a proper presidential candidate should.[34]

On November 7, 1848, America's first national election day, voters across the country went to the polls, but in markedly lower numbers than they had in the past two elections. The counting of the votes brought few surprises. Zachary Taylor received about 47 percent of the popular vote, but that was good enough to win him 163 electoral votes, a clear majority. Lewis Cass drew a little more than 42 percent, good for 127 electoral votes.[35]

Once again antislavery voters, discontented with the choices offered them by the two major parties, had at least threatened to make a difference. The Free-Soil Party drew just over 10 percent of the vote nationwide. Almost half of those votes came in New York State, where Free-Soil voters made up more than 26 percent of the electorate. Cass ran third with scarcely 25 percent of New York popular votes, and Taylor carried the state with only 36 percent of the vote, slightly fewer total votes than Clay had received in a losing effort in the state four years before. Van Buren pulled most of his New York votes away from Cass and the Democrats, adding nearly 105,000 votes to the 1844 Liberty Party tally of less than 16,000 in the state. The votes of those 105,000 Barnburners, added to Cass's total, would have been enough to carry the state for the Democratic candidate. New York's 36 electoral votes would have reversed the totals in the electoral college, giving Taylor 127 and Cass 163—and the presidency.[36]

Or so it seemed, but here matters became even more complicated. In Ohio and Indiana the existence of the Free-Soil Party had had an opposite effect. Enthusiasm for the new, bigger, and almost viable antislavery party lured a large number of antislavery Whigs in Ohio's Western Reserve—roughly the state's northern tier of counties—as well as in northern Indiana to abandon Taylor in favor of Van Buren, with the result that the two states probably shifted from the Whig to the Democratic column. The exchange of Ohio's 23 electoral votes and Indiana's 12 would have brought Taylor back up to 162 and Cass back down to 128. Thus the antislavery Conscience Whigs of Ohio had effectively canceled out the antislavery Barnburner Democrats of New York, leaving the outcome of the election as it would have been without the presence of the Free-Soil Party.[37]

In the final analysis, the election had been decided on the basis of traditional Whig and Democratic party issues and party loyalties, with the impact of slavery hitting both parties about equally. Cass won seven of fifteen slave states, Taylor seven of fifteen free states. Each candidate received a little more than 40 percent of his electoral votes from slave states. Thus, despite the inflammatory issue of the Wilmot Proviso and the question of what was to be done about slavery in the newly acquired territories of the Mexican Cession, the center was still holding. The result was especially ironic for Van Buren, defeated at least in part by the remarkable inherent stability of the two-party system he himself had done perhaps more than any other man to create. He had wanted to engineer a political system that would suppress issues too contentious for the safety of the nation, and now that he had become convinced that the most contentious of those issues would endanger the nation even more if the system continued to suppress it, he found that he had done his previous work all too well. The system suppressed him.[38]

Nevertheless, antislavery voters had once again decided the outcome at least in individual states. Now both major parties had experienced the growing difficulty of trying to hold down the political concern about the issue of slavery. The crowning irony was that this time it was Van Buren himself who had led the movement that strained and threatened to tear the fabric of the national political parties. At sixty-five, Van Buren was ready to retire from politics. The fate of the parties, and of the country, would lie in the hands of other men.[39]

Curiously, many thousands of the men who would, by their collective action, do much to decide the fate of their country in ways of which they never dreamed were even then diligently traveling at their best possible speed away from Washington, D.C., and the settled parts of the United States.

CHAPTER EIGHTEEN

The California Gold Rush

JOHANN AUGUSTUS SUTTER had big plans. California in the summer of 1847 might be well on its way from Mexican to United States rule, but Sutter—who signed himself John Sutter now that the old country was eight years behind him—hoped to prosper as much under the new regime as he had under the old. Frémont's Bear Flag Revolt was almost a year in the past. United States troops under Kearny and Stockton had put down the uprising of the Californios that winter, securing U.S. control of the province, but the economic and quasi-political empire Sutter had built up at the confluence of the Sacramento and American rivers in California's Central Valley was as thriving and prosperous as it had been three and a half years earlier when Frémont, Carson, and their band of half-starved explorers had first come down out of the Sierras and enjoyed Sutter's hospitality for several weeks.

More recently, indeed, in that very spring of 1847, another collection of Americans, the woebegone survivors of the Donner Party, had staggered out of the mountains and had also found much-needed aid with Sutter. It was now just four months since the last members of the ill-starred wagon train had reached Sutter's Fort and the sprawling settlement the Swiss émigré Sutter called New Helvetia. Not all wagon trains suffered such losses. Most came through unscathed. The country was growing up, and Sutter wanted to expand his own operations to match, making plans to produce more of the commodities that the burgeoning population would wish to buy.

Among his plans was the gristmill he hoped to build near his fort to make flour from the grain grown on his extensive fields. To the east, up the American River, where dense stands of evergreen timber covered the foothills of the Sierras, Sutter planned to build a sawmill to provide cut lumber for his own spread and for the growing markets of San Francisco Bay, fifty miles down the Sacramento and reachable by raft. To oversee the construction of the sawmill, Sutter in August 1847 hired James Marshall, a down-on-his-luck carpenter who had briefly owned a ranch in the

Central Valley. He had served in Frémont's California Battalion, come home to find his cattle stolen or strayed, and lost the ranch for debt. He needed work. Sutter needed a carpenter—he needed a skilled millwright, actually, but Marshall would have to do—and so they signed a contract that provided that each man would receive half the profit of the timber sawed in the new mill.[1]

Marshall chose a site for the sawmill on the American River about forty miles upstream from the fort in a valley that the local Indians called Coloma. For labor he used a number of recently discharged members of the Mormon Battalion. Mustered out of service at Los Angeles, they had started for Utah to join the Mormons who had established themselves there while the battalion was marching across the continent to help secure California for the United States. When they had reached the Sierra Nevada, however, a letter met them from the Mormon authorities, directing that all of the unmarried veterans stay in California for the time being, find employment, and send their earnings to Utah to help the sect establish itself there. On turning back toward the broad valley, they naturally encountered Sutter's domains. Sutter was glad to hire a number of them, since they made considerably more willing and reliable workers than the local Indians. He put one crew to work on his gristmill and sent another four men upstream to the site of his future sawmill to work for Marshall.[2]

They got started on the project while Scott and his army, far away to the south, were completing the conquest of Mexico City that fall, and they continued through the rainy California winter. The wet weather sometimes interfered with the work, but by January 1848 they had erected the mill and dug the headrace, the channel bringing water from the river above the mill and leading it under the mill's waterwheel. Marshall had his men dig a very rudimentary ditch to start the tailrace, the channel that would lead the water back to the river below the mill after it had done its work of turning the wheel. Then Marshall allowed the flowing water to finish the job of excavation. Each morning Marshall closed the sluice gate at the entrance of the headrace so that his men could have access to the machinery they were finishing up on the lower parts of the mill. When the millrace was dry, he would walk it, inspecting the additional erosion of the tailrace. On the morning of January 24 he noticed something unusual. From the bottom of the tailrace he saw the morning sun reflecting off small flecks of something bright, shiny, and yellow.[3]

Marshall later explained that with his knowledge of mineralogy, he knew the metallic lumps and flakes he picked up from the bottom of the tailrace could have been only one of two substances: either "sulphuret of iron"—pyrite, or fool's gold, which was "very bright and brittle"—or else "gold, bright yet malleable." He took two nearby rocks and hammered a nugget flat between them. It was undeniably malleable.[4]

Marshall went back to the mill and told his workmen he had found gold. At first they did not believe him, but after several more homespun tests, they too concluded that the find was genuine. All agreed it was a novelty, but if they did not get their mill built, they would not get paid. They went back to work, and Marshall told them they could look around for other nuggets and flakes after hours, if they wished. On the whole, the discovery of gold in the millrace seemed interesting but not particularly exciting. After all, it was not as if a fellow could make a living picking bits of gold out of streambeds.[5]

Nine days after Marshall made his mildly diverting discovery, Nicholas Trist met with representatives of the Mexican government at Guadalupe Hidalgo and worked out the details of the treaty that would end the Mexican War and officially make California part of the United States. By the time the treaty had received the formal ratification of both governments three months later, California was well on its way to being transformed forever in ways quite unrelated to its change of nominal ownership.

That spring two men walked into the headquarters of Colonel Richard B. Mason, the American army officer serving as acting governor of California. Mason's headquarters were located in Monterey, the sleepy capital of what had hitherto been a very sleepy and out-of-the-way province. Inside the headquarters, they met Mason's adjutant, Lieutenant William Tecumseh Sherman, who asked them their business. They said they were there on behalf of Sutter and had some very special business to transact with Mason in person. Sherman showed them in to Mason's office, and a short while later the colonel emerged, called the lieutenant in, and showed him about half an ounce of gold dust and nuggets that the men had brought. Sherman had been stationed in northern Georgia several years before and knew what placer gold looked like. He also suggested several simple tests they could use to authenticate the substance, much as Marshall and his workers had done the preceding January. In a few minutes, Sherman had confirmed to his and Mason's satisfaction that the substance in front of them was indeed gold.[6]

Then Mason handed Sherman the letter from Sutter that was the reason for the two men's visit. Sutter said the gold came from the tailrace of a mill he had built at Coloma on the American River, and he asked for

The California Gold Rush, 1849

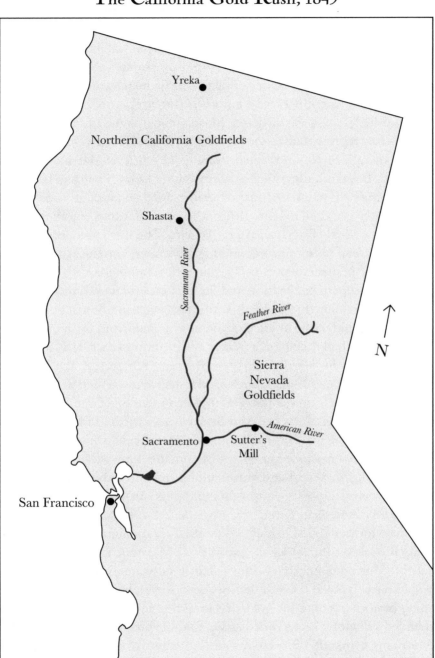

Yreka

Northern California Goldfields

Shasta

Sacramento River

Feather River

Sierra
Nevada
Goldfields

American River

Sacramento

Sutter's
Mill

San Francisco

N

the right of preemption—that is, the first right to purchase the land from the government—under U.S. law. Mason had Sherman draft his reply, stating that since no peace treaty had yet been ratified between Mexico and the United States, U.S. law did not yet apply in California, and therefore he could not grant Sutter the right of preemption. Still, Mason had Sherman write, because Sutter's mill was forty miles from the nearest settlement, "he was not likely to be disturbed by trespassers." When Sherman finished writing out the letter, Mason read it, signed it, and gave it to Sutter's two representatives to carry back to New Helvetia.[7]

Mason and Sherman reacted to the gold much as Marshall and his men had. It was an interesting curiosity but no more. They had heard of the discovery of small amounts of gold before, some of it at San Fernando, three hundred miles to the south and not far from another sleepy California coastal village called Los Angeles. The trace amounts of gold found there had been of no economic significance, and the army officers assumed the find at Coloma Valley would turn out the same.[8]

Such was not to be the case, and Sutter, for one, knew as much by this time. He had thought Marshall was crazy when he had reported the presence of gold in the tailrace of the new sawmill, and then, once convinced, he too had thought it a matter of little importance. His viewpoint changed when he learned that his Mormon laborers at the sawmill, prospecting in their off-duty hours as Marshall allowed, had worked their way downstream from the mill about fifteen miles to a large bar of sand and gravel that would henceforth be known as Mormon Island. There they found a tremendously rich deposit of placer gold, which had eroded from a vein somewhere up in the mountains and washed down the streams along with sand and gravel until it came to rest along with those humble materials in this and other bars and banks that fringed and bisected the American River.[9]

The Mormons of Marshall's crew told their coreligionists on the gristmill crew about the fabulous discovery at Mormon Island. Then both sets of Mormons informed Sutter that if he wanted their services, he would have to make it worth their while to spend their days doing something besides panning for gold. He raised their pay, but they soon demanded still more; it was raised again, and the process repeated until the Mormons demanded $10 a day. Sutter finally balked at such an outrageous price—ten times the going rate for skilled labor back in the States—and let the Mormons go, leaving both his mills standing almost finished.[10]

As spring gave way to summer, more and more reports filtered down to Monterey of the impressive amounts of gold found along the American River near Sutter's Mill. "Stories reached us of fabulous discoveries," Sherman recalled, "and spread throughout the land. Everybody was talking of 'Gold! gold!!' " It was like a fever, Sherman thought, as one man after another succumbed to the lure of the easy riches supposed to exist in the interior of the state. Soldiers began to desert and head for the goldfields, in one case a whole platoon at once. Sailors jumped ship to launch their own quests for gold. And seemingly every day one could see civilians fitting out wagons and pack mules with supplies and equipment and leaving for the Coloma Valley.[11]

Stories filtered back of men making as much as $50 in a single day, while a man back east would have to labor hard for two months or more to make that much money. Then came reports of some men making $500 a day, then thousands of dollars per day. Enough of the gold was finding its way to the coast to make the reports sound plausible. The cost of goods at Yerba Buena—San Francisco—was said to be rising steeply under the pressure of a steadily increasing gold supply. Prices skyrocketed for such items as tin pans, shovels, horses, mules, and anything else an eager gold seeker might use.[12]

Eventually it was too much for Sherman, and he caught the fever as well. He would not desert, but he did convince Mason "that it was our duty to go up and see with our own eyes," as he later explained it, "that we might report the truth to our Government." Mason agreed and near the end of June ordered Sherman to make preparations for an exploratory trip to the goldfields. They set off with horses, pack mules, four soldiers, and Colonel Mason's slave and personal servant, Aaron. They rode north along the coast to San Francisco, crossed the bay on a schooner while their horses and mules made the passage less stylishly in a cargo scow, and over the next several days rode on through Sonoma to the Sacramento and Sutter's Fort, where they remained several days so as to join Sutter for the first Fourth of July celebration in California as part of the United States. Settlers flocked in from miles around to join the celebration, with toasts and speeches and Sutter as the gracious host providing plenty of food and drink.[13]

The next day, Mason, Sherman, and their men continued their journey toward the Coloma Valley. At Mormon Island they found some three hundred Mormons present, all diligently working the diggings. At first the gold seekers had used pans, sloshing water and sediment around and around until the heavier gold had settled to the bottom and the lighter sand, silt, and gravel had slopped over the rim. The wholesale working of the placer beds required a larger instrument, and the army officers found the men using boxlike wooden structures called cradles. A team of four men worked each cradle, shoveling in sediment and dumping bucketfuls of water atop it while one of their number vigorously rocked the cradle to create the sloshing that would separate the lighter grains of quartz from the heavier gold. It was hard work, under a hot sun, often standing in icy water, hoisting buckets of water or shovels of waterlogged sand and gravel, but Sherman estimated that a team working a cradle could extract an average of one ounce of gold, then worth $16, per man per day.[14]

Hanging around the crowd at Mormon Island was Sam Brannan, chief official of the Mormon Church in California, collecting the tithes of the faithful. Brannan was not a veteran of the Mormon Battalion. He had been a Mormon for fifteen years by this time, having joined the followers of Joseph Smith at Kirtland and helped build the first Mormon temple there. A promising young man, Brannan received orders to travel to the East Coast to head up the Mormon publishing effort there, which he had done ably and with considerable profit to himself on the side. When the troubles broke out around Nauvoo leading to Smith's death, Mormon leadership at headquarters had directed Brannan to gather together all the East Coast Mormons he could and take them by ship to that sleepy, mostly empty northernmost province of Mexico, California. So it was that at age twenty-nine Brannan found himself once again on the soil of the United States as the ranking Mormon in California with the somewhat incongruous title of "elder."[15]

Brannan had played the gold rush ever so carefully from the very outset. One of his first actions on arriving in California had been to start a newspaper, *The California Star.* He also kept a small store near Sutter's Fort. When word had first arrived of gold on the American River, Brannan had gone to see it and had satisfied himself that the reports were indeed true. Then he had published just the opposite in the columns of *The Star.* The reports of gold, he wrote, were "all a sham . . . got up to guzzle the gullible." He continued to deprecate the news from the American River until he had bought up all of the picks, shovels, and pans he could find for twenty cents each. Then he took a bottle of the gold and rode into San Francisco, where he walked through the streets waving the bottle and shouting, "Gold! Gold on the American River!" He changed the tune of *The Star* to suit. When the news triggered the stampede of gold seekers he had anticipated, Brannan sold them picks, shovels, and pans for $16 each. He cleared $36,000 in profits in the next few months, outdoing the earnings of any of the men who stood day after day in the ice-cold waters doing the backbreaking work of washing gold dust out of the river-bottom sediment.[16]

As Mason toured the diggings around Mormon Island, one of the men working on the cradles asked him, "Governor, what business has Sam Brannan to collect the tithes here?"

"Brannan has a perfect right to collect the tax," Mason replied, "if you Mormons are fools enough to pay it."

"Then I for one won't pay it any longer," replied the prospector.

"This is public land," Mason added, "and the gold is the property of the United States; all of you here are trespassers, but, as the Government is benefited by your getting out the gold, I do not intend to interfere."[17]

Thereafter, Brannan was unable to collect much in the way of tithes, but the funds he had already gathered from the faithful never found their way to Salt Lake City. Brannan became one of the richest merchants in California, and some people were uncharitable enough to suggest that the tithes he pocketed were the cornerstone of his wealth. They underestimated him, but they were certainly correct in assuming that the misappropriated tithes had boosted Brannan's already impressive wealth.[18]

Mason and Sherman continued up the American to Coloma, finding scores of additional gold seekers all along its course and that of its tributaries, as well as along the nearby Yuba and Feather rivers and even the sand and gravel deposits in the beds of old rivers and creeks some distance from where the water now flowed. The return of Mason and Sherman to Monterey a few days later with confirmation of the accounts of gold in the interior fanned the fires of gold fever to even greater heat. Everyone in California who could do so seemed to be headed for the diggings. It took $300 a month to keep a hired laborer anywhere in the province, and increasing numbers of soldiers deserted from the two regular army companies that were, by that September, the only U.S. forces remaining in California. Almost all business in the province came to a halt, save the highly lucrative parallel businesses of digging for gold and supplying those who were digging for gold.[19]

As soon as they had returned to Monterey, Mason had Sherman write up a report to Washington relaying their findings. At Sherman's suggestion, he had purchased enough of the gold to fill an oyster can and sent it, along with the report, carried by an army officer, as a sample of the gold then being found in California.[20]

Mason had already sent news of the discovery of gold to Washington by the hand of Lieutenant Edward F. Beale, who arrived in the capital in mid-September. Mason and Sherman had hoped their full report along with the large sample of the gold would reach Polk in time for him to include the news in his annual State of the Union address that December. Mason entrusted the original of the report and the oyster can full of gold to Lieutenant Lucien Loeser, but the lieutenant was delayed in transit. On arriving in New Orleans, he used the telegraph, a five-year-old technology, to inform the War Department that he was on his way with important dispatches, but he did not arrive in Washington until two days after the president had sent his address over to Congress. A second messenger who Mason had dispatched several days later with a duplicate copy of the report did, however, arrive in time, and Polk was able to mention repeatedly in his address the "abundance of gold" in the lands newly acquired from Mexico. When Loeser arrived a few days later, Secretary of War William Marcy personally took the gold over to the White House to show to the president.[21]

For Polk, now a lame duck, the news was a pleasant culmination of the work of his administration. His political opponents had argued that California was too far away and too unimportant to be purchased at a price of millions of dollars. He had never imagined a discovery such as this, but had firmly believed California was worth the price without it. The arrival of gold from the new acquisition, together with a confirmed report that hundreds, perhaps thousands, of men were extracting an ounce per man per day from the streambeds and riverbanks of California, was added confirmation that he had acted wisely. Surely, it had indeed been America's Manifest Destiny to expand all the way to the golden shore of the Pacific. Delighted, the president prepared a special additional message to Congress, notifying that body, and the rest of the world, of the now thoroughly authenticated news of gold in California. "The accounts of the abundance of gold in that territory," Polk wrote, "are of such an extraordinary character as would scarcely command belief were they not corroborated by the authentic reports of officers in the public service who have visited the mineral district and derived the facts which they detail from personal observation."[22]

Polk's announcement, coming as it did on top of numerous reports from less impressive sources, launched a flood of immigration to California. Eager gold seekers flocked to North America's Pacific coast from almost every inhabited part of the globe—China, Australia, South America, Europe, and, of course, other parts of the United States. Nearly all of the foreigners came by sea, and so too did many of the Americans. Excitement ran high, and sometimes the departure of a ship bound for California had an almost carnival atmosphere. As one such vessel moved away from the wharf in Salem, Massachusetts, several of the passengers sang a ditty to the tune of "Oh! Susanna":

> *I shall soon be in Francisco,*
> *And then I'll look around,*
> *And when I see the gold lumps there,*
> *I'll pick them off the ground.*

> *I'll scrape the mountains clear, my boys,*
> *I'll drain the rivers dry,*
> *A "pocket full of rocks" bring home,*
> *So, brothers, don't you cry.*

> *Oh, California, that's the land for me.*
> *I'm going to Sacramento with my wash-bowl on my knee.*[23]

Not all departures for the goldfields were completely joyous occasions, at least not for those who remained behind. Some Americans bitterly opposed the decision of their family members to go to California, partially because they feared for the safety or morals of those who went and partially because they wondered what would become of the families left behind. Determined gold seekers did not let such concerns deter them. One frustrated young man wrote in a letter, "Mother o Mother, why do you still resist my going my mind is made up to go. Why o why cant you let me go with a cheerful heart, and with a well made up mind that I will try to do well."[24]

This was the great age of the clipper ship, the fastest and most graceful type of commercial sailing vessel ever built. The concept was thoroughly American, born in Baltimore in the early decades of the nineteenth century and come of age there by 1833, when the first true square-rigged clipper ship, the *Annie McKim*, slid down the builder's ways and into the waters of the Patapsco River. Clippers sacrificed carrying capacity for speed, and their every line announced that time was money. They specialized in carrying low-bulk, high-value cargoes over long voyages. A prime use for the clippers was in carrying tea from the Far East to the kitchens and parlors of North American and Europe, and they famously raced one another to be the first to arrive in New York with a shipment of the year's tea crop. With speeds of sixteen knots or even faster, they were also useful for carrying such valuable cargoes as spices or people. In 1849 many of them carried people who were in a great hurry to reach California before all the best gold claims were staked by others.

Not only clippers but ships of all descriptions were soon carrying passengers on the voyage to the West Coast. By December 21, 1848, a single New York newspaper ran advertisements for sixty-two different vessels preparing to depart for California and offering to take passengers. The cheapest berth on one of those ships went for $120, and that was "with sailor's rations."[25]

From the East Coast, the voyage to California led around Cape Horn, a prodigious trip of some seventeen thousand miles between New York and San Francisco. When William Tecumseh Sherman had traveled that route during the latter half of 1846 on board the sloop of war *Lexington,* one of the faster types of warships in the U.S. Navy, the journey had taken an excruciating 198 days and had had Sherman and his fellow officers contemplating "The Rime of the Ancient Mariner."[26]

Forty-niners traveling around the Horn could at least hope to make better time, and not only because of the finer lines of the clipper ships. In 1847 Matthew Fontaine Maury, a retired U.S. naval officer, had published his *Wind and Current Charts.* A devout Christian, Maury believed that God the Creator had revealed actual truth about the world in the Bible. When he read in the Eighth Psalm a reference to "the paths of the seas," he began to ask himself what those paths might be. Others might dismiss the reference as purely poetic and nothing more, but Maury had for many years pored over the logs of scores of ships. Eventually he discovered that there were indeed paths in the seas, and they were ocean currents. Maury's charts mapped them, enabling ship captains to cut their sailing times dramatically by choosing courses that kept them inside of favorable currents and outside of unfavorable ones. In 1851 the enterprising shipowners George and Nathaniel Griswold commissioned William Webb to build them the biggest, fastest clipper that had ever yet put to sea. They also hired the top captain in the trade and promised him a handsome bonus if he could make the transit to San Francisco in 90 days or less. He made it in 108, missing his bonus by 18 days due to heavy storms off Cape Horn.[27]

One could also make the voyage to California in the newfangled steamships, the best of which were meant to combine at least some of the finer lines of the clipper with the steady, reliable power of steam. They had a certain grace about them, even if bulky paddle-wheel housings amidships marred their appearance somewhat. Their advantage was that they could, as it were, make their breeze, churning on even when the vagaries of weather left their purebred cousins, the clippers, becalmed. If traveling by steamship, one might very well opt not to go around the Horn but instead to take the shortcut by way of the Isthmus of Panama. The American canal in Panama was still more than half a century in the future, and though the route via Panama cut twelve thousand miles off the sea voyage to California, the actual journey across the isthmus was not for the faint of heart.[28]

In 1847 Congress had, in response to the acquisition of Oregon and in anticipation of the acquisition of California, authorized subsidies for two lines of mail and passenger steamships, one to operate ships running from New York and New Orleans to the Atlantic shore of Panama and the other, smaller concern to ply its vessels from Panama's Pacific coast to the ports of California and Oregon. William H. Aspinwall submitted the winning bid for the Pacific mail steamship line, and his *California* was the first steamship on the western coast of the Americas. The *California* had to steam around the Horn to reach the Pacific. Departing New York on October 6, 1848, and using Maury's new charts of currents, she made splendid time down the eastern coast of South America without pushing her new and relatively untested engines to anything like their best speed. Having rounded Cape Horn and steamed up the west side of the continent, she arrived for her first visit at Panama City to find the town jam-packed with eager gold seekers desperate for passage to California. With the efficiency typical in ventures directed at least in part by a government, the mail steamer contracts had provided for more and larger ships on the Atlantic than on the Pacific. Consequently, it was much easier for travelers to get into Panama than to get out.[29]

The throngs impatiently awaiting passage on the Pacific shore of the isthmus had paid anywhere from $200 to $500 for their tickets to California. On disembarking on the Atlantic side of Panama, they had traveled by dugout canoe up the dangerous and temperamental Chagres River between banks cloaked in dense jungle foliage for about fifty winding miles. They had to cover the final twenty miles on rented mules or on foot over poorly maintained trails through jungles and mountains. The trip across the isthmus could take a week or more. All the while the travelers were in Panama, including while they waited at Panama City on the Pacific coast, they were at grave risk of contracting malaria, yellow fever, cholera, typhoid, or any number of other less well-known but at least equally deadly diseases. To make matters worse, the high demand generated by the crowds of strangers in town drove prices up to the point that boarding in Panama City cost $10 per day.[30]

On her first call at the port of Panama City, the new steamer *California* picked up some four hundred desperate passengers and set off for San Francisco, where she arrived on February 28, 1849. Her entire crew promptly deserted, leaving her stranded in the harbor. It was four months before her owner and her captain could hire another crew to take her back to sea. This aggravated the problem of the throngs of forty-niners waiting in Panama City to continue their journey to the goldfields, and the situation would only grow worse as the phenomenon of deserting crews became a chronic one in San Francisco Bay. No inducement seemed sufficient to keep the sailors—nor at times even their officers or the captain—on board as they envisioned unlimited wealth for the taking in the interior. The harbor became increasingly clogged with abandoned vessels riding forlornly at anchor.[31]

Despite such setbacks as the loss of the *California*'s crew, Aspinwall's steamship line provided a dramatic improvement over even what the best clipper ships could manage sailing around the Horn. When the *California*'s sister ship in the Aspinwall line, the *Oregon*, arrived at San Francisco on its maiden voyage, her captain wisely brought his ship close alongside the ship of the line *Ohio* at Saucelito and arranged with the warship's captain to transfer his crew to the *Ohio* as prisoners during his ship's stay in port, thus preventing the mass desertion that had plagued the *California* and many other ships. The *California* eventually got back into service, and by then she and the *Oregon* had been joined in Pacific waters by Aspinwall's third steamer, the *Panama*. When in January 1850 Lieutenant Sherman traveled back to the East Coast, he took the *Oregon*, crossed the isthmus, caught the mail steamer on the Atlantic side, and reached New York only thirty days out of San Francisco. The world was getting smaller.[32]

Many Americans eager to get to the gold of California in that heady year of 1849 could not afford the ticket for passage on a steamship or a berth on one of the elite new clippers or even the $120 that steerage passage might cost on a less than elite vessel. Unwilling to lose the six months that might be required for the voyage around the Horn on a plodding, old-fashioned cargo ship or, indeed, to wait for anything at all when their feet or their horses' hooves could be bringing them closer to the fabled riches of the Sierras, they set out for California overland. Whereas the immigrants flocking to California by sea came from nearly every corner of the globe, those who made the trek across the continent were nearly all Americans.[33]

They came from around the country. In DeKalb County, Georgia, a group of men advertised in the local papers that they were organizing a company to go out to California. In New York, a workingmen's California company organized itself, while another organization came together composed of young professional men, some of them leaving behind salaries as high as $1,500 a year to go to California. Still another California company sprang up out of the city's German and Swedish immigrant population. It was much the same in the rest of the states. Individually or in organized companies many thousands of Americans hastily prepared to cross the continent. Twelve "respectable young gentlemen" in Boston organized themselves as the New England Pioneers and set out for California. A Milwaukee journalist wryly noted in January 1849 that "Wisconsin has had the *yellow fever* attended with the usual delirium in such cases and a strong disposition to talk of California and of 'nothing else,' for about a month."[34]

The most obvious land route to California was the tried and proven—or, in the case of the Hastings Cutoff, disproven—California Trail, and a vastly increased volume of wagon trains set off early that spring from Independence or St. Joseph, Missouri, over the prairies of what would one day be Kansas, along the Platte River, through South Pass, and across the Basin and Range region to California.

The use of this route had an interesting side effect. Many gold seekers from northern states had, like most of their northern brethren, never visited a slave state or seen slavery in the flesh. Their trip to California brought them into the slave state of Missouri, through which most of them passed from St. Louis to the upper Missouri towns at the trailhead. For many of them the experience of actually seeing such events as a slave auction served to confirm and intensify their previous, often nearly dormant, feelings of distaste for the South's peculiar institution.

The second big shock of the journey (the first for those coming from the slave states) was the price of provisions in the trailhead towns. The guidebooks said things would be as cheap in St. Joseph and Independence as at St. Louis, but the massive increase in traffic along the trail bid up prices to levels of which the writers of the guidebooks had never dreamed. The hard-dealing Missouri merchants knew the travelers had no choice but to pay. As a crowning indecency, after the fleecing they suffered in the towns, the forty-niners had to pay a ferryman $50 to take them and their wagons across the wide Missouri.[35]

The massive influx of migrants had an effect on more than just prices. The tens of thousands of people, all traveling along rivers in the middle of a hot summer, became an ideal host community for deadly water-borne bacteria, particularly the *Vibrio cholerae,* the cause of the disease known as cholera. The summer of 1849 saw a massive outbreak along the rivers that were the highways of western travel. Nor were the migrants the only ones to suffer. People died in the towns along the way as well as on the lonely stretches of prairie. St. Louis was especially hard hit by the disease. Cholera struck with suddenness and, because no one then understood its cause, with stunning capriciousness. A man could be hale and hearty at breakfast, complain of cramps and nausea later in the morning, and then, after several hours of intense suffering, be dead before suppertime.[36]

Indians proved to be far less dangerous than microbes on the journey west, though they did sometimes engage in threatening behavior. The Indians were accustomed by now to travelers on the Oregon and California trails, but 1849 saw many times as many migrants as had the preceding years. Some of the travelers had tense moments with the tribesmen. One California-bound wagon train encountered a large group of Indians who demanded the payment of toll before they would allow the wagons to pass. The men of the wagon train discussed the matter among themselves and decided that since they were on a main thoroughfare within the public domain of the United States, they would pay no toll. They proceeded on, and the Indians did nothing.[37]

Not all of the forty-niners chose to take the established route. Those who viewed its trace on a map were liable to the same kinds of thoughts that had misled Lansford Hastings. As it meandered across the continent, the California Trail described anything but the straight line that everyone knew was the shortest route between the goldfields and a man who was bound and determined to make his fortune there, cost what it may. One simple alternative was the Hastings Cuttoff itself, now known as the Mormon Trail, since the Mormons had followed that route in reaching their new home around the Great Salt Lake. The followers of Brigham Young had cleared Emigration Canyon of much of the brush that had bedeviled the Donner Party's transit and made something like a road, but beyond the foot of the Wasatch and the new Zion of the Mormons, the Great Salt Lake Desert stretched out for miles, promising the same sort of grueling, dry crossing between water holes that the Donners had endured three years before. Nevertheless, many emigrants, eager not to lose a minute in reaching the goldfields, struggled across the deserts.[38]

For some gold seekers, the established overland trails seemed to make no sense. Why travel all the way north to the Missouri River towns at the head of the Oregon Trail, especially if one was starting out from the southern states? A Mississippi newspaper recommended that travelers to California take a route through northern Mexico, via Monterrey, Saltillo, and Mazatlán, while an Arkansas journalist urged the superiority of a route departing Fort Smith and ascending the Arkansas River and then the Canadian River across the southern plains and finally the Gila River route, which had so taxed Kearny and Carson's party two years before, as the final pathway to California.[39]

Other travelers sought to improvise their own routes, either from the Great Salt Lake or by traveling west from Texas. Some of them found their way into a deep valley at the eastern foot of the towering Sierra Nevada, south of the California Trail. They could not have known, but at 282 feet below sea level, this valley was the lowest dry land in North America—and very dry indeed, perhaps the driest spot on the continent and very possibly the hottest as well. In the early twentieth century, men would record temperatures in the valley of more than 130 degrees Fahrenheit. Coming on top of all they had suffered already in their journey, it seemed to the weary travelers nothing but a place of death. At least one man did die there and possibly others. The surviving forty-niners gave the place its name: Death Valley.[40]

By land and by sea, after easy voyages or difficult journeys, gold seekers flocked into California throughout 1849. The new arrivals found the previous arrivals still diligently extracting wealth from the ground or preparing to extract it from the new influx of gold seekers. Sutter had laid out a grid of town lots on his lands at New Helvetia and was selling them as part of a new municipality people were calling Sacramento City. Farther south, where additional goldfields had been discovered, Charles Weber was the proud owner of a settlement that was still known as French Camp but would soon come to be called Stockton. At the beginning of 1849, perhaps thirteen thousand non-Indian residents had inhabited California. Before the year was past, more than one hundred thousand lived there. Of the newcomers, thirty-nine thousand had come by sea, the rest across the continent.[41]

California was a wild and lawless community, for the new owner, the United States, had set up no territorial government, and the only authority in the entire province was to be found in the tiny garrisons of U.S. Army troops. Even their jurisdiction was limited and questionable. What order existed in California was the product of uprooted Americans banding together to establish rudimentary justice and equity. Miners improvised much of what later became standard American mining law. Some had prior experience in the legal profession, but all had experience in self-government. Sometimes criminals became so bold and outrageous in one locality or another that good men had to bond together into community uplift societies and use ropes to do the lifting. Vigilante justice was generally the only kind available.[42]

The most pressing question by the end of the year, both for Californians and for Americans in the eastern states and especially in the national capital, was how long this state of affairs would last. Answering that question would require somehow reconciling America's new empire of liberty with its persistent contradiction in the institution of slavery. Westward expansion had previously forced the country to attend to the unpleasant issue of slavery, but somehow the politicians had always found ways to dodge the issue. Now the acquisition of California—and its sudden peopling as a result of the gold rush—made the issue inescapable.

CHAPTER NINETEEN

California and the Expansion of Slavery

THE THIRTY-FIRST Congress convened in Washington, D.C.—Washington City, as Americans still called it in those days—on a snowy December 3, 1849. Its members had been elected thirteen months earlier, along with Whig president Zachary Taylor, in the wake of the Treaty of Guadalupe Hidalgo. The topic on the legislators' minds as they gathered in the national capital was the vast expanse of territory the United States had acquired under the terms of that treaty—or more specifically, the status of slavery in that region. It was not a new question, but recent developments in California had made it more pressing than ever before. Other points of contention existed between North and South, but California meant they would have to be dealt with sooner rather than later.

California had to have a government. Because it already contained nearly one hundred thousand people in a state of virtual anarchy, it needed that government at once. Under that new government, whatever it might be, slavery would either be allowed or it would not. Congress would ultimately have to make that decision. Thus the sudden expansion into California meant that Congress had to deal directly and immediately with the issue of slavery expansion.

The turmoil stemming from the Wilmot Proviso had never really subsided. After Wilmot had introduced it, and the Senate had swatted it down, near the start of the war back in August 1846, other northern representatives had resurrected its substance and attached it to new bills. Furious southern representatives and senators had killed it each time, aided by northern congressmen loyal to the administration of then president James K. Polk, who called the proviso "a mischievous & foolish amendment."[1]

As far as Polk was concerned, the whole question was irrelevant and had no place in discussions of ending the Mexican War. "What connection slavery had with making peace with Mexico," the exasperated president wrote, "it is difficult to conceive." As far as Polk was concerned, slavery was a side issue, an incidental matter unrelated to the great public benefit of extending the United States and the rule of its free institutions. The war that he had waged against Mexico had not been either for or against slavery. Of course, Polk was a Tennessee slaveholder who saw nothing wrong with the institution, so his complacence is perhaps understandable. Yet he was one of a dwindling number of Americans for whom slavery could conceivably be a side issue or irrelevant to any topic of public debate.[2]

Now the president was a Louisiana slaveholder, owner of more human chattel than Polk had ever claimed. Zachary Taylor had never clearly stated his views on slavery as a political issue or on the Wilmot Proviso, but southerners were confident and northerners disgusted at having a major slaveholder in the White House. The country would, it seemed, have to decide the issue of slavery in the Mexican Cession on his watch.

Southern political leaders had been ferocious in their attack on the Wilmot Proviso and the opposition to slavery that lay behind it. Leading the charge, not surprisingly, was John C. Calhoun. The Wilmot Proviso was unjust to southerners, he claimed, conveniently overlooking the 40 percent of southerners who were, in fact, slaves and the additional 30 percent who were whites who would not, during their lifetimes, be part of a slaveholding household. To Calhoun, a southerner was a slaveholder, and a slaveholder could not go into a territory without his slaves. If slavery was prohibited there, then southerners were prohibited, and that was manifestly a violation of their rights. It would, he said, give the free states "the monopoly of the public domain, to the entire seclusion of the slaveholding States."[3]

Calhoun actually welcomed the Wilmot Proviso and the movement it had spawned in the North as an opportunity to rally the South around the cause of slavery and force a showdown. "If the South act as it ought," he wrote to a political ally, "the Wilmot proviso, instead of proving to be the means of successfully assailing us and our peculiar institution, may be made the occasion of successfully asserting our equality and rights by enabling us to force the issue on the North. Something of the kind was indispensable to rouse and unite the South."[4]

Calhoun demanded that the Missouri Compromise line, established at latitude 36°30' north in 1820 as the border between slave and free territories in the Louisiana Purchase, be extended to the Pacific, with all the lands south of it being reserved for future slave states. To northerners this was entirely unsatisfactory. Most of the territory gained from Mexico lay south of the Missouri Compromise line, and the more Calhoun and other southerners clamored for slavery in those lands, the more credible to northerners became the claims of abolitionists that the entire Mexican War had been ginned up as part of an enormous plot to add slave territory to the Union.[5]

In this state of mind, the Thirty-first Congress had arrived in the national capital and taken up the suddenly pressing issue of California. The problems the senators and representatives would face had been made more pressing and immediate by events in California. In April 1849 General Bennett Riley had taken over from Colonel Richard Mason as military governor of California. Recognizing the impossibility of his task and aware of calls by some Californians for the establishment of civil government, Riley decided to anticipate Congress and on June 3 called for an election, to take place August 1, for the purpose of selecting delegates to a convention. This convention would, according to the general, have the option either of setting up a territorial government or of drawing up a state constitution and petitioning Congress for admission to the Union.[6]

The next day, June 4, Georgia congressman T. Butler King arrived in San Francisco on a mission from President Taylor, and though Riley had had no knowledge of Taylor's intent for King's mission, his action turned out to dovetail nicely with the president's plans. Back in April, the same month in which Riley had succeeded to command in California, Taylor had dispatched King, one of the relative handful of men in the country who actually owned more slaves than the president did, to go to California and encourage the settlers there to form a state government and petition Congress for immediate admission to the Union, bypassing territorial status. Taylor believed that such a move would completely sidestep the bothersome and potentially dangerous congressional debate over the issue of slavery in California. After all, both northerners and southerners admitted that Congress had no constitutional authority to legislate on the status of slavery in a state. Therefore, if California were to seek statehood, Congress should have nothing more to say in the matter. Clearly, Taylor was new to Washington.[7]

The people of California duly elected their delegates, and the delegates convened on Monday, September 3. One delegate had a copy of the constitution of New York, which the convention used as a template, adjusting the basic pattern as seemed appropriate. They debated and set the boundaries of their proposed state, wrote laws of property and marriage, and addressed various other issues. Most significantly from the point of view of contemporary politics, they determined that California would be a free state. The decision did not stem from an abundance of abolitionists among the forty-niners. In fact, there were few. Instead, most of the new Californians were nonslaveholding whites from various states who cared nothing at all about slavery save that they did not want to live next to or compete economically with blacks. In fact, a large number of them would have liked to exclude all blacks from the state, free as well as slave. Submitted to the voters of California, the proposed constitution, making California a free state, passed by an overwhelming margin.[8]

So it was that California's free-state constitution arrived in Washington just in time for the newly convened Thirty-first Congress to face the decision of what to do about it. Southern representatives and senators reacted with outrage. This was "worse than the Wilmot Proviso," Calhoun announced. "What the latter proposes to do openly the former is intended to do covertly and fraudulently." That is, admitting California as a free state was just another, more underhanded way of banning southerners (by which Calhoun always meant slaveholders) from the territories, just as the Wilmot Proviso had proposed to do. Almost half of California lay south of the Missouri Compromise line, heightening the slaveholders' sense of deprivation in seeing it become free soil.[9]

Most galling of all, perhaps, was the fact that California's admission as a free state would make a total of sixteen free states to fifteen slave. This was of great importance to southerners. Despite the advantage they received from the U.S. Constitution's three-fifths clause, they had never been able to equal the votes of the northern states in the House of Representatives, but they had for several decades managed to maintain equality in the Senate by refusing to allow the admission of any additional free state without that of a corresponding slave state. The Senate had become the South's bulwark, where any unwanted federal legislation could be stopped, just as southern senators, with a few compliant northern allies, had succeeded in quashing the Wilmot Proviso in each of its incarnations. California's admission as a free state would break the balance in the Senate, and few could imagine any way that the balance would ever be restored. The slaveholding states would then find themselves in a permanent minority. Calhoun and others like him were determined not to tolerate such a development.[10]

California was the most pressing and immediate of the problems facing the new Congress, but the issue of the proposed new state on the Pacific also served to drag forward other issues related to slavery and the results of the recently ended war with Mexico. The most obvious of these concerned the status of slavery in the rest of the Mexican Cession—that is, most or all of the modern-day states of New Mexico, Arizona, Nevada, and Utah and smaller portions of Colorado and Wyoming. As in California, slavery had been illegal in these areas under Mexican law prior to annexation by the United States. Unlike California, none of these areas, or all of them put together, had population enough to justify an application for statehood. That left the question of slavery within those areas squarely within Congress's jurisdiction, and Congress was likely to drag the question into its debates on the issue of California statehood and the future of slavery in the American West.

Further complicating the question of slavery in the Mexican Cession was the claim of Texas to half the province of New Mexico. At the time it had won its independence, back in 1836, Texas had claimed, and Santa Anna had accepted in the Treaty of Velasco, the boundary of the Rio Grande, well beyond the border of the old province of Tejas. The boundary dispute growing from this claim, as it impinged on Mexican claims to the south, had been the immediate cause for the outbreak of the Mexican War. Now the issue was Texas's Rio Grande boundary claim as it impinged on the province of New Mexico to the west, extending to the point that Texas claimed ownership of Santa Fe, capital of the neighboring province.

Now that the war with Mexico was over, that neighboring province belonged to the United States. Detracting from Texas's claim to the region was the fact that the inhabitants did not wish to be part of Texas and that the Republic of Texas had never succeeded in exerting any control over the region. Slavery entered the dispute because Texas was a slave state, whereas the territorial government of New Mexico, whenever Congress got around to setting it up officially, would either be open or closed to slavery, as the men in Washington might decide. Proslavery congressmen were determined that the disputed lands should remain part of Texas, safe for slavery and securely out of the reach of the Free-Soilers and their Wilmot Proviso. The situation had grown intense enough that Texas was threatening to use armed force, with New Mexico promising resistance and pleading with the federal government for protection. If California had not been forcing the slavery issue into the laps of the members of the Thirty-first Congress, the Texas–New Mexico border dispute would have been enough by itself.[11]

These issues joined the ongoing sources of slavery contention. Abolitionists wanted slavery, or at least the slave trade, banned in the District of Columbia and had been petitioning Congress for this for more than a decade. Slavery advocates, on the other hand, were angry at the personal liberty laws of northern states, which greatly increased the difficulty of catching runaway slaves and of kidnapping northern blacks into southern slavery. Some Yankees were going further and engaging in all but open obstruction of the Fugitive Slave Law. Proslavery forces in Congress were determined not only to block any attempt to limit slavery or the slave trade in the District of Columbia but also to force through a new and drastically stronger version of the Fugitive Slave Law that would stop once and for all personal liberty laws and every other northern attempt to interfere with the laudable efforts of southern slave catchers to put black people in their rightful place, which they deemed to be slavery.[12]

Before they could turn their attention to the problems confronting the country, the members of Congress had to organize their respective houses. The Senate quickly finished this task, but the House was a different story. Its chamber was an ill-designed and noisy acoustical disaster about which one member said, "It was not a hall—it was a cavern—a mammoth cave, in which men might speak in all parts, and be understood in none." This echoing Chamber of Babel might have been a good metaphor for the body of men attempting to organize themselves in it. The new House included 112 Democrats, 115 Whigs, and 13 Free-Soilers. Election of a Speaker required a majority vote, and the Free-Soilers held the balance of power. Worse, as far as harmony and efficient operations were concerned, each of the major parties was badly divided along North-South lines.[13]

With no faction possessing a clear majority, the representatives wrangled and argued over slavery as well as the traditional economic and constitutional issues that had divided Democrats from Whigs. Day after day congressmen made their way through the bitter cold from their various boardinghouses to the hot, stuffy, and windowless House chamber to continue the successive futile ballots and the increasingly acrimonious debate.[14]

They were well past the fortieth ballot when, on December 13, New York congressman William Duer remarked that he thought there were disunionists in the House. Virginia representative Thomas H. Bayly indignantly denied it: "There are no disunionists in this House."

"I wish I could think so," Duer replied, "but I fear there are."

Bayly demanded that Duer identify the alleged disunionists, and Duer indicated that one of them was Virginia Democrat Richard K. Meade.

Meade bristled. "It is false."

"You are a liar, Sir," replied Duer.

At that, Meade bolted from his seat and went for Duer. Each man's friends rushed in, and pandemonium broke out. The sergeant at arms of the House rushed in waving the official mace, symbol of the House's authority, high above his head. "Take away the Mace," came several shouts, "it has no authority here." Its authority proved sufficient, however, to induce the members to pause long enough for their good sense to return, and a mêlée was avoided.[15]

The issue of slavery was never far from the surface, even in such a seemingly mundane matter as the election of a Speaker of the House. The South's system of bondage was rapidly becoming the issue behind all other issues, the question that decided one's allegiance in all other disputes. One southern member who addressed the issue openly during these debates was Georgia Whig Robert Toombs. Big, bluff, and unkempt, his "long, glossy black hair" tossing wildly as he jerked his head this way and that in the intensity of his speech, Toombs roared at northern representatives, "I do not . . . hesitate to avow before this house and the country, and in the presence of the living God, that if by your legislation you seek to drive us from the territories of California and New Mexico, purchased by the common blood and treasure of the whole people, and to abolish slavery in this district, thereby attempting to fix a national degradation upon half the States . . . I am for disunion." Duer had been right.[16]

The balloting and debating dragged on through the middle weeks of December. A motion was made—and indignantly rejected—to select the Speaker by plurality. Another motion called for drawing names out of a hat. The House spurned it as well. Candidates rose and fell as individual vote totals fluctuated but never reached the necessary majority. Finally, on December 22, in preparation for the sixty-third ballot, the exhausted House agreed to allow election by plurality. Georgia Democrat Howell Cobb won the speakership with 102 votes.[17]

With the House at last organized, Congress was ready to receive the president's annual message. Ever since Thomas Jefferson, presidents had not appeared before Congress to read their State of the Union addresses but had instead forwarded a written message to be read by the clerk of the House. This definitely worked to Taylor's advantage, since no clerk could possibly have read the address as dryly as the president, with his well-known wooden style of oratory. The members of the House and Senate therefore listened to the clerk drone through the address. "We should abstain from the introduction of those exciting topics of a sectional character which have hitherto produced painful apprehensions in the public mind." With this in mind, he urged Congress to accept his plan of admitting California directly to statehood with whatever provisions its inhabitants might make on the subject of slavery. This, he urged, would avoid "all causes of uneasiness" and create "confidence and kind feeling."[18]

It did nothing of the sort. Taylor's plan for sectional harmony was to prove no more successful than similarly well-intended schemes introduced by far more savvy politicians. The southern reaction to the president's proposal was entirely predictable. Indeed, it had already begun, and it continued unabated after the president's address.

Southerners were especially angry because they felt betrayed. Was not Taylor one of them? Was he not a major slaveholder? Many southerners had supported him for exactly that reason. Georgia Whig congressman Alexander Stephens had been the leader and organizer of the Young Indians and felt more appalled than anyone else at this shocking turn of events. The president they thought would be the staunchest defender of slavery was now advocating a policy they saw as a backdoor implementation of the Wilmot Proviso. An angry Congressman Abraham W. Venable of North Carolina introduced a resolution demanding that the president turn over to Congress copies of whatever "instructions" he might have "given to any agents, civil or military, touching the organization of California into a state government"—a move that obviously had King's mission to California in mind. The resolution passed on the last day of 1849, and Taylor complied on January 21, explaining in his covering message, "In advising an early application by the people of these Territories for admission as States, I was actuated principally by an earnest desire to afford to the wisdom and patriotism of Congress the opportunity of avoiding occasions of bitter and angry dissensions among the people of the United States."[19]

Other southern political leaders did not see it that way. How could Taylor have turned on them? One reason was that Taylor's top political supporter and advisor, Kentucky's John J. Crittenden, had accepted the Whig nomination for governor of Kentucky in order to help Taylor carry that state in the election. It had worked, and Crittenden had also won his race for governor. Thus, in this first winter of Taylor's administration, Crittenden was not in Washington but five hundred miles away in Frankfort. In his absence Taylor had come to rely on the advice of another of his stalwart backers among the Whigs, Senator William H. Seward. Seward was an upstate New York politician of sufficiently flexible principles to have supported a slaveholder like Taylor for president, but he was still eager to take as strong an antislavery stand as he felt his constituents required. That made him all the more dangerous to southerners—an antislavery Yankee whispering in the ear of the ultimate political innocent, Zachary Taylor.

Stephens, together with his fellow Georgian Toombs, determined to take action. They were an odd couple, these two Georgia politicians. Toombs stood more than six feet tall, robust and rampant. "Little Alec" Stephens, though of average height for the day at five feet seven inches, weighed less than eighty pounds and was variously described as looking "frail and thin to painful meagerness," or like a "boyish invalid escaped from some hospital," or like a "well-preserved mummy." He had a pinched face, a pointed nose, protruding ears, and burning black eyes. He was a fierce little bantam, though, and he had, over the course of his career, issued five different challenges to duels, without getting any takers. He was a first-rate politician, and he and Toombs were fast friends and, in this case, strong political allies.

They decided to go and talk to the president about the issue of slavery and the evils of the Wilmot Proviso, however it might be disguised behind the supposed right of the people of California to choose their own government. The Georgians arranged an audience with Taylor and pressed on him the importance of vetoing any bill that would hinder the spread of slavery into the new territories, presumably including a California statehood bill if the new state was to be free rather than slave. Taylor informed them stoutly that he would sign any constitutional bill that landed on his desk—good Whig doctrine, that—and that it would then be his duty to enforce the law. Stephens and Toombs warned that if he did, the result might be the secession of the slave states. Taylor did not take well to threats, whether from Santa Anna or from this apparently mismatched pair of slavery advocates. He reacted vociferously, terminating the interview as the two Georgians beat as hasty a retreat as ever Mexican soldiers had done before Old Rough and Ready's batteries. A caller who came to the president's office a few minutes later found Taylor raging about the two "high priests in the inner councils of the slave power." They had made demands and threatened secession unless he gave in. Secession was treason, he roared, and he would hang every man who tried it.[20]

Many who hoped to avoid such drastic developments looked hopefully to the Senate. Meeting in its smaller and acoustically far more pleasing chamber on the other side of the Capitol, the Senate of that day was a highly respected body. Political oratory was then considered a prime form of entertainment, and the Senate was celebrated as the source of the finest political oratory of the time. The Senate of the Thirty-first Congress consisted of thirty-three Democrats and twenty-seven Whigs and Free-Soilers. Among its members were some new faces. Jefferson Davis was there, son-in-law to the president by his late wife and hero of Buena Vista. Stephen A. Douglas was there from Illinois, where a few years before, as a state judge, he had helped negotiate with Joseph Smith and the Mormons. So too was Seward, who had previously served as governor of New York. Yet another freshman senator was Ohio Free-Soiler Salmon P. Chase.

Yet it was not the new but the old faces who dominated the Senate, a body that prided itself on the longevity, experience, and wisdom of its members. Thomas Hart Benton was still there, holding, with thirty years' continuous service, the distinction of the longest uninterrupted Senate tenure in the history of the young Republic. But towering above Benton, at least figuratively, were all three of the men who had dominated the national government from one office or another—but not the presidency—for most of the past half century: Calhoun, Webster, and Clay.

Since John C. Calhoun had come to Washington as a U.S. representative in 1811, he had served in the House, as U.S. vice president, as secretary of war, and as secretary of state. Since 1832 he had been in the Senate, with a two-and-a-half-year hiatus to serve as Tyler's secretary of state. As a young man Calhoun had favored a strong national government at a time when it appeared that such a government would be controlled by the South. As it became increasingly apparent that the institution of slavery was incurring the disapproval of the rest of the country and the rest of the world, and that the South would not dominate the national government, Calhoun became a champion of a national government whose powers were, for the most part, starkly limited. He favored not states' rights but rather the rights of the South as a distinct—and distinctly slaveholding—section of the country. In an 1837 Senate speech he had announced that slavery was "a positive good." Calhoun was showing his age, and below his wild mane of hair his face looked downright cadaverous, save that his intense eyes still glared out from their deeply shadowed sockets. In fact, Calhoun, who that January was a few weeks short of his sixty-eighth birthday, was dying of tuberculosis.[21]

Daniel Webster, sometimes called Black Dan for his jet-black hair and bushy black eyebrows and somewhat swarthy visage, celebrated his sixty-eighth birthday that very month of January 1850. He had come to Washington as a U.S. representative in 1813, two years later than Calhoun and Clay, but whereas those two had been war hawks who had advocated war with Great Britain, Webster had been elected to represent his native New Hampshire on a wave of opposition to the War of 1812, which was very unpopular in New England.

After moving to Massachusetts, Webster had represented the voters of that state first in the House of Representatives and then, since 1827, in the U.S. Senate, except for a four-year break during most of which he had served as secretary of state under first Harrison and then Tyler. He had gained fame defending the cause of the Union in his celebrated Senate debate with Senator Robert Y. Hayne of South Carolina. Generally, throughout his years in Washington, Webster had been an advocate of a strong central government and of the interests of New England, as well as those of the Second Bank of the United States, from which he had received a regular stipend. He had for some years been at odds with Henry Clay, the other great man of the Whig Party, primarily because no one party could be big enough for two such outsized egos and sets of ambitions. Webster believed that he and Clay should both have had their turns in the presidency by this time. Embittered by his failure to win the presidency, Webster was gradually destroying his body and mind with alcohol and occasionally made a spectacle of himself by public intoxication.[22]

Towering over them all in reputation and popular acclaim was Henry Clay. Clay had not thought he'd return to the Senate when he had retired from that body in 1842. Rather, he had confidently expected to have reached his lifelong goal of the presidency. Since that time, however, he had failed in two separate presidential bids, and his favorite son, Henry Clay Jr., had died on the battlefield of Buena Vista in 1847. Clay was a sad old man when he returned to Washington in December 1849 to take the Senate seat to which the Kentucky legislature had unanimously elected him.

He said he was reluctant to return to government, and this time it seemed to be true. He knew now that he would never be president, and he could not quite shake the bitterness of it. "My relations to the Whigs are wholly changed by the events of the past year," he wrote, referring to the party's failure to nominate him in 1848. Whether out of duty or habit, or both, he accepted the seat and thus found himself in the nation's icy capital city that winter, returning to the Senate to which he had first come forty-three years before at the not-quite-constitutional (for a senator) age of twenty-nine. Since then he had been senator, representative, Speaker of the House, secretary of state, and six-time disappointed seeker of the presidency. He would be seventy-three in April, and he was beginning to look it. Men had called him the Great Compromiser and the Old Coon. They still did, but now some also called him Ancient Henry. What was left of his hair, though still hanging to his neck, was now gray, and his tall, lithe form had taken on a certain gauntness. He coughed far too much. In fact, Clay, like Calhoun, was suffering from tuberculosis.[23]

As he had been on similar occasions in the past, Clay was eager to achieve a compromise to the conflicts then plaguing the nation. He was a slaveholder from a border state that identified with its fellow slave states and yet looked largely to the Ohio River and the free states across it for its commerce. Clay had long been moderately, almost nominally, opposed to slavery, favoring the colonization of free blacks as a vague first step toward the most gradual emancipation imaginable, but also denouncing all abolitionists and Free-Soilers as public menaces. Clay was naturally in the center of the present debate, and, on top of that, he was a compromiser by nature and disposition. Thanks to his reputation, won with the Missouri Compromise of 1820 and the Compromise Tariff of 1833, men looked to Clay for some way out of the present impasse, and he was loath to disappoint.

CHAPTER TWENTY

The Struggle for Compromise

ON THE EVENING of a frosty January 21, Clay paid a surprise call on his old colleague and intraparty nemesis Daniel Webster to see if he could gain his support for a comprehensive compromise proposal. Webster was receptive. All the recent agitation about slavery in the territories had been, he thought, "mischievous," a sentiment that would have surprised the many earnest abolitionists among his New England admirers. To Webster, however, the Wilmot Proviso and similar efforts only served to create "heart burnings." Clay spelled out the details of the compromise program he planned to propose to Congress, and Webster promised his support.[1]

Eight days later, on January 29, 1850, Clay rose in the Senate to offer a set of resolutions aimed at settling all of the major disputes then dividing the two sections of the country and threatening the Union's continued survival. Word had spread that the Great Compromiser would be offering his solution that day, and massive crowds arrived early on what turned out to be a mild and pleasant winter day in the capital. The Senate's visitor galleries were packed, and senators had admitted special guests like Congressman Alexander Stephens and other members of the House of Representatives, who crowded the rear of the chamber's main floor. "Every aisle, nook and corner" was filled with humanity, Stephens wrote.[2]

Clay rose, and the packed galleries and crowded floor were soon reminded by his graceful figure, smooth, clear voice, and engaging words why he had become the most successful legislator in the Republic's history. Clay said that he would offer eight resolutions that, "taken together, in combination," would "propose an amicable arrangement of all questions in controversy between the free and the slave Sates, growing out of the subject of slavery." Together they formed a solution, he said, that the Senate could and should support.[3]

Point by point, Clay's resolutions addressed the hot spots of the slavery controversy. He first called for the admission of California as a state without restriction on the status of slavery there. Since California was already petitioning for admission as a free state, that is what it would become under Clay's plan. Next he proposed that in all the rest of the lands acquired from Mexico, territories were to be organized without restriction regarding the status of slavery. Ironically this imposed more or less the very same popular sovereignty that defeated presidential candidate Lewis Cass, now once again representing Michigan in this very chamber, had proposed two years before. Since, as Clay pointed out, slavery had not previously existed in these regions thanks in part to climate and in part to Mexican law, he conceded that it was unlikely to move into those areas under this new arrangement. The North should therefore feel no loss, and the South too could, in theory, shrug off the loss of the Mexican Cession since there had been little chance for slavery there in the first place. Next Clay proposed that Texas surrender its claims to half of New Mexico. Austin's writ had never run west of the Pecos anyway, and the local populace was decidedly opposed to inclusion in the Lone Star State.

So far, Clay's first three points had seemed somewhat to favor northern views. His last five would be quite different. In exchange for the surrender of its questionable claims in New Mexico, Texas was to have its entire preannexation debt paid by the federal government. At a whopping $10 million, the Texas debt represented a sum that was more than half of what the United States had paid for the entire Mexican Cession, including California, probably the last time such a high relative value would be placed on the empty expanse of the Llano Estacado between the Rio Grande and the modern-day Texas–New Mexico boundary.

Clay then turned his attention eastward to the long-standing disputes about slavery that had predated the Mexican War. The slave trade, he proposed, should be abolished in the District of Columbia. No longer would American statesmen have to blush with embarrassment when foreign diplomats pointed out slave auctions taking place within sight of the Capitol. This was a point for the North, but Clay's counterbalancing point followed immediately. Congress would promise never to abolish slavery itself in the District of Columbia without the consent of both of the neighboring states. Since these were the slave states of Maryland and Virginia, it was clear that such permission would never be forthcoming and slavery in the national capital would be guaranteed in perpetuity.

Another sore spot had involved the interstate slave trade, the steady and highly profitable commerce by which Upper South states like Virginia, Maryland, and Clay's own Kentucky sold the surplus increase of their slave populations to the more slave-hungry cotton and sugar planta-tions of the Deep South. Abolitionists had pointed out the obvious fact that the Constitution gave Congress the power to regulate interstate commerce and therefore every American was in conscience bound to advocate the banning of the interstate slave trade. Southerners differed sharply with that view, and Clay's compromise proposal called for Con-gress to declare, in violation of common sense and the plain text of the Constitution, that it in fact had no authority to regulate that particular part of interstate commerce known as the interstate slave trade. This last was a clear point for the cause of slavery, and worse was to come.

Clay's final point proposed a new and much stronger fugitive slave law. The new act would accomplish all that slaveholders had been demanding by way of shutting down the personal liberty laws of the northern states. So much for states' rights. It would also teach a lesson to northern magistrates, sheriffs, and common citizens who exercised their judgmental view of slavery and refused to cooperate in the capture and return of fugitives from bondage. From now on the law would require the cooperation of local sheriffs, the use of their jails, and, if necessary, the deputation of northern citizens, willing or not, to form posses to capture runaway slaves. It was all that the slaveholders could have asked for. Not only did it place the federal government's stamp of unambiguous approval on the institution of slavery, but it also proposed to force the self-righteous Yankees to soil themselves with what they were continually claiming was the guilt of slavery. Priceless.

Having presented his compromise proposal, Clay made an impas-sioned appeal to the Senate to adopt it. He admitted that his plan asked the North to sacrifice more than the South. This he said the North could afford to grant because it had a larger population than the South. "You are in the point of numbers . . . greater," Clay said, addressing his north-ern colleagues, "and greatness and magnanimity should ever be allied together." The North was not threatened, Clay maintained, and there-fore could afford to give in to more of the South's demands. Of course he made no mention of the slaves and just what they were to sacrifice or how they could afford it. Apparently they were expected to be very mag-nanimous indeed, not because they could afford it but because they had no choice.[4]

Clay concluded by displaying a piece of wood he said was a fragment of George Washington's coffin. In an argument that sounds to modern ears like something a personal injury trial lawyer would use in his final address to the jury, Clay argued that the relic was "a warning voice coming from the grave to the Congress now in session to beware, to pause, to reflect before they lend themselves to any purposes which shall destroy that Union which was cemented by his exertions and example." With a few more words urging compromise, Clay concluded his speech.[5]

The formal debate on Clay's proposals was scheduled to begin the following week, and Clay was slated to lead off. Once again the Senate chamber was packed with eager spectators as a weak and ailing Henry Clay made his way to his desk. In the galleries and the corridors outside, the crowds were so dense that several women fainted. Others screamed. When at one o'clock that afternoon Clay rose to speak, a roar of applause met him, and it took several minutes to restore order. Again calling on his old charm and eloquence, Clay spoke throughout the rest of that day's session, taking each point of his proposed compromise and arguing its merits at length. The next day he was back to continue the speech. In all, it lasted nearly five hours and left Clay utterly exhausted.[6]

Next to take the floor was a succession of southern senators who angrily denounced the compromise proposal. Despite such attractive features as the draconian new Fugitive Slave Act, they were bitterly unhappy with Clay's resolutions. Everything Clay's proposal gave the South was already the South's by right. Everything Clay's proposal gave the North was also the South's by right. Slaveholding senators were outraged. "You have awakened a feeling which can no longer be trifled with," growled Georgia senator John Berrien at his northern colleagues. "The South asserts, then, her right to participate in all of the territories which may be acquired by the United States. She asserts her right to emigrate to them, with her property of any description. That is the precise right which is denied by the North."[7]

"We want no compromise," declaimed Alabama's Jeremiah Clemens. Compromise just meant giving up the rights of the South. The Constitution guaranteed all that the South claimed. The proposed compromise gave all that away, said Clemens, and he was utterly opposed to it. And so it went, as one southern senator after another rose to denounce Clay and his compromise and complain of the plight of the poor, persecuted slaveholders whose rights were being trampled by the "many aggressions" of the North against the South. Meanwhile, similar scenes were taking place in the House, which had also taken up the same issues, with predictably less decorum and more raucousness—but similar lack of progress.[8]

On March 4 massive crowds once again packed the Senate chambers and gallery as the arch southerner himself, John C. Calhoun, was sched-

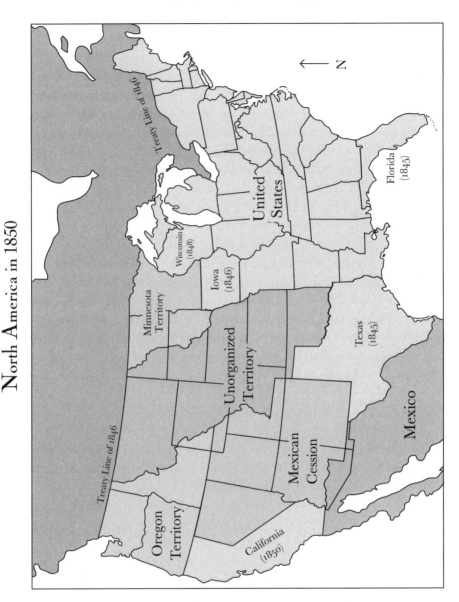

North America in 1850

uled to speak. The masses were hushed as the old man entered the Senate chamber supported by Virginia senator James M. Mason, who helped the dying man to his seat. Six feet two inches tall, but stooped and wizened, Calhoun appeared emaciated, almost shriveled. His deep-set eyes seemed to have sunk even farther into their dark sockets but gleamed out from under his beetling brows with still more intensity, and his gaunt visage resembled an animated skull surmounted with an extravagant mane of gray hair. Dour and humorless even on lighter occasions, Calhoun now looked positively sepulchral. A spectator thought him "pale and cadaverous, like a fugitive from a grave."[9]

Calhoun had never met a compromise proposal he did not hate. "I hold concession or compromise to be fatal," he had once said to a fellow proslavery partisan. To "concede an inch" would place the backers of slavery at a disadvantage from which they might never recover, so he had always held out for the unconditional surrender of the North. Nothing but complete northern submission to every southern demand had ever satisfied him in the past. Senators and spectators waited in suspense to see if slavery's chief spokesman for the past two decades would now join Clay in backing the compromise resolutions. Deathly silence gripped the packed chamber as the time came for Calhoun to take the floor.[10]

Unsteadily the tall, thin figure uncoiled from his seat. In a quavering voice that listeners had to strain to catch, he said that he had written out his remarks but did not have the strength to read them. He hoped the Senate would permit Mason, who occupied the seat behind Calhoun's, to read the address for him. No objection was raised, and Mason took the manuscript and rose to his feet as Calhoun slumped back into his chair.[11]

Slowly and emphatically, and in what one listener thought "a very haughty and defiant tone," Mason began to read: "I have . . . believed from the first that the agitation of the subject of slavery could, if not prevented by some timely and effective measure, end in disunion." Because neither the federal government nor the northern state governments had taken the steps necessary to still the voices of the abolitionists, Calhoun said, the crisis had come and the Union was endangered. The North was to blame for the country's troubles now. It had persecuted the South for generations, and the South was not going to take it anymore. Among the North's many sins was the Northwest Ordinance of 1787, banning slavery from the region north of the Ohio River and east of the Mississippi. Then there had been the Missouri Compromise of 1820, prohibiting slavery in the Louisiana Purchase above latitude 36°30' north. And now there was the attempt to foist the substance of the Wilmot Proviso on the South under the guise of Clay's odious compromise resolutions. All these laws violated the rights of slaveholders by preventing them from entering parts of the national domain with a particular type of property—slaves. They were also violations of the Constitution, according to Calhoun, notwithstanding their having in the first two cases been enacted by some of the same men who had helped write the Constitution.

What was to be done then? The only solution was for the North to submit, make its citizens stop talking about slavery, and enforce the Fugitive Slave Law with exemplary rigor. On top of that, in order to expiate its grievous sins and reassure the long-suffering slaveholders, the North must accept a constitutional amendment guaranteeing equilibrium in the federal government between the North and the South, by which Calhoun meant a system that would guarantee southern control. If the North would not do so, and especially if it insisted on admitting California with the constitution chosen by its inhabitants, Calhoun threatened that the South would break up the Union and it would be the North's fault. "The responsibility for saving the Union rests on the North," Mason read, "and not on the South." In conclusion, Calhoun wrote, "Having faithfully done my duty to the best of my ability, both to the Union and my section throughout this agitation, I shall have the consolation, let what will come, that I am free from all responsibility."[12]

The speech ended, and Mason resumed his seat. Calhoun, who had sat slumped and motionless, eyelids drooping, throughout the reading, now turned and looked around with grim satisfaction at his political allies. Despite his protestations of concern for the Union, Calhoun had to have realized that his proposed constitutional amendment would be a massive obstruction to any semiamicable settlement of the sectional troubles. Calhoun's stature was such that it would be very difficult for any other southern politician to take issue with him, and now he had staked them all to a position that could only bring secession. Like Clay, Calhoun had longed for decades to be president of the United States. Now that he clearly would not live to see another presidential election, he seemed intent on destroying the country he could not rule. When another southern senator several days later privately expressed dismay that Calhoun had not consulted his fellow southern leaders before making his speech, Calhoun replied, "I never did consult any man upon any speech I ever made. I make my speeches for myself."[13]

Northern senators had heard enough. Their replies began the next day. Democratic senators from Maine and Wisconsin responded with speeches calling for the immediate admission of California and the exclusion of slavery from the rest of the Mexican Cession. Southern senators repeatedly interrupted them with angry outbursts, and the northerners responded in kind. Emotions rose. A correspondent of *The New York Herald* wrote that the outbreak of violence and bloodshed on the Senate floor seemed imminent: "It is impossible for those at a distance to realize that their delegates in Congress are preparing for such scenes as have never been witnessed in our heretofore peaceable civil contests. The

Southern members are excited to the highest pitch. Men go armed, and are preparing for the contest and personal strife that will ensue before a week has passed. We are in the crisis so long and so justly dreaded."[14]

Senator Isaac P. Walker of Wisconsin held the floor when the March 7 session opened at noon. He looked around at the immense throng of visitors who packed the Senate chamber fuller even than it had been three days earlier for Calhoun's speech and knew what it meant. "Mr. President," Walker began, "this vast audience has not assembled to hear me." Word had gone out that on this day Daniel Webster, the great lion of the North, planned to address the Senate. Excitement raced through Washington at the thought of the North's foremost orator finally giving an answer to Calhoun and the whole baying pack of southern disunionists. Now with Webster present, as well as nearly everyone else in the capital city who could wedge himself into the chamber, Walker said he felt it both a duty and a pleasure to yield the floor to the distinguished senator from Massachusetts.[15]

Webster was a man of average height, distinctly shorter than Clay or Calhoun, but he was average in no other way. He had a way of rising majestically from his seat—"the godlike Daniel getting on his feet," someone had called it—that thrilled audiences. With his huge head, striking black eyes, broad shoulders, and deep chest, Webster possessed "enormous physical magnetism," according to a journalist. Another wrote, "When I first put eye upon him . . . I was as much awe-stricken as if I had been gazing on Bunker Hill Monument." Webster's voice matched his appearance, deep and resonant—"a voice of great power and depth," a contemporary called it, "a voice full of magnetism, a voice such as is heard only once in a lifetime." His oratory, another explained, was like "Vesuvius . . . in full blast." He was the pride of New England.[16]

Now assuming his accustomed stance, left hand under the tails of his blue claw-hammer coat, he launched into the speech all Washington had been waiting to hear. "Mr. President," intoned Webster, "I wish to speak today, not as a Massachusetts man, nor as a northern man, but as an American." He mentioned how fortunate the country was, in these turbulent times, to have the Senate, with its unshakable dignity, wisdom, and moderation, and said that his only purpose in speaking was to restore harmony. "I speak today for the preservation of the Union. 'Hear me for my cause.' "[17]

Several days before making this speech, Webster had paid a call on Calhoun, in hopes of setting the stage for sectional reconciliation, and he had come away from the two-hour meeting with the sense that harmony was possible. When Webster began his speech, the gravely ill South Carolina senator was not in the chamber, but some minutes later he entered through the door behind the president's chair, draped in a long black cloak, and took his accustomed seat. Webster, who was still speaking, had not seen him come in and mentioned "an honorable member whose health does not allow him to be here today."

"He is here," came the voice of another senator, and then from Calhoun himself, in a weak voice, "The Senator from South Carolina is in his seat." Webster paused, turned, and bowed. "I am very glad to hear that he is," Webster said. "May he long be in health and the enjoyment of it to serve his country."[18]

Continuing his speech, Webster mentioned, as Calhoun had done, the split six years before of the Methodist Church. Webster, who was a Unitarian, said that the whole thing had been unnecessary. The Methodists had had no differences worth parting company over—at least none that Webster apparently cared much about—and they had therefore been wrong to split the denomination. He proceeded then to the subject of the new territories. Like many others, he believed the dry climate of the Southwest would make slavery impossible in that region. The Wilmot Proviso was therefore unnecessary and served only to annoy the South, and Webster said he would not support it. Next he took up the question of fugitive slaves. Runaways were to be returned, he said. The Constitution was clear in this matter, and that ought to take precedence over everyone's conscience. It certainly did his. In this matter, he said, "the South . . . is right, and the North is wrong."

"Then, Sir, there are the Abolition societies," Webster continued. They were useless, and their members were well-meaning dupes. In response to the abolitionists, Webster said, southerners had rallied around the cause of slavery, curtailing what few freedoms blacks did have, so that "the bonds of the slave were bound more firmly than before, their rivets were more strongly fastened." This, Webster maintained, was the fault not of the slaveholders, who had done it, but of the abolitionists, who had hurt their feelings by criticizing the practice of owning one's fellow human beings. Northerners listening in the audience gasped in horror.

Webster next admonished the South. He had heard talk of secession, and he found this deplorable. Peaceful secession was a pipe dream. The separation of the United States into two or more republics living peacefully alongside each other was impossible and must never be attempted.

Then, after an eloquent appeal for patriotism and national unity, he concluded and resumed his seat, having spoken for some three hours.[19]

As soon as Webster sat down, Calhoun rose. As much as the Massachusetts senator's speech had been a betrayal of a vast number of his constituents, it was still not good enough for Calhoun. "Am I to understand him, that no degree of oppression, no outrage, no broken faith, can produce the destruction of this Union?" came the South Carolinian's weak and hollow voice. "No, sir!" Calhoun continued. "The Union can be broken. Great moral causes will break it, if they go on; and it can only be preserved by justice, good faith, and a rigid adherence to the Constitution."

Webster had clearly come out in favor of the compromise, and other proponents of the compromise, in the North and in the border states, heaped praise on him as news of his speech, including verbatim copies, spread rapidly across the country. Northeastern businessmen whose cotton mills processed the cotton grown by the slaves were happy to see the great Massachusetts senator standing in support of peace, tranquillity, and good profits. One thousand prominent Bostonians published a letter in support of Webster in the *Boston Courier,* and several hundred New York businessmen sent him another letter of support and a gold watch. Southerners praised the speech, a North Carolina newspaper hailing it as "the great speech from Mr. Webster."[20]

Reaction was much different among even moderate opponents of slavery. *The Boston Daily Atlas,* a Whig paper, moderate on sectional issues and previously supportive of Webster, sadly disagreed with nearly every point of his speech. Abolitionists were less measured in their response. The *Boston Emancipator and Republican* discussed the speech under the heading "Webster's Servility—Massachusetts Disgraced." Webster's betrayal was likened to that of Benedict Arnold and even of Lucifer himself.[21] John Greenleaf Whittier expressed the feelings of abolitionists most poignantly in his poem "Ichabod," the title of which was a Hebrew name from the Old Testament meaning "the glory is departed":

> *So fallen! So lost! The light withdrawn*
> *Which once he wore!*
> *The glory from his gray hairs gone*
> *Forevermore!*

Through several stanzas Whittier urged his readers to react neither with rage nor with ridicule—"Revile him not, the Tempter hath / A snare for all"—but rather with sorrow. He concluded with three stanzas rich in allusions both to the Bible and to Milton:

> *Of all we loved and honored, naught*
> *Save power remains;*
> *A fallen angel's pride of thought, still strong in chains.*
>
> *All else is gone; from those great eyes*
> *The soul has fled:*
> *When faith is lost, when honor dies*
> *The man is dead!*
>
> *Then, pay the reverence of old days*
> *To his dead fame;*
> *Walk backward, with averted gaze,*
> *And hide the shame!*[22]

Massachusetts congressman Horace Mann read the entire poem to the House of Representatives.[23]

And the debate went on. Not all northerners were as ready as Webster to prostrate themselves to southern demands and threats of disunion. One who was not was William H. Seward. Though a man of somewhat flexible principles, Seward knew what his constituents expected and did his best to deliver. He was no great orator, and no large crowds packed the gallery to hear his speech. He presented the views of the antislavery men of the North. "Yes; let California come in, in her robes of freedom," he said. No compromise was necessary for that purpose, and he would vote for none. The Fugitive Slave Law was immoral, and he would not vote for it either. Most shocking, in the midst of what was in many ways a very dry speech, he said, "There is a higher law than the Constitution."[24]

That statement aroused outrage among southerners and backers of the compromise, despite—or perhaps because of—the fact that the overwhelming majority of Americans did in fact believe that the law of God was superior to the Constitution. Those who wanted tolerance for slavery were particularly quick to denounce what Clay contemptuously called Seward's "wild, reckless and abominable theories," lest the American people, or at least those of them not unalterably committed to slavery, start to reflect on the truth of what the New York senator had said. Southern newspapers raged. The speech was, a Mississippi newspaper sneered, "a hypocritical appeal to the canting fanaticism of the North."

Southern senators rushed to express their outrage to Taylor, who hastily directed the editor of the *Republic,* the official organ of his administration, to lose no time in distancing him from anything that smacked of "higher law."[25]

Calhoun died quietly at his Washington lodgings on March 31, and the Senate paused for several days to observe his funeral. Clay and Webster served as two of his pallbearers, and they and others eulogized him in extravagant terms. "When," Clay asked rhetorically, "will that great vacancy . . . be filled by an equal amount of ability, patriotism, and devotion, to what he conceived to be the best interests of his country?" Thomas Hart Benton was not among the public eulogizers, and privately he remarked, "Calhoun died with treason in his heart and on his lips." But Benton would not denounce him publicly. "When God Almighty lays his hand upon a man, sir, I take mine off."[26]

Calhoun's strident insistence on the rights of slaveholders was more than represented in surviving southern senators, especially the forty-one-year-old Mississippian Jefferson Davis, who took up where Calhoun left off. Clay, who was himself a sick man, began to fear that little hope remained for his proposed compromise. Zachary Taylor was against it, with all the influence of the executive branch, maintaining that California should be admitted at once without any compromise. As the debates dragged on through April, Clay gave in to the urging of senatorial gadfly Henry S. Foote of Mississippi and agreed that all eight points of his compromise should be lumped into a single bill, the so-called Omnibus Bill, in a desperate effort to secure passage.[27]

Even taking that modest step required days of parliamentary wrangling. Emotions became still further aroused, especially where Foote was concerned. The annoying Mississippian made a sneering comment to freshman Arkansas senator Solon Borland on a Washington street and in return received a punch in the face. A few days later Foote became abusive to Benton on the Senate floor, calling the Missouri senator a blackguard, devoid of honor, who was too old and cowardly to fight a duel with him. This was unwise of Foote, who had suffered wounds in a number of duels but had never yet hit his opponent in a single one of them. When Foote continued to abuse Benton in the next day's session, the Missourian jumped up and charged him. Foote fled up the center aisle of the chamber, drawing a revolver, amid shouts for order and the constant pounding of Vice President Fillmore's gavel. Other senators succeeded in disarming Foote and restraining Benton, and eventually order was restored.[28]

The compromise proposals fared no better in the form of the Omnibus Bill. Indeed, it proved even more difficult to pass the large, clumsy piece of legislation, which, instead of giving everyone something to like, seemed to give every senator something to hate. In fiery debates Clay denounced the president and sparred vigorously, angrily, with opponents from both North and South, those who rejected the compromise because it was too friendly to slavery and those who rejected it because it was not friendly enough, yet he and his coterie of centrist senators could get nowhere. Southerners demanded, at a minimum, the extension of the Missouri Compromise line to the Pacific, dividing California into two states, free to the north and slave to the south.[29]

The nation seemed to teeter on the brink of civil war. Reports arrived in Washington that Texas was preparing for the military invasion of New Mexico. Taylor vowed to fight and sent reinforcements to the army garrisons in New Mexico. If necessary, he said, he would go there himself, "before those people shall go into that country or have a foot of that territory." The other slave states would almost certainly have backed Texas with armed force.[30]

Then on June 3 delegates from most of the slave states met in a convention at Nashville, Tennessee. The concept for the convention was an orphan idea of Calhoun's; he had called for a convention in Mississippi the previous year, which had in turn called for the Nashville convention. Its purpose was to agree on means of resistance by the slave states against northern aggression in the form of the Wilmot Proviso. Southern state legislatures had dispatched most of the delegations, and it was understood that the most likely means of resistance would be secession. The delegates met for eight days before adjourning on June 11, and though they stepped back from calling for secession, they did endorse the demand for the extension of the Thirty-six Thirty Line, with an ominous suggestion that they might assemble again that fall if the situation seemed to require it.[31]

The dog days came to Washington, and the senators sweltered on in their debates. Cholera would likely begin its depredations in the capital very soon, but no resolution seemed in sight. A delegation of compromise-minded southern Whigs appealed to Taylor in late June, but the president remained firm.[32]

The Fourth of July that year saw the ceremony for the laying of the cornerstone of the Washington Monument, and the president was in attendance. The day was oppressively hot, and Taylor mentioned having a headache and feeling dizzy before leaving his carriage at the monument site. Nonetheless, he sat on the sun-drenched platform for three hours, including a wearisome two-hour Henry Foote speech. Back at the White House, Taylor compensated himself by downing prodigious amounts of cherries, wild berries, iced milk, and iced water. That evening he suffered a severe attack of gastroenteritis, with cramps, vomiting, and diarrhea, and canceled his attendance at a party. In the days that followed, fever set in, and the president's condition looked grim. Anxious crowds kept vigil outside the White House, receiving hourly updates on his condition. In the predawn hours of July 9, the old warrior rallied. Church bells rang in response to the good news, and happy crowds lit bonfires. Shortly after midday, however, he took a sudden and dramatic turn for the worse, and the physicians gave up hope. Congress adjourned early that afternoon in respect, and at 10:35 that night Taylor expired. His last words were "I am prepared; I have endeavored to do my duty." A bell at the State Department tolled out the news around midnight, and soon all across the city the bells that had celebrated the president's apparent recovery less than twenty-four hours before rang again, this time in mourning.[33]

For only the second time in the history of the Republic, a president had died in office. Portly, dapper Millard Fillmore took the oath of office in a somber ceremony in the House chamber. Taylor received an impressive state funeral, with Winfield Scott on hand, resplendent in full uniform, and an honor guard of fifteen hundred troops. Public mourning was profound, for Taylor had been not only the chief magistrate but also one of the foremost heroes of the recent war. Bands played, bells tolled, and cannon boomed in salute as the president's remains were borne to a temporary resting place, pending removal to the family burying ground in Kentucky when cooler weather should come.[34]

The Omnibus Bill scarcely survived the president who had opposed it. By the end of the month its senatorial foes had succeeded in parliamentary maneuvers to take it apart and discard the pieces. The compromise seemed to be dead. Not quite despairing but feeling that after speaking in defense of the measure some seventy times on the Senate floor he could do no more for it, the ailing Henry Clay left Washington for the more healthful climate of Newport, Rhode Island.[35]

But the compromise was not dead. Out of the wreckage of the Omnibus Bill, thirty-six-year-old Illinois senator Stephen A. Douglas, an early and enthusiastic supporter of compromise, took all eight separate parts and, much as Clay had originally intended, began to work them through Congress in ones and twos. A bill for organizing the Utah Terri-

tory on the basis of popular sovereignty passed quickly. Another for settling the Texas–New Mexico boundary dispute with a handsome payment to Texas followed soon thereafter. The California statehood bill
passed with thirty-four yeas, only four of them from southern senators.
The other pieces of the compromise followed in one bill after another,
and each passed. By the end of August, what would come to be called the
Compromise of 1850 had passed the Senate and was headed for the
House. By the end of the first week in September, that body had added
its approval, and the legislation was signed by an eager President Fillmore. Cannon salutes, fireworks, and parades celebrated the accomplishment that most Americans believed would bring peace and union for
their time.[36]

How had Douglas succeeded in one month where the great Clay had
failed in six? Congressional fatigue and rising fear of secession had
helped pave the way. So too had a newly supportive White House, for
unlike Taylor, Fillmore was a compromiser. Most important was Douglas's insight in keeping the pieces separate or uniting them in well-
conceived small packages. This allowed him to use shifting coalitions to
pass the different measures. Only five senators voted for every piece of
the compromise, and the ratio was similar in the House. A majority of
northerners voted against the Fugitive Slave Act, and a large majority
of southerners voted against California statehood. But Douglas and his
small band of compromisers voted first with one sectional bloc and then
with the other to push the compromise through, piece by piece.[37]

The public at large received the Compromise of 1850 with a collective
sigh of relief. Few Americans wanted to see the Union break up if they
could feel that their rights were reasonably respected within it. The fact
that Congress had finally worked out a compromise seemed to indicate
that such was the case. The public received this reassurance gratefully.
Slave controversy seemed to have been banished from the national political arena. The threatened second gathering of the Nashville convention,
or some successor gathering for the purpose of orchestrating southern
secession, did not take place.

And yet the settlement of 1850 was a mirage. In contrast to previous
compromises, it did not come about as a result of adherents of two contending positions reaching the conclusion that they were satisfied to meet
each other halfway. A large majority of the members of Congress had
held steadfastly to the position that at least some elements of the compromise were completely unacceptable, regardless of what inducements
might be placed alongside them. That majority, though holding to oppo-

site positions, had never backed down, never accepted the key claims of the opposing side, never compromised. In effect, the settlement of 1850 had not been a true compromise but rather a peace arrangement forced on the two contending parties by parliamentary legerdemain. It was a truce. It would delay a final showdown and give the country and its leaders a reprieve—of what length no one could say—during which they might or might not be able to change the course that history had taken during the 1840s and steer clear of national cataclysm.

When the decade of the 1840s had started, slavery was one issue among many in American national politics. It was a contentious issue, but one that politicians had succeeded in containing within safe boundaries. The two-party system had been a key element of that containment. It assured that each party, in order to be competitive with the other, would either suppress issues of sectional difference or else try to present them in a form that would be acceptable to both sections of the country. As the early futile political efforts of the abolitionists demonstrated, it was an effective system.

Territorial expansion was a far more exciting issue for most Americans. The American people had believed since before independence that it was their destiny to spread westward into the interior of the continent. As the nineteenth century dawned and matured, they came to believe that they and the free system of government they carried with them were meant to expand all the way across the continent to the shores of the Pacific. In the 1840s they had found expression for that belief in the words of John L. O'Sullivan and others, and they had found a way to make it happen. Or perhaps the way simply opened in front of them. An unstable Mexican government, a Texas boundary dispute, an ambitious president or two, and the sheer, unquenchable westering urge of countless ordinary Americans willing to take great risks in order to win better lives for themselves and their families had all combined to create a mighty surge of expansion by which the United States actually had "overspread the continent."

But there was a snake in this garden. The very surge of expansion that led to the realization of the long-held American dream of a continent-wide empire of liberty also served to intensify and focus the national disagreement over slavery to the point that none of the old political methods sufficed to contain it anymore. Acquiring new territory forced the question of what slavery's status would be in that new territory, and with that, the fatal flaw, the starkest inconsistency in America's system of free government, became impossible to evade. The crowning irony of the decade of the 1840s was that it brought the culmination of American hopes and thereby brought the country to the brink of the conflict it long had dreaded.

Tensions had been building, and the great clash might have come eventually even without the rapid expansion of that momentous decade. Perhaps gradual and peaceful change was as impossible as the permanent continuance of the country, in words Lincoln would frame eight years later, "half slave and half free." The events of the 1840s guaranteed that a clash would come sooner rather than later, and that it would henceforth be extremely difficult to avoid. The politicians had succeeded in cobbling together a political truce by the narrowest of margins, and even the man who had engineered its final passage, Stephen Douglas, did not realize how slender was the thread by which that sectional cease-fire hung—as he would demonstrate, to his grief and the country's, four years hence. The 1840s had brought the nation to the brink of civil war and left it teetering there precariously. At decade's end the chances of avoiding secession and war were drastically lower than they had seemed at its outset. America had reached its territorial culmination, but it was about to reap the fruits of its own internal contradiction.

NOTES

CHAPTER I
THE LOG CABIN AND HARD CIDER CAMPAIGN

1. Thomas Jefferson to John Holmes, April 22, 1820, Manuscript Division, Library of Congress. Donald B. Cole, *Martin Van Buren and the American Political System* (Princeton, N.J.: Princeton University Press, 1984), 37, 96, 127.
2. Robert Gray Gunderson, *The Log-Cabin Campaign* (Lexington: University of Kentucky Press, 1957), 113–14; Cole, *Martin Van Buren*, 9–31.
3. Cole, *Martin Van Buren*, 37, 96, 127; James C. Curtis, "In the Shadow of Old Hickory: The Political Travail of Martin Van Buren," *Journal of the Early Republic* 1, no. 3 (Autumn 1981): 256–57.
4. Norma Lois Peterson, *The Presidencies of William Henry Harrison and John Tyler* (Lawrence: University Press of Kansas, 1989), 21; Milton Friedman, *A Program for Monetary Stability* (New York: Fordham University Press, 1960), 10.
5. Cole, *Martin Van Buren*, 292, 297.
6. Theodore Roosevelt, quoted in H. W. Brands, *T.R.: The Last Romantic* (New York: Basic Books, 1997), 601.
7. Gunderson, *The Log-Cabin Campaign*, 57–58.
8. Robert V. Remini, *Henry Clay: Statesman for the Union* (New York: W. W. Norton, 1991), 549; Peterson, *Presidencies*, 21; Gunderson, *The Log-Cabin Campaign*, 43, 45–47, 58–64.
9. Gunderson, *The Log-Cabin Campaign*, 44–45, 47, 52–54, 58–64; Joel H. Silbey, *Martin Van Buren and the Emergence of American Popular Politics* (Lanham, Md.: Rowman and Littlefield, 2002), 143; Remini, *Henry Clay*, 539–46, 554.
10. Freeman Cleaves, *Old Tippecanoe: William Henry Harrison and His Time* (New York: Charles Scribner's Sons, 1939), 318; Peterson, *Presidencies*, 21, 24–26; Gunderson, *The Log-Cabin Campaign*, 57–62; Remini, *Henry Clay*, 548–52.
11. Cleaves, *Old Tippecanoe*, 5–29.
12. Cleaves, *Old Tippecanoe*, 30–102.
13. Cleaves, *Old Tippecanoe*, 102–318; Peterson, *Presidencies*, 18; Gunderson, *The Log-Cabin Campaign*, 111–12.
14. Gunderson, *The Log-Cabin Campaign*, 62; Cleaves, *Old Tippecanoe*, 318; Remini, *Henry Clay*, 552.
15. Dan Monroe, *The Republican Vision of John Tyler* (College Station: Texas A&M University Press, 2003), 84–87.
16. Silbey, *Martin Van Buren*, 137–38.
17. Peterson, *Presidencies*, 20, 26–27; Gunderson, *The Log-Cabin Campaign*, 62–64; Remini, *Henry Clay*, 553.

18. Peterson, *Presidencies*, 27; Cleaves, *Old Tippecanoe*, 319; Gunderson, *The Log-Cabin Campaign*, 65, 73.

19. Gunderson, *The Log-Cabin Campaign*, 93. On the positions of both national parties toward slavery within the South, see William J. Cooper Jr., *Liberty and Slavery: Southern Politics to 1860* (New York: McGraw-Hill, 1993).

20. Gunderson, *The Log-Cabin Campaign*, 68–69; Remini, *Henry Clay*, 554.

21. Remini, *Henry Clay*, 554–55.

22. Gunderson, *The Log-Cabin Campaign*, 68–69; Cleaves, *Old Tippecanoe*, 318; Remini, *Henry Clay*, 556.

23. Gunderson, *The Log-Cabin Campaign*, 74; Cleaves, *Old Tippecanoe*, 320–21.

24. *Daily National Intelligencer* (Washington, D.C.), December 20, 1839, issue 8377, col. C; *Fayetteville Observer* (Fayetteville, N.C.), January 1, 1840, issue 1178, col. C; *Raleigh Register, and North-Carolina Gazette* (Raleigh, N.C.), February 21, 1840, issue 17, col. C; *Tennessee Whig* (Jonesborough, Tenn.), March 5, 1840, issue 42, col. D; Gunderson, *The Log-Cabin Campaign*, 74–75.

25. Gunderson, *The Log-Cabin Campaign*, 94–95; Edward P. Crapol, *John Tyler: The Accidental President* (Chapel Hill: University of North Carolina Press, 2006), 18.

26. *Cleveland Daily Herald* (Cleveland, Ohio), July 13, 1840, issue 265, col. A; Gunderson, *The Log-Cabin Campaign*, 101–5; Cole, *Martin Van Buren*, 344–45.

27. Cole, *Martin Van Buren*, 345.

28. *Boston Courier* (Boston, Mass.), July 16, 1840, issue 1694, col. F; *Daily National Intelligencer* (Washington, D.C.), July 23, 1840, issue 8561, col. C, and July 30, 1840, issue 8567, col. D; *Fayetteville Observer* (Fayetteville, N.C.), July 29, 1840, issue 1208, col. A; Gunderson, *The Log-Cabin Campaign*, 105–7.

29. Gunderson, *The Log-Cabin Campaign*, 65.

30. *Daily National Intelligencer* (Washington, D.C.), May 1, 1840, issue 8490, col. E, and May 4, 1840, issue 8492, col. D; *Raleigh Register, and North-Carolina Gazette* (Raleigh, N.C.), May 1, 1840, issue 27, col. D; *Pennsylvania Inquirer and Daily Courier* (Philadelphia, Pa.), May 5, 1840, issue 108, col. B; *The North American and Daily Advertiser* (Philadelphia, Pa.), May 6, 1840, issue 347, col. B; Gunderson, *The Log-Cabin Campaign*, 1–3.

31. Gunderson, *The Log-Cabin Campaign*, 4.

32. Gunderson, *The Log-Cabin Campaign*, 4–5.

33. Gunderson, *The Log-Cabin Campaign*, 79–80.

34. Cleaves, *Old Tippecanoe*, 294.

35. Gunderson, *The Log-Cabin Campaign*, 79–83; Silbey, *Martin Van Buren*, 148.

36. Peterson, *Presidencies*, 27.

37. *Cleveland Daily Herald* (Cleveland, Ohio), June 13, 1840, issue 243, col. A.

38. *New-York Spectator* (New York, N.Y.), June 15, 1840, col. B; *Cleveland Daily Herald* (Cleveland, Ohio), June 15, 1840, issue 244, col. A; Cleaves, *Old Tippecanoe*, 324–25.

39. Silbey, *Martin Van Buren*, 143–44.

40. Remini, *Henry Clay*, 564.

41. *The Log Cabin* (New York, N.Y.), October 24, 1840, issue 26, col. A; *Cleveland Daily Herald* (Cleveland, Ohio), June 15, 1840, issue 244, col. A; Gunderson, *The Log-Cabin Campaign*, 131–34, 148; Cleaves, *Old Tippecanoe*, 325–26.

42. Gunderson, *The Log-Cabin Campaign*, 245–46; Peterson, *Presidencies*, 28–29; Silbey, *Martin Van Buren*; Crapol, *John Tyler*, 18; Cleaves, *Old Tippecanoe*, 326.

43. Merton L. Dillon, *The Abolitionists: The Growth of a Dissenting Minority* (De Kalb: Northern Illinois University Press, 1974), 131.

44. Peterson, *Presidencies*, 27.

45. Gunderson, *The Log-Cabin Campaign*, 253–55.

46. Cole, *Martin Van Buren*, 373; Crapol, *John Tyler*, 17.

47. Gunderson, *The Log-Cabin Campaign*, 246–47.

CHAPTER 2

TYLER, CLAY, AND THE DURABILITY OF THE TWO-PARTY SYSTEM

1. Norma Lois Peterson, *The Presidencies of William Henry Harrison and John Tyler* (Lawrence: University Press of Kansas, 1989), 31.

2. Freeman Cleaves, *Old Tippecanoe: William Henry Harrison and His Time* (New York: Charles Scribner's Sons, 1939), 329; Peterson, *Presidencies*, 31–32; Robert V. Remini, *Henry Clay: Statesman for the Union* (New York: W. W. Norton, 1991), 568–69.

3. Peterson, *Presidencies*, 31–32; Dan Monroe, *The Republican Vision of John Tyler* (College Station: Texas A&M University Press, 2003), 83–84; Cleaves, *Old Tippecanoe*, 329–30.

4. Remini, *Henry Clay*, 571–72.

5. Peterson, *Presidencies*, 32–33; Remini, *Henry Clay*, 571, 574.

6. Cleaves, *Old Tippecanoe*, 334; Remini, *Henry Clay*, 572.

7. Cleaves, *Old Tippecanoe*, 334–36; Peterson, *Presidencies*, 33–36.

8. Cleaves, *Old Tippecanoe*, 336.

9. Peterson, *Presidencies*, 33–36; Cleaves, *Old Tippecanoe*, 336–37.

10. Peterson, *Presidencies*, 37–39; Monroe, *Republican Vision*, 84; Cleaves, *Old Tippecanoe*, 338–39; Remini, *Henry Clay*, 572.

11. Monroe, *Republican Vision*, 80; Peterson, *Presidencies*, 37–39.

12. Peterson, *Presidencies*, 37–39; Cleaves, *Old Tippecanoe*, 339; Remini, *Henry Clay*, 575–76.

13. Peterson, *Presidencies*, 41–42; Monroe, *Republican Vision*, 80; Cleaves, *Old Tippecanoe*, 341–42.

14. Cleaves, *Old Tippecanoe*, 342–43.

15. Edward P. Crapol, *John Tyler: The Accidental President* (Chapel Hill: University of North Carolina Press, 2006), 8–11.

16. Peterson, *Presidencies*, 45–50; Crapol, *John Tyler*, 11–13.

17. Crapol, *John Tyler*, 30–41; Remini, *Henry Clay*, 582.

18. Peterson, *Presidencies*, 54–55, 57; Crapol, *John Tyler*, 16; Remini, *Henry Clay*, 580–81.

19. Peterson, *Presidencies*, 59–60; Monroe, *Republican Vision*, 88–89; Remini, *Henry Clay*, 581.

20. Peterson, *Presidencies*, 59–60; Monroe, *Republican Vision*, 83.

21. Remini, *Henry Clay*, 582–83.

22. Remini, *Henry Clay*, 583–84.

23. Remini, *Henry Clay*, 578–79, 584–86.

24. Peterson, *Presidencies*, 63–65; Monroe, *Republican Vision*, 93–94; Remini, *Henry Clay*, 586–87.

25. Crapol, *John Tyler*, 19; Remini, *Henry Clay*, 587.

26. Peterson, *Presidencies*, 65–70; Monroe, *Republican Vision*, 95–99; Remini, *Henry Clay*, 587–90.

27. Monroe, *Republican Vision*, 103–4; Remini, *Henry Clay*, 590.

28. Monroe, *Republican Vision*, 103–4.

29. Crapol, *John Tyler*, 20.

30. Peterson, *Presidencies*, 71–90; Monroe, *Republican Vision*, 100.

31. Remini, *Henry Clay*, 594–96.

32. Peterson, *Presidencies*, 91; Monroe, *Republican Vision*, 101; Remini, *Henry Clay*, 597.

33. Monroe, *Republican Vision*, 108.

34. Monroe, *Republican Vision*, 108.

35. Peterson, *Presidencies*, 91.

36. Peterson, *Presidencies*, 89–90.

37. Peterson, *Presidencies*, 95–112; Monroe, *Republican Vision*, 140–41; Remini, *Henry Clay*, 600–10.

38. Peterson, *Presidencies*, 107.

CHAPTER 3

ABOLITIONISM

1. John R. McKivigan, *The War Against Proslavery Religion: Abolitionism and the Northern Churches, 1830–1865* (Ithaca, N.Y.: Cornell University Press, 1984), 80, 116, 132; Merton L. Dillon, *The Abolitionists: The Growth of a Dissenting Minority* (De Kalb: Northern Illinois University Press, 1974), 30.

2. Dillon, *The Abolitionists*, 36.

3. Dillon, *The Abolitionists*, 38–39.

4. Dillon, *The Abolitionists*, 39–40.

5. William Lee Miller, *Arguing About Slavery: The Great Battle in the United States Congress* (New York: Alfred A. Knopf, 1996), 93–103; James C. Curtis, "In the Shadow of Old Hickory: The Political Travail of Martin Van Buren," *Journal of the Early Republic* 1, no. 3 (Autumn 1981): 256–57; Edward P. Crapol, *John Tyler: The Accidental President* (Chapel Hill: University of North Carolina Press, 2006), 43–49.

6. Miller, *Arguing About Slavery*, 8–454; Donald B. Cole, *Martin Van Buren and the American Political System* (Princeton, N.J.: Princeton University Press, 1984), 96, 280–81; Curtis, "Shadow," 257; Henry H. Simms, *Emotion at High Tide: Abolition as a Controversial Factor, 1830–1845* (Richmond, Va.: William Byrd Press, 1960), 93–119, 144–70.

7. Dillon, *The Abolitionists*, 134–35.

8. Dillon, *The Abolitionists*, 135.

9. Dillon, *The Abolitionists*, 135.

10. Stanley Harrold, *American Abolitionists* (Harlow, England: Pearson Education, 2001), 67–68; *The Liberator* (Boston, Mass.), November 30, 1849, issue 48, col. E; McKivigan, *Proslavery Religion*, 38, 162–63. In 1853 Michigan Central College moved from Spring Arbor to Hillsdale, Michigan, and changed its name to suit. It is still in operation and still maintains its heritage of eschewing all racial discrimination.

11. Dillon, *The Abolitionists*, 150–52.

12. Harrold, *American Abolitionists*, 36.

13. Harrold, *American Abolitionists*, 37; Simms, *Emotion at High Tide*, 171–79; McKivigan, *Proslavery Religion*, 61–73.

14. Chris Padgett, "Hearing the Anti-Slavery Rank-and-File: The Wesleyan Methodist Schism of 1843," *Journal of the Early Republic* 12, no. 1 (Spring 1992): 65–67, 70; Walter Brownlow Posey, "Influence of Slavery upon the Methodist Church in the Early South and Southwest," *The Mississippi Valley Historical Review* 17, no. 4 (March 1931): 530–39; Lewis M. Purifoy, "The Southern Methodist Church and the Proslavery Argument," *The Journal of Southern History* 32, no. 3 (August 1966): 325; McKivigan, *Proslavery Religion*, 25.

15. Lucius C. Matlack, *The Life of Rev. Orange Scott* (New York: C. Prindle and L. C. Matlack, 1847), 31; Padgett, "Hearing," 69; Henry C. Sheldon, *History of the Christian Church*, 5 vols. (Peabody, Mass.: Hendrickson, 1988), 5:239–40.

16. Sheldon, *Christian Church*, 5:239–41.

17. Sheldon, *Christian Church*, 5:239–41; Nathan Bangs, *History of the Methodist Episcopal Church*, 4 vols. (New York: G. Lane and P. P. Sandford for the Methodist Episcopal Church, 1853), vol. 4, chap. 15.

18. McKivigan, *Proslavery Religion*, 84–85; Bangs, *Methodist Episcopal Church*, vol. 4, chap. 15; Matlack, *Orange Scott*, 166–86.

19. Padgett, "Hearing," 64.

20. Orange Scott, *The Grounds of Secession from the M. E. Church* (New York: C. Prindle, 1848), 3–191; Matlack, *Orange Scott*, 187–215; Sheldon, *Christian Church*, 5:241; *Vermont Chronicle* (Bellows Falls, Vt.), November 6, 1844; issue 45, p. 178, col. B; Padgett, "Hearing," 66, 71, 74–84; McKivigan, *Proslavery Religion*, 85.

21. George G. Smith, *The Life and Letters of James Osgood Andrew* (Nashville, Tenn.: Southern Methodist Publishing House, 1882), 336–39; Padgett, "Hearing," 76; McKivigan, *Proslavery Religion*, 85–87.

22. Smith, *James Osgood Andrew*, 338–81; Purifoy, "Southern Methodist Church," 325–26; Simms, *Emotion at High Tide*, 211.

23. Dillon, *The Abolitionists*, 157; McKivigan, *Proslavery Religion*, 26.

24. Sheldon, *Christian Church*, 5:292; C. C. Goen, "Broken Churches, Broken Nation: Regional Religion and North-South Alienation in Antebellum America," *Church History* 52, no. 1 (March 1983): 24; McKivigan, *Proslavery Religion*, 87–88.

25. Simms, *Emotion at High Tide*, 200; McKivigan, *Proslavery Religion*, 84.

26. Goen, "Broken Churches, Broken Nation," 22; Simms, *Emotion at High Tide*, 212.

CHAPTER 4
THE OREGON TRAIL

1. Ray Allen Billington, *Westward Expansion: A History of the American Frontier*, 4th ed. (New York: Macmillan, 1974), 399–406.

2. Billington, *Westward Expansion*, 432–33; David Dary, *The Oregon Trail: An American Saga* (New York: Alfred A. Knopf, 2004), 8–9; David Sievert Lavender, *Westward Vision: The Story of the Oregon Trail* (New York: McGraw-Hill, 1963), 26, 62–67, 82–127; Stephen E. Ambrose, *Undaunted Courage: Meriwether Lewis, Thomas Jefferson, and the Opening of the American West* (New York: Simon and Schuster, 1996).

3. Billington, *Westward Expansion*, 438; Dary, *The Oregon Trail*, 56–57.

4. Billington, *Westward Expansion*, 438–39; Dary, *The Oregon Trail*, 57; John B. Horner, *Oregon: Her History, Her Great Men, Her Literature* (Portland, Ore.: J. K. Gill, 1919), 69.

5. Billington, *Westward Expansion*, 439–42; Randol B. Fletcher, "Oregon or the Grave," *Columbia Magazine* (Washington Historical Society, Tacoma, Washington), Winter 2006; Dary, *The Oregon Trail*, 61–62; Lavender, *Westward Vision*, 271, 278–79; Horner, *Oregon*, 75.

6. Billington, *Westward Expansion*, 441–42; Dary, *The Oregon Trail*, 62–63; Bernard DeVoto, *Across the Wide Missouri* (Boston: Houghton Mifflin, 1947), 246.

7. Billington, *Westward Expansion*, 431.

8. Horner, *Oregon*, 79, 82–83; Ralph Friedman, *Tracking Down Oregon* (Caldwell, Idaho: Caxton Printers, 1978), 105–6; Dale L. Walker, *Pacific Destiny: The Three-Century Journey to the Oregon Country* (New York: Forge, 2000), 303–4; S. A. Clarke, *Pioneer Days of Oregon History*, 2 vols. (Portland, Ore.: J. K. Gill, 1905), 2:445–46; Fletcher, "Oregon or the Grave"; DeVoto, *Across the Wide Missouri*, 445; Lavender, *Westward Vision*, 332.

9. Thomas J. Farnham, *Travels in the Great Western Prairies, the Anahuac and Rocky Mountains, and in the Oregon Territory*, 2 vols. (London: Richard Bentley, 1843), 1:45; Fletcher, "Oregon or the Grave"; DeVoto, *Across the Wide Missouri*, 380–81; Friedman, *Tracking Down Oregon*, 106.

10. Farnham, *Travels*, 46–55; Clarke, *Pioneer Days*, 2:446; Fletcher, "Oregon or the Grave"; DeVoto, *Across the Wide Missouri*, 381; Friedman, *Tracking Down Oregon*, 107; Lavender, *Westward Vision*, 333.

11. Farnham, *Travels*, 67.

12. Farnham, *Travels*, 58, 65–80; Clarke, *Pioneer Days*, 2:442; Fletcher, "Oregon or the Grave"; DeVoto, *Across the Wide Missouri*, 381; Friedman, *Tracking Down Oregon*, 106–7; Lavender, *Westward Vision*, 333–34.

13. Farnham, *Travels*, 90–91; Clarke, *Pioneer Days*, 2:443; Fletcher, "Oregon or the Grave"; DeVoto, *Across the Wide Missouri*, 381; Walker, *Pacific Destiny*, 304; Lavender, *Westward Vision*, 334.

14. Farnham, *Travels*, 96–98; Clarke, *Pioneer Days*, 2:443, 446, 448; Fletcher, "Oregon or the Grave"; Farnham, *Travels;* Walker, *Pacific Destiny*, 304; DeVoto, *Across the Wide Missouri*, 381–82; Friedman, *Tracking Down Oregon*, 107–8; Lavender, *Westward Vision*, 334.

15. Clarke, *Pioneer Days*, 2:443, 446, 448; Fletcher, "Oregon or the Grave"; Farnham, *Travels*, 99–380; Walker, *Pacific Destiny*, 304; DeVoto, *Across the Wide Missouri*, 381–82; Friedman, *Tracking Down Oregon*, 107–8.

16. Fletcher, "Oregon or the Grave"; Clarke, *Pioneer Days*, 2:406, 443.

17. Edward P. Crapol, *John Tyler: The Accidental President* (Chapel Hill: University of North Carolina Press, 2006), 20–26.

18. Ferol Egan, *Frémont: Explorer for a Restless Nation* (Garden City, N.Y.: Doubleday, 1977), 50–57.

19. Egan, *Frémont*, 8–48, 60–61; John Charles Frémont, *Memoirs of My Life* (New York: Cooper Square Press, 2001), 18–29; Charles Wentworth Upham, *The Life, Explorations, and Public Services of John Charles Frémont* (New York: Livermore and Rudd, 1856), 11; Samuel M. Smucker, *The Life of Col. John Charles Fremont and His Narrative of Explorations and Adventures in Kansas, Nebraska, Oregon and California* (New York: Miller, Orton and Mulligan, 1856), 7–13.

20. Egan, *Frémont*, 8–48, 60–61; Smucker, *John Charles Fremont*, 12–15; Frémont, *Memoirs*, 30–78.

21. Oliver Hampton Smith, *Early Indiana Trials and Sketches* (Cincinnati: Moore, Wilstach, Keys, 1858), 571.

22. Clarke, *Pioneer Days,* 2:406–7; Dary, *The Oregon Trail,* 78; Walker, *Pacific Destiny,* 315.

23. Clarke, *Pioneer Days,* 2:407; Walker, *Pacific Destiny,* 316; Billington, *Westward Expansion,* 445–46.

24. Lansford W. Hastings, *The Emigrants' Guide to Oregon and California, Containing Scenes and Incidents of a Party of Oregon Emigrants* (New York: Da Capo Press, 1969), 6–7; Clarke, *Pioneer Days,* 2:407; Walker, *Pacific Destiny,* 316; Dary, *The Oregon Trail,* 78; Billington, *Westward Expansion,* 446; Lavender, *Westward Vision,* 354.

25. Hastings, *Emigrants' Guide,* 8; Walker, *Pacific Destiny,* 311.

26. Dary, *The Oregon Trail,* 81.

27. Hastings, *Emigrants' Guide,* 9; Lavender, *Westward Vision,* 353, 355; Dary, *The Oregon Trail,* 79; Walker, *Pacific Destiny,* 316.

28. Hastings, *Emigrants' Guide,* 9; Lavender, *Westward Vision,* 353, 355–56; Dary, *The Oregon Trail,* 79.

29. Dary, *The Oregon Trail,* 60.

30. Hastings, *Emigrants' Guide,* 10–17; Clarke, *Pioneer Days,* 2:461; Lavender, *Westward Vision,* 356.

31. Hastings, *Emigrants' Guide,* 10–17; Lavender, *Westward Vision,* 356; Egan, *Frémont,* 87–88; Frémont, *Memoirs,* 114–16.

32. Egan, *Frémont,* 101–18; Dary, *The Oregon Trail,* 83; Walker, *Pacific Destiny,* 331; Smucker, *John Charles Fremont,* 163.

33. Hastings, *Emigrants' Guide,* 19–20; Clarke, *Pioneer Days,* 2:461–63.

34. Hastings, *Emigrants' Guide,* 20–21; Walker, *Pacific Destiny,* 316.

35. Lavender, *Westward Vision,* 358; Clarke, *Pioneer Days,* 2:461–63.

36. Clarke, *Pioneer Days,* 2:407.

37. Clarke, *Pioneer Days,* 2:473–75; Walker, *Pacific Destiny,* 317; Lavender, *Westward Vision,* 361–62.

38. Clarke, *Pioneer Days,* 2:473–75; Lavender, *Westward Vision,* 361–62.

39. Clarke, *Pioneer Days,* 2:473–75; Lavender, *Westward Vision,* 361–62; Walker, *Pacific Destiny,* 317–18.

40. Billington, *Westward Expansion,* 443; Lavender, *Westward Vision,* 344, 359–62; Walker, *Pacific Destiny,* 315, 317–18.

41. Clarke, *Pioneer Days,* 2:473–75; Walker, *Pacific Destiny,* 318.

42. Billington, *Westward Expansion,* 447; Lavender, *Westward Vision,* 367–68; Walker, *Pacific Destiny,* 360.

43. Walker, *Pacific Destiny,* 359–61.

44. Billington, *Westward Expansion,* 447; Hubert Howe Bancroft, *History of Oregon* (San Francisco: History Company, 1890), 395; Lavender, *Westward Vision,* 370; Dary, *The Oregon Trail,* 80; Walker, *Pacific Destiny,* 342.

45. Lavender, *Westward Vision,* 370; Dary, *The Oregon Trail,* 84–85.

46. Lavender, *Westward Vision,* 369–70; Bancroft, *History of Oregon,* 396.

47. Lavender, *Westward Vision,* 370, 372.

48. Lavender, *Westward Vision,* 371–72.

49. Lavender, *Westward Vision,* 372.

50. Lavender, *Westward Vision,* 373; Billington, *Westward Expansion,* 447.

51. Lavender, *Westward Vision,* 366, 373; Dary, *The Oregon Trail,* 84; Egan, *Frémont,* 123.

52. Lavender, *Westward Vision*, 373–74; Bancroft, *History of Oregon*, 396–97.

53. Lavender, *Westward Vision*, 375–76; Clarke, *Pioneer Days*, 2:475–85; Walker, *Pacific Destiny*, 368; Bancroft, *History of Oregon*, 397.

54. Lavender, *Westward Vision*, 343, 376–79; Clarke, *Pioneer Days*, 2:475–85; Walker, *Pacific Destiny*, 368–69; Bancroft, *History of Oregon*, 399.

55. Clarke, *Pioneer Days*, 2:475–85; Bancroft, *History of Oregon*, 401–16.

56. Clarke, *Pioneer Days*, 2:454; Billington, *Westward Expansion*, 447.

57. Clarke, *Pioneer Days*, 2:454; Billington, *Westward Expansion*, 447; Bancroft, *History of Oregon*, 415.

CHAPTER 5
THE ALLURE AND THE DANGER OF CALIFORNIA

1. Ray Allen Billington, *Westward Expansion: A History of the American Frontier*, 4th ed. (New York: Macmillan, 1974), 469–80; Bernard DeVoto, *The Year of Decision: 1846* (Boston: Little, Brown, 1943), 19.

2. Richard Henry Dana Jr., *Two Years Before the Mast* (New York: D. Appleton, 1912). Quotation on p. 186.

3. Billington, *Westward Expansion*, 481.

4. Billington, *Westward Expansion*, 481.

5. Billington, *Westward Expansion*, 482.

6. Lansford W. Hastings, *The Emigrants' Guide to Oregon and California, Containing Scenes and Incidents of a Party of Oregon Emigrants* (New York: Da Capo Press, 1969).

7. Gene A. Smith, *Thomas Ap Catesby Jones: Commodore of Manifest Destiny* (Annapolis, Md.: Naval Institute Press, 2000), 105–20.

8. Dale L. Walker, *Pacific Destiny: The Three-Century Journey to the Oregon Country* (New York: Forge, 2000), 332.

9. John Charles Frémont, *Memoirs of My Life* (New York: Cooper Square Press, 2001), 198–223.

10. Ferol Egan, *Frémont: Explorer for a Restless Nation* (Garden City, N.Y.: Doubleday, 1977), 147–54; Frémont, *Memoirs*, 230–35.

11. Egan, *Frémont*, 157–223; Walker, *Pacific Destiny*, 332; Samuel M. Smucker, *The Life of Col. John Charles Fremont and His Narrative of Explorations and Adventures in Kansas, Nebraska, Oregon and California* (New York: Miller, Orton and Mulligan, 1856), 372–401; Frémont, *Memoirs*, 233–351.

12. John S. D. Eisenhower, *So Far from God: The U.S. War with Mexico, 1846–1848* (New York: Random House, 1989), 203; Walker, *Pacific Destiny*, 332–33; Egan, *Frémont*, 224–25; Thomas J. Schoonover, *The Life and Times of General John A. Sutter* (Sacramento: D. Johnson, 1895), 1–28; Smucker, *John Charles Fremont*, 401–23; Albert L. Hurtado, *John Sutter: A Life on the North American Frontier* (Norman: University of Oklahoma Press, 2006), 127–29; H. W. Brands, *The Age of Gold: The California Gold Rush and the New American Dream* (New York: Random House, 2002), 4; Frémont, *Memoirs*, 351–54.

13. Egan, *Frémont*, 227–32; Schoonover, *John A. Sutter*, 27–28.

14. Eliza P. Donner Houghton, *The Expedition of the Donner Party and Its Tragic Fate* (Lincoln: University of Nebraska Press, 1997), 1–2, 4.

15. Charles Fayette McGlashan, *History of the Donner Party: A Tragedy of the Sierra* (Sacramento: H. S. Crocker, 1907), 27; DeVoto, *The Year of Decision*, 119–21.

16. McGlashan, *History*, 25–26; Houghton, *Expedition*, 7–8, 11–18, 24–26.
17. Hubert H. Bancroft, *California Inter Pocula* (San Francisco: History Company, 1888), 94.
18. McGlashan, *History*, 29; Houghton, *Expedition*, 30–33; Bancroft, *California Inter Pocula*, 94.
19. McGlashan, *History*, 31; Houghton, *Expedition*, 33–34.
20. McGlashan, *History*, 31–32; Houghton, *Expedition*, 34–35.
21. Houghton, *Expedition*, 35–36; Bancroft, *California Inter Pocula*, 95.
22. McGlashan, *History*, 32–33; Houghton, *Expedition*, 36–37; Bancroft, *California Inter Pocula*, 95.
23. McGlashan, *History*, 33–39; Houghton, *Expedition*, 40–44; Bancroft, *California Inter Pocula*, 95–96.
24. McGlashan, *History*, 39–56; Houghton, *Expedition*, 37, 44–49, 58.
25. McGlashan, *History*, 51–55; Houghton, *Expedition*, 54–56; Bancroft, *California Inter Pocula*, 98.
26. McGlashan, *History*, 54–56; Houghton, *Expedition*, 56–58.
27. McGlashan, *History*, 56–57; Houghton, *Expedition*, 59; Bancroft, *California Inter Pocula*, 98–99.
28. McGlashan, *History*, 57–63; Houghton, *Expedition*, 60–61.
29. McGlashan, *History*, 64–112; Houghton, *Expedition*, 77–90; Bancroft, *California Inter Pocula*, 99–102.
30. McGlashan, *History*, 112–224; Houghton, *Expedition*, 61–76.

CHAPTER 6
THE MORMONS AND THEIR MIGRATION

1. Richard Abanes, *One Nation Under Gods: A History of the Mormon Church* (New York: Four Walls Eight Windows, 2002), 3–4, 9–10, 28; Leonard J. Arrington and Davis Bitton, *The Mormon Experience: A History of the Latter-day Saints* (New York: Vintage Books, 1980), 3–5; Robert V. Remini, *Joseph Smith* (New York: Penguin, 2002), 1–8, 17; Alice Felt Tyler, *Freedom's Ferment: Phases of American Social History to 1860* (Minneapolis: University of Minnesota Press, 1944), 68–69, 86.
2. Abanes, *One Nation Under Gods*, 28; Remini, *Joseph Smith*, 48–51; Ernest H. Taves, *Trouble Enough: Joseph Smith and the Book of Mormon* (Buffalo, N.Y.: Prometheus Books, 1984), 17–24; Tyler, *Freedom's Ferment*, 87–88; Arrington and Bitton dispute the accounts of Smith's treasure-digging activities (*The Mormon Experience*, 10–11).
3. Arrington and Bitton, *The Mormon Experience*, 8–9, 12–14; Remini, *Joseph Smith*, 38, 52–56; Taves, *Trouble Enough*, 25–31; Tyler, *Freedom's Ferment*, 89–90.
4. Remini, *Joseph Smith*, 57–71; Taves, *Trouble Enough*, 34–43; Richard Lyman Bushman, *Joseph Smith: Rough Stone Rolling* (New York: Alfred A. Knopf, 2005), 71; Tyler, *Freedom's Ferment*, 90.
5. Taves, *Trouble Enough*, 34–48; Tyler, *Freedom's Ferment*, 90–93.
6. Arrington and Bitton, *The Mormon Experience*, 21; Remini, *Joseph Smith*, 65–100, 120–21; Taves, *Trouble Enough*, 62–75, 99–100; Bushman, *Joseph Smith*, 180–83, 323–25; Tyler, *Freedom's Ferment*, 94–97.
7. Bushman, *Joseph Smith*, 178–80; Arrington and Bitton, *The Mormon Experience*, 21; Remini, *Joseph Smith*, 108–17; Taves, *Trouble Enough*, 91–97; Tyler, *Freedom's Ferment*, 97–98.

8. Arrington and Bitton, *The Mormon Experience,* 21; Remini, *Joseph Smith,* 108–17; Taves, *Trouble Enough,* 91–97; Bushman, *Joseph Smith,* 235–50.

9. Remini, *Joseph Smith,* 112–13, 115–20; Taves, *Trouble Enough,* 81–82; Bushman, *Joseph Smith,* 150–51, 215–19, 310–19, 328–29.

10. Remini, *Joseph Smith,* 122–27; Taves, *Trouble Enough,* 112–16; Bushman, *Joseph Smith,* 329–32; Tyler, *Freedom's Ferment,* 98–99.

11. Arrington and Bitton, *The Mormon Experience,* 21–22; Remini, *Joseph Smith,* 127–28; Taves, *Trouble Enough,* 118–19.

12. Remini, *Joseph Smith,* 128–34; Taves, *Trouble Enough,* 119–26; Bushman, *Joseph Smith,* 342–58; Tyler, *Freedom's Ferment,* 100.

13. Taves, *Trouble Enough,* 118–28, 130–31; Remini, *Joseph Smith,* 134–38; Bushman, *Joseph Smith,* 358–65.

14. Remini, *Joseph Smith,* 134–38; Taves, *Trouble Enough,* 130–47; Bushman, *Joseph Smith,* 365–91.

15. Remini, *Joseph Smith,* 140–50; Taves, *Trouble Enough,* 149–58; Tyler, *Freedom's Ferment,* 100–103.

16. Remini, *Joseph Smith,* 150–51, 157–58; Taves, *Trouble Enough,* 159–61.

17. Remini, *Joseph Smith,* 151–54; Taves, *Trouble Enough,* 177–84; Tyler, *Freedom's Ferment,* 104.

18. Remini, *Joseph Smith,* 160–66; Taves, *Trouble Enough,* 158–59; Tyler, *Freedom's Ferment,* 104; Norton Jacob, *The Mormon Vanguard Brigade of 1847: Norton Jacob's Record,* ed. Ronald O. Barney (Logan: Utah State University Press, 2005), 33.

19. Remini, *Joseph Smith,* 164; Taves, *Trouble Enough,* 157–58, 169–75.

20. Remini, *Joseph Smith,* 167; Taves, *Trouble Enough,* 198–206; Tyler, *Freedom's Ferment,* 105.

21. Remini, *Joseph Smith,* 167–74; Taves, *Trouble Enough,* 206–13.

22. Taves, *Trouble Enough,* 220; Jacob, *Mormon Vanguard,* 42–44; Leonard J. Arrington, *Brigham Young: American Moses* (New York: Alfred A. Knopf, 1985), 119–21.

23. Arrington, *Brigham Young,* 122–23.

24. Egan, *Frémont,* 155; Arrington, *Brigham Young,* 123–24.

25. Jacob, *Mormon Vanguard,* 44–48; Arrington, *Brigham Young,* 124–25; Taves, *Trouble Enough,* 220.

26. Taves, *Trouble Enough,* 220; Arrington, *Brigham Young,* 126.

27. Taves, *Trouble Enough,* 220–22.

28. Arrington, *Brigham Young,* 126–27; Jacob, *Mormon Vanguard,* 61, 70.

29. Arrington, *Brigham Young,* 127–29.

CHAPTER 7

TYLER AND TEXAS

1. Edward P. Crapol, *John Tyler: The Accidental President* (Chapel Hill: University of North Carolina Press, 2006), 20.

2. Crapol, *John Tyler,* 176; H. W. Brands, *Lone Star Nation: How a Ragged Army of Volunteers Won the Battle for Texas Independence and Changed America* (Garden City, N.Y.: Doubleday, 2004).

3. Crapol, *John Tyler,* 176; Richard Bruce Winders, *Crisis in the Southwest: The United States, Mexico, and the Struggle over Texas* (Wilmington, Del.: Scholarly Resources,

2002), 73–76, 78–79, 94; Dan Monroe, *The Republican Vision of John Tyler* (College Station: Texas A&M University Press, 2003), 149, 156–57.

4. Brands, *Lone Star Nation*, 4–112.

5. Winders, *Crisis in the Southwest*, 5–7; Brands, *Lone Star Nation*, 76–80, 98, 140, 180–84.

6. Winders, *Crisis in the Southwest*, 8–12; Brands, *Lone Star Nation*, 115–240.

7. Winders, *Crisis in the Southwest*, 12–23; Brands, *Lone Star Nation*, 41–42, 78–80, 138–42, 181–84, 226–37.

8. Winders, *Crisis in the Southwest*, 23–28; Brands, *Lone Star Nation*, 333–463.

9. Winders, *Crisis in the Southwest*, 30–34; Brands, *Lone Star Nation*, 467–92.

10. Winders, *Crisis in the Southwest*, 71–81; Brands, *Lone Star Nation*, 480–502; Henry H. Simms, *Emotion at High Tide: Abolition as a Controversial Factor, 1830–1845* (Richmond, Va.: William Byrd Press, 1960), 180–98.

11. William Lee Miller, *Arguing About Slavery: The Great Battle in the United States Congress* (New York: Alfred A. Knopf, 1996), 284–98; Simms, *Emotion at High Tide*, 180–98.

12. Norma Lois Peterson, *The Presidencies of William Henry Harrison and John Tyler* (Lawrence: University Press of Kansas, 1989), 186–94; Monroe, *Republican Vision*, 161.

13. Peterson, *Presidencies*, 185–200; Brands, *Lone Star Nation*, 502.

14. Peterson, *Presidencies*, 183–92; Crapol, *John Tyler*, 51, 202. Crapol argues that Upshur came over to Tyler's point of view.

15. Peterson, *Presidencies*, 191–93.

16. Monroe, *Republican Vision*, 163–64.

17. Peterson, *Presidencies*, 197–200; Crapol, *John Tyler*, 207.

18. Lee M. Pearson, "The 'Princeton' and the 'Peacemaker': A Study in Nineteenth-Century Naval Research and Development Procedures," *Technology and Culture* 7, no. 2 (Spring 1966): 164–65.

19. Pearson, "The 'Princeton' and the 'Peacemaker,'" 169–70; Crapol, *John Tyler*, 208.

20. *Pennsylvania Inquirer and National Gazette* (Philadelphia, Pa.), September 8, 1843, issue 59, col. B; *The Boston Daily Atlas* (Boston, Mass.), September 11, 1843, issue 61, col. G; *The New York Herald* (New York, N.Y.), September 5, 1843, issue 243, col. F.

21. *Pennsylvania Inquirer and National Gazette* (Philadelphia, Pa.), October 21, 1843, issue 96, col. D.

22. *Pennsylvania Inquirer and National Gazette* (Philadelphia, Pa.), December 20, 1843, issue 147, col. E; *Daily National Intelligencer* (Washington, D.C.), January 22, 1844, issue 9649, col. B, and February 19, 1844, issue 9673, col. E; *The Cleveland Herald* (Cleveland, Ohio), February 7, 1844, issue 190, col. B.

23. *Daily National Intelligencer* (Washington, D.C.), February 19, 1844, issue 9673, col. C; Crapol, *John Tyler*, 207.

24. Thomas Hart Benton, *Thirty Years' View*, 2 vols. (New York: D. Appleton, 1856), 2:567; Ann Blackman, "Fatal Cruise of the *Princeton*," *Navy History*, September 2005; Peterson, *Presidencies*, 202; Katharine Anthony, *Dolly Madison: Her Life and Times* (Garden City, N.Y.: Doubleday, 1949), 388; Crapol, *John Tyler*, 207–8.

25. Blackman, "Fatal Cruise"; *Daily National Intelligencer*, (Washington, D.C.), February 29, 1844, issue 9682, col. C; Crapol, *John Tyler*, 208.

26. Crapol, *John Tyler*, 208.

27. Benton, *Thirty Years' View*, 2:567–68; Blackman, "Fatal Cruise"; Peterson, *Presidencies*, 203.

28. Benton, *Thirty Years' View*, 2:568; Peterson, *Presidencies*, 203.

29. Benton, *Thirty Years' View*, 2:568; Blackman, "Fatal Cruise"; Peterson, *Presidencies*, 203; *Daily National Intelligencer* (Washington, D.C.), February 29, 1844, issue 9682, col. C; *The New York Herald* (New York, N.Y.), March 1, 1844, issue 61, col. A; *The Scioto Gazette* (Chillicothe, Ohio), March 7, 1844, issue 48, col. F.

30. Blackman, "Fatal Cruise"; Anthony, *Dolly Madison*, 388.

31. Peterson, *Presidencies*, 203–11; Crapol, *John Tyler*, 209.

32. *Greenville Mountaineer* (Greenville, S.C.), March 1, 1844, issue 42, col. D; Peterson, *Presidencies*, 203–11; Monroe, *Republican Vision*, 172–73; Crapol, *John Tyler*, 211.

33. *Daily National Intelligencer* (Washington, D.C.), March 7, 1844, issue 9688, col. C; Peterson, *Presidencies*, 206.

34. *Greenville Mountaineer* (Greenville, S.C.), March 1, 1844, issue 42, col. F, and March 8, 1844, issue 43, col. D; *The Liberator* (Boston, Mass.), March 1, 1844, issue 9, p. 34, col. C; *The Cleveland Herald* (Cleveland, Ohio), March 4, 1844, issue 212, col. B; *Daily National Intelligencer* (Washington, D.C.), March 4, 1844, issue 9685, col. D; *The New York Herald* (New York, N.Y.), March 7, 1844, issue 67, col. A.

35. Peterson, *Presidencies*, 206–7.

36. Crapol, *John Tyler*, 13, 204.

37. Peterson, *Presidencies*, 207–9; Monroe, *Republican Vision*, 170–71; *The Liberator* (Boston, Mass.), March 1, 1844, issue 9, col. A; *The New York Herald* (New York, N.Y.), March 7, 1844, issue 67, col. D; Crapol, *John Tyler*, 37–38, 204–6.

38. *Mississippi Free Trader and Natchez Gazette* (Natchez, Miss.), March 6, 1844, issue 56, col. C.

39. Peterson, *Presidencies*, 213; Crapol, *John Tyler*, 212.

40. Peterson, *Presidencies*, 214.

41. Monroe, *Republican Vision*, 174; Crapol, *John Tyler*, 215.

42. Peterson, *Presidencies*, 217; Monroe, *Republican Vision*, 174–75.

43. Peterson, *Presidencies*, 217–18; Benton, *Thirty Years' View*, 2:207–19; Monroe, *Republican Vision*, 174–75.

44. Peterson, *Presidencies*, 218.

45. Benton, *Thirty Years' View*, 2:619.

CHAPTER 8
THE ELECTION OF 1844

1. Norma Lois Peterson, *The Presidencies of William Henry Harrison and John Tyler* (Lawrence: University Press of Kansas, 1989), 219.

2. *Emancipator and Weekly Chronicle* (Boston, Mass.), July 3, 1844, issue 10, p. 40, col. A; Peterson, *Presidencies*, 220–21; Dan Monroe, *The Republican Vision of John Tyler* (College Station: Texas A&M University Press, 2003), 175.

3. Joel H. Silbey, *Martin Van Buren and the Emergence of American Popular Politics* (Lanham, Md.: Rowman and Littlefield, 2002), 166–67, 172–73; Donald B. Cole, *Martin Van Buren and the American Political System* (Princeton, N.J.: Princeton University Press, 1984), 390–91; Peterson, *Presidencies*, 219–20; *The Ohio Statesman* (Columbus, Ohio), January 2, 1844, issue 33, col. D; Monroe, *Republican Vision*, 175.

4. Peterson, *Presidencies*, 221.

5. Peterson, *Presidencies*, 221–22.

6. Peterson, *Presidencies*, 222–23; Silbey, *Martin Van Buren*, 174–75; Cole, *Martin Van Buren*, 392–95.

7. Peterson, *Presidencies*, 222–25; Silbey, *Martin Van Buren*, 175.

8. Edward P. Crapol, *John Tyler: The Accidental President* (Chapel Hill: University of North Carolina Press, 2006), 183–94.

9. Peterson, *Presidencies*, 222–25; Silbey, *Martin Van Buren*, 175.

10. Peterson, *Presidencies*, 223.

11. Silbey, *Martin Van Buren*, 176–77.

12. Cole, *Martin Van Buren*, 396.

13. Silbey, *Martin Van Buren*, 177; Cole, *Martin Van Buren*, 396–97.

14. Peterson, *Presidencies*, 225; Cole, *Martin Van Buren*, 397.

15. Crapol, *John Tyler*, 219.

16. Peterson, *Presidencies*, 225, 241.

17. Peterson, *Presidencies*, 226–33.

18. *The New York Herald* (New York, N.Y.), August 22, 1844, issue 233, col. D.

19. Peterson, *Presidencies*, 234.

20. Henry Clay, *The Private Correspondence of Henry Clay*, ed. Calvin Colton (New York: A. S. Barnes, 1856), 490–91; *Weekly Ohio Statesman* (Columbus, Ohio), August 14, 1844, issue 6, col. D; Peterson, *Presidencies*, 234.

21. *New-Orleans Commercial Bulletin* (New Orleans, La.), July 25, 1844, issue 196, col. C.

22. *The Liberator* (Boston, Mass.), July 26, 1844, issue 30, p. 118, col. A.

23. *Weekly Ohio Statesman* (Columbus, Ohio), August 14, 1844, issue 6, col. D; *Emancipator and Weekly Chronicle* (Boston, Mass.), August 14, 1844, issue 16, p. 62, col. A.

24. *New-Orleans Commercial Bulletin* (New Orleans, La.), August 29, 1844, issue 226, col. C.

25. *The Mississippian* (Jackson, Miss.), September 6, 1844, issue 43, col. B; *Emancipator and Weekly Chronicle* (Boston, Mass.), September 11, 1844, issue 20, p. 80, col. A; *Weekly Ohio Statesman* (Columbus, Ohio), September 11, 1844, issue 10, cols. E and H, and September 18, 1844, issue 11, col. G; Clay, *Private Correspondence*, 493.

26. *Weekly Ohio Statesman* (Columbus, Ohio), September 11, 1844, issue 10, cols. E and H, and September 18, 1844, issue 11, col. G.

27. *Weekly Ohio Statesman* (Columbus, Ohio), September 11, 1844, issue 10, col. A.

28. Crapol, *John Tyler*, 219.

29. Peterson, *Presidencies*, 243.

30. Peterson, *Presidencies*, 243–44.

31. Clay, *Private Correspondence*, 495–96.

CHAPTER 9

TEXAS ANNEXATION

1. Peterson, *The Presidencies of William Henry Harrison and John Tyler* (Lawrence: University Press of Kansas, 1989), 245–46.

2. Peterson, *Presidencies*, 245; H. W. Brands, *Lone Star Nation: How a Ragged Army of Volunteers Won the Battle for Texas Independence and Changed America* (Garden City, N.Y.: Doubleday, 2004).

3. John S. D. Eisenhower, *So Far from God: The U.S. War with Mexico, 1846–1848* (New York: Random House, 1989), 17–19; Peterson, *Presidencies,* 252, 256.

4. Eisenhower, *So Far from God,* 19–20; Peterson, *Presidencies,* 255–57; Edward P. Crapol, *John Tyler: The Accidental President* (Chapel Hill: University of North Carolina Press, 2006), 220–21.

5. Peterson, *Presidencies,* 251; William Lee Miller, *Arguing About Slavery: The Great Battle in the United States Congress* (New York: Alfred A. Knopf, 1996), 476–82.

6. Peterson, *Presidencies,* 259; Crapol, *John Tyler,* 220–21.

7. Eisenhower, *So Far from God,* 22, 24–25.

8. Eisenhower, *So Far from God,* 26; Richard Bruce Winders, *Crisis in the Southwest: The United States, Mexico, and the Struggle over Texas* (Wilmington, Del.: Scholarly Resources, 2002), 88; *The North American and Daily Advertiser* (Philadelphia, Pa.), July 14, 1845, issue 1958, col. B.

9. *Daily National Intelligencer* (Washington, D.C.), March 5, 1845, issue 9997, col. C; Eisenhower, *So Far from God,* 22–23.

10. Eisenhower, *So Far from God,* 23; Bernard DeVoto, *The Year of Decision: 1846* (Boston: Little, Brown, 1943), 26.

11. Eisenhower, *So Far from God,* 23.

12. James K. Polk, *The Diary of James K. Polk During His Presidency, 1845–1849,* ed. Milo Milton Quaife, 4 vols. (Chicago: A. C. McClurg, 1910), 1:2–5; Eisenhower, *So Far from God,* 23, 34; DeVoto, *The Year of Decision,* 24.

13. Eisenhower, *So Far from God,* 30–35; Winders, *Crisis in the Southwest,* 92; Robert W. Johannsen, *To the Halls of the Montezumas: The Mexican War in the American Imagination* (New York: Oxford University Press, 1985), 7; DeVoto, *The Year of Decision,* 14.

14. Napoleon Jackson Tecumseh Dana, *Monterrey Is Ours!: The Mexican War Letters of Lieutenant Dana, 1845–1847,* ed. Robert H. Ferrell (Lexington: University Press of Kentucky, 1990), 2, 5; Ephraim Kirby Smith, *To Mexico with Scott: Letters of Captain E. Kirby Smith to His Wife,* ed. Emma Jerome Blackwood (Cambridge, Mass.: Harvard University Press, 1917), 18–19.

15. Winders, *Crisis in the Southwest,* 93.

16. Winders, *Crisis in the Southwest,* 93.

17. Eisenhower, *So Far from God,* 42–43; Polk, *Diary,* 1:71–72.

18. Polk, *Diary,* 1:83–84; Eisenhower, *So Far from God,* 43–44; DeVoto, *The Year of Decision,* 21.

19. Eisenhower, *So Far from God,* 44–46; DeVoto, *The Year of Decision,* 16; Polk, *Diary,* 1:33–35.

20. Eisenhower, *So Far from God,* 44; Polk, *Diary,* 1:93–94.

21. Eisenhower, *So Far from God,* 46; DeVoto, *The Year of Decision,* 16–17.

22. Eisenhower, *So Far from God,* 44–45.

23. Eisenhower, *So Far from God,* 47; DeVoto, *The Year of Decision,* 27–28.

24. Eisenhower, *So Far from God,* 46–47; Polk, *Diary,* 1:327–37.

25. Eisenhower, *So Far from God,* 47; Winders, *Crisis in the Southwest,* 94–95.

26. Eisenhower, *So Far from God,* 47–48; Polk, *Diary,* 1:191–92.

27. Eisenhower, *So Far from God,* 48–50; Polk, *Diary,* 1:8–9.

CHAPTER 10
ARMIES ALONG THE RIO GRANDE

1. John S. D. Eisenhower, *So Far from God: The U.S. War with Mexico, 1846–1848* (New York: Random House, 1989), 50–52; Ephraim Kirby Smith, *To Mexico with Scott: Letters of Captain E. Kirby Smith to His Wife*, ed. Emma Jerome Blackwood (Cambridge, Mass.: Harvard University Press, 1917), 19.
2. Smith, *To Mexico with Scott*, 23.
3. Eisenhower, *So Far from God*, 52–53, 56.
4. John Corey Henshaw, *Recollections of the War with Mexico*, ed. Gary F. Kurutz (Columbia: University of Missouri Press, 2008), 41; Smith, *To Mexico with Scott*, 27–31.
5. Eisenhower, *So Far from God*, 52–54; Smith, *To Mexico with Scott*, 31; Henshaw, *Recollections*, 41–43; Smith, *To Mexico with Scott*, 32.
6. Eisenhower, *So Far from God*, 54–57; Napoleon Jackson Tecumseh Dana, *Monterrey Is Ours!: The Mexican War Letters of Lieutenant Dana, 1845–1847*, ed. Robert H. Ferrell (Lexington: University Press of Kentucky, 1990), 39; Philip Norbourne Barbour, *Journals of the Late Brevet Major Philip Norbourne Barbour, Captain in the 3rd Regiment, United States Infantry, and His Wife, Martha Isabella Hopkins Barbour, Written During the War with Mexico—1846*, ed. Rhoda van Bibber Tanner Doubleday (New York: G. P. Putnam's Sons, 1936), 17; Smith, *To Mexico with Scott*, 33–34; Henshaw, *Recollections*, 44.
7. Eisenhower, *So Far from God*, 54–57; Barbour, *Journals*, 17–20; Henshaw, *Recollections*, 45.
8. Barbour, *Journals*, 20–23; Eisenhower, *So Far from God*, 60–61; Richard Bruce Winders, *Crisis in the Southwest: The United States, Mexico, and the Struggle over Texas* (Wilmington, Del.: Scholarly Resources, 2002), 93–94; Henshaw, *Recollections*, 44.
9. Eisenhower, *So Far from God*, 63–64; Barbour, *Journals*, 32, 34, 36; Smith, *To Mexico with Scott*, 37.
10. Eisenhower, *So Far from God*, 63–64.
11. Eisenhower, *So Far from God*, 63–65; Henshaw, *Recollections*, 47–48; Dana, *Monterrey Is Ours!*, 46, 48; Barbour, *Journals*, 32–33, 41–43; Winders, *Crisis in the Southwest*, 95; *Raleigh Register, and North-Carolina Gazette* (Raleigh, N.C.), May 12, 1846, issue 38, col. E; Smith, *To Mexico with Scott*, 39.
12. Eisenhower, *So Far from God*, 65; Barbour, *Journals*, 46–47; Henshaw, *Recollections*, 48–49; Smith, *To Mexico with Scott*, 39–42.
13. Eisenhower, *So Far from God*, 65–66; Robert W. Johannsen, *To the Halls of the Montezumas: The Mexican War in the American Imagination* (New York: Oxford University Press, 1985), 8; *Daily National Intelligencer* (Washington, D.C.), May 11, 1846, issue 10364, col. B.
14. James K. Polk, *The Diary of James K. Polk During His Presidency, 1845–1849*, ed. Milo Milton Quaife, 4 vols. (Chicago: A. C. McClurg, 1910), 1:379–80, 1:382–85.
15. Polk, *Diary*, 1:386; Eisenhower, *So Far from God*, 65–66; *Raleigh Register, and North-Carolina Gazette* (Raleigh, N.C.), May 12, 1846, issue 38, col. D.
16. Polk, *Diary*, 1:390–91; Eisenhower, *So Far from God*, 66–68; Winders, *Crisis in the Southwest*, 99; *Pensacola Gazette* (Pensacola, Fla.), May 30, 1846, issue 9, col. F; *New-Hampshire Statesman and State Journal* (Concord, N.H.), May 15, 1846, issue 1303, col. F.

17. *Mississippi Free Trader and Natchez Gazette* (Natchez, Miss.), May 9, 1846, issue 56, col. C, and May 28, 1846, issue 65, col. A; *The North American* (Philadelphia, Pa.), May 14, 1846, issue 2218, col. H; *Raymond Gazette* (Raymond, Miss.), May 8, 1846, issue 47, col. B; *Boston Courier* (Boston, Mass.), May 28, 1846, issue 3213, col. C; *The Cleveland Herald* (Cleveland, Ohio), May 22, 1846, issue 293, col. A; *Daily National Intelligencer* (Washington, D.C.), May 21, 1846, issue 10373, col. E.

18. Eisenhower, *So Far from God*, 71–72; Winders, *Crisis in the Southwest*, 96; Barbour, *Journals*, 51.

19. Eisenhower, *So Far from God*, 64, 73.

20. Eisenhower, *So Far from God*, 74–75; Smith, *To Mexico with Scott*, 44.

21. Eisenhower, *So Far from God*, 73–75; Henshaw, *Recollections*, 53–55; Dana, *Monterrey Is Ours!*, 58.

22. Eisenhower, *So Far from God*, 75; Barbour, *Journals*, 52; Smith, *To Mexico with Scott*, 44.

23. Eisenhower, *So Far from God*, 75–76; Winders, *Crisis in the Southwest*, 96; Barbour, *Journals*, 52; Henshaw, *Recollections*, 56; Smith, *To Mexico with Scott*, 44–45.

24. Henshaw, *Recollections*, 56; Dana, *Monterrey Is Ours!*, 59–60.

25. Dana, *Monterrey Is Ours!*, 61; Henshaw, *Recollections*, 55–59.

26. Dana, *Monterrey Is Ours!*, 61; Henshaw, *Recollections*, 59–61.

27. Henshaw, *Recollections*, 61; Dana, *Monterrey Is Ours!*, 62.

28. Eisenhower, *So Far from God*, 76; Barbour, *Journals*, 53; Smith, *To Mexico with Scott*, 45.

29. Eisenhower, *So Far from God*, 76; Winders, *Crisis in the Southwest*, 96; Barbour, *Journals*, 54.

30. Eisenhower, *So Far from God*, 77; Winders, *Crisis in the Southwest*, 97; Barbour, *Journals*, 54.

31. Eisenhower, *So Far from God*, 79.

32. Eisenhower, *So Far from God*, 79; Barbour, *Journals*, 55; Smith, *To Mexico with Scott*, 45, 48.

33. Eisenhower, *So Far from God*, 79; Smith, *To Mexico with Scott*, 49; Brooks D. Simpson, *Ulysses S. Grant: Triumph over Adversity, 1822–1865* (Boston: Houghton Mifflin, 2000), 31.

34. Eisenhower, *So Far from God*, 79; Smith, *To Mexico with Scott*, 49.

35. Eisenhower, *So Far from God*, 79–80; Winders, *Crisis in the Southwest*, 97; Barbour, *Journals*, 56, 171; Smith, *To Mexico with Scott*, 49.

36. Henshaw, *Recollections*, 63–64.

37. Eisenhower, *So Far from God*, 81; Barbour, *Journals*, 57; Smith, *To Mexico with Scott*, 46.

38. Barbour, *Journals*, 58; Smith, *To Mexico with Scott*, 50.

39. Barbour, *Journals*, 57; Dana, *Monterrey Is Ours!*, 75–76; Mike Stroud, "James S. McIntosh," Historical Markers Database, http://www.hmdb.org/marker.asp?marker=5403.

40. Eisenhower, *So Far from God*, 83; Winders, *Crisis in the Southwest*, 97–98.

41. Eisenhower, *So Far from God*, 83.

42. Eisenhower, *So Far from God*, 83; Barbour, *Journals*, 60.

43. Barbour, *Journals*, 60; Smith, *To Mexico with Scott*, 51–52.

44. Eisenhower, *So Far from God*, 84; Winders, *Crisis in the Southwest*, 98; Dana, *Monterrey Is Ours!*, 62–63; Barbour, *Journals*, 61; Smith, *To Mexico with Scott*, 52.

45. Henshaw, *Recollections*, 65–67; Dana, *Monterrey Is Ours!*, 64.
46. Eisenhower, *So Far from God*, 84; Dana, *Monterrey Is Ours!*, 62.

CHAPTER 11

THE MONTERREY CAMPAIGN

1. John S. D. Eisenhower, *So Far from God: The U.S. War with Mexico, 1846–1848* (New York: Random House, 1989), 86–89.
2. Eisenhower, *So Far from God*, 89–94.
3. Eisenhower, *So Far from God*, 89–97.
4. Philip Norbourne Barbour, *Journals of the Late Brevet Major Philip Norbourne Barbour, Captain in the 3rd Regiment, United States Infantry, and His Wife, Martha Isabella Hopkins Barbour, Written During the War with Mexico—1846*, ed. Rhoda van Bibber Tanner Doubleday (New York: G. P. Putnam's Sons, 1936), 67; John Corey Henshaw, *Recollections of the War with Mexico*, ed. Gary F. Kurutz (Columbia: University of Missouri Press, 2008), 70; Napoleon Jackson Tecumseh Dana, *Monterrey Is Ours!: The Mexican War Letters of Lieutenant Dana, 1845–1847*, ed. Robert H. Ferrell (Lexington: University Press of Kentucky, 1990), 80–81.
5. Eisenhower, *So Far from God*, 98–103; Henshaw, *Recollections*, 70–71.
6. Eisenhower, *So Far from God*, 101–2.
7. Barbour, *Journals*, 105–6.
8. Eisenhower, *So Far from God*, 105; Richard Bruce Winders, *Crisis in the Southwest: The United States, Mexico, and the Struggle over Texas* (Wilmington, Del.: Scholarly Resources, 2002), 101.
9. Dwight L. Clarke, *Stephen Watts Kearny: Soldier of the West* (Norman: University of Oklahoma Press, 1966), 3–84, 108.
10. Eisenhower, *So Far from God*, 205–6, 242; Clarke, *Stephen Watts Kearny*, 108–9; Abraham Robinson Johnston, Marcellus Ball Edwards, and Philip Gooch Ferguson, *Marching with the Army of the West, 1846–1848*, ed. Ralph P. Bieber (Glendale, Calif.: Arthur H. Clark, 1936), 115; George Rutledge Gibson, *Journal of a Soldier Under Kearny and Doniphan, 1846–1847*, ed. Ralph P. Bieber (Glendale, Calif.: Arthur H. Clark, 1935), 125.
11. Gibson, *Journal*, 125; Joseph G. Dawson III, *Doniphan's Epic March: The 1st Missouri Volunteers in the Mexican War* (Lawrence: University Press of Kansas, 1999), 52–53; Eisenhower, *So Far from God*, 205–6; Clarke, *Stephen Watts Kearny*, 113–14.
12. Dawson, *Doniphan's Epic March*, 53–64; Gibson, *Journal*, 141.
13. Dawson, *Doniphan's Epic March*, 53–64; Johnston, Edwards, and Ferguson, *Marching*, 83, 85, 129; Henry Smith Turner, *The Original Journals of Henry Smith Turner with Stephen Watts Kearny to New Mexico and California, 1846–1847*, ed. Dwight L. Clarke (Norman: University of Oklahoma Press, 1966), 61; Gibson, *Journal*, 136, 147, 151.
14. Dawson, *Doniphan's Epic March*, 53–64; Johnston, Edwards, and Ferguson, *Marching*, 83, 85, 129; Turner, *Original Journals*, 61; Gibson, *Journal*, 147; Clarke, *Stephen Watts Kearny*, 131.
15. Dawson, *Doniphan's Epic March*, 65–78; Johnston, Edwards, and Ferguson, *Marching*, 94, 98–99; Gibson, *Journal*, 181, 191.
16. Dawson, *Doniphan's Epic March*, 65–78; Turner, *Original Journals*, 66–72; Johnston, Edwards, and Ferguson, *Marching*, 99–103; Clarke, *Stephen Watts Kearny*, 105,

124–25, 127; Gibson, *Journal*, 202–3; Eisenhower, *So Far from God*, 207–9; Winders, *Crisis in the Southwest*, 101.

17. Dawson, *Doniphan's Epic March*, 65–78; Turner, *Original Journals*, 66–72; Johnston, Edwards, and Ferguson, *Marching*, 99–103; Clarke, *Stephen Watts Kearny*, 105, 124–25, 127; Gibson, *Journal*, 202, 205, 209; Eisenhower, *So Far from God*, 207–9; Winders, *Crisis in the Southwest*, 101.

18. Eisenhower, *So Far from God*, 196–97.

19. Gibson, *Journal*, 209–10; Johnston, Edwards, and Ferguson, *Marching*, 162–65; Turner, *Original Journals*, 74.

20. Dawson, *Doniphan's Epic March*, 77, 83–87; Eisenhower, *So Far from God*, 209–10; Clarke, *Stephen Watts Kearny*, 148–49.

21. Eisenhower, *So Far from God*, 104–5.

22. Eisenhower, *So Far from God*, 105–11; Dana, *Monterrey Is Ours!*, 99–100.

23. Eisenhower, *So Far from God*, 111–12; Dana, *Monterrey Is Ours!*, 108–9; George Wilkins Kendall, *Dispatches from the Mexican War*, ed. Lawrence Delbert Cress (Norman: University of Oklahoma Press, 1999), 97.

24. Eisenhower, *So Far from God*, 111–12; Dana, *Monterrey Is Ours!*, 108–9; Winders, *Crisis in the Southwest*, 103.

25. Dana, *Monterrey Is Ours!*, 111; Winders, *Crisis in the Southwest*, 103.

26. Dana, *Monterrey Is Ours!*, 115–19.

27. Eisenhower, *So Far from God*, 116.

28. Eisenhower, *So Far from God*, 57–58, 91.

29. Eisenhower, *So Far from God*, 114–16.

30. Eisenhower, *So Far from God*, 120–21.

31. Eisenhower, *So Far from God*, 120–21.

32. Henshaw, *Recollections*, 80.

33. Kendall, *Dispatches*, 110, 121–22.

34. Eisenhower, *So Far from God*, 125–28; Dana, *Monterrey Is Ours!*, 125; Winders, *Crisis in the Southwest*, 104; Barbour, *Journals*, 107; Kendall, *Dispatches*, 110–11, 122.

35. Dana, *Monterrey Is Ours!*, 129; Henshaw, *Recollections*, 80; Kendall, *Dispatches*, 122–23.

36. Kendall, *Dispatches*, 123–24.

37. Eisenhower, *So Far from God*, 128–30; Kendall, *Dispatches*, 124–25; Dana, *Monterrey Is Ours!*, 129–30; Henshaw, *Recollections*, 80.

38. Eisenhower, *So Far from God*, 131; Dana, *Monterrey Is Ours!*, 130–31; Henshaw, *Recollections*, 81; Kendall, *Dispatches*, 125–28.

39. Eisenhower, *So Far from God*, 131–32.

40. Kendall, *Dispatches*, 129–30.

41. Kendall, *Dispatches*, 130–31; Dana, *Monterrey Is Ours!*, 131–32.

42. Eisenhower, *So Far from God*, 132–33; Kendall, *Dispatches*, 131; Dana, *Monterrey Is Ours!*, 131; Henshaw, *Recollections*, 83.

43. Eisenhower, *So Far from God*, 133; Kendall, *Dispatches*, 132; Dana, *Monterrey Is Ours!*, 133.

44. Eisenhower, *So Far from God*, 135.

45. Eisenhower, *So Far from God*, 135–37; Winders, *Crisis in the Southwest*, 104–5.

46. Eisenhower, *So Far from God*, 137–38; Winders, *Crisis in the Southwest*, 105; William C. Cooper Jr., *Jefferson Davis, American* (New York: Alfred A. Knopf, 2000), 136–37.

47. Kendall, *Dispatches*, 133.
48. Eisenhower, *So Far from God*, 139; Winders, *Crisis in the Southwest*, 105; Dana, *Monterrey Is Ours!*, 134–35; Kendall, *Dispatches*, 133–34.
49. Eisenhower, *So Far from God*, 140; Dana, *Monterrey Is Ours!*, 135–36; Henshaw, *Recollections*, 83.
50. Eisenhower, *So Far from God*, 141; Cooper, *Jefferson Davis*, 138.
51. Eisenhower, *So Far from God*, 141–42; Cooper, *Jefferson Davis*, 138.
52. Henshaw, *Recollections*, 84–85; Kendall, *Dispatches*, 137–38.
53. Eisenhower, *So Far from God*, 142–43; Dana, *Monterrey Is Ours!*, 137–38; Winders, *Crisis in the Southwest*, 106; Kendall, *Dispatches*, 138–39.
54. Eisenhower, *So Far from God*, 144–45; Kendall, *Dispatches*, 140.
55. Eisenhower, *So Far from God*, 145–46.
56. Eisenhower, *So Far from God*, 145–47.
57. Eisenhower, *So Far from God*, 150–51.
58. Eisenhower, *So Far from God*, 150; Dana, *Monterrey Is Ours!*, 138.
59. Henshaw, *Recollections*, 87; Winders, *Crisis in the Southwest*, 106–7; Eisenhower, *So Far from God*, 149–51; Kendall, *Dispatches*, 114–15.
60. Eisenhower, *So Far from God*, 152–53; Winders, *Crisis in the Southwest*, 106–7.
61. Eisenhower, *So Far from God*, 155–59.

CHAPTER 12
NEW MEXICO, CHIHUAHUA, AND CALIFORNIA

1. Joseph G. Dawson III, *Doniphan's Epic March: The 1st Missouri Volunteers in the Mexican War* (Lawrence, University Press of Kansas, 1999), 1–6.
2. Dawson, *Doniphan's Epic March*, 6–11.
3. Dawson, *Doniphan's Epic March*, 7, 11, 20–21, 28.
4. Dawson, *Doniphan's Epic March*, 30, 32–33, 39.
5. Richard Bruce Winders, *Crisis in the Southwest: The United States, Mexico, and the Struggle over Texas* (Wilmington, Del.: Scholarly Resources, 2002), 107; John S. D. Eisenhower, *So Far from God: The U.S. War with Mexico, 1846–1848* (New York: Random House, 1989), 235.
6. James A. Crutchfield, *Tragedy at Taos: The Revolt of 1847* (Plano: Republic of Texas Press, 1995), 95–100.
7. Crutchfield, *Tragedy at Taos*, 57–58.
8. Eisenhower, *So Far from God*, 234–37; Crutchfield, *Tragedy at Taos*, 103–5.
9. Crutchfield, *Tragedy at Taos*, 110–11.
10. Eisenhower, *So Far from God*, 237–40; Winders, *Crisis in the Southwest*, 110–11; Crutchfield, *Tragedy at Taos*, 115–32.
11. Dawson, *Doniphan's Epic March*, 106–9; Abraham Robinson Johnston, Marcellus Ball Edwards, and Philip Gooch Ferguson, *Marching with the Army of the West, 1846–1848*, ed. Ralph P. Bieber (Glendale, Calif.: Arthur H. Clark, 1936), 199–200; George Rutledge Gibson, *Journal of a Soldier Under Kearny and Doniphan, 1846–1847*, ed. Ralph P. Bieber (Glendale, Calif.: Arthur H. Clark, 1936), 282–98.
12. Dawson, *Doniphan's Epic March*, 110–11; C. H. Kribben to M. L. Clark, December 26, 1846, in *Raymond Gazette* (Raymond, Miss.), March 12, 1847, issue 38, col. A; Johnston, Edwards, and Ferguson, *Marching*, 228; Winders, *Crisis in the Southwest*, 107–8; Gibson, *Journal*, 300.

13. Dawson, *Doniphan's Epic March*, 111; Johnston, Edwards, and Ferguson, *Marching*, 229–30.
14. Dawson, *Doniphan's Epic March*, 110–12; Johnston, Edwards, and Ferguson, *Marching*, 230–32.
15. Dawson, *Doniphan's Epic March*, 112–13; Johnston, Edwards, and Ferguson, *Marching*, 230; Gibson, *Journal*, 303.
16. Dawson, *Doniphan's Epic March*, 113; Gibson, *Journal*, 303.
17. Dawson, *Doniphan's Epic March*, 114; C. H. Kribben to M. L. Clark, December 26, 1846, in *Raymond Gazette* (Raymond, Miss.), March 12, 1847, issue 38, col. A; Johnston, Edwards, and Ferguson, *Marching*, 231.
18. Dawson, *Doniphan's Epic March*, 114–15; Johnston, Edwards, and Ferguson, *Marching*, 231, 235; Gibson, *Journal*, 305.
19. Dawson, *Doniphan's Epic March*, 115–17, 120; Johnston, Edwards, and Ferguson, *Marching*, 231–37; Winders, *Crisis in the Southwest*, 107–8; Gibson, *Journal of a Soldier*, 306–7.
20. Dawson, *Doniphan's Epic March*, 115–17, 120; Johnston, Edwards, and Ferguson, *Marching*, 238–39; Winders, *Crisis in the Southwest*, 107–8.
21. Dawson, *Doniphan's Epic March*, 120–41; Gibson, *Journal of a Soldier*, 325, 334–36.
22. Dawson, *Doniphan's Epic March*, 142–44; Winders, *Crisis in the Southwest*, 108; Eisenhower, *So Far from God*, 241–43.
23. Dawson, *Doniphan's Epic March*, 144–45; Johnston, Edwards, and Ferguson, *Marching*, 261.
24. Dawson, *Doniphan's Epic March*, 145; Gibson, *Journal*, 343–44.
25. Dawson, *Doniphan's Epic March*, 145–49; Johnston, Edwards, and Ferguson, *Marching*, 261–63.
26. Dawson, *Doniphan's Epic March*, 149–53; Gibson, *Journal*, 345–49.
27. Dawson, *Doniphan's Epic March*, 153–56; Johnston, Edwards, and Ferguson, *Marching*, 263–66.
28. Dawson, *Doniphan's Epic March*, 156–57; Winders, *Crisis in the Southwest*, 108; Eisenhower, *So Far from God*, 241–43.
29. Dawson, *Doniphan's Epic March*, 163–71, 179–83; Winders, *Crisis in the Southwest*, 108; Eisenhower, *So Far from God*, 241–50.
30. Henry Smith Turner, *The Original Journals of Henry Smith Turner with Stephen Watts Kearny to New Mexico and California, 1846–1847*, ed. Dwight L. Clarke (Norman: University of Oklahoma Press, 1966), 79–80; Dwight L. Clarke, *Stephen Watts Kearny: Soldier of the West* (Norman: University of Oklahoma Press, 1966), 166–68; Ferol Egan, *Frémont: Explorer for a Restless Nation* (Garden City, N.Y.: Doubleday, 1977), 374.
31. Eisenhower, *So Far from God*, 200.
32. Eisenhower, *So Far from God*, 200–202.
33. Eisenhower, *So Far from God*, 203.
34. Eisenhower, *So Far from God*, 211–12.
35. Eisenhower, *So Far from God*, 212–14.
36. Eisenhower, *So Far from God*, 212–13.
37. Eisenhower, *So Far from God*, 213.
38. Eisenhower, *So Far from God*, 214.
39. Eisenhower, *So Far from God*, 214–15.

40. Eisenhower, *So Far from God*, 215–16.
41. Eisenhower, *So Far from God*, 217–19; Clarke, *Stephen Watts Kearny*, 175–76; Egan, *Frémont*, 372.
42. Eisenhower, *So Far from God*, 219–22; Turner, *Original Journals*, 90.
43. Turner, *Original Journals*, 117–18; Eisenhower, *So Far from God*, 219–22.
44. Turner, *Original Journals*, 119–23; Eisenhower, *So Far from God*, 219–22.
45. Turner, *Original Journals*, 122–23; Clarke, *Stephen Watts Kearny*, 192–93, 195–201, 204–7.
46. Clarke, *Stephen Watts Kearny*, 195–201.
47. Clarke, *Stephen Watts Kearny*, 201–3.
48. Clarke, *Stephen Watts Kearny*, 203.
49. Clarke, *Stephen Watts Kearny*, 207–12.
50. Clarke, *Stephen Watts Kearny*, 212–13.
51. Clarke, *Stephen Watts Kearny*, 212–17.
52. Clarke, *Stephen Watts Kearny*, 217–19.
53. Clarke, *Stephen Watts Kearny*, 220–23; Eisenhower, *So Far from God*, 224–25.
54. Clarke, *Stephen Watts Kearny*, 223–29; Eisenhower, *So Far from God*, 225–26.
55. Eisenhower, *So Far from God*, 226–27.
56. Clarke, *Stephen Watts Kearny*, 242.
57. Clarke, *Stephen Watts Kearny*, 245–48; Winders, *Crisis in the Southwest*, 110.
58. Clarke, *Stephen Watts Kearny*, 249–52.
59. Eisenhower, *So Far from God*, 229–30; Winders, *Crisis in the Southwest*, 110; Clarke, *Stephen Watts Kearny*, 253–54.
60. Clarke, *Stephen Watts Kearny*, 256–58; Eisenhower, *So Far from God*, 230.
61. Clarke, *Stephen Watts Kearny*, 258–70; Eisenhower, *So Far from God*, 230.
62. Leonard J. Arrington, *Brigham Young: American Moses* (New York: Alfred A. Knopf, 1985), 128.
63. Clarke, *Stephen Watts Kearny*, 165.
64. Clarke, *Stephen Watts Kearny*, 270–79; Eisenhower, *So Far from God*, 231.
65. Clarke, *Stephen Watts Kearny*, 299–303.
66. Clarke, *Stephen Watts Kearny*, 305–10.
67. Clarke, *Stephen Watts Kearny*, 310–11.
68. Eisenhower, *So Far from God*, 231–32.

CHAPTER 13
BUENA VISTA

1. David Lavender, *Climax at Buena Vista: The Decisive Battle of the Mexican-American War* (Philadelphia: University of Pennsylvania Press, 2003), 96–97.
2. Lavender, *Climax at Buena Vista*, 122–35.
3. Lavender, *Climax at Buena Vista*, 130–34.
4. Thomas Hart Benton, *Thirty Years' View*, 2 vols. (New York: D. Appleton, 1856), 2:693–94; James K. Polk, *The Diary of James K. Polk During His Presidency, 1845–1849*, ed. Milo Milton Quaife, 4 vols. (Chicago: A. C. McClurg, 1910), 2:219–23, 239.
5. Polk, *Diary*, 2:222–23, 231; Timothy D. Johnson, *A Gallant Little Army: The Mexico City Campaign* (Lawrence: University Press of Kansas, 2007), 15.

6. Polk, *Diary*, 2:222–23, 231.

7. Polk, *Diary*, 2:228–29, 231, 239; Benton, *Thirty Years' View*, 2:693–94.

8. Polk, *Diary*, 2:241–44; Lavender, *Climax at Buena Vista*, 142.

9. Polk, *Diary*, 2:244–45; John S. D. Eisenhower, *So Far from God: The U.S. War with Mexico, 1846–1848* (New York: Random House, 1989), 161–65.

10. Polk, *Diary*, 2:301–10; Lavender, *Climax at Buena Vista*, 143.

11. Lavender, *Climax at Buena Vista*, 152.

12. Eisenhower, *So Far from God*, 166–67, 172–75; Lavender, *Climax at Buena Vista*, 152–53.

13. Eisenhower, *So Far from God*, 166–67, 172–75; Lavender, *Climax at Buena Vista*, 152–54, 158, 161; *Raleigh Register, and North-Carolina Gazette* (Raleigh, N.C.), February 5, 1847, issue 11, col. D; Polk, *Diary*, 2:307.

14. Eisenhower, *So Far from God*, 173–76; Lavender, *Climax at Buena Vista*, 153.

15. Lavender, *Climax at Buena Vista*, 163–64.

16. Lavender, *Climax at Buena Vista*, 164; Peter F. Stevens, *The Rogue's March: John Riley and the St. Patrick's Battalion* (Washington, D.C.: Brassey's, 1999), 1–165; George Wilkins Kendall, *Dispatches from the Mexican War*, ed. Lawrence Delbert Cress (Norman: University of Oklahoma Press, 1999), 107.

17. Lavender, *Climax at Buena Vista*, 165.

18. Eisenhower, *So Far from God*, 182–83.

19. Eisenhower, *So Far from God*, 178–81; Lavender, *Climax at Buena Vista*, 160–68.

20. Lavender, *Climax at Buena Vista*, 167–69.

21. Eisenhower, *So Far from God*, 178–81; Lavender, *Climax at Buena Vista*, 169–71.

22. Lavender, *Climax at Buena Vista*, 168–69.

23. Eisenhower, *So Far from God*, 181.

24. Lavender, *Climax at Buena Vista*, 171–72.

25. Eisenhower, *So Far from God*, 185.

26. Lavender, *Climax at Buena Vista*, 172; William C. Cooper Jr., *Jefferson Davis, American* (New York: Alfred A. Knopf, 2000), 147.

27. Eisenhower, *So Far from God*, 178–81; Lavender, *Climax at Buena Vista*, 172–73; Benjamin Franklin Scribner, *Camp Life of a Volunteer: A Campaign in Mexico* (Philadelphia: Grigg, Elliot, 1847), 59.

28. Lavender, *Climax at Buena Vista*, 177–78.

29. Eisenhower, *So Far from God*, 185–87; Lavender, *Climax at Buena Vista*, 179.

30. Lavender, *Climax at Buena Vista*, 175; Eisenhower, *So Far from God*, 185–87.

31. Cooper, *Jefferson Davis*, 148.

32. Lavender, *Climax at Buena Vista*, 179; Eisenhower, *So Far from God*, 185–87; Scribner, *Camp Life*, 59.

33. Eisenhower, *So Far from God*, 185–87; Lavender, *Climax at Buena Vista*, 185–86.

34. Lavender, *Climax at Buena Vista*, 186.

35. Eisenhower, *So Far from God*, 187; Lavender, *Climax at Buena Vista*, 186–87; Scribner, *Camp Life*, 59, 62.

36. Eisenhower, *So Far from God*, 187; Lavender, *Climax at Buena Vista*, 188.

37. Eisenhower, *So Far from God*, 187–88; Lavender, *Climax at Buena Vista*, 190, 195.

38. Eisenhower, *So Far from God*, 187–88; Lavender, *Climax at Buena Vista*, 190–91; Scribner, *Camp Life*, 61.

39. Scribner, *Camp Life*, 60–61.

40. Eisenhower, *So Far from God*, 187–88.
41. Scribner, *Camp Life*, 61.
42. Lavender, *Climax at Buena Vista*, 192.
43. Eisenhower, *So Far from God*, 189; Lavender, *Climax at Buena Vista*, 192.
44. Lavender, *Climax at Buena Vista*, 192–94; Stevens, *The Rogue's March*, 190–92.
45. Lavender, *Climax at Buena Vista*, 195; Cooper, *Jefferson Davis*, 151.
46. Lavender, *Climax at Buena Vista*, 198; Stevens, *The Rogue's March*, 191–92.
47. Lavender, *Climax at Buena Vista*, 198.
48. Lavender, *Climax at Buena Vista*, 198–99.
49. Lavender, *Climax at Buena Vista*, 199; Scribner, *Camp Life*, 61, 63.
50. Lavender, *Climax at Buena Vista*, 199.
51. Lavender, *Climax at Buena Vista*, 200–201; Cooper, *Jefferson Davis*, 152.
52. Lavender, *Climax at Buena Vista*, 201–2; Stevens, *The Rogue's March*, 191–94; Scribner, *Camp Life*, 63–64.
53. Lavender, *Climax at Buena Vista*, 202; Eisenhower, *So Far from God*, 189; Scribner, *Camp Life*, 63; Cooper, *Jefferson Davis*, 153.
54. Scribner, *Camp Life*, 65; Cooper, *Jefferson Davis*, 153.
55. Lavender, *Climax at Buena Vista*, 203; Scribner, *Camp Life*, 65; Stevens, *The Rogue's March*, 194–96; Cooper, *Jefferson Davis*, 153.
56. Scribner, *Camp Life*, 65.
57. Lavender, *Climax at Buena Vista*, 204.
58. Eisenhower, *So Far from God*, 189; Lavender, *Climax at Buena Vista*, 207.
59. Eisenhower, *So Far from God*, 189–90.
60. Eisenhower, *So Far from God*, 190; Scribner, *Camp Life*, 66.
61. Eisenhower, *So Far from God*, 190.
62. Eisenhower, *So Far from God*, 191.

CHAPTER 14

VERACRUZ, CERRO GORDO, AND THE POLITICS OF EXPANSION

1. John S. D. Eisenhower, *So Far from God: The U.S. War with Mexico, 1846–1848* (New York: Random House, 1989), 286.
2. Eisenhower, *So Far from God*, 286.
3. Eisenhower, *So Far from God*, 286; Joel H. Silbey, *Party over Section: The Rough and Ready Presidential Election of 1848* (Lawrence: University of Kansas Press, 2009), 31–32.
4. Eisenhower, *So Far from God*, 286–87.
5. Eisenhower, *So Far from God*, 253–57; Timothy D. Johnson, *A Gallant Little Army: The Mexico City Campaign* (Lawrence: University Press of Kansas, 2007), 9, 20; John Corey Henshaw, *Recollections of the War with Mexico*, ed. Gary F. Kurutz (Columbia: University of Missouri Press, 2008), 110.
6. Johnson, *A Gallant Little Army*, 20; Ephraim Kirby Smith, *To Mexico with Scott: Letters of Captain E. Kirby Smith to His Wife*, ed. Emma Jerome Blackwood (Cambridge, Mass.: Harvard University Press, 1917), 108.
7. Smith, *To Mexico with Scott*, 108–10; Robert Anderson, *An Artillery Officer in the Mexican War, 1846–7: Letters of Robert Anderson* (Freeport, N.Y.: Books for Libraries Press, 1911), 71.

8. Johnson, *A Gallant Little Army*, 11, 22–23; Eisenhower, *So Far from God*, 257–59.

9. Johnson, *A Gallant Little Army*, 10; Napoleon Jackson Tecumseh Dana, *Monterrey Is Ours!: The Mexican War Letters of Lieutenant Dana, 1845–1847*, ed. Robert H. Ferrell (Lexington: University Press of Kentucky, 1990), 189; Henshaw, *Recollections*, 112; Smith, *To Mexico with Scott*, 112; Anderson, *Artillery Officer*, 69, 72.

10. Smith, *To Mexico with Scott*, 113; J. Jacob Oswandel, *Notes of the Mexican War, 1846–1848* (Philadelphia, 1885), 67–68.

11. Johnson, *A Gallant Little Army*, 10; Oswandel, *Notes*, 68; Smith, *To Mexico with Scott*, 114.

12. Johnson, *A Gallant Little Army*, 10; Oswandel, *Notes*, 68.

13. Johnson, *A Gallant Little Army*, 10, 21–22; Eisenhower, *So Far from God*, 259; Smith, *To Mexico with Scott*, 114; Oswandel, *Notes*, 70; Henshaw, *Recollections*, 114; George Wilkins Kendall, *Dispatches from the Mexican War*, ed. Lawrence Delbert Cress (Norman: University of Oklahoma Press, 1999), 158–59; Anderson, *Artillery Officer*, 74.

14. Johnson, *A Gallant Little Army*, 25–27; Oswandel, *Notes*, 71–72.

15. Oswandel, *Notes*, 74–75.

16. Johnson, *A Gallant Little Army*, 28; Oswandel, *Notes*, 76–79; Henshaw, *Recollections*, 115; Dana, *Monterrey Is Ours!*, 189–91; Smith, *To Mexico with Scott*, 117.

17. Johnson, *A Gallant Little Army*, 28–29; Oswandel, *Notes*, 76–78; Smith, *To Mexico with Scott*, 117.

18. Anderson, *Artillery Officer*, 92.

19. Johnson, *A Gallant Little Army*, 32.

20. Johnson, *A Gallant Little Army*, 32.

21. Johnson, *A Gallant Little Army*, 32–38; Kendall, *Dispatches*, 168–69; Oswandel, *Notes*, 89.

22. Johnson, *A Gallant Little Army*, 38–39; Eisenhower, *So Far from God*, 259–64.

23. Johnson, *A Gallant Little Army*, 38–43; Oswandel, *Notes*, 90; Eisenhower, *So Far from God*, 259–64; Kendall, *Dispatches*, 172–73; Henshaw, *Recollections*, 117–18; Smith, *To Mexico with Scott*, 125.

24. Johnson, *A Gallant Little Army*, 38–43; Oswandel, *Notes*, 90; Eisenhower, *So Far from God*, 259–64; Kendall, *Dispatches*, 175–76; Anderson, *Artillery Officer*, 97.

25. Henshaw, *Recollections*, 121; Eisenhower, *So Far from God*, 259–64; Johnson, *A Gallant Little Army*, 47–49; Kendall, *Dispatches*, 179–81; Anderson, *Artillery Officer*, 93–94.

26. Eisenhower, *So Far from God*, 264–65; Johnson, *A Gallant Little Army*, 48–51.

27. Johnson, *A Gallant Little Army*, 16, 52–58.

28. Eisenhower, *So Far from God*, 269–71.

29. Eisenhower, *So Far from God*, 271–72.

30. Johnson, *A Gallant Little Army*, 59–68; Kendall, *Dispatches*, 207; Henshaw, *Recollections*, 126; Dana, *Monterrey Is Ours!*, 201–2.

31. Johnson, *A Gallant Little Army*, 68–69; Henshaw, *Recollections*, 128.

32. Johnson, *A Gallant Little Army*, 69; Henshaw, *Recollections*, 128; Dana, *Monterrey Is Ours!*, 202; Kendall, *Dispatches*, 207; Craig L. Symonds, *Joseph E. Johnston: A Civil War Biography* (New York: W. W. Norton, 1992), 58.

33. Johnson, *A Gallant Little Army*, 70–73; Eisenhower, *So Far from God*, 274–76; Henshaw, *Recollections*, 129.

34. Nathaniel Cheairs Hughes Jr. and Roy P. Stonesifer, Jr., *The Life and Wars of Gideon J. Pillow* (Chapel Hill: University of North Carolina Press, 1993), 23–66; Eisenhower, *So Far from God,* 274–76.

35. Eisenhower, *So Far from God,* 274–76.

36. Johnson, *A Gallant Little Army,* 74.

37. Eisenhower, *So Far from God,* 276–77; Oswandel, *Notes,* 113.

38. Oswandel, *Notes,* 113–14; Henshaw, *Recollections,* 129.

39. Eisenhower, *So Far from God,* 277–78; Johnson, *A Gallant Little Army,* 76–77.

40. Johnson, *A Gallant Little Army,* 77–78; Hughes and Stonesifer, *Gideon J. Pillow,* 67–69; Henshaw, *Recollections,* 130.

41. Eisenhower, *So Far from God,* 279.

42. Eisenhower, *So Far from God,* 278.

43. Kendall, *Dispatches,* 213; Eisenhower, *So Far from God,* 278–79; Johnson, *A Gallant Little Army,* 80.

44. Johnson, *A Gallant Little Army,* 80.

45. Eisenhower, *So Far from God,* 278–79; Johnson, *A Gallant Little Army,* 80.

46. Johnson, *A Gallant Little Army,* 80; Oswandel, *Notes,* 116; Henshaw, *Recollections,* 132.

47. Johnson, *A Gallant Little Army,* 80–81.

48. Johnson, *A Gallant Little Army,* 83.

49. Johnson, *A Gallant Little Army,* 82–83; Oswandel, *Notes,* 117–19; Henshaw, *Recollections,* 132.

50. Oswandel, *Notes,* 122.

51. Eisenhower, *So Far from God,* 280–82; Johnson, *A Gallant Little Army,* 85–87; Henshaw, *Recollections,* 133; Kendall, *Dispatches,* 217.

52. Johnson, *A Gallant Little Army,* 87–88; Kendall, *Dispatches,* 216.

53. Hughes and Stonesifer, *Gideon J. Pillow,* 70–71.

54. Hughes and Stonesifer, *Gideon J. Pillow,* 71–73; Eisenhower, *So Far from God,* 281–82; Johnson, *A Gallant Little Army,* 88–91; Oswandel, *Notes,* 126.

55. Oswandel, *Notes,* 124–26.

56. Oswandel, *Notes,* 124–26.

57. Hughes and Stonesifer, *Gideon J. Pillow,* 72–73; Johnson, *A Gallant Little Army,* 92; Oswandel, *Notes,* 127.

58. Eisenhower, *So Far from God,* 282–83; Oswandel, *Notes,* 129; Henshaw, *Recollections,* 134–35; Kendall, *Dispatches,* 213, 215.

59. Eisenhower, *So Far from God,* 290–91.

CHAPTER 15
TO THE GATES OF MEXICO CITY

1. John S. D. Eisenhower, *So Far from God: The U.S. War with Mexico, 1846–1848* (New York: Random House, 1989), 292–95; Timothy D. Johnson, *A Gallant Little Army: The Mexico City Campaign* (Lawrence: University Press of Kansas, 2007), 96–97; J. Jacob Oswandel, *Notes of the Mexican War, 1846–1848* (Philadelphia, 1885), 133; John Corey Henshaw, *Recollections of the War with Mexico,* ed. Gary F. Kurutz (Columbia: University of Missouri Press, 2008), 134.

2. Eisenhower, *So Far from God,* 292–97; Johnson, *A Gallant Little Army,* 100–101.

3. Eisenhower, *So Far from God*, 298–301; Johnson, *A Gallant Little Army*, 113–15.

4. Johnson, *A Gallant Little Army*, 105–9; Henshaw, *Recollections*, 138; George Wilkins Kendall, *Dispatches from the Mexican War*, ed. Lawrence Delbert Cress (Norman: University of Oklahoma Press, 1999), 219.

5. Oswandel, *Notes*, 141–45; Johnson, *A Gallant Little Army*, 105–9.

6. Henshaw, *Recollections*, 139; Johnson, *A Gallant Little Army*, 112.

7. Johnson, *A Gallant Little Army*, 117–18, 139–40; Eisenhower, *So Far from God*, 297–98; Ephraim Kirby Smith, *To Mexico with Scott: Letters of Captain E. Kirby Smith to His Wife*, ed. Emma Jerome Blackwood (Cambridge, Mass.: Harvard University Press, 1917), 149.

8. Johnson, *A Gallant Little Army*, 119–24, 131; Kendall, *Dispatches*, 269–70, 274; Henshaw, *Recollections*, 143–45; Oswandel, *Notes*, 206–11.

9. Johnson, *A Gallant Little Army*, 127, 142–43.

10. Eisenhower, *So Far from God*, 302–7; Johnson, *A Gallant Little Army*, 142–43; Kendall, *Dispatches*, 308–11.

11. Eisenhower, *So Far from God*, 306–8.

12. Johnson, *A Gallant Little Army*, 149.

13. Johnson, *A Gallant Little Army*, 127–28.

14. Robert Anderson, *An Artillery Officer in the Mexican War, 1846–7: Letters of Robert Anderson* (Freeport, N.Y.: Books for Libraries Press, 1911), 278–86; Oswandel, *Notes*, 244; Eisenhower, *So Far from God*, 311; Johnson, *A Gallant Little Army*, 152; Henshaw, *Recollections*, 152; Kendall, *Dispatches*, 319; Smith, *To Mexico with Scott*, 192.

15. Johnson, *A Gallant Little Army*, 153; Anderson, *Artillery Officer*, 287.

16. Eisenhower, *So Far from God*, 312–14; Johnson, *A Gallant Little Army*, 154–56.

17. Johnson, *A Gallant Little Army*, 154–56; Kendall, *Dispatches*, 283; Smith, *To Mexico with Scott*, 193.

18. Johnson, *A Gallant Little Army*, 157.

19. Eisenhower, *So Far from God*, 312–14; Johnson, *A Gallant Little Army*, 157; Henshaw, *Recollections*, 157; Kendall, *Dispatches*, 325–26; Smith, *To Mexico with Scott*, 194; Anderson, *Artillery Officer*, 290.

20. Eisenhower, *So Far from God*, 316; Johnson, *A Gallant Little Army*, 158–60; Kendall, *Dispatches*, 326–27; Smith, *To Mexico with Scott*, 196–97.

21. Eisenhower, *So Far from God*, 316; Johnson, *A Gallant Little Army*, 158–60; Kendall, *Dispatches*, 326–27.

22. Eisenhower, *So Far from God*, 318; Johnson, *A Gallant Little Army*, 160–62; Kendall, *Dispatches*, 327.

23. Eisenhower, *So Far from God*, 319; Johnson, *A Gallant Little Army*, 162; Kendall, *Dispatches*, 328; Anderson, *Artillery Officer*, 294; Nathaniel Cheairs Hughes Jr. and Roy P. Stonesifer Jr., *The Life and Wars of Gideon J. Pillow* (Chapel Hill: University of North Carolina Press, 1993), 82.

24. Johnson, *A Gallant Little Army*, 162–63; Hughes and Stonesifer, *Gideon J. Pillow*, 83.

25. Eisenhower, *So Far from God*, 316–17; Johnson, *A Gallant Little Army*, 160–63.

26. Johnson, *A Gallant Little Army*, 165; Kendall, *Dispatches*, 328; Hughes and Stonesifer, *Gideon J. Pillow*, 83.

27. Johnson, *A Gallant Little Army*, 165; Hughes and Stonesifer, *Gideon J. Pillow*, 86.

28. Hughes and Stonesifer, *Gideon J. Pillow*, 83.

29. Eisenhower, *So Far from God*, 319–20.

30. Eisenhower, *So Far from God*, 320–21; Johnson, *A Gallant Little Army*, 167–69; Kendall, *Dispatches*, 329, 344.

31. Eisenhower, *So Far from God*, 322–23; Johnson, *A Gallant Little Army*, 169.

32. Eisenhower, *So Far from God*, 322–23; Johnson, *A Gallant Little Army*, 169–70.

33. Johnson, *A Gallant Little Army*, 170–72; Henshaw, *Recollections*, 160–61; Kendall, *Dispatches*, 329–30.

34. Eisenhower, *So Far from God*, 321–24; Johnson, *A Gallant Little Army*, 172–74; Kendall, *Dispatches*, 330–31.

35. Eisenhower, *So Far from God*, 321–24; Johnson, *A Gallant Little Army*, 169, 174–76.

36. Eisenhower, *So Far from God*, 324; Johnson, *A Gallant Little Army*, 177.

37. Eisenhower, *So Far from God*, 325; Johnson, *A Gallant Little Army*, 179–82.

38. Eisenhower, *So Far from God*, 325; Johnson, *A Gallant Little Army*, 179–82.

39. Peter F. Stevens, *The Rogue's March: John Riley and the St. Patrick's Battalion* (Washington, D.C.: Brassey's, 1999), 189–233; Johnson, *A Gallant Little Army*, 182.

40. Henshaw, *Recollections*, 163; Kendall, *Dispatches*, 332; Johnson, *A Gallant Little Army*, 182; Stevens, *The Rogue's March*, 238; Smith, *To Mexico with Scott*, 201.

41. Johnson, *A Gallant Little Army*, 182.

42. Johnson, *A Gallant Little Army*, 183–84; Smith, *To Mexico with Scott*, 199–200.

43. Johnson, *A Gallant Little Army*, 184–86; Kendall, *Dispatches*, 332; Smith, *To Mexico with Scott*, 201; Anderson, *Artillery Officer*, 294.

44. Johnson, *A Gallant Little Army*, 186.

45. Smith, *To Mexico with Scott*, 214.

46. Johnson, *A Gallant Little Army*, 187–88.

47. Johnson, *A Gallant Little Army*, 188–89; Smith, *To Mexico with Scott*, 202–3; Jeffry D. Wert, *General James Longstreet: The Confederacy's Most Controversial Soldier: A Biography* (New York: Simon and Schuster, 1993), 44.

48. Eisenhower, *So Far from God*, 325–27; Johnson, *A Gallant Little Army*, 188–89; Stevens, *The Rogue's March*, 241–43; Henshaw, *Recollections*, 165; Kendall, *Dispatches*, 334.

49. Johnson, *A Gallant Little Army*, 190–91.

50. Johnson, *A Gallant Little Army*, 191–92.

CHAPTER 16

A CONQUERED CAPITAL AND A NEGOTIATED PEACE

1. John S. D. Eisenhower, *So Far from God: The U.S. War with Mexico, 1846–1848* (New York: Random House, 1989), 328–29; Timothy D. Johnson, *A Gallant Little Army: The Mexico City Campaign* (Lawrence: University Press of Kansas, 2007), 194–95.

2. Eisenhower, *So Far from God*, 328–29; Johnson, *A Gallant Little Army*, 194–95; Ephraim Kirby Smith, *To Mexico with Scott: Letters of Captain E. Kirby Smith to His Wife*, ed. Emma Jerome Blackwood (Cambridge, Mass.: Harvard University Press, 1917), 181, 205; George Wilkins Kendall, *Dispatches from the Mexican War*, ed. Lawrence Delbert Cress (Norman: University of Oklahoma Press, 1999), 340, 350–52, 360–63.

3. Eisenhower, *So Far from God*, 328–29; Johnson, *A Gallant Little Army*, 194–95.

4. Eisenhower, *So Far from God*, 329–30; Johnson, *A Gallant Little Army*, 194–95.

5. Eisenhower, *So Far from God*, 331; Johnson, *A Gallant Little Army*, 197–98; Kendall, *Dispatches*, 340, 350–52, 360–63; Smith, *To Mexico with Scott*, 207.

6. Eisenhower, *So Far from God*, 331–32; Johnson, *A Gallant Little Army*, 200–201; John Corey Henshaw, *Recollections of the War with Mexico*, ed. Gary F. Kurutz (Columbia: University of Missouri Press, 2008), 165; Ralph W. Kirkham, *The Mexican War Journal and Letters of Ralph W. Kirkham*, ed. Robert Ryal Miller (College Station: Texas A&M University Press, 1991), 56; Kendall, *Dispatches*, 341–42, 369–70; Smith, *To Mexico with Scott*, 215–16; Robert Anderson, *An Artillery Officer in the Mexican War, 1846–7: Letters of Robert Anderson* (Freeport, N.Y.: Books for Libraries Press, 1911), 308.

7. Johnson, *A Gallant Little Army*, 201.

8. Eisenhower, *So Far from God*, 334–36; Johnson, *A Gallant Little Army*, 201–2; Kirkham, *Mexican War*, 56; Kendall, *Dispatches*, 371.

9. Johnson, *A Gallant Little Army*, 202–3; Kendall, *Dispatches*, 371–72; Smith, *To Mexico with Scott*, 217.

10. Johnson, *A Gallant Little Army*, 203–4.

11. Johnson, *A Gallant Little Army*, 204–5.

12. Johnson, *A Gallant Little Army*, 205–6; Kirkham, *Mexican War*, 57–58; Henshaw, *Recollections*, 168; Smith, *To Mexico with Scott*, 217.

13. Johnson, *A Gallant Little Army*, 206–7; Anderson, *Artillery Officer*, 311–13; Brooks D. Simpson, *Ulysses S. Grant: Triumph over Adversity, 1822–1865* (Boston: Houghton Mifflin, 2000), 42.

14. Johnson, *A Gallant Little Army*, 207.

15. Eisenhower, *So Far from God*, 334–36; Kirkham, *Mexican War*, 58.

16. Johnson, *A Gallant Little Army*, 207–8; Kendall, *Dispatches*, 375; Kirkham, *Mexican War*, 60.

17. Johnson, *A Gallant Little Army*, 207–8.

18. Peter F. Stevens, *The Rogue's March: John Riley and the St. Patrick's Battalion* (Washington, D.C.: Brassey's, 1999), 247–69; Eisenhower, *So Far from God*, 341–42; Kirkham, *Mexican War*, 60; Kendall, *Dispatches*, 343, 349.

19. Stevens, *The Rogue's March*, 269.

20. Eisenhower, *So Far from God*, 337–38, 341–42.

21. Johnson, *A Gallant Little Army*, 210–11.

22. Johnson, *A Gallant Little Army*, 212; Kendall, *Dispatches*, 380.

23. Eisenhower, *So Far from God*, 337–38; Johnson, *A Gallant Little Army*, 212–13; Nathaniel Cheairs Hughes Jr. and Roy P. Stonesifer Jr., *The Life and Wars of Gideon J. Pillow* (Chapel Hill: University of North Carolina Press, 1993), 96.

24. Eisenhower, *So Far from God*, 338–40; Johnson, *A Gallant Little Army*, 213.

25. Eisenhower, *So Far from God*, 338–39; Johnson, *A Gallant Little Army*, 214–15; Kendall, *Dispatches*, 381.

26. Johnson, *A Gallant Little Army*, 216.

27. Henshaw, *Recollections*, 171.

28. Johnson, *A Gallant Little Army*, 216.

29. Eisenhower, *So Far from God*, 339; Johnson, *A Gallant Little Army*, 217; Stevens, *The Rogue's March*, 270–73.

30. Eisenhower, *So Far from God*, 341–42.

31. Johnson, *A Gallant Little Army*, 219; Craig L. Symonds, *Joseph E. Johnston: A Civil War Biography* (New York: W. W. Norton, 1992), 69.

32. Johnson, *A Gallant Little Army*, 220.

33. Eisenhower, *So Far from God*, 340–41; Jeffry D. Wert, *General James Longstreet: The Confederacy's Most Controversial Soldier: A Biography* (New York: Simon and Schuster, 1993), 45.

34. Symonds, *Joseph E. Johnston*, 69.

35. Eisenhower, *So Far from God*, 341; Symonds, *Joseph E. Johnston*, 70; Kirkham, *Mexican War*, 62.

36. Eisenhower, *So Far from God*, 342; Stevens, *The Rogue's March*, 275–76.

37. Eisenhower, *So Far from God*, 342.

38. Johnson, *A Gallant Little Army*, 227–31; Kendall, *Dispatches*, 383.

39. Johnson, *A Gallant Little Army*, 230–32; Kendall, *Dispatches*, 383.

40. Johnson, *A Gallant Little Army*, 233.

41. Johnson, *A Gallant Little Army*, 233–34.

42. Kirkham, *Mexican War*, 63–64; Kendall, *Dispatches*, 383.

43. Johnson, *A Gallant Little Army*, 235–36; Simpson, *Ulysses S. Grant*, 43–44.

44. Johnson, *A Gallant Little Army*, 236–37; Kirkham, *Mexican War*, 65–66.

45. Eisenhower, *So Far from God*, 342; Johnson, *A Gallant Little Army*, 237–39; Kendall, *Dispatches*, 384; Stevens, *The Rogue's March*, 277.

46. Eisenhower, *So Far from God*, 345–46; Henshaw, *Recollections*, 174; Kirkham, *Mexican War*, 66; Kendall, *Dispatches*, 384–85.

47. Eisenhower, *So Far from God*, 346–49.

48. Eisenhower, *So Far from God*, 350–55; Anderson, *Artillery Officer*, 338; Hughes and Stonesifer, *Gideon J. Pillow*, 106–20.

49. Eisenhower, *So Far from God*, 358–61.

50. Eisenhower, *So Far from God*, 361.

51. Eisenhower, *So Far from God*, 363.

52. Eisenhower, *So Far from God*, 365–66.

53. Eisenhower, *So Far from God*, 366–67; Joel H. Silbey, *Party over Section: The Rough and Ready Presidential Election of 1848* (Lawrence: University Press of Kansas, 2009), 30.

54. Eisenhower, *So Far from God*, 367.

CHAPTER 17
THE ELECTION OF 1848

1. Joel H. Silbey, *Party over Section: The Rough and Ready Presidential Election of 1848* (Lawrence: University Press of Kansas, 2009), 37.

2. Donald B. Cole, *Martin Van Buren and the American Political System* (Princeton, N.J.: Princeton University Press, 1984), 398–408; Silbey, *Party over Section*, 36–37.

3. K. Jack Bauer, *Zachary Taylor: Soldier, Planter, Statesman of the Old Southwest* (Baton Rouge: Louisiana State University Press, 1985), 221.

4. Bauer, *Zachary Taylor*, 221.

5. Cole, *Martin Van Buren*, 409–11.

6. Cole, *Martin Van Buren*, 412.

7. Silbey, *Party over Section*, 37–38, 49, 62.

8. Silbey, *Party over Section*, 38–39.

9. Silbey, *Party over Section*, 40–41.

10. Silbey, *Party over Section*, 62–63; Willard Carl Klunder, *Lewis Cass and the Politics of*

Moderation (Kent, Ohio: Kent State University Press, 1996), 183; W. L. G. Smith, *Fifty Years of Public Life: The Life and Times of Lewis Cass* (New York: Derby and Jackson, 1856), 648.

11. Silbey, *Party over Section*, 63–64; Klunder, *Lewis Cass*, 175–86; Smith, *Fifty Years*, 652–53.

12. Klunder, *Lewis Cass*, 1–118; Andrew Cunningham McLaughlin, *Lewis Cass* (Boston: Houghton, Mifflin, 1891), 1–220; Silbey, *Party over Section*, 50–53; Smith, *Fifty Years*, 13–647.

13. McLaughlin, *Lewis Cass*, 231; Klunder, *Lewis Cass*, 168–70; Silbey, *Party over Section*, 52–53.

14. Silbey, *Party over Section*, 64.

15. Robert V. Remini, *Henry Clay: Statesman for the Union* (New York: W. W. Norton, 1991), 706; Silbey, *Party over Section*, 53–59, 68; Bauer, *Zachary Taylor*, 235.

16. Remini, *Henry Clay*, 680–86.

17. Remini, *Henry Clay*, 687–95, 703; Bauer, *Zachary Taylor*, 232.

18. Silbey, *Party over Section*, 53–60; Remini, *Henry Clay*, 691; Bauer, *Zachary Taylor*, 218; Michael A. Morrison, *Slavery and the American West: The Eclipse of Manifest Destiny and the Coming of the Civil War* (Chapel Hill: University of North Carolina Press, 1997), 88.

19. Remini, *Henry Clay*, 691; Bauer, *Zachary Taylor*, 217; John S. D. Eisenhower, *Zachary Taylor* (New York: Times Books, 2008), 74–75.

20. Bauer, *Zachary Taylor*, 219.

21. Silbey, *Party over Section*, 69–70; Remini, *Henry Clay*, 706–7; Bauer, *Zachary Taylor*, 235–37.

22. Silbey, *Party over Section*, 70–71; Remini, *Henry Clay*, 709–11.

23. Cole, *Martin Van Buren*, 413–14; Silbey, *Party over Section*, 72–73.

24. Cole, *Martin Van Buren*, 414.

25. Silbey, *Party over Section*, 39–40; Cole, *Martin Van Buren*, 414.

26. Cole, *Martin Van Buren*, 414–15; Silbey, *Party over Section*, 74–76; John Niven, *Salmon P. Chase: A Biography* (New York: Oxford University Press, 1995), 108–9; Frederick J. Blue, *Salmon P. Chase: A Life in Politics* (Kent, Ohio: Kent State University Press, 1987), 63; *The New York Herald* (New York, N.Y.), July 8, 1848, col. B; *The Cleveland Herald* (Cleveland, Ohio), August 9, 1848, issue 193, col. D; *The Boston Daily Atlas* (Boston, Mass.), August 10, 1848, issue 34, col. C; *Daily National Intelligencer* (Washington, D.C.), August 10, 1848, issue 11063, col. E.

27. Eric Foner, *Free Soil, Free Labor, Free Men: The Ideology of the Republican Party Before the Civil War* (New York: Oxford University Press, 1995), 125; Niven, *Salmon P. Chase*, 109–10; Blue, *Salmon P. Chase*, 64.

28. Cole, *Martin Van Buren*, 414–15; Silbey, *Party over Section*, 76–79; Niven, *Salmon P. Chase*, 110–11; Blue, *Salmon P. Chase*, 64–66.

29. Silbey, *Party over Section*, 79–80.

30. Silbey, *Party over Section*, 79–80.

31. Silbey, *Party over Section*, 80–82.

32. Cole, *Martin Van Buren*, 416.

33. Silbey, *Party over Section*, 84; William C. Cooper Jr., *Jefferson Davis, American* (New York: Alfred A. Knopf, 2000), 176–78.

34. Silbey, *Party over Section*, 94–95; Bauer, *Zachary Taylor*, 239; Blue, *Salmon P. Chase*, 66.

35. Cole, *Martin Van Buren*, 417; Bauer, *Zachary Taylor*, 245.

36. Cole, *Martin Van Buren*, 417; Silbey, *Party over Section*, 144–45; Remini, *Henry Clay*, 712; Klunder, *Lewis Cass*, 232.

37. Cole, *Martin Van Buren*, 418; Silbey, *Party over Section*, 144–45; Klunder, *Lewis Cass*, 231.

38. Silbey, *Party over Section*, 132–45.

39. Cole, *Martin Van Buren*, 419.

CHAPTER 18

THE CALIFORNIA GOLD RUSH

1. H. W. Brands, *The Age of Gold: The California Gold Rush and the New American Dream* (New York: Random House, 2002), 2–7; *The New York Herald* (New York, N.Y.), June 27, 1849, col. C.

2. Brands, *The Age of Gold*, 8–11; William Tecumseh Sherman, *Memoirs of General W. T. Sherman* (New York: Library of America, 1990), 73; *The New York Herald* (New York, N.Y.), June 27, 1849, col. C.

3. Brands, *The Age of Gold*, 13–16; Sherman, *Memoirs*, 74; *The New York Herald* (New York, N.Y.), June 27, 1849, col. C.

4. Brands, *The Age of Gold*, 16; *The New York Herald* (New York, N.Y.), June 27, 1849, col. C.

5. Brands, *The Age of Gold*, 16–17; Leonard L. Richards, *The California Gold Rush and the Coming of the Civil War* (New York: Alfred A. Knopf, 2007), 3–4.

6. Sherman, *Memoirs*, 64–65.

7. Sherman, *Memoirs*, 65.

8. Sherman, *Memoirs*, 65.

9. Sherman, *Memoirs*, 74–75; Richards, *California Gold Rush*, 5.

10. Sherman, *Memoirs*, 75.

11. Sherman, *Memoirs*, 70; Richards, *California Gold Rush*, 13; Rosemarie Mossinger, *Woodleaf Legacy: The Story of a California Gold Rush Town* (Nevada City, Calif.: Carl Mautz Publishing, 1995), 21.

12. Sherman, *Memoirs*, 70.

13. Sherman, *Memoirs*, 71–72.

14. Sherman, *Memoirs*, 76–77.

15. Richards, *California Gold Rush*, 12.

16. Mossinger, *Woodleaf Legacy*, 21.

17. Sherman, *Memoirs*, 76–77.

18. Sherman, *Memoirs*, 77; Richards, *California Gold Rush*, 12–13.

19. Sherman, *Memoirs*, 78–80.

20. Sherman, *Memoirs*, 81–82.

21. Malcolm J. Rohrbough, *Days of Gold: The California Gold Rush and the American Nation* (Berkeley: University of California Press, 1997), 22–23; Sherman, *Memoirs*, 81–82; Brands, *The Age of Gold*, 47; Richards, *California Gold Rush*, 19–20; Walter R. Borneman, *Polk: The Man Who Transformed the Presidency and America* (New York: Random House, 2008), 332.

22. Borneman, *Polk*, 332; Brands, *The Age of Gold*, 70.

23. Rohrbough, *Days of Gold*, 28–32; Brands, *The Age of Gold*, 47–92; *Milwaukee Sentinel and Gazette* (Milwaukee, Wis.), January 10, 1849, issue 226, col. B.

24. Rohrbough, *Days of Gold*, 33–37.

25. Brands, *The Age of Gold*, 104; *Milwaukee Sentinel and Gazette* (Milwaukee, Wis.), January 1, 1849, issue 219, col. C; *Daily National Intelligencer* (Washington, D.C.), January 2, 1849, issue 11186, col. C.

26. *Daily National Intelligencer* (Washington, D.C.), January 1, 1849, issue 11185, col. C; Sherman, *Memoirs*, 38–44.

27. Brands, *The Age of Gold*, 104–6, 121.

28. *Daily National Intelligencer* (Washington, D.C.), January 1, 1849, issue 11185, col. C; *The Mississippian* (Jackson, Miss.), January 5, 1849, issue 2, col. E.

29. *Daily National Intelligencer* (Washington, D.C.), January 5, 1849, issue 11189, col. D; *Milwaukee Sentinel and Gazette* (Milwaukee, Wis.), January 6, 1849, issue 223, col. B.

30. Brands, *The Age of Gold*, 72–85; *The Mississippian* (Jackson, Miss.), January 5, 1849, issue 2, col. E.

31. Brands, *The Age of Gold*, 85; Mossinger, *Woodleaf Legacy*, 22; *Milwaukee Sentinel and Gazette* (Milwaukee, Wis.), January 1, 1849, issue 219, col. C.

32. Sherman, *Memoirs*, 90, 106; Steven E. Woodworth, *Sherman* (New York: Palgrave Macmillan, 2009), 20.

33. Brands, *The Age of Gold*, 122.

34. *Daily National Intelligencer* (Washington, D.C.), January 2, 1849, issue 11186, col. C; *Arkansas State Democrat* (Little Rock, Ark.), January 5, 1849, issue 34, col. C; *The Boston Daily Atlas* (Boston, Mass.), January 11, 1849, issue 163, col. B; *Milwaukee Sentinel and Gazette* (Milwaukee, Wis.), January 11, 1849, issue 227, col. C.

35. Brands, *The Age of Gold*, 133, 135–36.

36. Brands, *The Age of Gold*, 136–38; Richards, *California Gold Rush*, 50–54.

37. Brands, *The Age of Gold*, 139–41; Richards, *California Gold Rush*, 49–50.

38. Brands, *The Age of Gold*, 148–49.

39. *The Mississippian* (Jackson, Miss.), January 5, 1849, issue 2, col. G; *The Natchez Semi-Weekly Courier* (Natchez, Miss.), January 9, 1849, issue 4, col. C.

40. Brands, *The Age of Gold*, 179–87.

41. Sherman, *Memoirs*, 83; *The New York Herald* (New York, N.Y.), June 27, 1849, col. C; Rohrbough, *Days of Gold*, 8; Mossinger, *Woodleaf Legacy*, 22.

42. Mossinger, *Woodleaf Legacy*, 27–28.

CHAPTER 19
CALIFORNIA AND THE EXPANSION OF SLAVERY

1. John C. Waugh, *On the Brink of Civil War: The Compromise of 1850 and How It Changed the Course of American History* (Wilmington, Del.: Scholarly Resources, 2003), 22, 27, 43.

2. Waugh, *Brink*, 22.

3. John Niven, *John C. Calhoun and the Price of Union: A Biography* (Baton Rouge: Louisiana State University Press, 1988), 306–8; William M. Meigs, *The Life of John Caldwell Calhoun*, 2 vols. (New York: Da Capo, 1970), 2:398–99; Waugh, *Brink*, 23.

4. Niven, *John C. Calhoun*, 310; Meigs, *John Caldwell Calhoun*, 2:396–97; Waugh, *Brink*, 23.

5. *Bangor Daily Whig and Courier* (Bangor, Maine), March 7, 1850, issue 211, col. B; Waugh, *Brink*, 24.

6. Leonard L. Richards, *The California Gold Rush and the Coming of the Civil War* (New York: Alfred A. Knopf, 2007), 69.

7. *Boston Courier* (Boston, Mass.), January 7, 1850, issue 3590, col. C; Richards, *California Gold Rush,* 69; *Daily National Intelligencer* (Washington, D.C.), January 22, 1850, issue 11515, col. E; Waugh, *Brink,* 40–41.

8. *Vermont Patriot* (Montpelier, Vt.), January 10, 1850, issue 3/211, col. A; *North American and United States Gazette* (Philadelphia, Pa.), January 16, 1850, issue 16830, col. F; Richards, *California Gold Rush,* 71–82, 91.

9. *Bangor Daily Whig and Courier* (Bangor, Maine), February 25, 1850, issue 202, col. A; *Daily Morning News* (Savannah, Ga.), January 26, 1850, issue 11, col. D; Waugh, *Brink,* 27–29.

10. Waugh, *Brink,* 29.

11. *The Weekly Herald* (New York, N.Y.), December 1, 1849, issue 48, p. 380, col. C; Waugh, *Brink,* 29.

12. Waugh, *Brink,* 29–30.

13. *The Boston Daily Atlas* (Boston, Mass.), December 1, 1849, issue 129, col. G; *The Weekly Herald* (New York, N.Y.), December 8, 1849, issue 49, p. 388, col. B; *The Boston Daily Atlas* (Boston, Mass.), December 11, 1849, issue 137, col. A; Waugh, *Brink,* 43–44.

14. Richards, *California Gold Rush,* 95; Waugh, *Brink,* 44–50.

15. *The Boston Daily Atlas* (Boston, Mass.), December 17, 1849, issue 142, col. B; Waugh, *Brink,* 50–51.

16. *Bangor Daily Whig and Courier* (Bangor, Maine), December 12, 1849, issue 138, col. A; Waugh, *Brink,* 51, 55.

17. *The Ohio Observer* (Hudson, Ohio), December 26, 1849, issue 51, col. E; *The Scioto Gazette* (Chillicothe, Ohio), December 26, 1849, issue 39, col. A; Richards, *California Gold Rush,* 97; Waugh, *Brink,* 49–52.

18. Waugh, *Brink,* 53–54.

19. *Boston Courier* (Boston, Mass.), January 7, 1850, issue 3590, col. C; *Daily National Intelligencer* (Washington, D.C.), January 22, 1850, issue 11515, col. E; Waugh, *Brink,* 54–55.

20. Waugh, *Brink,* 38–39, 55–59.

21. *The Natchez Semi-Weekly Courier* (Natchez, Miss.), February 5, 1850, issue 12, col. A; Niven, *John C. Calhoun,* 1–305.

22. Robert V. Remini, *Daniel Webster: The Man and His Time* (New York: W. W. Norton, 1997), 27–661, 682–83; Waugh, *Brink,* 68.

23. Waugh, *Brink,* 63, 66.

CHAPTER 20

THE STRUGGLE FOR COMPROMISE

1. Robert V. Remini, *Henry Clay: Statesman for the Union* (New York: W. W. Norton, 1991), 731–32; Robert V. Remini, *Daniel Webster: The Man and His Time* (New York: W. W. Norton, 1997), 665; John C. Waugh, *On the Brink of Civil War: The Compromise of 1850 and How It Changed the Course of American History* (Wilmington, Del.: Scholarly Resources, 2003), 74.

2. Waugh, *Brink,* 74–75.

3. Remini, *Henry Clay,* 732; Waugh, *Brink,* 74–75.

4. *Bangor Daily Whig and Courier* (Bangor, Maine), February 1, 1850, issue 182, col. E; Remini, *Henry Clay,* 732–33; Waugh, *Brink,* 75.

5. Waugh, *Brink,* 75–76.

6. *Vermont Chronicle* (Bellows Falls, Vt.), February 19, 1850, issue 8, p. 31, col. C; Remini, *Henry Clay,* 735–37; Waugh, *Brink,* 76–78.

7. *Vermont Chronicle* (Bellows Falls, Vt.), February 26, 1850, issue 9, p. 35, col. A; *Bangor Daily Whig and Courier* (Bangor, Maine), February 25, 1850, issue 202, col. A; Leonard L. Richards, *The California Gold Rush and the Coming of the Civil War* (New York: Alfred A. Knopf, 2007), 104; Waugh, *Brink,* 78–79.

8. *Bangor Daily Whig and Courier* (Bangor, Maine), February 25, 1850, issue 202, col. A; *Vermont Chronicle* (Bellows Falls, Vt.), February 26, 1850, issue 9, p. 35, col. A; *Fayetteville Observer* (Fayetteville, N.C.), February 26, 1850, issue 1708, col. A; Waugh, *Brink,* 79–90.

9. John Niven, *John C. Calhoun and the Price of Union: A Biography* (Baton Rouge: Louisiana State University Press, 1988), 337–38; William M. Meigs, *The Life of John Caldwell Calhoun,* 2 vols. (New York: Da Dapo, 1970), 2:449–50; Waugh, *Brink,* 85–90.

10. Waugh, *Brink,* 89–90.

11. Niven, *John C. Calhoun,* 340; Meigs, *John Caldwell Calhoun,* 2:450; Richards, *California Gold Rush,* 105; Waugh, *Brink,* 90.

12. *Daily Morning News* (Savannah, Ga.), March 9, 1850, issue 45, col. C; *The Raleigh Register, and North-Carolina Gazette* (Raleigh, N.C.), March 9, 1850, issue 20, col. A; *Milwaukee Sentinel and Gazette* (Milwaukee, Wis.), March 8, 1850, issue 273, col. A; *The Scioto Gazette* (Chillicothe, Ohio), March 7, 1850, issue 81, col. C; Meigs, *John Caldwell Calhoun,* 2:450–56; Richards, *California Gold Rush,* 105; Waugh, *Brink,* 90–93.

13. Waugh, *Brink,* 93–94.

14. *Daily National Intelligencer* (Washington, D.C.), March 8, 1850, issue 11554, col. F; Waugh, *Brink,* 85, 97.

15. *The Boston Daily Atlas* (Boston, Mass.), March 11, 1850, issue 213, col. D; Remini, *Daniel Webster,* 669; Maurice G. Baxter, *One and Inseparable: Daniel Webster and the Union* (Cambridge, Mass.: Harvard University Press, 1984), 413; Waugh, *Brink,* 97–98.

16. Waugh, *Brink,* 98–101.

17. *The Boston Daily Atlas* (Boston, Mass.), March 11, 1850, issue 213, col. D; Remini, *Daniel Webster,* 669; Waugh, *Brink,* 102–3.

18. *The Boston Daily Atlas* (Boston, Mass.), March 11, 1850, issue 213, col. D; Baxter, *One and Inseparable,* 415–16; Meigs, *John Caldwell Calhoun,* 2:457; Waugh, *Brink,* 105.

19. *The Boston Daily Atlas* (Boston, Mass.), March 11, 1850, issue 213, col. D; *Daily Morning News* (Savannah, Ga.), March 12, 1850, issue 47, col. C; Daniel Webster, *Daniel Webster, "The Completest Man,"* ed. Kenneth E. Shewmaker (Hanover, N.H.: University Press of New England, 1990), 121–30; Baxter, *One and Inseparable,* 416; Waugh, *Brink,* 105.

20. *Daily National Intelligencer* (Washington, D.C.), March 16, 1850, issue 11560, col. C; *The Weekly Raleigh Register, and North-Carolina Gazette* (Raleigh, N.C.), March 13, 1850, issue 23, col. C; *Fayetteville Observer* (Fayetteville, N.C.), March 12, 1850, issue

1710, col. B; *Daily National Intelligencer* (Washington, D.C.), March 18, 1850, issue 11561, col. E; Remini, *Daniel Webster,* 673–75; Waugh, *Brink,* 105–7.

21. *The Boston Daily Atlas* (Boston, Mass.), March 9, 1850, issue 212, col. A, and March 11, 1850, issue 213, col. E; *The Daily Ohio Statesman* (Columbus, Ohio), March 11, 1850, issue 796/704, col. A; *Emancipator and Republican* (Boston, Mass.), March 14, 1850, issue 46; col. D; Baxter, *One and Inseparable,* 418; Remini, *Daniel Webster,* 675–78; Waugh, *Brink,* 105–6.

22. John Greenleaf Whittier, *The Complete Poetical Works of John Greenleaf Whittier* (Boston: Houghton Mifflin, 1894); Remini, *Daniel Webster,* 677.

23. Remini, *Daniel Webster,* 677.

24. *North American and United States Gazette* (Philadelphia, Pa.), March 13, 1850, issue 16878, col. A; William H. Seward, *The Works of William H. Seward,* ed. George E. Baker, 5 vols. (New York: Redfield, 1853), 1:70–93.

25. *The Raleigh Register* (Raleigh, N.C.), March 20, 1850, issue 23, col. B; *Fayetteville Observer* (Fayetteville, N.C.), March 26, 1850, issue 1712, col. C; *The Natchez Semi-Weekly Courier* (Natchez, Miss.), March 26, 1850, issue 26, col. E; Waugh, *Brink,* 113–14.

26. *Milwaukee Sentinel and Gazette* (Milwaukee, Wis.), April 4, 1850, issue 295, col. A; *The Boston Daily Atlas* (Boston, Mass.), April 5, 1850, issue 235, col. E; *Fayetteville Observer* (Fayetteville, N.C.), April 2, 1850, issue 1713, col. C; *North American and United States Gazette* (Philadelphia, Pa.), April 1, 1850, issue 16894, col. A; *The Scioto Gazette* (Chillicothe, Ohio), April 1, 1850, issue 102, cols. A and D; *The Daily Ohio Statesman* (Columbus, Ohio), April 1, 1850, issue 814/722, col. C; *Daily National Intelligencer* (Washington, D.C.), April 1, 1850, issue 11573, col. A, and April 3, 1850, issue 11575, col. A; *North American and United States Gazette* (Philadelphia, Pa.), April 4, 1850, issue 16897, col. H; Niven, *John C. Calhoun,* 343; Meigs, *John Caldwell Calhoun,* 2:462; Remini, *Henry Clay,* 743; Waugh, *Brink,* 129–30.

27. *Missouri Courier* (Hannibal, Mo.), March 7, 1850, issue 42, col. C; Remini, *Henry Clay,* 744; Waugh, *Brink,* 131.

28. *Mississippi Free Trader and Natchez Gazette* (Natchez, Miss.), March 30, 1850, issue 16, col. C; *Boston Courier* (Boston, Mass.), April 1, 1850, issue 3613, col. F; *The Boston Daily Atlas* (Boston, Mass.), April 3, 1850, issue 233, col. G; *Milwaukee Sentinel and Gazette* (Milwaukee, Wis.), April 10, 1850, issue 300, col. A; *The Natchez Semi-Weekly Courier* (Natchez, Miss.), April 5, 1850, issue 29, col. E; Richards, *California Gold Rush,* 103; Remini, *Henry Clay,* 745; Waugh, *Brink,* 132–41.

29. *Bangor Daily Whig and Courier* (Bangor, Maine), February 25, 1850, issue 202, col. A; *Daily Morning News* (Savannah, Ga.), January 26, 1850, issue 11, col. D; Waugh, *Brink,* 143–52.

30. Waugh, *Brink,* 153–54.

31. *The Natchez Semi-Weekly Courier* (Natchez, Miss.), February 15, 1850, issue 15, col. A; Waugh, *Brink,* 158.

32. Waugh, *Brink,* 159–60.

33. *The Cleveland Herald* (Cleveland, Ohio), July 9, 1850, issue 161, col. A, and July 15, 1850, issue 166, col. B; *The Daily Ohio Statesman* (Columbus, Ohio), July 9, 1850, issue 887/791, col. F; *Emancipator and Republican* (Boston, Mass.), July 11, 1850, issue 11, col. A; *The Boston Daily Atlas* (Boston, Mass.), July 10, 1850, issue 8, col. D; Waugh, *Brink,* 163–65.

34. *Daily National Intelligencer* (Washington, D.C.), July 12, 1850, issue 11659, col. B, and July 13, 1850, issue 11660, col. B; Waugh, *Brink*, 165–67.

35. Remini, *Henry Clay*, 756–57; Waugh, *Brink*, 173–77.

36. Robert W. Johannsen, *Stephen A. Douglas* (New York: Oxford University Press, 1973), 294–97; Waugh, *Brink*, 177–84.

37. Richards, *California Gold Rush*, 110.

INDEX

Page numbers in *italics* refer to maps.

A NOTE ABOUT THE AUTHOR

Steven E. Woodworth was born in Ohio and grew up in the Midwest. He earned his Ph.D. in history at Rice University in 1987 and is the author, coauthor, or editor of twenty-eight books on American history, including *Nothing but Victory: The Army of the Tennessee, 1861–1865*. He is currently a professor of history at Texas Christian University in Fort Worth, Texas.